Agricultural Literature :

Proud Heritage--Future Promise

A Bicentennial Symposium

September 24-26, 1975·

Edited By:
- *Alan Fusonie*
- *Leila Moran*

SPONSORED BY THE:

- *Agricultural History Society*
- *American Association of Nurserymen, Inc.*
- *American Poultry Historical Association*
- *Associates of the National Agricultural Library, Inc.*
- *Graduate School, U.S. Dept. of Agriculture*
- *Massey-Ferguson, Inc.*

Washington, D.C.

Associates of the National Agricultural Library, Inc.

and the

Graduate School Press, U.S. Dept. of Agriculture

Library of Congress Card Number 76-47084
ISBN Number 87771-010-4

Published and sold by the Graduate School Press, U.S. Department of Agriculture, Washington, D.C. 20250.

Contents

Introduction

      Alan Fusonie

      Leila Moran 1

A Bicentennial Welcome from the Tower

      Richard A. Farley 7

A Modified Heritage: The Colonial Economy and Social Order as Seen in Literary and Non-Literary Sources

      Aubrey C. Land 9

The Converging Paths of Agricultural and Early American History: A Commentary and Speculation

      Edward C. Carter II 25

The Agricultural Literature of the Gentleman Farmer in the Colonies

      Alan Fusonie 33

In Praise of the Historical: A Commentary

      John D. Macoll 57

John Banister: Seventeenth Century Scholar, Minister, Farmer, Artist, and Naturalist

      Joseph Ewan 63

Western Movement—Its Literature

      Jeff Dykes 71

Agriculture with Hoof and Horn: An Analysis of the Historical Literature of the Cattle Industry

Walter Rundell, Jr.
Anne M. Butler 87

Horticultural Heritage: The Influence of U.S. Nurserymen

Elisabeth Woodburn 109

Horticultural Heritage—The Influence of U.S. Nurserymen: A Commentary

Charles van Ravenswaay 143

Past and New Directions in Agricultural Education

John B. Holden 149

Leadership in American Agriculture: The Published Documentary Heritage

Harold T. Pinkett 159

Who's A Leader? The Published Documents: A Commentary

John T. Schlebecker 169

The Making of an Agricultural Publisher: Edwin T. Meredith and the Development of *Successful Farming* Magazine

Peter L. Petersen 173

Great Men and Enduring Farm Magazines: A Commentary

Earl W. McMunn 193

Agricultural People

John J. McKelvey, Jr. 213

The History of Agricultural Libraries in the United States

J. Richard Blanchard 219

The Development of Agricultural Libraries in the Unites States: A Commentary

Richard A. Farley 237

Historical Research within the College of Agriculture

Irvin M. May, Jr. 243

Historical Research within the College of Agriculture: A Commentary

Vivian Wiser 259

Agriculture in Communist China

Gilbert C. Fite 263

Oral History as Agricultural Literature: Creativity and the Labormanagement Resource

Gould P. Colman 273

A Folklorist, not a Farmer: A Commentary

George G. Carey 289

The Mechanization of American Agriculture

Wayne D. Rasmussen 295

Commentary on the Mechanization of American Agriculture

Roy Bainer 317

Man Made Famines: Past, Present, and Future

William A. Dando 323

Commentary on "Man Made Famines: Past, Present, and Future"

Surinder M. Bhardwaj 341

Index 353

Introduction

At the time of the American Revolution about 90 percent of the American people were farmers, many of them small farmers possessing little more than the family Bible for reading material. Yet, there were also a small number of gentleman farmers and planters who found time for reading, writing, and experimentation in agriculture and its related fields. As time passed, immigrants and land-seeking pioneers were lured by a wilderness rich in farmland potential, forests, and other natural resources. The growing application of an increasingly innovative science and technology gradually yielded an expanding agricultural production while, at the same time, curtailing the amount of physical labor required. By 1974, only 4.4 percent of the nation's labor force was engaged in agriculture, producing enough farm products to take care of our domestic consumption at home while also producing enough agricultural output to export abroad.

Today, the United States is the only former European colony to ever become both one of the most powerful and one of the most agriculturally productive nations in the world. This unprecedented progress in agriculture on the part of the United States is reflected in its rich body of agricultural literature — from one of the first American imprints on American agriculture entitled *Essays Upon Field Husbandry* by Jared Eliot to the immense and diverse literature of today. The U.S. Department of Agriculture's National Agricultural Library has accumulated over 1.5 million volumes of this reading material.

The idea for a symposium focusing upon the historical as well as the continual importance of American agricultural literature to the world community was conceived in the winter of 1974; by May of the following year, with the theme defined and suggestions for papers and commentaries under way, the possibilities for multiple sponsorship and identifying potential audiences were developed along with a registration brochure, publicity, and other related matters. As the program became more formalized six groups agreed to serve as joint sponsors: the Associates of the National Agricultural Library, Inc.; the Agricultural History Society; the American Poultry Historical Society; the Graduate School, U.S. Department of Agriculture; Massey-Ferguson, Inc., and the American Association of Nurserymen, Inc. The symposium, planned for three days — September 24 to 26, 1975 — was both informative and entertaining. It

1

was attended by 106 registrants of whom over half were affiliated with either universities or the government. The remaining individuals came from such diverse areas as botanical gardens, museums, nurseries, state archives, and included bookdealers as well as publishers. During the three-day period, there was a sincere effort by those in attendance to search for and to reassess the sense of order, continuity, and change in the rural landscape of America within the milieu of the realities of today and speculations about tomorrow.

The National Agricultural Library (NAL) in cooperation with the symposium sponsors provided meeting space, equipment, a list of available NAL publications, and its *Guide to Services*. The Agricultural History Center at the University of California, Davis, and the Agricultural History Group of the U.S. Department of Agriculture had an exhibit table with lists and samples of bibliographies available from the Center. Finally, the Cucumber Book Shop, Rockville, Maryland, put on a book exhibit of current imprints in American agriculture.

The Symposium brought together 27 speakers from various fields who offered papers and commentaries to review and interpret sources, histories, and other writings on the American colonial economy and society, the westward movement, horticultural heritage, agricultural heritage, agricultural libraries, mechanization, and food supplies. Participants included book dealers, editors, folklorists, geographers, historians, librarians, scientists, and others.

In his welcoming remarks, Richard Farley, Director of the National Agricultural Library, set the tone for the Symposium, alluding to the Vermont tradition of the town meeting at which there exists a sense of community responsibility and sharing of views. The first session, chaired by Ralph H. Estey, was entitled "A Modified Heritage: The Colonial Economy and Social Order as Seen in Literary and Non-literary Sources." In his paper, Aubrey Land delivered an analysis of the differing characteristics in the colonial economy as well as an overview synthesis of such valuable works as Bidwell and Falconer's *History of Agriculture in the Northern United States, 1620–1860* and Gray's *History of Agriculture in the Southern United States to 1860*. He provided a lucid account of the interaction of the heritage from abroad, local conditions, continuity, and change upon the colonial society and economy. Edward Carter, in his commentary, made the observation that now might be the time to undertake substantial sociological studies directed towards reconstructing life as it existed in early American agrarian societies. The next paper, "Agricultural Literature of the Gentlemen Farmer in the Colonies" by Alan Fusonie relied heavily upon primary source

2

materials in re-examining the role of correspondence, imprint literature, and the press in communicating the latest developments in agriculture. John Macoll presented a most persuasive commentary expressing the need for each generation of scholars to re-investigate and interpret for themselves the rich body of original source materials. The luncheon speaker, Joseph Ewan, delivered a captivating presentation on "John Banister: 17th Century Scholar, Minister, Farmer, Artist, Naturalist" which highlighted some of Banister's contributions as well as his relationships with his colleagues. It was a fitting tribute to the man who brought the first accounts of the plants of Virginia to the attention of European collectors.

The afternoon session was chaired by Robert Kiger. The first paper, "Westward Movement — Its Literature," by Jeff Dykes demonstrated not only the author's immense awareness and understanding of the informational value of the primary source imprint materials of the period but also his understanding and appreciation of the Southwest frontier — the land as well as the men whose history it became. Westward expansion captured the interest and imagination of Americans as no other aspect of their history. The commentary by Walter Rundell and Anne Butler entitled "Agriculture with Hoof and Horn: An Analysis of Historical Literature on the Cattle Industry" added a unique dimension of both atmosphere and content, giving a descriptive overview of 13 prominent literary studies involving the cattle industry. The development of an emerging cattle industry had been not only an important frontier enterprise but also a contributing factor in the closing of the frontier by the 1890s. The second paper, "Horticultural Heritage: The Influence of the U.S. Nurserymen," by Elisabeth Woodburn was most effective in illuminating the value of both the pre-1860 horticultural imprint literature and the dedicated individuals who helped contribute to its rich history. In general, the diverse patterns in the growth of horticultural literature was evidenced in the gradually increasing number of seedmen engaged in the writing of treatises on gardening. Charles Van Ravenswaay, in commenting on this paper, also pointed out the importance of the gardening and/or horticultural catalogues of the seed houses and nurseries as valuable sources of information. Following the Luau dinner that evening at the University of Maryland's Rossborough Inn, John Holden, in his paper "Past and New Directions in Agricultural Education," gave an overview presentation of some of the more important developments in agricultural education with special attention to the Cooperative Extension Service and the Graduate School of the U.S. Department of Agriculture.

The story of American agriculture and those individuals who

3

helped to make it is indeed a proud one. In the Thursday morning session chaired by Roe C. Black, the first paper entitled "Leadership in American Agriculture: The Published Documentary Heritage" by Harold Pinkett vividly portrayed the leadership of a number of individuals inclusive of Washington, Jefferson, and their colleagues abroad, outstanding journalists of the 19th century, individuals in the Department of Agriculture, and shed illumination on pertinent published documentary materials. John Schlebecker's commentary re-emphasized the importance of autobiographies, diaries, and journals as well as the often overlooked poetry and novels as source materials.

The many outstanding editors of the farm press in America from John Stuart Skinner of the *American Farmer* founded in 1819 to the agricultural editors of today have provided a unique medium for the advancement of potentially useful agricultural knowledge. Peter Peterson in his paper "The Making of an Agricultural Publisher: Edwin T. Meredith and the Development of *Successful Farming* Magazine" presented a well-documented human interest story of the rise of a young farm boy from Iowa to a position of successful publisher and knowledgeable agriculturist. In his commentary, Earl McMunn expanded further upon the aspect of publishing by surveying the development of numerous farm journals and agricultural editors. The luncheon speaker, John McKelvey, Jr., in his paper "Agricultural People" praised not only the contributions of scientists, explorers, and adventurers to agricultural literature but also literary figures such as Joseph Conrad, Robert Burns, Robert Frost, Tolstoy, and others.

In 1954, Norman Cousins, educational and literary editor, defined a library as " . . .the delivery room for the birth of ideas — a place where history comes to life." The first of the afternoon sessions which was chaired by Foster Mohrhardt focused upon the role of the library in the agricultural community. In his paper "The History of Agricultural Libraries in the United States," Richard Blanchard dealt with the problem of the proliferation of agricultural libraries which has increased proportionally to the development of agricultural literature; the latter, in turn, has progressed from early cuneiform inscriptions to the immense and varied resources of today. In his commentary, Richard Farley utilized some unique historical policy documents relating to the development of the U.S. Department of Agriculture Library in the late 19th century which involved the issue of centralization versus decentralization; he also touched upon the present and future need for NAL to strike a balance between the national and the international demands of the

4

agricultural community. The final paper of the afternoon, "Historical Research Within the College of Agriculture," by Irvin May, Jr.
offered some insights into the present and possible future roles of a
research historian at the Texas Agricultural Experiment Station. In
her commentary, Vivian Wiser provided a national view, focusing
attention upon the evolution of historical work within the colleges of
agriculture. At the evening dinner which was held at the University
of Maryland's Center of Adult Education, the guest speaker, Gilbert Fite, delivered an informative paper entitled "Agriculture in
Communist China" based upon his recent trip through some of the
agricultural regions in China.

The sessions on the concluding day were chaired by Theodore
Byerley and began with a paper "Oral History as Agricultural Literature: Creativity and the Labormanagement Resource" by Gould
Colman, in which he not only discussed the status of oral history but
also provided a demonstration of the successful use of the tape recorder in documenting the labormanagement activities of a family
farm operation over an extended period of time. George Carey's
commentary praised this technique as a useful approach for both the
oral historian and the folklorist; in his presentation, he also offered
some rather humorous examples of anecdotes collected by the folklorist.

The last decade of the 19th Century experienced the full emergence of the Industrial Revolution in America; at the same time a
revolution was also taking place in agriculture as well. In his paper
"Mechanization of American Agriculture," Wayne Rasmussen presented a balanced analysis of agricultural production and focused attention upon both the benefits and the social implications resulting
from the process of mechanization. Roy Bainer, in his commentary,
elaborated upon many of the improvements which are involved in
the mechanization process. The final papers of the Symposium dealt
with the critical problem facing the world today — man and the food
supply. One hundred years ago, one farmer supplied the food and
fiber required by about 5 persons. Today, we are being asked to
share our abundance with millions of hungry people in other nations. In his illustrated presentation entitled "Man-Made Famines:
Past, Present, and Future," William Dando gave a critical analysis
of man's experience with hunger, starvation, and famine from
primitive times to the present; he identified future areas of potential
famine and made an urgent plea for cooperation in developing an
international anti-famine strategy. Surinder Bhardwaj, in his commentary, provided numerous examples of man as the principal in-
strumentality who caused both hunger and famine. As Dando had

done, Bhardwaj also emphasized the imperative need for global reform.

This Symposium on Agricultural Literature produced an informative and useful group of scholarly papers. All papers have been slightly revised to accommodate a potential reading audience. However, due to the interdisciplinary nature of the Symposium the diverse styles of footnoting were left as submitted reflecting the intent and integrity of the originators. There were many supportive hands involved in this Symposium: Patrick Brennen of the University of South Dakota, Shirley Gaventa, Nancy Lewis, Irene White and other staff members of the National Agricultural Library. A special debt of gratitude is owed to Irene Glennon and Sharon Crutchfield of NAL for their time and effort in preparing the index to these proceedings, to Gerald Ogden of the Agricultural History Group of the U.S. Department of Agriculture for his bibliographic review of portions of some of the papers, and to Donna Fusonie for her editorial assistance in reviewing manuscript.

Alan Fusonie
Leila Moran
Editors

A Bicentennial Welcome from the Tower

The first recorded town meeting was in Dorchester, Massachusetts, in 1633. I am told that Vermont, which is steeped in a great sense of tradition, is often referred to as town meeting country. Every year on the first Tuesday in March, voters throughout the state meet in their town halls or community buildings to share their views.

Today, some two hundred years after the inception of the new nation, some thoughtful people are gathered here at the National Agricultural Library for a town meeting to analyze, discuss, and interpret the implications of agricultural literature past, present, and future.

On behalf of Secretary Butz and the staff of the National Agricultural Library, I welcome you and assure you that we will do everything possible to make your brief stay with us productive, profitable, and pleasant.

RICHARD A. FARLEY
Director
National Agricultural Library
U.S. Department of Agriculture

A Modified Heritage: The Colonial Economy and Social Order as seen in the Literary and Non-Literary Sources

By
Aubrey C. Land

Anyone who undertakes to comment on early American agriculture, either briefly or at length, faces a two-fold problem. On the one hand the literature is large; on the other it does not usually answer the questions that often tease his mind. All students must stand, if not in awe, at least in a respectful posture before the monumental work of Lewis C. Gray and that of Percy W. Bidwell and John I. Falconer.[1] Gray's monumental two-volume study of the South — the agricultural region par excellence in the eyes of mercantilist Englishmen — is almost too good to be true, combining readability with complete mastery of the literary sources of every kind, from contemporary technical manuals and reports to the most casual observations of travelers passing briefly through the area. His bibliography is enough to frighten the beginner, who might easily conclude that nothing is left to be done. Bidwell and Falconer's single volume seems only a trifle less formidable. Their first chapter, "Field Husbandry," has sixteen sections ranging from land clearing to vegetable and fruit crops, each one a model essay but heavily

Dr. Land is a Research Professor, Department of History, University of Georgia, Athens, Georgia.

History of Agriculture in the Southern United States To 1860

BY

Lewis Cecil Gray

ASSISTED BY

Esther Katherine Thompson

With an Introductory Note by

Henry Charles Taylor

VOLUME I

Published by the Carnegie Institution of Washington
Washington 1933

History of Agriculture in the Northern United States 1620-1860

BY

Percy Wells Bidwell, Ph.D.
ECONOMIST, UNITED STATES TARIFF COMMISSION
FORMERLY
ASSISTANT PROFESSOR OF ECONOMICS, YALE UNIVERSITY

AND

John I. Falconer, Ph.D.
PROFESSOR OF RURAL ECONOMY, OHIO STATE UNIVERSITY

Published by the Carnegie Institution of Washington
Washington, May, 1925

factual and not always easy to construe. In a work that is at once comprehensive and pioneering, one cannot expect all questions to be answered, not even all the important ones. It is no criticism of Bidwell and Falconer for the North and Gray for the South that they restricted their research to New World phenomena. Merely ascertaining the facts and putting them into some array was itself a formidable task. Gray does considerably more than the counterpart volume for the North with the difficult matters of Indian agriculture, surely an important resource for early settlers in providing lessons in clearing, cultivation, and even food crops suitable to New World conditions. I mention this in passing as an illustration of what you all know very well, namely that agriculture is shaped by many stimuli and examples, some not easy to assess especially when imperfectly known.[2] Both Gray and Bidwell and Falconer deserve high praise for their accomplishments. But major tasks still remain ahead, work for many hands and brains. One may include among these the philosophy of the subject, or, put another way, the interpretation or construction of early American agricultural experience. How in short did a tradition develop strong enough not only to endure but also to prevail?

Prominent among the ingredients of this tradition, the matter of heritage stands among the foremost questions needing fuller investigation. Facile answers will not serve. Students of political thought would never claim that Tom, Dick, and Harry migrated to the Atlantic frontier as walking textbooks of English law and the constitution. At most, the humble immigrant had a conception of the fairness and equity covered by the large umbrella that he called British liberties. By analogy, the British tradition in agriculture must have been, to many newcomers, similarly vague, particularly in matters of detail. By no means all immigrants came from farms. Many had been city folk — tailors, artisans, even younger children of professional men — or inhabitants of villages, who could cope with the limited tasks demanded by kitchen garden or flower garden, but who could hardly have opened a furrow with the unwieldy English plow of that day.[3]

Yet whatever his background and occupation at home, each immigrant was bound for a New World where he wrung all or part of his living from the soil. In the first years of colonization crops — either for subsistence or for market — and capital formation kept all hands in colonial households almost fully occupied. Even as late as the American War for Independence, well over ninety percent of the population were engaged in agriculture. Accordingly, the agri-

11

cultural tradition brought by the immigrants and its adaptation to conditions in the wilderness demands analysis.

Fortunately a talented group of scholars has provided a wealth of knowledge about the state of British agriculture in the seventeenth and eighteenth centuries. Some of these studies might well serve as models for similar investigations in the colonial period, for they go beyond crops, tools, and organization into the more difficult and treacherous realm of work attitudes and social bearings of husbandry.[4]

If I have read them correctly, these studies tell of an agriculture solidly based on ancient traditions—crops, farm buildings, animals, and many of the routines—but undergoing a slow change from medieval to what may be called, in a rough way, modern organization associated with the transition from subsistence, or at least a kind of self-sufficient, agriculture to something more nearly functional to the capitalistic economy of the modern age. Yet within the characteristic British stability and sturdiness there was a balance so delicate that the limited Enclosure Movement of the 16th century created a social problem of national visibility and of such concern that contemporary publicists debated the pros and cons with passion.[5]

After the nation had adjusted to the initial social consequences of this First Enclosure Movement, the 17th century was relatively stable, though not unchanging.[6] Drainage of the fens added over 300,000 acres to English arable land and the growth of London, as a metropolitan center of consumption, altered the character of husbandry on the purlieu of the city.[7] The next remarkable change came with the eighteenth century enclosure movement which brought new methods of tillage and improved farm animals.

The seaboard colonies were settled, then, before the effects of the eighteenth century agricultural revolution could be felt among immigrants coming from either countryside or urban places in Britain. The heritage and traditions they brought had varying careers according to the area along the seaboard where they settled. Three general areas may be identified to test the durability and the applicability of the British heritage: New England, the Middle Colonies, and the seaboard from the Chesapeake southward. Each has its own history and within each a careful reader of the literary accounts can discern considerable local variations, some flourishing in subordinate sectors no larger than a county, or even part of a county. Parenthetically local variation entails on students of early American agriculture microanalysis as well as the "big picture" approach that survives in college courses which give pupils such bland generalizations as "the middle colonies were the bread colonies."

One day it may be possible to construct a model that will admit of quantitative scoring under the two heads, durability and applicability of the English heritage, taking into account the literary (usually descriptive) evidence and the non-literary materials, which are still comparatively unexploited. For the present a much less ambitious procedure must suffice. And, first, I may offer the proposition that only in New England — named and appropriately so by John Smith in his post-Virginia career with the "other" company — did something close to the British tradition survive for any period of time. Next, let me offer the qualification that even in New England the tradition suffered a sea change, though not into something rich and strange, because New England agriculture never afforded a base for wealth and prosperity comparable to the colonies farther south. In broad terms New England was atypical, never developed the profitable commercial agriculture of the planting colonies or the middle colonies. Consequently to the end of British dominion, New England remained, at best, the poor relation too nearly like rural England and at worst Peck's Bad Boy when the Yankees turned for their economic salvation to shipping and fishing competitive with English occupations.

But, to get to specifics on the question of continuity and change, we must first notice that the New England settlers were a special breed, Puritans, whose conceptions first imposed a characteristic pattern on their settlements, which were cohesive — the orderly township division of land with modest family farms — and secondly shaped their lifestyles with a work ethic at variance with the prevalent rural attitudes at home. There must have been a few New Englanders who were downright lazy and more who would have enjoyed a laxer regimen — the extra hour in bed. But neither climate, doctrine, nor the presiding elders favored such soft and easy ways. They worked as English farm labor did not; township discipline would have been visited upon laggards.[8]

It was well that the Puritans of New England had the particular disposition that led to compact settlement and Spartan discipline. It was their salvation in the face of the task before them. For they faced a land that the passage of centuries would make it difficult for anyone today to call up realistically. "The whole country is a perfect forest," marvelled one eyewitness. Every acre was won to arable

13

from the forest primeval, which meant days of heavy labor with ax and mattock and even then, when settlers had made a small clearing, they had no more than a bare beginning towards a farmstead. They still lacked house, barn, fences, which consumed many more hours of exhausting work. Capital formation thus competed with cultivation as never before in the previous experience of early settlers. Back home, farmers had nibbled away at moors and forests along the lines that divided the desert from the sown. But these tiny bites were fringe encroachments on wastes that lay adjacent to established farms and hamlets. In New England, save for occasional clearings Indians had made here and there for their small-scale planting, settlers carved their beachhead from the perfect forest that stretched from high tide and shingle on back into a hinterland of a thousand miles. Their task was formidable, their performance was heroic.

To descend from this Olympian view to the close-up—in the language of the media, to zoom-in—reveals details of a process that, if it did not essentially alter the English tradition, nevertheless gave it in time a flavor as distinctive as Yankee speech. There were the hot debates for years over the proper way to clear fields—whether to girdle trees for immediate planting about their bases or to "stub" all growth in order to make a field that could take the plow immediately.[9] The immediate adoption of a totally new high-yield crop, maize, from the Indians—and, at least temporarily, the method of fertilizing it with fish—is a fact well publicized in sixth-grade readers, even when its implications are not. The addition of salt hay to fodder for livestock was another small Americanizing feature of New England agriculture. This is merely to underscore the obvious, that local conditions are bound to affect the heritage in some degree. But, in the main, continuity prevailed over change. An English farmer moving to Massachusetts in the mid-1700's would have found the familiar: the plow, fields of small grain (for New Englanders refused to subsist wholly and indefinitely on hasty pudding), farms similar in size to those back home, with barns and homes patterned on English models. One has only to refer to Professor Darrett Rutman's attractive monograph, *Husbandmen of Plymouth,* for confirmation in detail.[10]

The planting colonies from the Chesapeake on south to the Spanish borderlands stand at the opposite pole. Here English tradition first worked mischief and then underwent sharp change. Almost annual crises occured at Jamestown for a dozen years after 1607 when in late winter settlers faced actual starvation. Yet, paradoxically, they took time, and plenty of it for, "pastimes and merry exercise," one of which included playing bowls in the streets. In a brilliant and provocative article, Professor Edmund Morgan argues that this behavior does not indicate an epidemic of lunacy but rather reflects prevailing English work attitudes and practices.[11] The labor problem at Jamestown was further aggravated by the quasi-military character of the expedition in an age when military service meant idleness, inefficiency, malnutrition, and lack of incentive. None of the company programs succeeded, either the industrial or the agricultural, however harsh the laws, and "Dale's laws" — essentially a military code — have become legendary for their brutality. Nor did this complexion of affairs improve until the Virginia Company decided on a division of land, investing each adventurer with his own freehold from the company's vast holdings.[12] Only then were minimum conditions provided for both a society and an economy.

John Rolfe's experiments had pointed a direction. The future of Virginia was to be — according to different views — the stinking weed or the sovereign remedy but, in any case, tobacco, a cash crop commanding high prices yet requiring beyond constant attention, no sophisticated culture. At first sight it is remarkable that within a dozen years the basics of tobacco culture — from seed beds through transplanting, worming and suckering, cutting and curing, to final prizing (that is packing in hogsheads for export) — had settled into a pattern that continued without real change throughout the seventeenth century.[13] Tobacco culture adapted itself ideally to the spirit of routine and its predominance, first in Virginia then, a decade or so later, in Maryland gives agriculture in the Chesapeake region a strikingly unprogressive aspect, a seeming imperviousness to experimentation and innovation.[14] Only a few years ago, in a symposium similar to this, I attempted to identify the obstacles to change and progress in the Chesapeake region as a combination of crops, labor, and technology or, rather, the lack of it. I still think this explanation has considerable validity, however sharp or unflattering to our forefathers who struggled with this threefold tangle that constituted the problem as I saw it then. But it omitted another ingredient that seems to me highly significant: the ineluctable effect of a system or superstructure erected on this agricultural base. If, in that paper, there are hints, wisps and strays of evidence, that might suggest to a reader that some other element was at work — as in physics, a new particle not identified but obviously affecting the experiment — the author did not make that factor explicit. My subsequent study of the

Carolinas and the Middle Colonies has given me a sharper conception of this process. Within a very few years tobacco culture called up a set of commercial arrangements, at first rather fragile but with every passing decade stronger and more permanent. To describe this organization of commerce — for such it was — would transcend the scope of this paper and repeat much that I and others have said elsewhere. A schematic outline will suffice here.

The unit of production was the field crop of a "hand," the first producer who cleared a few acres called a plantation somewhere in the endless forest. There, singlehandedly, he produced a crop with an upward limit of about 2,000 pounds of marketable leaf. Most crops ran to far less weight, some as small as a third of this upper limit. Of course, additional increments of labor — a member of the household or an indentured servant — enlarged the total output of the production unit. These small producers were the planters — the typical planters of the Chesapeake — and they formed the bulk of the population throughout the colonial period. They were small operators, primitively housed, carving out and then cultivating their plantations with, for the most part, nothing more than an ax and hoe, destitute of capital and often illiterate. Small planters could produce respectable crops. Indeed, during the early years, they made good money, for prices were high.[15] But, beyond raising crops, they were helpless. To sustain a commercial agriculture other and different hands were essential — the middle men in a network, still vestigial for some time, stretching from a collection point in Virginia or Maryland across 3,000 miles to the tobacco merchants of Britain. On the Tobacco Coast these persons were locals — whether recent immigrants or, as time went on, "country born," as the phrase went. The essential commercial organization was the work of their hands and brains: they assembled tobacco crops for cargoes, almost universally extended credit to small producers, sold them the necessities (hardware and textiles) and occasionally some small luxury (rum or sugar), and finally reaped the profits or went bankrupt. In the speech of the day such men were merchants in the general sense that they performed mercantile functions without which the Chesapeake economy could never have grown to the dimension it achieved at the end of the second hundred years.[16]

The merchant element — and numerically it was tiny — reaped the largest economic harvests. Some became moderately affluent and a few rich, at least by the standards of the time. They also acted as a brake on experimentation and helped harden the cake of custom; that is they clamped the monoculture on their provinces, kept the planter to his routine producing a crop they "understood" as later, in the black belt and on into the twentieth century, bankers in the cotton south held freehold farmers and tenants alike to the staple. After all, the merchants had woven a tissue of understandings and book operations that made any departure both a hazard and a threat.

And yet, paradoxically, they were also the exclusive experimenters and innovators. Their very system had been an innovation, an entrepreneural exercise. Moreover, they were innovators in labor: they bought the blacks in the early days of chattel slavery and, consequently, figured as innovators in a new labor system. Finally, some of them experimented with alternate crops—wheat, rye, hemp—and with more advanced technology. The diary of Landon Carter, second generation wealth from a bustling ancestor, tells us that in his own father's time—the early eighteenth century—wheat was a hoeing culture. Carter, of course, used the plow in cultivating the wheat he produced for market.[17]

By contrast the poorer planters had no margin for experimental innovation. Whatever time they had remaining after tending their tobacco went first to food crops to sustain their families—maize, required by law in early days to prevent famine, garden vegetables—and secondly to capital formation—houses, tobacco drying barns, outbuildings, fences, orchards.[18] These were, in the common speech of the time, "improvements." But even given abundant leisure, would their case have been different? Unlettered, when not illiterate, the ordinary planter had nothing beyond hearsay to pull him into the quickening stream of thought about such agricultural improvements as were reported in the volumes coming from English presses. But even had they been the studious type, given to books and with the money to buy them, they would have found none that addressed itself to tobacco. Assuredly, the cards were stacked against the small planters.[19]

In sum, the agricultural experience of the Chesapeake region was one of sharp change from the English heritage. Local crops demanded radically different husbandry which, after quick and early establishment, resisted change for the overwhelming majority of planters. In certain respects agriculture in the Carolinas and later in coastal Georgia followed a different course from that of the Chesapeake. The earliest Carolina settlements came in the second wave of colonial enterprise just after the Restoration and the immigrant population fumbled for several decades with subsistence agriculture and herding before finding in rice a true bonanza. But rice culture (even further from the English tradition than tobacco) evoked a husbandry and commercial organization at variance with Chesapeake agriculture.[20]

This is not the place to enter into a description of rice culture, even in summary fashion. Gray and others have provided a quite complete account.[21] But after the student has learned very nearly all there is to know about the details—of tidal and riverine cultivation, of upland planting, of the application of slave labor, and the like— questions still tease his mind. Why, for instance, did planters in the rice country keep up a constant dialogue on methods of cultivating and processing their crop for market? From earliest years (around the turn of the century) a succession of pamphlets, and later newspaper essays, speak of inventions and patents, of methods of drilling and weeding. This even while the staple was creating the rice millionaires.[22]

Indeed, the agricultural history of this southern flank of the English seaboard was one of change and innovation. One might say of revolutions if the term were not too much abused. Well after rice had laid the foundation for a kind of bonanza economy, indigo—an even more technically demanding crop—opened new possibilities for wealth. Then, of course, finally short staple cotton eclipsed them both.

To what stimuli this more adventuresome response can be attributed is not clear. To be sure, Carolina settlers began arriving six decades after the initial settlement at Jamestown and some of them, at least, did not come directly from the British Isles but from the West India Islands where they had known slave labor at first hand. Those who came directly from Britain—and over the first thirty years they were in the majority—had hopes of cultivating commodities such as silk and wine, which were not at all suited to the Carolina climate. They must have experienced some trauma when they began to clear and plant and to bow to the yoke of pastoral and subsistence agriculture.[22] We know little in detail about these three decades; for example, there exists no single micro-study of a parish unit. Once rice became the staple, Carolina agriculture fell into a pattern of large plantations, slave labor, and the commercial net centering on the merchant princes in Charleston, the only real port and city in the planting south until the rise of Baltimore after the Revolution.

Perhaps the term agribusiness to describe South Carolina commercial agriculture would be pretentious and inexact as applied to this area. And yet more than a suggestion of this description appears

18

in the well-known contemporaneous source, the anonymous *American Husbandry,* which was originally published in 1776.[23] The author conveys his message in the form of a model—a do-it-yourself guide to success in rice culture—which is as thoroughly capitalistic as a manual for establishing and enlarging a textile plant in England. First, the entrepreneur invests a certain sum of money in land, labor (slaves), and equipment. After each successive crop, he plows back the profits into his enterprise. At the end of several years he has made the grade and levelled out on the fair plateau of endless affluence—the good life. Even today, one reading this work has the urge to leap from his chair, run out, and buy a rice plantation. Such projections were not uncommon in the eighteenth century—for the sugar colonies, the cocoa walks of the islands, and the enterprises in Virginia and Maryland.[24] They lie in the zone between the nascent science of economics and that of promotional literature. Whatever they tell us about the realities (chances of failure, pure hard work) in occasional digressions, the emphasis, the sweep to almost certain success, is as compelling as the tale of the Sleeping Beauty where the princess wakes to bliss. Shadowy background figures are hardly seen or scarcely noticed. A few principals carry the story. But what of the invisible people without whom the drama of kings and queens would have no context and could hardly carry out the play?

Unfortunately next to nothing is known about these common men or their families. The literary sources contain abundant data on the great planters with their attractive life-styles. Classes beneath them lie just below the level of visibility, at least, in the literary sources which scarcely mention them. Accordingly, for studies of this huge segment of the population, students have only the resources of the probate records: the wills, inventories, and accounts. Articles and monographs will not come easily from these intractable materials, but only from them can we find what statisticians call central tendencies, something more nearly the "average." I would argue that here the agricultural tradition is made and perpetuated, reasoning from the Chesapeake case. Without these studies we shall not see Carolina agriculture whole, merely the elite, which is important, but not all.

We are in better case with the last and, in some ways, most interesting, element in the colonial heritage. Professor Richard H. Shryock in a classic article has imprinted indelibly the contrast between German and English traditions on the thinking about early American agriculture. He takes us to Pennsylvania where the moving Germans debarked. However, his findings have wider geographical implications, because the Germans moved downwards across western Maryland and Virginia on into the Carolinas.[25] Almost poetically, he evokes a picture of sturdy stone barns and houses, of fat lands for which the Germans had an infallible eye, and fields cleared not by halfway measures of girdling but by the backbreaking labor of grubbing out even the largest trees. German husbandry proved enduring, even more so than their language now all but gone or their personal names transformed from Mueller to Miller, Kuester to Custer, or Boettler to Butler.[26] Disbelievers can see physical proof of this durability simply by driving along the arc of fertile soils from Lancaster, Pennsylvania, through Frederick, Maryland, and on to Greensboro, North Carolina.

The Shryock image has not stood without challenge. Professor James T. Lemon has argued with a formidable array of evidence that the Germans had no keener eye for fertile land, no greater superiority in farming techniques (fertilizing, for instance), no better husbandry than neighboring English, Scotch-Irish, and Welsh in Pennsylvania. Nor, he claims, does the evidence support the stereotype of German frugality and industry that supposedly made for worldly success. He finds other neighboring ethnic groups in the fertile area he studied — southeastern Pennsylvania — enjoying prosperity equally with the Germans in both degree and kind.[27]

Yet the testimony of contemporary eyewitnesses cannot be discounted. Benjamin Franklin and Richard Rush, though not infallible, were shrewd observers. Moreover hard-headed businessmen — the Dulanys, Carrolls, and other landlords — had similar impressions, firm enough that they sought to attract the Germans southward into the western parts of Maryland and Virginia where soil and climate resembled those of Pennsylvania.[28] Perhaps too much has been made of ethnic contributions to the agricultural heritage of the Germanic element in this western arc. Possibly the hypothesis to explain the development of the West should include the factor of fusion of traditions, both British and German. At any rate the area of the Middle Colonies and the fertile back country slanting southwest had, in colonial times, a special character.

Throughout this area the people practiced commercial agriculture and their cash crop, grain, was well adapted to the soil. Without the temptations inherent in bonanza crops to abuse the soil and turn agriculture into an extractive enterprise, they held to a balance of cash crops, subsistence crops, and farm animals for dairy and meat. The Germans proved somewhat more picturesque among the contributors with their massive stone barns that have lasted until today as outward and visible signs of an inner spirit: stolid, dogged, temperamentally suited to the routine of farm toil. One can think of worse models.

The Germans were not the only non-English element in the Middle Colonies lying between Maryland and Connecticut. All of this middle group belongs to the restoration wave of colonization. The English won New York by conquest from the Dutch who had already made some settlements along the Hudson and had taken to a kind of farming not unlike that of the Germans later.[29] The Swedes along the Delaware and the smaller Finnish population were already within Dutch dominions. Finally, in the 1680's, with the establishment of Pennsylvania the foundations were complete. The Middle Colony area, then, had from the first a polyglot character and William Penn's immigration policy—his promotion of his colony—accentuated the variety. Not only the Germans but Welsh, Scotch-Irish, and English either settled or passed through Pennsylvania, while Philadelphia became, after 1710, a veritable distributing point for land-hungry Europeans bound for the south and west.[30]

Whatever their ethnic background and agricultural heritage, settlers in the Middle Colonies gravitated towards a balanced mixture of grain and livestock that has come to represent an important strand in American agricultural history, repeated in the West just across the mountains and still later in the Prairie States.[31] In a world today hungry for bread, cereal production still figures as prominently as in recorded history back to the time when a Hebraic dreamer prophesied and forestalled famine in Egypt and saved not only the land of Pharaoh but also surrounding world as well. This tradition of grain and livestock husbandry descends from the fusion of heritages—British, German, and others. The scale of farm operations in America was larger but the farmsteads had many resemblances in detail to old world counterparts, not only buildings but also orchards, kitchen gardens, fencing, and drainage. The fusion of traditions in the Middle Colonies proved durable in the new mixture and receptive to improvements as they came.[32]

Charles A. Beard once wisely observed that the philosophy of a subject is found at its perimeters. I take this aphorism to mean that the true master has assimilated—brought under control both detail and rational construction—a solid core from which he endeavors to push outward the boundaries of knowledge by further hypothesis and testing in research. On this analysis, students of early American agriculture do not show a very impressive track record. To be sure

21

they see other rich and fascinating fields to harvest: a) the wave of agricultural improvement between Jackson and the War, b) the expansion and mechanization after the War and, of course, c) the multiform patterns of the twentieth century that have made the United States the foremost agricultural nation as well as the leading industrial nation. These form the main stream and patently deserve — as they have had — major attention. But serious students of beginnings — those interested in the source of the stream, the first springs without which there can be no stream at all — find some irony in the neglect of a subject that touched our colonial forebears more closely than legislatures, constitutions, and social structure: their daily bread. In any terms, the task of setting forth this early adventure still challenges the brain and pen of those who can tell of transferring an agricultural tradition from a land of gentle rainfall to an area where clouds pile upon the firmament, the heavens crash, and the deluge pours down. Or, from the green and pleasant arable of manicured farms to a continent of almost limitless virgin forest. In this crucible, the heritage — the raw materials — began the fusion into something new. The story has not been perfectly told.

REFERENCES

1. Louis Cecil Gray, *History of Agriculture in the Southern United States to 1860*, 2 vols., Contributions to American Economic History (Washington: Carnegie Institution of Washington, 1933; reprint ed., Gloucester, Mass.: Peter Smith, 1958). Percy Wells Bidwell and John I. Falconer, *History of Agriculture in the Northern United States, 1620–1860*, Contributions to American Economic History (Washington: Carnegie Institution of Washington, 1925; reprint ed., New York: Peter Smith, 1941).
2. C. Melvin Herndon, "Indian Agriculture in the Southern Colonies," *North Carolina Historical Review* 44 (Summer 1967): 283–297 assembles many of the scattered scraps of information for the southern seaboard, with emphasis on the Chesapeake.
3. Research in this area presents real problems of place of origin, not to mention occupation or degree of skill.
4. Joan Thirsk, *English Peasant Farming: The Agrarian History of Lincolnshire from Tudor to Recent Times* (London, 1957); Joan Thirsk, ed., *The Agrarian History of England and Wales, 1500–1640*, vol. X (Cambridge, 1967) — see especially Chapter III, "Farming Techniques," Chapter IX, "Enclosing and Engrossing," and Chapter VIII, "Farm Laborers." Other pertinent studies include: Eric Kerridge, *Agrarian Problems in the Seventeenth Century and After* (London, 1969); Alan Harris, *The Rural Landscape of the East Riding of Yorkshire, 1700–1850; A Study in Historical Geography* (Oxford, 1961); J.R. Ravensdale, *Liable to Floods: Village Landscape on the Edge of the Fens, A.D. 450–1850* (Cambridge, 1974); Arthur G. Ruston and Denis Whitney, *Hooten Pagnell: The Agricultural Evolution of a Yorkshire Village* (New York, 1934); Alan R.H. Baker and Robin A. Butlin, eds., *Studies of Field Systems in the British Isles* (Cambridge, 1973). The work of George E. Fussell, *The English Rural Labourer* (London, 1949) is well-known as is the older study (1907) by Gilbert Slater, *The English Peasantry and the Enclosure of the Common Fields* (reprint ed., New York, 1968). See also W.G. Hoskins, *The Midland Peasant: The Economic and Social Structure of a Leicestershire Village* (London, 1957). Recent journal literature on British

economic history includes works by H.J. Habakkuk, G.E. Mingay, E.L. James, B.A. Holderness, F.J. Fisher, and others.

5. Richard H. Tawney, *The Agrarian Problem of the Sixteenth Century* (London, 1912), pp. 313–409. Eric Kerridge, *The Agricultural Revolution* (New York, 1968), disputes Tawney's interpretation but does not offer a different picture of the hubbub that attended this early enclosure movement.

6. Kerridge argues that beneath the comparatively calm surface important changes were taking place.

7. F. J. Fisher, "The Sixteenth and Seventeenth Centuries: The Dark Ages in English Economic History?" *Economica,* new series, 24 (February 1957): 2–18.

8. The literature on Puritan New England has taken a new direction during the past two and a half decades and the monographs and journal articles on town studies have brought new insights even though their authors were not primarily investigating agricultural history. The following are representative of a large body of studies: Sumner C. Powell, *Puritan Village: The Formation of a New England Town* (Anchor Books, Garden City, N. Y., 1965); Kenneth A. Lockridge, *A New England Town: The First Hundred Years, Dedham, Massachusetts, 1636–1736* (New York, 1970); Richard L. Bushman, *From Puritan to Yankee: Character and the Social Order in Connecticut, 1690–1765* (Cambridge, 1967), and Philip Greven, Jr., "Old Patterns in the New World: The Distribution of Land in 17th Century Andover," *Essex Institute Historical Collections* 101 (April 1965): 133–148.

9. John Pynchon, as late as 1668–1680, was careful to specify the method of "stubbing" his land for plowing. See Bidwell and Falconer, *Agriculture in the Northern United States,* p. 9.

10. Darrett B. Rutman, *Husbandmen of Plymouth: Farms and Villages in the Old Colony, 1620–1692* (Boston, 1967), pp. 28–62.

11. Edmund S. Morgan, "The Labor Problem at Jamestown, 1607–18," *American Historical Review* 76 (June 1971): 595–611.

12. Sigmund Diamond, "From Organization to Society: Virginia in the Seventeenth Century," *American Journal of Sociology* 63 (March 1958): 457–475.

13. Philip A. Bruce, *Economic History of Virginia in the Seventeenth Century,* 2 vols. (New York, 1896), I: 252–255, 279–280, 295, 303–308.

14. Aubrey C. Land, "The Tobacco Staple and the Planter's Problems: Technology, Labor, and Crops," *Agricultural History* 43 (January 1969): 69–81.

15. Edmund S. Morgan, "The First American Boom, Virginia 1618–1630," *William and Mary Quarterly,* ser. 3, 28 (April 1971): 169–198.

16. Aubrey C. Land, "Economic Base and Social Structure: The Northern Chesapeake in the Eighteenth Century," *Journal of Economic History* 25 (December 1965): 639–654.

17. Landon Carter, *The Diary of Colonel Landon Carter of Sabine Hall, 1752–1778,* ed. by Jack P. Greene, 2 vols. (Charlottesville, 1965), I, 260–261, and *passim.*

18. Some of this capital formation was forced; as for example, by landlords who specified the improvements—buildings, fences, and orchards—the tenant was obliged to make. See Aubrey C. Land, *Bases of the Plantation Society* (New York, 1969), pp. 40–42.

19. The literature for English farming is considerable. See G.E. Fussell, *The Old English Farming Books from Fitzherbert to Tull, 1523 to 1730* (London, 1947).

20. Gray, *Agriculture in the Southern United States,* I: 41–59 for beginnings, 277–290 for rice.

21. *Ibid.,* 280–284.

22. Converse D. Clowse, *Economic Beginnings in South Carolina, 1670–1730* (Columbia, S.C., 1971), especially pp. 1–94.

23. Harry J. Carmen, ed., *American Husbandry* (New York, 1936), pp. 291–306.

24. An unusual example can be found in Land, *Bases of the Plantation Society,* pp. 143–145. On the opportunities in sugar see Richard S. Dunn, *Sugar and Slaves: The Rise of the Planter Class in the English West Indies, 1624–1713* (Chapel Hill, 1972), pp. 182–223.

25. Richard H. Shryock, "British Versus German Traditions in Colonial Agriculture," *Mississippi Valley Historical Review* 26 (June 1939): 39–54. See also Albert B. Faust, *The*

German Element in the United States, 2 vols. (Boston, 1909), especially I: 177–211, 212–233 on Virginia and the Carolinas and II: 34–38 on the quality of farmers.

26. On the characteristics of Germans outside Pennsylvania see Dieter Cunz, *The Maryland Germans, A History* (Princeton, 1948), pp. 57, 191, 200–237.

27. James T. Lemon, "The Agricultural Practices of National Groups in Eighteenth-Century Southeastern Pennsylvania," *Geographical Review* 56 (October 1966): 467–496.

28. Aubrey C. Land, *Dulanys of Maryland* (Baltimore, 1968), pp. 170–184.

29. Thomas J. Wertenbaker, *The Founding of American Civilization: The Middle Colonies* (New York, 1938), pp. 86–99, 138–142, 214–228.

30. Wayland F. Dunaway, "Pennsylvania as an Early Distributing Center of Population," *Pennsylvania Magazine* 55 (1931): 134–169.

31. Bidwell and Falconer, *Agriculture in the Northern United States,* pp. 69–114.

32. *Ibid.,* 115–131.

The Converging Paths of Agricultural and Early American History: A Commentary and Speculation

By
Edward C. Carter II

The transit of culture across the Atlantic and its modification in the New World is perhaps the most important process studied by early American historians. Aubrey C. Land, the doyen of 17th and 18th century Chesapeake economic and social history, has provided us with a thoughtful, elegant essay in which he swiftly sketches the nature and configuration of four major early American agricultural experiences while posing problems for future investigation and also urging those engaged in research "to push outward the boundaries of knowledge by further hypothesis and testing . . . "[1] Like all good historians, Professor Land is interested in studying change over a significant period of time. He understands that the agricultural achievements of New England, the Chesapeake, the Carolina-coastal Georgia area, and the Middle Colonies were largely governed by the settlers' cultural baggage and the physical characteristics of their regions of settlement. Yet, Land suggests there are factors still to be discovered that account for the unusual proclivity

Dr. Carter is Associate Professor of early American History, the Catholic University of America, Washington, D.C., and Editor-in-Chief, The Papers of Benjamin Henry Latrobe.

25

for change and innovation of Carolina planters, and indeed also of the Pennsylvania German grain and livestock farmers. If his overview is traditional, Land suggests that until we analyze the social elements of that picture further and with greater precision, no amount of technical data will push early American agricultural history much beyond its present level of maturity and sophistication. Essentially, he implies that we need a history of agrarian society upon which to fashion agricultural history. To accomplish this, Land would have us move from descriptive history to conceptualization. The thrust of my remarks is that this process is already underway, propelled by two forces: the conscious efforts of particular historians, and certain new intellectual demands of American historical studies themselves.

My observations are those of a general early American historian who is more familiar with the idiosyncrasies of 18th century political institutions and ideology. But I brushed against Aubrey Land's topic recently while editing Benjamin Henry Latrobe's Virginia journals and sketchbooks, 1796–98, and teaching a course in the sociology and political economy of 17th century English colonization in North America and the Caribbean. Thus at most, I was only one step ahead of those aforementioned "bread colonies" professors when I agreed to serve as commentator. Clearly a crash course in the historiography of early American agriculture was indicated.

I began with the pertinent bibliographical sections of Brooke Hindle's informative *Technology in Early America*[2] and then turned to a rapid survey of the last two decades of *Agricultural History*. I discovered and read with great interest the papers of two earlier symposia that were related to our topic: the first, on Eighteenth-Century Agriculture (October 1967); the second, on American Agriculture, 1790–1840 (September 1970).[3] Especially impressive in the former are G. E. Fussell's "Science and Practice in Eighteenth-Century British Agriculture;" Conway Zirkle's paper on plant hybridization and breeding in America and his valuable commentary that postulates early American agriculture was fortunate to escape widespread use of the plow; Rodney C. Loehr's "Arthur Young and American Agriculture;" Land's own paper to which he refers above, "The Tobacco Staple and the Planter's Problems: Technology, Labor, and Crops;" and Merrill Jensen's views on the interrelationship between the Revolution and American agriculture. The latter symposium, while extending beyond 1815 (the customary date that political historians accept as the conclusion of early American history),[4] produced papers that are more relevant to

26

my observations, in particular: the historiographical review of northern agriculture by Wayne D. Rasmussen, a scholar whose patient and careful work should place us all in his debt; the stimulating, theoretical "Suggestions for the Geographical Study of Agricultural Change in the United States," by Andrew Hill Clark, a geographer; and Paul W. Gates' "Problems in Agricultural History." It is Gates who raises the most interesting questions and demonstrates that agricultural history possesses broad and significant dimensions when approached with imagination and a firm grounding in economic and social history. This, together with a bibliography published in conjunction with the symposium, should be required reading for all beginning American history graduate students.[5]

I was struck by several things in reviewing this material. American agricultural history is healthy and productive but appears to be in an early stage of development when compared to those other areas of American history with which I am familiar. Scholars are engaged in verifying data, editing documentary sources, and writing basic articles and monographs. Very little comparative work is being done yet and not much large scale synthesis undertaken. My survey corroborates Land's judgment concerning the paucity of the discipline's "philosophy." Nevertheless, there is a large volume of sound scholarship being produced similar in scope and structure to early American political and social history as it was written 25 years ago. Also, agricultural history has followed the same path in reaching a state similar, if slightly less advanced, to the history of technology.[6] Most disturbing is the fact that agricultural historians and their confreres in early American economic and social history are often investigating the same phenomenon, totally oblivious of each others' ongoing research or published results.[7] The next assignment of early American and Caribbean history must be predicated upon ever increasing research into what heretofore has been the domain of the agricultural historians. I shall consider the reasons for and implications of this development for the balance of this essay.

With Aubrey Land's paper and the problems he deems worthy of investigation, let us briefly note some complementary research that early American social and economic historians have undertaken recently. It is erroneous to assume that American agriculture was static and changeless during the 17th or 18th centuries or that Land's overview does not acknowledge significant intraregional variations of production and technology. Even in New England commercial export agriculture existed from the beginning in certain riverine areas and places such as Cape Cod. Following the Revolution, land was reclaimed or improved, crops diversified, and production increased in eastern Massachusetts. Sumner Powell has shown in *Puritan Village* that the founders of Sudbury did not have to hack their fields from the wilderness and that they successfully experimented with several systems of land distribution. Philip Greven has combined demography with an analysis of land distribution in a study of Andover that has important implications for agricultural historians.[8] These and similar monographs give weight to Paul Gates' prediction that the imaginative use of quantitative data extracted from probate records will allow us to "arrive at a clearer understanding of the land distribution process, the farming procedures, the changes in agriculture, . . . " of this area.[9] The Chesapeake was never totally a tobacco monoculture. Indeed, as Jacob Price has recently demonstrated, Norfolk grew to prominence during the revolutionary era specializing in the West Indian trade (forest products, Indian corn, pork, and beef) and becoming the major exporter of Virginia wheat to southern Europe.[10] Land is particularly intriguing when speculating about technological and entrepreneurial innovation and change in the Carolinas and Georgia as evidenced by the continual dialogue between the literate rice planters, and the development of rice, indigo, and short-staple cotton economies. These planters had more of a West Indian heritage than merely the use of slave labor and heavy capitalization upon which to draw. As Richard Dunn has made patently clear, the planters of Barbados and, to a lesser degree, those of the Leeward Islands had pioneered this pattern in their search for a cash crop by experimenting first with tobacco, then with cotton, before finally settling on sugar.[11] Peter Wood has recently shown that the amazing success of South Carolina's rice culture can be attributed largely to the fact that much of the region's slave labor came from the West coast of Africa and was "widely familiar with rice planting."[12] Here another non-European agricultural heritage merged with American tradition much as Indian production and techniques had done previously. At the 1975 annual meeting of the American Historical Association, there was a stimulating session on "Economic Change in America: Agricultural Productivity and Community Organization, 1700–1840" whose papers fulfilled Paul Gates' prophecy by utilizing statistical analysis of probate inventory records and tax valuation lists to describe accurately long-term patterns of land use, crop mix, crop yield per acre, average quantities of livestock held, and changing methods of farming.[13]

28

All this, however, is merely the beginning of a major historiographical movement that will result in the convergence of agricultural and early American history. Simply stated, the impact of the French school of *Annales* history on graduate training in the United States at such institutions as Johns Hopkins and Princeton is producing a generation of scholars dedicated to a new form of social history that seeks to explore three areas of human experience: "the basic conditions of life . . . the structure of economic and social life . . . [and] 'collective mentalities,' the belief systems and perceptual frameworks that determine the ways people interpret the routine and the extraordinary of their lives."[14] Inspired by both the philosophy and methodological practices of such great scholars as Marc Bloch, Lucien Febvre, Fernand Braudel, and Pierre Goubert, young American historians are dedicating themselves to a formidable task — the total reconstruction of past societies. As 90 percent of Americans in 1776 lived on the land, there will be an intellectual probing of agrarian life by early American historians as never before. To address such important problems as long-term economic developments, configuration of classes and social groups, "collective mentalities," or "modernization" (shift from an agricultural to an industrial society), these younger historians must first reconstitute the total life of the small scale American farmer together with his family structure. The record of the past, as Marc Bloch has so brilliantly illustrated, comes down to us in many forms — material as well as literary. Historians must not only master local archival resources, exploit the rare book and pamphlet collections of the American Antiquarian Society, Cornell University Library, Library Company of Philadelphia, and the National Agricultural Library, but they must actually learn how early agricultural artifacts functioned. John Demos' *A Little Commonwealth* is a good example of how archaeology and anthropology can help construct an outline sketch of a small society when the literary and legal documentation is scarce. Recently, Kenneth Lockridge has published preliminary results of his research on literary in New England that suggest there was nearly universal literacy among back-country farmers by 1790.[15] Was there any relationship between this phenomena and the reversal of exploitive farming practices, the adaption of reformers' ideas, and the increase of production that Robert Gross claims took place in parts of New England about this time? Thus the job at hand is the reconstruction of a variety of early American agrarian societies including that of the white yeoman farmer as well as the "inarticulate" black slave.

How can this story be more perfectly told? The time has come for two important American institutions, one private the other federal, to take an active role in speeding the process. The Institute of Early American History and Culture should sponsor a conference on the needs and opportunities for study of early American agriculture. Bernard Bailyn's seminal work, *Education in the Forming of American Society,* composed of interpretative and bibliographical essays, grew out of such a conference. By broadening the definition of education and moving beyond the boundaries of "institutional" history, Bailyn changed the entire direction of early American educational history and, in addition, stimulated the study of the family.[16] If the proper scholar can be found to undertake a similar review of the sources and literature of early American agrarian societies, the intellectual results may be equally as dramatic. Clearly, it is now possible for early American historians to consider issues of perhaps greater centrality than the niceties of federal theology and the Americanization of the classical tradition in law, literature, and architecture. I also propose that the National Historical Publications and Records Commission sponsor an historical editing project dealing with the literary, visual, and physical materials of these agrarian societies. Rather than letterpress, I suggest a microform publication with a highly sophisticated and inclusive printed guide and index. Such a project could also have its roots in the Institute conference and be held at a university such as Maryland, which boasts an outstanding history department already engaged in historical editing and a strong, research-oriented school of agriculture. Proximity to the National Agricultural Library would insure excellent bibliographical support. A modest proposal, but a surely proper tribute to that rising nation of early American farmers we memorialize this year.

REFERENCES

1. Land correctly is celebrated for his many books and articles on the economic and social structure of the Chesapeake, its tobacco culture, and plantation societies in general. Among his more important works are: *The Dulanys of Maryland* (Baltimore, 1968); ed., *Bases of the Plantation Society* (New York, 1969); and "Economic Base and Social Structure: The Northern Chesapeake in the Eighteenth Century," *Journal of Economic History* 25 (December 1965): 639–654.

2. Published in 1966 by the University of North Carolina Press, this work is one of the Needs and Opportunities for Study Series of The Institute of Early American History and Culture in Williamsburg. These volumes are outgrowths of conferences that explored special historical fields "which scholars have neglected or indifferently exploited or in which renewed interest has developed in our own times" (Brooke Hindle, *Technology in Early America* [Chapel Hill, 1966], p. vii). Further mention of these conferences and their resulting publications will be made below.

3. See *Agricultural History* 43 (January 1969): 1–186, and *ibid.*, 46 (January 1972): 1–223.

4. Hindle, however, makes a strong case for 1850 as the terminus of early American technology.

5. Douglas Bowers, comp., *A List of References for the History of Agriculture in the United States, 1790–1840* (Davis, California, 1969).

6. It is instructive to read *Agricultural History* and *Technology and Culture* in tandem and observe how each journal has moved relentlessly towards "professionalism." Representing two of the newer divisions of American historical studies, their earlier articles were written by agricultural specialists, engineers, and informed laymen. Gradually, the academicians began to contribute until a generation of university-trained scholars whose main preoccupation was agricultural or technological history made its appearance. The questions to which each group addressed itself were similar, as were their organizational methods as reflected by their meetings and policy statements appearing in their respective journals.

7. Gates points out the value to agricultural historians of the current New England 17th and 18th century community research of such younger scholars as Sumner C. Powell, Darrett B. Rutman, Philip J. Greven, Kenneth A. Lockridge, and Richard L. Bushman, who through the ingenious use of such varied things as land records, wills, and anthropological techniques have been able to reconstruct much of the life of this agrarian society. Land has also noted their contributions above.

8. Sumner C. Powell, *Puritan Village: The Formation of a New England Town* (Middletown, Conn., 1963); Philip J. Greven, *Four Generations: Population, Land, and Family in Colonial Andover, Massachusetts* (Ithaca, N.Y., 1970).

9. Paul W. Gates, "Problems of Agricultural History, 1790–1840," *Agricultural History* 46 (January 1972): 50.

10. Of great interest is the author's discussion of the rise of secondary coastal urban centers in the 4,000–8,000 population range such as Norfolk, New London, and Providence, that carried on the West Indian trade efficiently. The slightly larger port towns of 6,000–12,000 such as Charleston, Baltimore, and Newport sustained a significant European export trade by 1776. These port towns served farmers not only in the immediate hinterland but also up and down adjacent coast lines. See Jacob M. Price, "Economic Function and the Growth of American Port Towns in the Eighteenth Century," *Perspectives in American History* 8 (1974): 123–186.

11. Richard S. Dunn, *Sugar and Slaves: The Rise of the Planter Class in the English West Indies, 1624–1713* (Chapel Hill, N.C., 1972). The economies and social structures of North American and Caribbean plantation societies of this period should be considered comparatively. For a valuable review of current major literature see Jack P. Greene, "Society and Economy in the British Caribbean During the Seventeenth and Eighteenth Centuries," *American Historical Review* 79 (December 1974): 1499–1517.

12. Peter H. Wood, *Black Majority: Negroes in Colonial South Carolina from 1670 Through the Stono Rebellion* (New York, 1974), chapter II.

13. Of particular interest were two papers: Robert A. Gross, "The Agricultural Crisis of Eighteenth-Century New England," and Duane E. Bell, "Agricultural Organization, Output, and Productivity: Chester County, Pennsylvania in the Eighteenth Century." See Rosemary Brana-Shute, ed., *Abstracts of Papers Presented at the Ninetieth Annual Meeting of the American Historical Association, Atlanta, Georgia, December 28–30, 1975*, Session 64.

14. See Jack P. Greene, "The 'New History': From Top to Bottom" *New York Times,* January 8, 1975, p. 31. Johns Hopkins Graduate Study Program in Atlantic History and Culture proposed to examine the shared experience of societies bordering the Atlantic ocean by training students in both historical and anthropological methods. The first years of the program have focused on the study of roles of non-elite and non-European groups, the institution of slavery, transposition of European and African institutions to the New World, trade and technology, and colonization. Recently, the Johns Hopkins University Press has begun to publish edited translations of special issues of the *Annales: Economies, Societies, Civilizations* that will undoubtedly further popularize and accelerate research on early Ameri-

can agrarian society. See *Biology of Man in History* (Baltimore, Md., 1975) edited by Robert Forster and Orest Ranum and translated by Elborg Forster and Patricia M. Ranum, the first selection from the *Annales,* 24 (November–December 1969); another selection soon to be published is *Family and Society* (1976) from the *Annales,* 27 (July–October 1972).

15. John Demos, *A Little Commonwealth: Family Life in Plymouth Colony* (New York, 1970); Kenneth A. Lockridge, *Literacy in Colonial New England: An Enquiry into the Social Context of Literacy in the Early Modern West* (New York, 1974).

16. Bernard Bailyn, *Education in the Forming of American Society* (Chapel Hill, N.C., 1960).

The Agricultural Literature of the Gentleman Farmer in the Colonies

By
Alan E. Fusonie

The purpose of this essay is to present a selective view of the utilization of agricultural literature — both published and unpublished — by a number of American agriculturists during the early years of our nation. In particular, emphasis will be placed upon George Washington. It is especially fitting that we should look back to the time of the American Revolution, nearly six generations ago, a period when the American colonists were engaged in a political struggle to secure independence and establish a novel system of government — one which most European nations at the time characterized as absurd and unworkable. Today, however, it is apparent that aside from the military and political struggle for national survival, the scientific exchange of ideas between Colonialists and the Englishmen of the mother country continued to varying degrees and at an accelerated rate after the Revolution. This was particularly true in agriculture and its related fields where the articulate gentlemen farmers in the Colonies kept in communication with leading agriculturists across the Atlantic. These men kept themselves informed of the latest developments occurring in agriculture abroad,[1] through correspondence as well as by acquiring outstanding books,

Dr. Fusonie is a curator of Manuscripts and Rare Books at the National Agricultural Library, and Lecturer in American History at Prince George's Community College in Maryland.

treatises, and journals for use in their own private working libraries and for the libraries of agricultural societies.[2]

For the gentlemen farmers who comprised only a fraction of colonial society, it was an era of experimentation in such areas as land use, animal husbandry, seed cultivation, crop rotation, plantation management, farm implements, and harvesting. The small, often inarticulate, proprietor or yeoman farmer with meager hand tools and log cabin was less fortunate, for he could not afford the luxury of experimentation which would involve any risk of failure. Virginia, with its elite landed aristocracy possessing large acreage, cattle, fine horses, slave labor, servants, and crops such as maize, wheat, and tobacco for export, provided ideal conditions for early experimental developments in Colonial agriculture.

Certainly Thomas Jefferson—the designer of the neoclassical Monticello and the scientific farmer who perfected "the moldboard of least resistance"—ranks as one of the most outstanding examples of experimental progress. Another member of this distinguished seaboard gentry and one of the subjects of this essay was George Washington who, at the age of seventeen, started his career as county surveyor of Culpepper, Virginia. Born on February 22, 1732, at Wakefield Plantation in Westmoreland County, about 38 miles east of Fredericksburg, Washington later developed an intense concern with and dedication to improvements in agriculture. He manifested a deep scientific curiosity and a practical as well as an experimental interest not only in the latest developments taking place abroad but also in the limited number of outstanding improvements taking place within the Colonies. On his Mount Vernon estate which at one time entailed over eight thousand acres including Mansion House Farm, Union Farm, Dogue Run Farm, Muddy Hole Farm, and River Farm, Washington tested many reported improvements in agriculture. Even during the eight years of the American Revolution when his overseeing of farm experiments had been replaced by his duties as Commander and Chief of the Continental Army, he tried to keep himself informed about the management of his farm. He also had a public interest in promoting the work of agricultural societies as well as an official governmental concern for eliciting federal support for agriculture.

In the area of personal interest, Washington's desire to become a successful farmer was well matched by his ever-present spirit of inquiry. When at home, Washington could often be found seated at his desk in the Mansion House library corresponding with leading agriculturists in Britain,[3] the most notable of these being Arthur

A replica of a small-scale farm house of the 1770's at the end of a country lane with rail fence, located at Turkey Run Farm in McLean, Virginia. (Picture courtesy, Economic Research Service, U. S. Department of Agriculture)

A small farm dwelling illustrative of some in existence around the time of the American Revolution. (Picture courtesy, National Park Service)

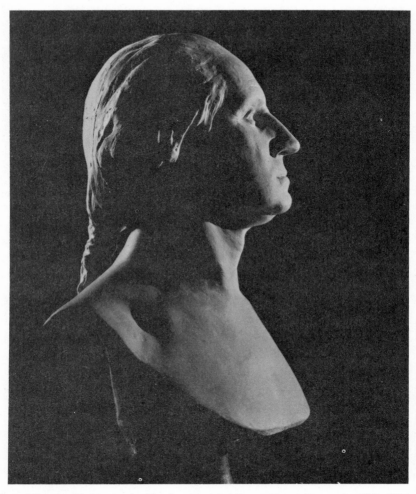

Bust of George Washington by Houdon, modeled live at Mount Vernon in 1785. (Picture courtesy, Mount Vernon Ladies, Association, Mount Vernon, Virginia)

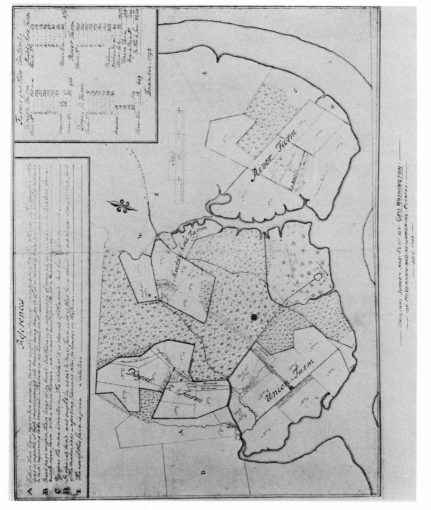

Courtesy Huntington Library, San Marino, California. Reproduction by permission.

37

Young. Through his reading and notetakings from Young's *Annals of Agriculture* . . . in such areas as barley, clover, carrots, cattle, hogs, lucerne, manures, oats, ploughing, ploughs, potatoes, rye, and turnips,[4] he became convinced of the superiority of the English system of husbandry and believed that the *Annals* might provide a guide for improved husbandry in the Colonies.[5] Young's *Annals* also included journalistic accounts of his own tours as well as statistical information relating to imports, exports, scarcity of food, and the status of the poor.[6] Washington also exchanged ideas with Sir John Sinclair, a Scottish agriculturist and the first President of the British Board of Agriculture. The correspondence of these two agriculturists with Washington was published in 1801.[7]

Although Washington was not known as an avid reader, he did study and assiduously extract information from published agricultural works based primarily on experiments. His discriminating approach to agricultural literature was clearly evident in the following excerpt from his letter of August 6, 1786 to Arthur Young: " . . . of the many volumes which have been written on this subject [husbandry], few of them are founded on experimental knowledge."[8] It is with this type of scrutiny that Washington took notes from the works of Jethro Tull, an English agriculturist, from Henry Home, an outstanding Scotch lawyer often addressed as Lord Kaimes, from Henri Louis Duhamel du Monceau, a most remarkable French economist and botanist of the eighteenth century. Washington's working library — the focal point for the direction and management of his farming operations — included published works by the following agriculturally related pioneers: John Abercrombie (Scottish-born horticulturist, 1726–1806); Matthew Allen (English farrier); James Anderson (Scottish economist and agriculturist, 1739–1808); William Gibson (English veterinary surgeon, 1680–1750); John Kennedy (English nurseryman, literary horticulturist, 1759–1842); William Marshall (English agriculturist, planter-farmer and philosopher, 1745–1818); Robert Maxwell (Scottish agricultural writer, 1695–1765); John Robinson (English politician and agriculturist, 1727–1802).[9] After reflecting upon what he had learned through correspondence and reading, Washington would conduct small experiments on various plots of soil on his farms as well as in his "Botanical Garden" behind the Mansion House. Since Washington did take notes from the writings of a number of agriculturists, it might be of interest to survey the work of several of them.

Jethro Tull was a pioneer in helping to improve methods of farming both through his inventions of the horse-hoe plough and the

A reproduction of George Washington's Library. (Picture courtesy, Mount Vernon Ladies Association, Mount Vernon, Virginia)

drill machine. In 1731, after years of study, observation, and actual experimentation in the field, Tull set to print his revolutionary and often controversial methods in his landmark work, *The Horse-Hoeing Husbandry.*[10] Years later, Washington, interested in Tull's ideas, began transcribing notes from his own third edition copy of Tull's work. He took careful and copious notes on Chapters I through XX but, apparently, not on the remaining three chapters and Appendix.[11] In his notes, which were taken from Chapter VI entitled "Of Hoeing," can be found Tull's description of the use of hoeing as an improved alternative to common tillage due to the fact that hoeing reduced the amount of time needed for the growth of plants and trees.[12] Washington did not agree with all of Tull's principles but found his spirit of experimentation worthy of emulation.

Washington also took extensive notes from Henry Home's (Lord Kaimes') book entitled, *The Gentleman Farmer: . . . ,* first published in 1776. This treatise includes descriptions of agricultural implements, cattle and horses, the preparation of farmland for planting, grass and plant cultures, crop rotation, reaping and storage of corn and hay crops, the feeding of farm cattle, manures, and also plant food, soil fertility, and the various means of fertilizing soil. In particular, Washington made detailed sketches of the Brake or Drage-Harrow (Plate 1), the Second Harrow (Plate 2), as well as the tables dealing with a six-year crop rotation plan for clay soil and also free soil, entailing the use of fallow, wheat, peas, barley, soy, oats, and pasture. Washington noted from Home's work that he considered the proper use of crop rotation to be the most important aspect of good husbandry.[13] Continually experimenting with crop rotation, Washington sketched out his own seven-year plan from 1793 to 1799 for his Dogue Run Farm entailing the use of buckwheat, corn, clover, grass, manure, and potatoes — illustrative of but one of his many efforts at diversified farming.[14]

The French influence upon Washington's interest in agriculture is largely attributable to Henri Louis Duhamel du Monceau who, in turn, was influenced by and tried to improve upon the drill plough invented by Jethro Tull, one of England's earliest and most notable writers on agriculture whose works were based upon actual experiments in the field. A member of the Royal Academy of Sciences in Paris, Duhamel wrote a number of books dealing with agriculture, forestry, and horticulture. One of his most outstanding works entitled *A Practical Treatise of Husbandry: . . .* was first published in 1759. Washington took careful notes from his translated second

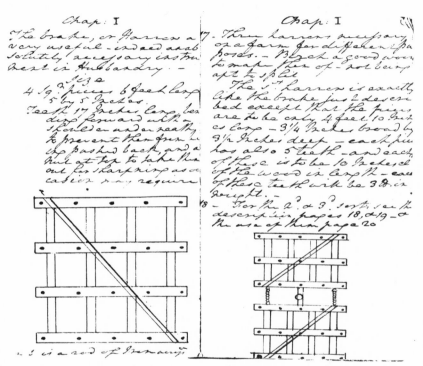

Hand sketched illustration of brake of drage-harrow (Plate 1), (Plate 2) from *George Washington Papers*. (Courtesy, Library of Congress, Manuscript Division)

41

141 - pasture, a single plough
with good cattle will be
sufficient to command
the remainder till sown

142 - Rotation in a Clay soil

	1775	1776	1777	1778	1779	1780
1	Fallow	Wheat	Pease	Barley	Hay	Oats
2	Wheat	Pease	Barley	Hay	Oats	Fallow
3	Pease	Barley	Hay	Oats	Fallow	Wheat
4	Barley	Hay	Oats	Fallow	Wheat	Pease
5	Hay	Oats	Fallow	Wheat	Pease	Barley
6	Oats	Fallow	Wheat	Pease	Barley	Hay
7	Pasture	Pasture	Pasture	Pasture	Pasture	Pasture

When the rotation is com=
pleted, the 7th enclosure having
been 6 years in pasture is rea=
dy to be taken up for a rotation
of crops, which begins with
Oats in the year 1781, and pro=
ceeds as in the 6th enclosure. —
In the same year 1781 the 5th enclosure
is made pasture; for which it
is prepared, by sowing pasture
grass-seeds with the Barley
of the year 1780. And in this
manner may the rotation be
carried on without end. —
Here the labour is equally
distributed; and there is no turn

or confusion. — But the
chief property of this rotation
is, that two exhausting or
white Corn Crops, are never
found together: By a due mix=
ture of crops, the soil is pre=
served in good heart without
any adventitious manure —
at the same time the land is al=
ways producing plentiful
crops: neither Hay nor pasture
get time to degenerate. —
The whole dung is laid up
on the fallow.
Every farm that takes a
grass-crop into the rotation
must be enclosed, which is peculiar=
ly necessary in a clay soil
as nothing is more hurtful
to clay than poaching —

Rotation in a free soil

	1775	1776	1777	1778	1779	1780
1	Turnip	Barley	Hay	Oats	Fallow	Wheat
2	Barley	Hay	Oats	Fallow	Wheat	Turnip
3	Hay	Oats	Fallow	Wheat	Turnip	Barley
4	Oats	Fallow	Wheat	Turnip	Barley	Hay
5	Fallow	Wheat	Turnip	Barley	Hay	Oats
6	Wheat	Turnip	Barley	Hay	Oats	Fallow
7	Pasture	Pasture	Pasture	Pasture	Pasture	Pasture

Hand sketched illustration of tables of six-years rotation plan from *George Washington Papers*. (Courtesy, Library of Congress, Manuscript Division)

edition copy printed in 1762, with the exception of the following parts: Part II, Chapter V; Part III, Chapters II, III, IV; Part IV, Chapters IV, V.[15] An examination of Washington's notes reveals that he was greatly interested in the emphasis which Duhamel placed upon the benefits to be derived from the use of tillage as opposed to the old reliance upon the use of dung.[16] Washington was impressed not only with Duhamel's estimate of the usefulness of the Rotherham or patent plough[17] but also with his description of the drill plough[18] and the basic essentials necessary for the operation of all ploughs.[19] Washington purchased a Rotherham or patent plough and it served his purposes well until finally giving way to wear, tear, and poor maintenance.[20] By synthesizing both his notes and his own innovative thoughts, Washington moved on to the testing and experimental stages and was successful in devising his own "barrel plough" for sowing corn, wheat, and oats. His invention was thought to be based, in part, upon the ideas of Duhamel and those expressed by Arthur Young in his *Annals of Agriculture*.[21]

Washington also took an active interest in the agricultural improvements being made within the Colonies. As an example, he kept in touch with his good friend, John Beale Bordley, a Maryland jurist and agriculturist whose own inquiring mind and zeal for experimentation had turned his 1600 acre farm on Wye Island into one of the first successful agricultural experiment stations in the Colonies.[22] The Wye Island Estate had been bequeathed to Bordley's first wife, Margaret Chew, by her bachelor brother, Philemon Lloyd Chew. In reference to the various experiments by the gentlemen farmers, Washington once told Bordley that:

> Experiments must be made, and the practice (of such of them as are useful) must be introduced by Gentlemen who have leisure and ability to devise and wherewithal to hazard something. The common farmer will not depart from the old road 'till the new one is made so plain and easy that he is sure it cannot be mistaken.[23]

Like Washington, Bordley was an enthusiastic student of British experiments in agriculture; in particular, he was also stimulated by the published works of both Jethro Tull and Arthur Young. In his own published work, *Sketches on Rotation of Crops . . .* , Bordley specifically expressed his indebtedness to these two men.[24]

Bordley was among the first in the Colonies to publish the results of his own research and experimentation in agriculture. In his work, *A Summary View of Courses of Crops . . .* , Bordley compared the English Norfolk system of crop rotation with the inferior practices

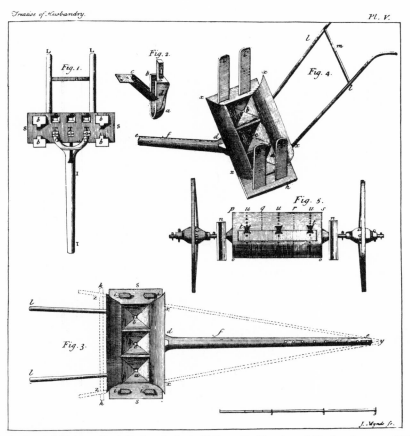

Illustration of Duhamel's drill-plough from Duhamel's *Treatise of Husbandry* . . . 1762. (Courtesy, National Agricultural Library, Rare Book Collection)

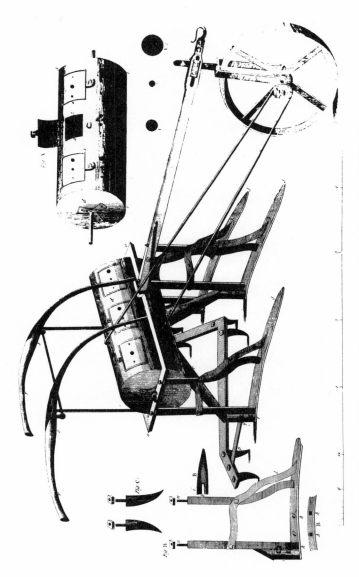

Illustration of drill-plough from Young's *Annals of Agriculture*, Vol. 3, 1785. (Courtesy, National Agricultural Library, Rare Book Collection)

45

Bordley's first wife, Margaret Chew, who died November 11, 1773. She was bequeathed by her bachelor brother, Philomon Lloyd Chew, an estate on Wye Island.

Elizabeth Bordley, daughter of John Beale Bordley and his second wife, the Widow Sara Mifflin by Gilbert Stuart.

(Courtesy, Papers of the Philadelphia Society for Promoting Agriculture, University of Pennsylvania Library, Rare Book Room)

John Beale Bordley at age twenty-one by Wallaston.

used in Maryland. Bordley also offered his eight-field system as an alternative solution to the problem of soil exhaustion.[25] On May 14, 1785, Bordley presented 60 copies of his *Summary Views . . .* to the Philadelphia Society for Promoting Agriculture for distribution to those members who had not already obtained a copy.[26] In his treatise on . . . *Rotation of Crops . . . ,* Bordley discussed and compared not only the old and new systems of crop rotation, which were then in practice in both England and America (including the use of maize, clover seed, the bean drill, and the sowing of wheat on clover),[27] but also the value of and plans for the utilization of farm-yard manure, cattle stalls, barns, and ice houses.[28] Washington must have appreciated the opportunity to read the experiments and observations of this remarkable Maryland farmer; he took notes from the beginning pages of his first edition copy of Bordley's *Essay and Notes on Husbandry* concerning the use of various types of trees for shade in pasture land as well as the required growing time and use of clover and timothy in a type of rotation system. This particu-lar book represented one of the first published accounts of scientific agriculture in America.[29] It should be mentioned that personal contact between agriculturists was an important aspect in the dis-semination of agricultural literature. John Singleton, a gentleman farmer from Easton, Maryland, in a letter of March 8, 1785, to his friend, Bordley, mentioned that he had read . . . *Notes on Husban-dry* and, at his uncle's home, had been able to show his copy to Charles Varlo, an English agriculturist, on tour through America. According to Singleton, he had been asked by Varlo to subscribe to his volume on husbandry entitled *A New System of Husbandry . . .* (1785).[30]

Washington's public and official governmental interest in encour-aging an improved and more wide-spread use of agriculture in the Colonies was greatly stimulated by the advice of Sir John Sinclair who, in corresponding with America's first President, pointed out the need for establishing both state and local agricultural societies throughout the United States as well as a National Board of Agricul-ture at the Federal level. In England, similar societies had already proved themselves to be instrumental in promoting much needed knowledge and improvements within the field of agriculture.[31]

With the expanding cultivation of land along the eastern sea-board,[32] the need for establishing societies for promoting agricul-tural improvements within the Colonies had already become in-creasingly apparent to many gentlemen farmers. As early as 1766, the New York Society gave substantial attention to the improvement of agriculture.[33] Nine years later, in 1775, a number of gentlemen farmers in Pennsylvania reportedly expressed an interest in establishing a similar society.[34] Another ten years passed before the first organization to be concerned exclusively with the promotion of agricultural reform in America was finally established in Philadelphia — the Philadelphia Society for Promoting Agriculture.

The preliminary work on the formation of this Society actually was begun during the winter of 1784–1785 by a group of prominent men among whom were such notables as John Beale Bordley and John Cadwalader, both of whom owned farms in Maryland. The Society itself was partially modeled after the agricultural societies which had already been formed in Europe. Its initial membership was concerned with the state of agriculture in America, more specifically with what was believed to be, " . . . our great inferiority . . . ,"[35] and the need for " . . . more skillful and fortunate management . . . ."[36] The Society, therefore, developed a set of rules and regulations which would act as guidelines and which were national in scope.[37] In paying tribute to the potential value of this undertaking, Washington, an honorary member of this particular Society, said, "[it] . . . promises extensive usefulness if it is prosecuted with spirit."[38] Two years later, on July 3, 1787, it was noted that George Washington, acting in behalf of Arthur Young, deposited with the Society six volumes of the *Annals of Agriculture*.[39]

By 1789, the Society's membership began to assume a national dimension for, in addition to the some 23 Marylanders, it included individuals from such states as Delaware, Kentucky, Massachusetts, New Hampshire, New York, Rhode Island, South Carolina, and Virginia.[40] The Society embarked immediately upon a plan of acquiring outstanding works on agriculture for its library. In addition, various communications pertinent to the advancement of agriculture were selected for publication in monograph as well as article form for inclusion in almanacs, newspapers, and other types of periodical literature. Illustrative of this effort was the pamphlet entitled *Agricultural Enquiries on Plaister of Paris . . . (1797)* by Judge Richard Peters, a practical farmer and first president of the Philadelphia Society for Promoting Agriculture. Peters had collaborated with Bordley and other members of the Society in establishing a number of model farms in Pennsylvania for experimentation with grains, plants, shrubs, and trees.[41]

In the preface of his pamphlet, Peters stressed the need to establish a state society of agriculture which would encourage communication, experimentation, and recognition for valuable ideas and deeds. He expressed dismay, however, at the "ineffectual" attempts by former legislatures, consisting mostly of farmers, to encourage research in agriculture.[42] In hope of stimulating some improvements, Peters, in his pamphlet, contrasts these conditions with the "incalculable" advantages gained not only by England as a result of its Board of Agriculture but also by France where support and encouragement for the advancement of agriculture was a part of the government's national policy.[43] Peters, also profoundly interested in agriculture abroad, corresponded with Washington and ultimately dedicated this small volume to him. Washington, appreciative of this gesture, asked Peters for several additional copies.[44]

The Philadelphia Society found the press a particularly important medium for the communication of agricultural information. *The Pennsylvania Mercury and Universal Advertiser* in its June 8, 1787 issue carried the reprint of a letter to the Society from Colonel George Morgan, farmer and owner of "Prospect," a 300-acre farm now a part of Princeton University, proposing the establishment of a committee to conduct some onsight inspections of a number of fields infected by the Hessian Fly and to develop some preventive measures.[45] The Hessian Fly, a destructive insect first appearing in Long Island, was reportedly brought into this country in the straw bedding used by Hessian soldiers.[46] In a limited way, the Philadelphia Society for Agriculture did become a vehicle for communication in the area of agricultural education although the Society had little or no influence over either the small proprietor or the yeoman or dirt farmer who continued to follow their traditional methods of exhausting the soil.

At the Federal level, Washington's efforts to evoke support for the promotion of agriculture had little immediate effect for, at the time, there were too many other national problems which demanded the attention of Congress. In 1794, Washington, in a letter to Sir John Sinclair, explained the situation in the following way:

> It will be sometime, I fear before an Agricultural Society
> with Congressional aid will be established in the Country; we
> must walk as other countries have done before we can
> run . . . .[47]

In spite of his pessimistic outlook on this matter, Washington, in his "Farewell Address" in 1796, recommended to Congress that public funds be appropriated to assist in the development of a National Board of Agriculture for the purpose of collecting and disseminating agricultural information.[48] He even asked if Sir John Sinclair would

Colonel George Morgan. (Courtesy, Papers of the Philadelphia Society for Promoting Agriculture, University of Pennsylvania Library, Rare Book Room)

Richard Peters (1744–1828), lawyer, Revolutionary patriot, judge, farmer. (Courtesy, University of Pennsylvania Rare Book Room)

remain available to advise and to assist future members of the proposed Board in its actual establishment and implementation.[49] Certainly Washington should be remembered as one of the leading national figures of his time who was fully aware of " . . . the importance of National encouragement to Agriculture."[50] On December 14, 1799, Washington died and was buried in the family vault at Mount Vernon.

Washington's proposed Board was not seriously considered during his lifetime, although the idea endured through the years due in part to the efforts of agricultural societies. Throughout the first half of the 19th century, interest in the development of agriculture in America continued to grow at both the state and local levels where an increasing number of agricultural societies were actively acquiring books, correspondence, magazines, and newspapers for their own libraries.[51] It was a common practice among the societies to list in their publications their latest acquisitions in agriculture.[52] To a certain degree, these societies made Congress more aware of the national importance of both agriculture and the American farmer. In 1852, a privately supported United States Agricultural Society was formed based upon the principles originally laid down in Washington's "Farewell Address."[53] At each of its annual meetings, the Society, along with the Maryland Agricultural Society and many other state and local societies, urged the establishment of a separate federally funded national Department of Agriculture.

Finally, in 1862, some 66 years after Washington's recommendation, the first national milestone in agriculture was achieved with Abraham Lincoln's historic signing of the Organic Act establishing a separate federally funded Department of Agriculture inclusive of a Library. This Act presented, in part, an historic testament to the development of a rich body of American imprint literature of the Revolutionary Period, 1783–1800, including works by the following agriculturally related pioneers: John Adlum (pioneer in viticulture, 1759–1836); John Bartram (first native American botantist, 1679–1777); William Bartram (traveler and naturalist, 1739–1823); John Binnes (Virginia farmer, 1781–1813); Metcalf Bowler (agriculturist, 1726–1789); William Coxe (pomologist, 1762–1831); William Darlington (botanist, 1782–1863); Samuel Deane (clergyman and agriculturist, 1733–1814); Oliver Evans (pioneer in the design of mills, 1755–1819); Timothy Pickering (soldier, administrator, politician, and agriculturist, 1745–1829); Timothy Pitkin (statesman, historian, economist, 1766–1842); Job Roberts (pioneer agriculturist, 1756–1851); Benjamin Rush (physician, patriot, humanitarian, and agriculturist, 1745–1813); John Taylor (political writer and agriculturist, 1753–1824); Thomas Walters (early American botanist, 1740–1789); Elkanah Watson (merchant, canal promoter, and agriculturist, 1758–1842). It was also the reflection of as well as take-off point from the initial interest and experimental efforts of both the agriculturists in the Colonies and the generations of agriculturists who succeeded them.[54]

REFERENCES

1. Wayne D. Rasmussen, "The American Revolution and Agriculture: A Comment," [Eighteenth Century Agriculture: A Symposium] *Agricultural History,* 43 (January 1969): 125; see also Rodney Loehr, "Arthur Young and American Agriculture," *Agricultural History,* 43 (January 1969): pp. 46–47.

2. For a list of agricultural books included in George Washington's Library see *The Boston Athenaeum Catalog of Washington's Collection in the Boston Athenaeum* (Cambridge: Massachusetts University Press for J. Wilson, 1897), pp. 9–10, 26–29, 32, 77, 88–97, 100, 102, 114, 126, 137, 148–151, 161–167, 299–300, 542–548 located in Library of Congress, Rare Book Room; see also *Inventory of the Contents of Mount Vernon 1810, With Prefatory Note by Worthington Chauncey Ford* (Portland, Ore.: Printed by Keldam Stationery and Printing Co., 1909), pp. 15–40; the inventory was reportedly printed from a manuscript owned by Mr. W. K. Bixby of St. Louis who donated his copies to the Mount Vernon Ladies' Association of the Union. Copy cited here is located at the Mount Vernon Ladies' Association Research and Reference Library, Mount Vernon, Virginia.

3. Cecil Wall, "George Washington Country Gentleman," *Agricultural History,* 43 (January 1969): 5.

4. According to Presidential Papers Microfilm: George Washington Papers, Series 8A-P, Notes, Reel 124, Library of Congress, Manuscript Division [hereinafter cited as LCMD, GWP 8A-D Notes, Reel 124], Washington definitely took handwritten notes from Young's work, *Annals of Agriculture.*

5. Letter from George Washington to Arthur Young, August 6, 1786. *The Writings of George Washington From the Original Manuscript Sources 1745–1799.* John C. Fitzpatrick, Editor (Wash., D. C.: Government Printing Office, 1938) [hereinafter cited as Fitzpatrick], 28, p. 511.

6. G. E. Fussell, "Early Farming Journals," *Economic History Review,* III (April 1932): 28; for a discussion of the influence of eighteenth-century British agriculture on American farming with special focus upon Arthur Young see Rodney C. Loehr, "Arthur Young and American Agriculture," [Eighteenth Century Agriculture: A Symposium] *Agricultural History,* 43 (January 1969): 43–56; in same journal see also article by Carl Woodward entitled, "A Discussion of Arthur Young and American Agriculture," pp. 57–67.

7. *Letters from His Excellency George Washington to Arthur Young, esq. F.R.S., and Sir John Sinclair, bart., M.P.* (London, 1801: Alexandria, Virginia, 1803). National Agricultural Library, Rare Books [hereinafter cited as NAL, RB]; for a comprehensive examination of Young's life as a public and private figure see *The Life of Arthur Young, 1741–1820* by J. G. Gazley. (Philadelphia: The American Philosophical Society, 1973), 727 p.

8. Letter from George Washington, Mt. Vernon to Arthur Young, August 6, 1786, Fitzpatrick, *XXIX,* p. 511.

9. Descriptive annotations to works by these and other authors of the period are contained in *A Selective Bibliography on George Washington's Interest in Agriculture* compiled by Alan E. and Donna Jean Fusonie (Davis, Calif.: Agricultural History Center, University of California, 1976), pp. 46. These works were either known to and/or read by many American gentlemen farmers.

10. For a biographical account of Tull's life see Earl Cathcart, "Jethro Tull: His Life, Times and Teaching," *Journal of the Royal Agricultural Society of England* (London, 1891): II, 1–4;

see also G. E. Fussell's book, *Jethro Tull: His Influence on Mechanized Agriculture*. (Reading: Osprey, 1973), 133 p.

11. According to LCMD, GWP 8A-D Notes, Reel 124, Washington definitely took handwritten notes from chapters 1-4 and 6-20 in Jethro Tull's book entitled *Horse-Hoeing Husbandry: or, An Essay on the Principles of Vegetation and Tillage. Designed to Introduce a New Method of Culture; Whereby the Produce of Land Will be Increased, and the Usual Expence Lessened. Together with Accurate Descriptions and Cuts of the Instruments Employed In It*. 3rd edition, very carefully corrected. To Which Is Prefixed, a New Preface by the Editors, Addressed to All Concerned in Agriculture. (London: Printed for A. Millar, 1751). Microfilm checked against rare edition copy at NAL, RB.

12. LCMD, GWP 8A-D Notes, Reel 124, pp. 47, 57.

13. An examination of LCMD, GWP 8A-D, Notes, Reel 124 reveals Washington's careful sketching and notetaking from Henry Home's (also referred to as Kaimes or Lord Kaimes) *The Gentleman Farmer: Being An Attempt to Improve Agriculture by Subjecting It To The Test of Rational Principles* (Edinburgh: Printed for W. Creech, 1776), Plates 1, 2, pp. 124, 129, 131. Microfilm checked against rare edition copy at NAL, RB.

14. Paul L. Haworth, *George Washington Country Gentleman; Being An Account of His Home Life and Agricultural Activities* (Indianapolis: Bobbs-Merrill Company, 1925), p. 121; for additional information concerning Washington's farms and efforts at crop rotation, see LCMD, GWP, Series 4, Reels 100, 104, 105, 106.

15. An examination of LCMD, GWP 8A-D Notes, Reel 124 reveals that Washington took notes from the following chapters in Henri Louis du Monceau Duhamel's book, *A Practical Treatise of Husbandry: Wherein Are Contained, Many Useful and Valuable Experiments and Observations in the New Husbandry, Collected During a Series of Years . . . Also, the Most Approved Practice of the Best English Farmers, In the Old Method of Husbandry* (London: Printed for C. Hitch and L. Hawes, 1762); Part I, Chapters 1-14; Part II, Chapters 1-5; Part III, Chapters 1, 5-7, 9-12; Part IV, Chapters 1-3. Microfilm checked against rare edition copy at NAL, RB.

16. *Ibid*., pp. 11-12.

17. *Ibid*., p. 49.

18. *Ibid*., p. 59.

19. *Ibid*., p. 421.

20. Benjamin Henry Latrobe, *Being the Notes and Sketches of an Architect, Naturalist and Traveler in the United States from 1796 to 1820*. (New York: Burt Franklin, c1905, 1971), pp. 60-61; Walter Brooke, *The Agricultural Papers of George Washington* (Boston: R. G. Badger, 1919), pp. 22-23; see also E. W. Hamilton, "George Washington, Farmer," *American Thresherman*, 33 (February 1931): 5, 18 — one of the illustrations reportedly details the Rotherham plough brought over from England.

21. Haworth, *op. cit*., p. 107; an examination of LCMD, GWP 8A-D Notes, Reel 124 reveals that Washington took notes from the first four volumes of Arthur Young's *Annals of Agriculture and Other Useful Arts*; his notes included information on ploughs and ploughing.

22. Stevenson Whitcomb Fletcher, *The Philadelphia Society for Promoting Agriculture, 1785-1955* (Philadelphia: The Philadelphia Society for Promoting Agriculture, 1959), pp. [34], [35]. For biographical sketch of the life of John Beale Bordley see *The Biographical Cyclopedia of Representative Men of Maryland and District of Columbia* (Baltimore: National Biographical Publishing Co.; 1879), pp. 49-50. Some other works which Bordley is credited with having published include: *Purport of a Letter on Sheep. Written in Maryland, March 30th, 1789*. [Copy located in Boston Athenaeum]; *Yellow Fever* (1793); *Intimations on Manufactures, Agriculture, and Trade* (1794); *Queries from the Board of Agriculture of London, with Answers by J. B. Bordley* (1797); *On Pasturing Cattle* (1798); *Husbandry Dependent on Livestock* (1800); *Epitome of Forsyth on Fruit Trees, with Notes by an American Farmer* (1803). See Elizabeth Bordley Gibson, *Biographical Sketches of the Bordley Family*. (Philadelphia, 1865), pp. 120-121, Paper of the Philadelphia Society for Promoting Agriculture, University of Pennsylvania, Rare Book Room [hereinafter cited as UPL, RBR] in October, 1934, the Philadelphia Society for Promoting Agriculture made

plans to celebrate their 150 year anniversary which included a pilgrimage to Wye Island. Due to poor road conditions, the idea had to be abandoned. Today, however, there is a paved road and Wye Island remains an area of land rich in agriculture.

23. Letter to John Beale Bordley from George Washington, August 17, 1788. LCMD, GWP, Series 2, P-8, V15-P219, Reel 197; Washington, through his private secretary, Tobias Lear, also corresponded with Oliver Evans, inventor and author of the work entitled *The Young Mill-Wright & Miller's Guide. In Five Parts Embellished with Twenty-Five Plates . . . .* (Philadelphia, Pa.: The Author, 1795) concerning the possible improvements to be made in his mill at Dogue Creek as well as inquiring into the future employment of a first-rate miller. At this time, growing interest in the construction and use of the grist mill in Northern Virginia indicated an expanding market for the agricultural products of wheat. For an article on the status of tobacco in Maryland and Virginia, 1720–1770, see Aubrey C. Land, "The Tobacco Staple and the Planter's Problems: Technology, Labor and Crops" [Eighteenth-Century Agriculture: A Symposium] *Agricultural History* 43 (January 1969): 69–81.

24. John Beale Bordley, *Sketches on Rotations of Crops and Other Rural Matters. To Which Are Annexed Invitations of Manufactures; On the Fruits of Agriculture; And On New Sources of Trade, Interfering With Products of the United States of America in Foreign Markets* (Philadelphia: Charles Cist, 1797), p. 66. NAL, RB.

25. Bordley, *A Summary View of the Courses of Crops, In The Husbandry of England and Maryland; With a Comparison of Their Products; And A System of Improved Courses Proposed for Farms in America* (Philadelphia: Charles Cist, 1784), pp. [3] – 22, NAL, RB.

26. *Minutes Book 1787–1810* [Manuscript], p. 60. UPL, RBR.

27. Bordley, *Sketches* . . . , pp. 1–38.

28. *Ibid.*, pp. 38–66.

29. LCMD, GWP 8A-D Notes, Reel 124, John Beale Bordley, *Essay and Notes on Husbandry* (Philadelphia: Budd and Bartram for Dobson, 1799), pp. 5–7, 12–17, Contents checked against 2nd ed. copy, 1801, located at NAL, RB; see also Ulysses P. Hedrick, *A History of Horticulture in America To 1860* (New York: Oxford University Press, 1950), p. 473.

30. Letter from John Singleton to John Beale Bordley, March 8, 1785, *Minutes Book of The Philadelphia Society For Promoting Agriculture* [Marked "The Folio"], Papers of the Philadelphia Society for Promoting Agriculture, UPL. RBR.

31. Donald McDonald, *Agricultural Writers From Sir Walter of Henley to Arthur Young, 1200–1800* (London: n.p., 1908), p. 4.

32. Rodney True, "Sketch of the History of the Philadelphia Society for Promoting Agriculture," *Memoirs of the Philadelphia Society for Promoting Agriculture* (Philadelphia Society for Promoting of Agriculture, 1939), VI, p. 5.

33. *New York Gazette*, March 13, 1766; *New York Mercury*, March 10, 1766; *Weekly Post Boy*, March 13, 1766.

34. *American Husbandry. Containing An Account of the Soil, Climate, Production and Agriculture, of the British Colonies in North America and the West Indies; With Observations on the Advantages of Settling in Them, Compared with Great Britain and Ireland* (London: J. Bew, 1775), I, p. 180. This is an anonymous book in which the author appears to have been familiar with the agriculture of Maryland and Virginia. It has been suggested that possibly Dr. John Mitchell, an English physician and naturalist, who lived in Virginia for a time may have been the author. NAL, RB.

35. *An Address from the Philadelphia Society for Promoting Agriculture; With a Summary of Its Laws and Premiums Offered* (Philadelphia: The Philadelphia Society for Promoting Agriculture, 1785), p. A2. NAL, RB.

36. *Ibid.*, p. A2.

37. *Ibid.*, p. 9.

38. Letter from George Washington to James Warren, October 7, 1785. LCMD, GWP, Series 2, Letterbook, Vol. 12, p. 247 (Original).

39. *Minutes Book 1787–1810* [Manuscript], p. 60. Papers of The Philadelphia Society for Promoting Agriculture. UPL, RBR.

40. *Laws of the Philadelphia Society for Promoting Agriculture; As Revised and Enacted by*

the *Said Society, February 18th, 1789, with the Premiums Proposed, February 3rd, 1789. To which is Prefixed a List of the Members of the Society* (Philadelphia: The Philadelphia Society for Promoting Agriculture, 1787), pp. 3–9. NAL, RB.

41. Ulysses P. Hedrick, *A History of Horticulture in America To 1860* (New York: Oxford University Press, 1950), p. 147.

42. Richard Peters, *Agricultural Enquiries On Plaister of Paris. Also, Facts, Observations and Conjectures on that Substance* [!] *when Applied as Manure. Collected, Chiefly from the Practice of Farmers in Pennsylvania, and Published as Much with a View to Invite, as to Give Information,* [iii].

43. *Ibid.,* [iv]; for an insight into Judge Peters' approach to soil exhaustion see his article, "Improvements of Worn Out Lands," *Columbian Magazine* (January 1791): 27–31; *American Museum,* IX (January 1791): 41–44; *American Museum,* IX (February, 1791): 109–111.

44. Letter from George Washington to Richard Peters, January 21, 1797, in Fitzpatrick, XXXV, p. 371.

45. *The Pennsylvania Mercury and Universal Advertiser* (June 8, 1787); September 14, 1787, issue gives a descriptive account of an on-sight observation of the Hessian Fly on Long Island.

46. Bordley, *Essays and Notes* . . . ., p. 242; Wayne D. Rasmussen, "The Farmer In The Evolution of a New Nation, 1763–1788," [Mimeographed. Copy, courtesy of the author], (June 27, 1960), p. 11.

47. Letter from George Washington to Sir John Sinclair, July 20, 1794. LCMD, GWP, Series 2, Reel 7.

48. "Farewell Address" by George Washington, December 7, 1796, in Fitzpatrick, XXXV, pp. 315–16.

49. Letter from George Washington to Sir John Sinclair, December 10, 1796. LCMD, GWP, Series 2, Reel 8.

50. Letter from George Washington to Sir John Sinclair, January 20, 1799, in Fitzpatrick, XXXVI, p. 97.

51. Loehr, *op. cit.,* p. 55.

52. For an example of this practice see *Memoirs of the Philadelphia Society for Promoting Agriculture* (Philadelphia: Benjamin Warner, 1818), IV, pp. xi–xx; see also *The Massachusetts Agricultural Repository and Journal* (Boston: Walls and Lilly, 1819), V, pp. 393–400. NAL, RB.

53. *The Journal of Agriculture: Comprising the Transactions and the Correspondence of the United States Agricultural Society,* III, i (April 1860), p. 161. NAL, RB.

54. For a selective list of monographs, periodicals, and works of agricultural societies published prior to 1860 see *Heritage of American Agriculture: A Bibliography of Pre-1860 Imprints,* compiled by the Author.

In Praise of the Historical:
A Commentary

By
John D. Macoll

Alan Fusonie has offered an unusual sight and sound presentation by showing colorful slides (see illustrations in Dr. Fusonie's paper) with his description of the agricultural literature of the colonial gentleman farmer. More than a unique presentation, his paper contains two major points for our consideration: communications and sources.

We learn that while persons of like interests initiated and maintained contact with each other during the colonial era, rarely did they meet face to face. We are also informed that these same gentlemen communicated directly through correspondence and indirectly through distribution of the printed word. Given the manner, expense, and time involved in using the mails of the 1970s, one ought to be profoundly stirred that a letter or package sent in an earlier age ever reached its destination.

Fusonie provides several examples of how literate men exchanged ideas on improving agriculture, be it soil, crops, or tools. That the number of this circle of interest was rather small cannot be denied; what is also undeniable is the wealth of material created and, incidently, left behind in which future researchers can indulge themselves to their hearts' content.

Dr. Macoll is Chief of the Records Division, Federal Trade Commission, Washington, D,C.

One has only to recall historians of the first order who used original primary source documents to write landmark histories that broke new ground and led the way to conclusions that have generally stood the test of time — revisionists and quantitative historians notwithstanding. So many come to mind: Frederick Jackson Turner, Solon J. Buck, Arthur M. Schlesinger, Sr., and other historians availed themselves of the raw resources of history at a time when there was not as much available comparatively as there is today.

Unfortunately for those who are addicted to the historical drug generically termed primary sources, the heart's content of one historian is not necessarily that of another. To put it bluntly, because the drive for publication has created a glut of books and articles based primarily on other books and articles, we have been swamped by the secondary source syndrome and hung up on the historical hysterics of challenging interpretations. These, in turn, are based upon interpreting a revisionist's interpretation of an earlier interpretation. Likened to the situation of the fish caught in tightly woven nets, it is virtually impossible to resist the temptation to wreak havoc on another historian's work for, the more eminent the historian-victim, the more significant the catch.

The reliance upon self-indulgent interpretations without returning to the basis of history — the original written word — is creating an irresistible irrelevance to the fabric of history in the original first person. So much is now being written about historical interpretations that we have lost sight of the primary principles of the historical context.

Quite properly, monographs and other writings provide the reader with facts — as should any good work. But we have become enamored with where the direction in thinking is going. This is not necessarily bad — there is just too much of it! The basic elements of research have been sacrificed for seeming convenience and conformity. The *nouveau* researcher, if he or she may be dignified by that scarred yet sacred word, revels in the latest monograph based on conclusions, dubious or otherwise, of some historians who have not had the decency or energy to avail themselves of the rich primary resources in this country. Unhappily, many doctoral dissertations are barren of essential primary source documentation. One can only conclude that the secondary source syndrome has established a firm beachhead in the graduate schools.

The only apparent exception to this state of affairs is the wholly unrealistic demand by certain individuals in the historical profession that current government records be thrown open to investigation and research. Some historians have suggested a ten-year moratorium on the destruction of all Federal records. Since the United States Government generates six to seven million cubic feet of records annually, the thought of such a ban staggers even my highly imaginative flights and convinces me that those who support such a move have used government archives infrequently and, therefore, to be as diplomatic as possible, do not know what they are talking about.

Government records aside, only in the relatively recent past have there been intensive efforts to uncover the rich documentary sources in American history. The first effort was the one volume *Guide to Archives and Manuscript Collections in the United States,* compiled under the editorial supervision of the late Philip M. Hamer, first executive director of the recently reorganized National Historical Publications and Records Commission, and published by Yale University Press in 1961. The Hamer *Guide* is a boon to researchers because it not only lists concisely the holdings of key repositories but also describes the holdings of many hitherto ignored small collections scattered throughout the country. At about the same time, the Library of Congress began the monumental multi-volume *National Union Catalog of Manuscript Collections,* affectionately known as NUCMC, edited by the late Arline Custer. Unlike the Hamer *Guide,* NUCMC lavishly details holdings, including significant names of senders and recipients. Unless lightning strikes the Library of Congress, NUCMC will continue to report the ever-increasing holdings in American repositories. And, with a revised edition — hopefully continued one volume — of the Hamer *Guide* in the near future, intrepid researchers cannot plead ignorance of available primary resources. Such an admission — and there are many everyday — acknowledges stupendous failure.

Let us assume our intrepid researcher has consulted the appropriate reference works. He is still not satisfied. He refuses to dirty his hands with old manuscripts or archives unless it is all laid out for him. Anything less than that is poor boy's work. Assuming further that our researcher has a strong interest in the papers of an early American statesman, he decides to apply pressure on a certain historical documentary editing letterpress project that is partially supported by Federal grants. To our ever-anxious researcher, this project does not appear to publish quickly enough, even though the scholarship — deep, abiding scholarship — has broken new ground and has set new standards of historical investigation. Primary sources abound in these volumes, just the thing to lead the inquisitive researcher to more fertile ground such as other manuscript collections, newspapers and, particularly, archives—those nasty, dirty records that are never in the order a researcher wishes!

Nevertheless, our researcher, in true audacious fashion, demands access to yet unpublished documents collected by the project, despite the facts that this can only slow the project considerably and that an editor who receives Federal funds is under no obligation to accede to such demands unless he so wishes. If a researcher is so impatient, then let him soil his hands at the same repositories that the editor did. What a pampered lot we are—expecting someone else to do all the work for us! These pertinent and, to some who read these lines, impertinent comments are asides to my basic argument, which is the overemphasis on secondary works as sources of raw information at the expense of research into primary source material.

To relate directly to this Symposium, there have been bibliographical publications of secondary sources on American agricultural history. In recent years, there have also been lists published of early agricultural experiments and experiences, the latest of which has been compiled by Alan Fusonie himself. This is good and should be encouraged, but it represents only the tip of the proverbial iceberg. Some thought should be given to compiling and publishing an annotated list of manuscript and archival resources in agricultural history. Certainly NUCMC and the Hamer *Guide* list papers of individuals and firms connected with agriculture, and the National Archives and other major repositories make no secret of their holdings related to the history of American agriculture. If such a compilation has begun, it would be a most encouraging sign that researchers are coming of age. Perhaps small historical documentary editing projects could be established concerning some of the men cited by Fusonie in his paper. If this is not economically feasible, then a selected annotated series of documents could be published in historical journals, a method which used to be a significant outlet for such information. This suggestion may fall on barren ground for, excepting certain regional or state historical journals, most editors are rather adamant in their refusal to publish documents.

Even if the necessary conditions existed, it is doubtful that there would be the same excitement generated over the publication of primary sources, either as documents or as lists, as there is over the latest secondary work. Alluding to an earlier inference, one has little patience for those who contemptuously refuse to delve into the

60

raw resources. They are a swindle to those devoted to the heartbeat of agricultural or any other history. Researchers are the doctors investigating the body historical, not each other.

Alan Fusonie's topic reflects the significance of agriculture in American history. And the people that populate his paper were important because the colonial period depended upon such individuals to exchange ideas necessary to improve agriculture. Another historian may use the same sources as Fusonie and draw different conclusions, but at least the challenger availed himself of the same documentation. In this era of the American Bicentennial, we should be returning to first principles in historical research, namely, the original documentary sources — the life blood of solid, dependable history.

John Banister: Seventeenth Century Scholar, Minister, Farmer, Artist, and Naturalist

By
Joseph Ewan

In 1597, John Gerard addressed his "courteous and well willing" listeners stating that "among the manifold creatures of God none *provoked* men's studies more, or *satisfied* their desires so much as plants have done." Quite a testimony for plants!

Between John Gerard and today there is a chapter in American botanical history of greater significance than is generally realized. The story begins at Oxford, the site of the first botanical garden in England, and centers around a student, John Banister, age 17, who was "on campus" for about ten years from 1667 to 1678 when he left to take a ministry in Virginia. From 1678 until 1692, when he was accidentally shot while a member of an exploring party to the Roanoke River, Banister, the scholar, was a minister, planter-farmer, artist, and a naturalist.[1]

What was happening during those formative years when Banister lived at Oxford? Whom did he meet? How did these Oxonians give direction to Virginian, and thus American, plant studies?

Henry Compton, Queen's College, later Bishop of Oxford and then of London, was to make possible Banister's Virginia ministry.

Dr. Ewan is Professor of Botany, Tulane University, New Orleans, Louisiana.

Compton grew many of the novelties that Banister found in the New World. The bishop's garden at Fulham Palace had been famous since Bishop Grindal (in Elizabeth's time) and had introduced such novelties as tamarisk from the Near East. Compton later "had a thousand species of exotic plants in his stoves and gardens . . . There were but few days in the year, till towards the latter part of his life, but he was actually in his garden, ordering and directing . . . "[2]

In 1657, Robert Plot entered Magdalen College, where Banister was later a student, and it was surely Plot who gave a model for the "Natural History of Virginia" which Banister had in progress at his death. Plot's *Natural History of Oxfordshire* was published in 1677 while Banister was still at Oxford and his assistance was acknowledged in the preface. This folio was the first broadly conceived provincial natural history, a form widely adapted for other English districts in the century to follow. Plot became the first keeper of the Ashmolean Museum, and another Oxonian, Edward Lhwyd, of fossil fame, became Plot's assistant.

The Bobarts, father and then son, were in charge of the Physick Garden at Oxford. The father initiated a catalogue of the garden in 1648, which was published in 1658; two other authors, Dr. Philip Stephens, principal of Magdalen Hall, and William Browne, native of Oxford and Senior Fellow of Magdalen College, were co-authors. When Banister entered Magdalen, in 1667, there existed a botanical tradition. Leonard Plukenet, who was to publish Banister's drawings of Virginia plants, matriculated at Hart Hall, Oxford, in 1662. He was then 22 years of age. In 1658, the same year that the second edition of the catalogue of the botanic garden was published, John Locke entered Christ Church as a student. Locke was at Oxford, as a student, then a medical practitioner, from 1658 to 1684, and, over those years, brought together an exceptional library of about 3000 volumes. His library has been described in detail by Harrison and Laslett.[3] It contained many botanical titles by Gesner, Bauhin, Morison, Morin, etc. Among them was a copy of Bobart's *Catalogue* of 1658.

Banister took his Master's degree in 1674. Then for three years, as a fellow, he served as chorister, clerk, and chaplain. In 1677, probably on his departure for Virginia, Jacob Bobart presented him with a sixth edition copy of John Evelyn's *Kalendarium Hortense* which had been published the year before. In 1677, one of the most important figures in British botany, William Sherard, matriculated in St. John's College; although Sherard and Banister were at Oxford that year, there is no record that they ever met. Both probably studied under Robert Morison. The same year in which Banister left Magdalen, John Clayton took his bachelor's degree at Merton. Later, as Rev. John Clayton, the two met in Virginia in 1686.

While John Tradescant the younger had taken plants from Virginia to England, Hariot and John White had already brought back a few specimens in 1586 and 1587. The bald cypress was growing in the Oxford Physick Garden and the black walnut was also probably his introduction. Tradescant the elder is reputed to have been sought as head gardener before Jacob Bobart the elder was appointed. He was succeeded by his son. Banister took snippets in the garden during his studies and mounted them in a blank folio. Along the curve of a stem or margin of a leaf, he had labeled specimens with their Latin mononomial or phrase name and the author who coined them. He also carefully entered these plant names in a small notebook. The dried plants went with him to the New World to serve as a guide to unknown Virginia plants he would later discover but the notebook had been left with Professor Robert Morison, who less was engrossed in his *Universal History of Plants* updating Caspar Bauhin's *Pinax*. It is probable that Morison recommended to Bishop Compton that Banister be sent to Virginia, perhaps on "a Virginia fellowship." Both he and Compton coveted exotic plants. Thus, to Morison, until his accidental death in 1683, and then to Leonard Plukenet and John Ray went plants, and to Martin Lister and Edward Lhwyd went shells, fossils, and insects for scientific study. Chiefly to Compton, to his gardener, George London, and also to the younger Jacob Bobart, went seeds and roots of promising garden subjects.

Few figures in English botany hold more variety and importance for us than Robert Morison, yet no full biography has ever been attempted. Born and educated in Aberdeen, Morison first enters the Oxford scene, on September 2, 1670, when he lectured at Oxford. During his long Cromwellian exile he had studied at Montpellier under Vespacion Robin (remember *Robinia*). The gardens of the Duke of Blois were then under Morison's charge. Morison published *Hortus Blesensis,* or an account of the garden at Blois, supplementing it with what he called "hallucinations of Caspar Bauhin,' and the 'animadversions of [his brother] Johann Bauhin." Morison's criticism was called by some invidious and by others deserved. Then three days after he arrived at Oxford, in the words of historian Anthony à Wood, Morison "was translated to the Physic Garden, where he read in the middle of it (with a table before him) on herbs and plants thrice a week."[4] He lectured for five weeks in 1670, again in 1673, surely to Banister among others but, for the next thirteen years, he "prosecuted his large design of publishing the Universal Knowledge of Simples." His design, however, was cut short by his accidental death in 1683. He left us besides his folio *Plantarum historiae universalis Oxoniensis*,[5] the first account of a plant family, the parsleys, ever to be monographically treated. When, in any event, you next drive through St. James Park, remember that it was Robert Morison who laid out the park for Charles II. It was Morison perhaps more than any other botanist back in England who, stirred the professional loyalties of Banister concerning Virginia botany. It was to Morison that Banister wrote a beautifully detailed letter from "The Falls" of the James River; fortunately this letter of April 6, 1679, one of a number which he must have written, has survived, and offers an important source of information of the James River country. Listen now to Banister:

> I take it [to be] Apocynum Americanum Latifolium. [*Apocynum cannabinum*]. The peel when dry and beaten becomes a very fine Shining Something between hair & Silk; the Indians dye it of Several Colours, & weave it into Baskets & Cohobbes, a thing of about a hands breadth in the middle which comes upon their breast, & is prettily wrought terminating in two long strings with which they bind up their truck [That which they carry.] at their backs. Of this well spun & woven Chamoletwise [Camlet, originally a fine cloth woven of camel's hair and silk, then goat's hair and silk, now of wool and cotton.] might be made a very neat & I daresay lasting Stuff. We sow here most sorts of English Grain besides those proper to the Country, as Maize of which there are divers kinds (not to mention its accidental differences (if they are no more) I mean its coloured, red blew, yellow, white & mixt.) whereof there are but two I think commonly planted among us: the one we call Flint Corn which is of a rounder form & harder substance, the other She-Corn, this is more soft & feminine, on whose Superficies Nature has impress'd the Signature ♀. The Indians have two Sorts more of Rath-ripe Corn, [Early ripe Zea mays L.] the ears of ye lesser Sort are no bigger than ye haft of a knife, & its stalks not much higher than ones middle, of these they can make two Crops in a Year.[6]

Banister was fond of watermelons. He called them a "very pleasant and innocent fruit. I have eaten near half a score of them in an afternoon." On tobacco and its impact on Virginia society, hear him again:

> Virginia is a country naturally so fertile, that it does or might
> be made yield anything that may conduce to the pleasure or
> necessity of life: but the great crops of Tobacco some strive
> to make, & the number of Planters which daily increases,
> and more by reason of a silly, fond, & withall a proud
> humour that generally possesseth the poorer sort of people
> (as it is reported of the Muscovites) that they had rather see
> their children starve at home, than put them out to learn
> anything abroad: These things, I say, hinder its improve-
> ment, for all arts & trades, if not propogated by communicat-
> ing them to others, die with, if not before their masters.[7]

From Banister's manuscript account of wild fruits and nuts let us
listen to this:

> Our old fields & woods abound with Strawberries, Mulber-
> ries, Pascimmons, grapes & hurtle-berries of several kinds;
> besides wallnuts black and white, haselnuts, chestnuts, Chin-
> quapins, the Indian name of small dwarf chestnuts; hence we
> also call small bits royal or piece of eight Chinquapins. Also
> our Island sandy rich low grounds yield us abundance of very
> good hops without the labour of planting, hilling, or weed-
> ing: nor are our Orchards less kind, affording us plenty of
> excellent apples, pears, plums, apricots, Nectarines, *Meloco-
> tones,* & several other very good sorts of Peaches that do,
> and do not, cleave to the stone, which I am persuaded are
> spontaneous somewhere or other on this Continent, for the
> Indians have & ever had more abundance & greater variety
> of them than we.[8]

Hedrick suggests that peaches were introduced by the Spanish to
Mexico and Florida during the sixteenth century and were spread so
rapidly by the Indians that they had become established in Virginia
before Jamestown was settled.[9] Peter Collinson on the flyleaf of his
copy of John Lawson's *History of Carolina* (1714), wrote

> It is very much doubted if Peaches are an American Fruit — it
> is more probable It was brought by the French who for some
> years attempted a Settlement on the Bay of Mexico on the
> Coast of Florida . . . under John Ribald anno 1562. They
> brought all sorts of Grains and Fruits to sustain their new
> colony — and it is to be Observed that the Peaches are
> planted by those Florida Indians & from Whom may have
> passed to the Indians of South Carolina but on our first
> Settling Virginia & Carolina & New England, Peach Stones

was carried from England & Sett on all those Colonies — & throve & bear Wonderfully.

Collinson annotated page 16 of this copy of Lawson "Father Hennepin first discovered the Messasipi, the greatest River of all Florida anno 1680 — In passing through the Indian Nations for many Hundred Miles on that River: mentions no peaches."

Banister taught himself to draw because, as he wrote, Providence had thrown him upon the "confines of a new world of plants of which wherein as yet a very small discovery has been made." Leonard Plukenet published 64 of Banister's drawings, to which we may add 11 attributable to him. Banister's skill contrasts with the crudity of other artists whom Plukenet employed in illustrating his *Phytographia*.

In short, this first botanist of Virginia described 340 plants of which 266 may be noted as first described in his manuscript catalogue. In the course of his descriptions, he cited older authors, Hariot, Tradescant, Gerard, Parkinson, Clusius, and so on, 74 times. John Ray, in his oft mentioned *Historia plantarum*,[10] published Banister's catalogue and listed 125 plants; they were only the new species from Virginia detected by Banister up to 1679, and they did not account for the species he had discovered by 1692, or such as the tulip tree, known to Europe before Banister's coming to Virginia.

One asks about Banister's ministry. I quote five words from his manuscript: "it tedders me too short." So we leave John Banister, scholar, minister, farmer, artist, and naturalist, with only this sampling of his talents, sketched against the background of his Oxford associations. A memorandum I once found in the Bancroft Library, perhaps the words of Governor John Evans of Colorado, perhaps only something Governor Evans collected in his wide reading, reads:

> A man's achievements are the measure of his powers. Circumstances may create apparent exceptions to the rule. Other things being equal results will be in favor of him who has the most talent and makes the best exertions. The use made of acquisitions indicates character . . . There are various kinds of talent. Some have but one, others are endowed with many. One who possesses a single talent highly developed can accomplish much but whoever has many is an Agamemnon.

REFERENCES

1. Joseph and Nesta Ewan, *John Banister and his Natural History of Virginia, 1678–1692* (Urbana: Univ. of Illinois Press, 1970) 485 pp.

2. Stephen Switzer, *Ichnographia rustica: or the nobleman, gentleman, and gardener's recreation. Containing directions for the general distribution of a country seat, into rural and extensive gardens, parks, paddocks, and a general system of agriculture, illustrated with great variety of copper-plates, done by the best hands, from the author's drawings.* (London: Dr. Brown, B. Barker, C. King, W. Mears, . . . , 1718), vol. 1, p. 70

3. John Harrison and Peter Laslett, *Library of John Locke ([Oxford]: Univ. Press, 1965).*

4. Anthony A. Wood, *Athenae Oxonienses. An exact history of all the Writers and Bishops who have had their education in the most ancient and famous university of Oxford, from . . . 1500 to the end of the year 1960. To which are added, the Fasti or Annals of the said University, for the same time.* (London: Tho. Bennet, 1691, 92) vol.2, "Fasti," 161, quoted from ed. 2 (1721) p.178.

5. Volume Two, the only volume published before his death.

6. Ewan and Ewan, p. 40.

7. *Ibid.* p. 361.

8. *Ibid.* p. 355. "meloctones," acc. to Oxford English Dictionary, a Cydonian apple or a peach grafted on a quince, described in 1719 by London and Wise as "not worth anyone's planting"

9. Ulysses P. Hedrick, *A History of Horticulture in America to 1860* (New York: Oxford University Press, 1950) p.19

10. John, Ray, *Historia plantarum; species hactenus editas aliasque insuper multas noviter inventas & descriptas complectens. In qua agitur primo de plantis in genere, earumque partibus, accidentibus & differentiis; deinde genera omnia tum summa tum subalterna and species usque infimas, notis suis certis & characteristicis definita, methodo naturae vestigiis insistente disponuntur . . . .* (London: typis M. Clark, prostant apud H. Faithorne, 1686–1704.) 3 Vols. "Catalogus stirpium rariorum" in vol. 2 (1688) pp. 1926–1928. Ivar Tidestrom privately published *Banister's Catalogue of Virginia Plants* (Washington, D.C.: the author, 1907) without-notes: see Ewan and Ewan, p. 141.

Western Movement — Its Literature

By
Jeff Dykes

The literature of the western movement in this country is so varied and so vast that in the time allotted on this program, we can only hit the high spots. In trying to find a way to limit the discussion to a manageable segment, serious consideration was given to mentioning only those books that influenced the movement. To have done so would have eliminated some of the best of the literature — in fact, practically all the books written in the last 100 years. The influence of the literature on the movement has received considerable thought on the selections that follow but has not been limiting.

Numerous events and situations were of great historical significance in the westward movement — among those of particular importance I have listed: The Louisiana Purchase; the Lewis and Clark Expedition; the fur trade; the Santa Fe market; the Annexation of Texas followed by the Mexican War and the Gadsden Purchase; the Opening of the Oregon Trail, followed by the settling of the United States-Canada boundary dispute; the railroad surveys and other official exploring expeditions; the persecution of the Mormons in Missouri and Illinois; the discovery of gold in California; the growth of the Texas Longhorn herds during the Civil War; the completion of the trans-continental railroad; the Battle of Palo Duro Canyon

Mr. Dykes is a collector and bibliographer of Western Americana, of College Park, Maryland.

71

and General A. Miles' winter campaign following the Battle of the Little Big Horn. Please note that only a few of the important happenings listed occurred after 1850. The early writings about the pre-1850 events and situations nearly all had some influence on the westward movement.

It is here recognized that the westward movement really began with the first moves inland from the seacoast colonial settlements and that the further expansion from the Appalachians to the Mississippi was another important step on the way to the Pacific. However, only a few books on the beginnings will be mentioned here as our emphasis today is on the West from the Mississippi. In 1817, Morris Birkbeck's *Notes on a Journey in America . . . To The Territory of Illinois* was issued in Philadelphia. It includes the first description known to me of the true or tallgrass prairie — probably the greatest natural grassland area in the world, stretching from Lake Winnipeg in Canada to the Gulf of Mexico. Birkbeck was an English land scout and later led a band of English settlers to their new homes in Illinois. His book was reprinted several times in England and in Ireland and there was a German edition in 1818 and a Dutch printing in 1820. In 1822, Birkbeck issued *An Address to the Farmers of Great Britain, with an Essay on the Prairies of the Western Country* in London, an expansion of his description of the prairie in his 1817 book.

Theodore Roosevelt's four volume set, *Winning the West* (N.Y., 1889–1894–1896) is entirely devoted to the Appalachian to Mississippi frontier. It was the first segment of a planned set that was to have covered the entire Western movement — the author's duties after 1896 did not permit him to finish the job.

The first important event in the expansion across the Mississippi was the purchase of Louisiana — making the exploration of the new territory a matter of extreme urgency. The literature of the first of the expeditions — by Lewis and Clark — is extensive indeed. Patrick Gass was a member of the party and his book was the earliest first-hand account of the expedition — it was issued in Pittsburg in 1807 with the title, *Journal of Voyages and Travels*. The first British edition came out in 1808 and Wright Howes' selective bibliography in *U.S. Iana, 1650–1950* (N.Y., 1962) calls it the "best" and claims that the map included in the French edition of 1810 was the "best of the Lewis and Clark route done up to this date." The authorized report was issued in Philadelphia in 1814 and was reprinted many times — the most scholarly being that of 1893. President Jefferson's message to Congress in 1806, *Communicating Discoveries — By*

Captains Lewis and Clark, Dr. Sibley and Mr. Dunbar was issued by both the House (believed to be the earlier) and the Senate. The message does not include much on the Lewis and Clark Expedition but is important for the information on the Louisiana-Texas frontier and the southern portion of the Louisiana Purchase.

The Canadians dominated the fur trade prior to the Louisiana Purchase — however, the Yankees challenged them almost immediately. A party of trappers enroute to fur country met Lewis and Clark on their return trip. John Colter decided to forego the hero's welcome awaiting the Lewis and Clark party in the East to return to the mountains to trap. During the period 1805–1845 the Mountain Men wrote much history on the land if not on paper. They trapped and traded to be sure, but they explored, found mountain passes, blazed trails, produced maps, served as scouts and guides to official exploring parties and later the army — they were the forerunners of the western settlers. Much has been written about Jed Smith, Hugh Glass, Old Bill Williams, Joe Walker, Ewing Young, Kit Carson, Jim Bridger, Broken Hand Fitzpatrick, and others of the valiant band. If they found little time to write they had their Boswells. Washington Irving's *The Rocky Mountains — Adventures In The Far West* (Philadelphia, 1837) was based on Captain Bonneville's papers and other sources. So far as I know all of the numerous reprints used the title, *Adventures of Captain Bonneville.* The previous year (1836), Irving's *Astoria* was released at Philadelphia. It is the story of the 1811 American attempt at settlement on the Pacific coast to bolster our claim to Oregon. Many years later Hiram M. Chittenden's *The American Fur Trade of the Far West* (N.Y., 1902) was issued in three volumes — it must be regarded as the classic on the subject. I freely confess, however, that I find some still later books more readable including *The Travels of Jedediah Smith* (Santa Ana, Calif., 1934) edited by Maurice S. Sullivan and printing for the first time Jed's own journals; Dr. LeRoy Hafen's *Broken Hand* (Denver, 1931), a biography of Thomas Fitzpatrick, and Walter S. Campbell's (writing as Stanley Vestal) biographies of *Joe Meek* (Caldwell, Idaho, 1952) and *Kit Carson,* (Boston, 1928).

Rumors trickled back to the States that there was a ready market for American goods in Santa Fe. It was only 800 miles from Independence on the Missouri to Santa Fe, so naturally, the American merchants set out to supply the market despite the dangers of the trail including the Comanches. Much of the literature on the trail and on Santa Fe is superb. Josiah Gregg's two volume account, *Commerce on the Prairies* (New York, 1844) is a classic. R. L.

Duffas' *The Santa Fe Trail* (New York, 1930) is a top job as is *El Gringo, or New Mexico and Her People* (New York, 1857) by William W. H. Davis. Willa Cather's *Death Comes for the Archbishop* (New York, 1927) is a moving piece of writing with a historical base. I can particularly recommend to you *Southwest on the Turquoise Trail: the First Diaries on the Road to Santa Fe* (Denver, 1933) edited, with bibliographical resume, 1810–1825, by Archer Butler Hulbert.

In the meantime, much else was happening in the Southwest — the Texas Revolution, including such dramatic events as the fall of the Alamo, the Run-a-way Scrape, and the victory at San Jacinto made Texas a Republic. The annexation of Texas in 1845 made war with Mexico almost a certainty since the U. S. adopted the Texas position in the still hot boundary dispute. When the war was over, the Southwest including California was a part of the United States. The Gadsden Purchase ended the boundary dispute between the United States and Mexico and the road was clear for further westward expansion. John R. Bartlett's *Personal Narrative of Explorations — in Texas, New Mexico, California, etc. — with the United States and Mexican Boundary Commission* (N.Y., 1854) is a nicely illustrated two-volume set that tells about marking the boundary from the Texas line to the Pacific.

Many visitors and new settlers from the States and Europe came to Texas during the days of the Republic and the early days of statehood. Much was printed about the resources of Texas and those who did not write books spread the news by letter or word of mouth. It was a letter to my own grandfather from one of his Georgia cousins who had settled near Gonzales, Texas, that encouraged him to continue his move westward. My grandfather had left Georgia and was raising cotton in the red hill country of Mississippi when the letter came from his cousin praising the deep, rich soils of Texas and mentioning that the prairie grasses were stirrup high as he rode horseback through them. My grandfather made it as far west as southern Arkansas — he stopped to spend the night with one of the Cotham families near "Rough and Ready" (now Monticello) fell in love with my grandmother, then the sixteen year old laughing-eyed, poetry-writing daughter of the family. He stayed on to court and marry her but had to agree to settle in Arkansas as the family thought my grandmother far too young to go to "wild" Texas. Grandfather was killed during the Civil War and Reconstruction days were not easy, even in southern Arkansas. Grandmother stuck it out until about 1870 when she traded 640 acres of land for a covered wagon and a yoke of oxen, took her four boys and finished the westward movement my grandfather had started when he left Georgia in the early 1840's. It is impossible to say how much the letter from the Texas cousin influenced her move but my father strongly believed that it was an important factor—my grandmother took the letter to Texas with her, gave it to my father, who gave it to me. I still have it.

Among the books, Mary Austin Holley's *Texas* (Baltimore, 1833) seems to have been written to encourage emigration to the colony of her cousin, Stephen F. Austin. It was rewritten and reissued in Lexington, Kentucky in 1836 with the primary purpose of seeking recognition of the infant Republic by the United States. Jacob De Cordova's *Texas: Her Resources and Her Public Men* (Philadelphia, 1858) was another emigration pitch. De Cordova owned much land script that he was anxious to market—despite the obvious profit motive it is a good book. Not all the promotional books on Texas were published in this country—Dr. Ferdinand von Roemer's *Texas* was issued in German in Bonn in 1849 and included the first geological map of the state. Roemer, a paleontologist, came to Texas in 1845 and spent two years gathering material for his book, not printed in English until 1935.

A number of excellent books were issued about the Mexican War. My favorites are *Sketches of The Campaign in Northern Mexico* (N.Y., 1835), probably by Major Luther P. Giddings but also attributed to M. E. Curwen; Capt. W. S. Henry's *Campaign Sketches of the War with Mexico* (N.Y., 1847) and *The Scouting Expeditions of McCulloch's Texas Rangers* (Philadelphia, 1847) by Samuel G. Reid, Jr., a Louisiana lawyer who served with Mc-Culloch in Mexico. Justin H. Smith's two volume set, *The War With Mexico, 1846–48* (N.Y., 1919) is very good formal history.

The Mormon trek and the settling of Utah was a dramatic episode in the westward movement. Many of those who went to other parts of the West were seeking a quick fortune with the thought of returning to their homes in the East. The Mormons, driven out of Missouri and later out of Illinois, sought asylum and a permanent place to establish their homes. They actively sought new members and, thus, new citizens for the West in this country and in Western Europe primarily through tracts and missionaries. My favorite book on the subject is Vardis Fisher's *Children of God* (N.Y., 1939)—it comes nearer than any book I know to covering the entire history of the Mormons up to 1890. It is so readable that one is unaware of the history lesson one gets. It was the Harper 1939–40 prize novel and was maligned by both the Mormons and the Utah "gentiles" — a good indication that the erudite author (raised in the church but a backslider) had been both sharp and analytical in his historical novel. However, if one prefers, history the slower and harder way, one should try *The Rocky Mountain Saints: a Full and Complete History of the Mormons* (New York, 1873) by T. B. H. Stenhouse.

The boundary problem with Canada was settled by treaty while the Mexican War was in progress. Long before this, however, a number of Americans had made their way overland via the Oregon Trail to settle in the Willamette Valley — a few others made the trip around the Horn by boat. The Hudson's Bay Company factor at Fort Vancouver on the north bank of the Columbia, Dr. John McLoughlin, did his best to hold Oregon for England. Stripping the country south of the Columbia of furs was the strategy used by Dr. McLoughlin to discourage the Americans. However, these Americans were interested in land and homes rather than furs and the strategy failed. A number of the Mountain Men, including Ewing Young and Joe Meek, gave up their traps to settle in the rich valley. When Dr. McLoughlin refused to sell cows to the settlers, Ewing Young led a party south to Mexican California to buy some. The story of the 1837 trail drive from California is well told in Col. Phillip I. Edwards' *California in 1837* (Sacramento, 1890). Richard Henry Dana's *Two Years Before the Mast* (N.Y., 1840) has something to say about ranching in Mexican California and has long been considered the classic on the hide and tallow trade. My favorite books about ranching in Spanish and later Mexican California were both written by Stewart Edward White: *Ranchero* (Garden City, N.Y., 1933) and *Folded Hills* (Garden City, N.Y., 1934). In these carefully researched novels the author continues the saga of Mountain Man Andy Burnett's personal westward trek that he started in *The Long Rifle* (Garden City, N.Y., 1932).

I suppose it would be considered treason to ignore Francis Parkman's *The California and Oregon Trail* (N.Y., 1849) and, beginning with the fourth edition in 1872, shortened to *The Oregon Trail*. I am inclined to agree with my old friend, J. Frank Dobie, who commented in his *Guide to Life and Literature of the Southwest* (Austin, 1943): "A good book but not so good as fifty others in these lists" I do admire the 1892 edition with the handsome Frederic Remington illustrations.

The discovery of gold in California early in 1848 turned a trickle of emigrants to the new territory into a torrent. Gold lured them to California but many of them became permanent residents. Gold was the single greatest stimulant to emigration in the history of the West. Samuel Clemens or if you prefer, Mark Twain, was there during most of the exciting doings and, in my opinion, *Roughing It* (Hartford, 1872) is the single best book about the gold era, the miners, mining and the people of early American California and Nevada. The critics have pointed out the bold and brash reporting as well as the frontier journalistic style. I do not fault the book for them—Twain told it like it was. It has been a personal favorite for well over sixty years and its seems unlikely that it will ever be replaced. Baynard Taylor's *El Dorado* (N.Y., 1850) is a classic by a distinguished writer, world traveller, and competent artist that appeared twenty-two years before *Roughing It*. Doubtlessly it had more influence on the westward movement but Taylor was a reporter covering a news story while Twain lived it. William M'Ilvaine's *Sketches of Scenery and Notes of Personal Adventure in California and Mexico* (Philadelphia, 1850) is nearly as good as *El Dorado* and the illustrations are better. M'Ilvaine had a Master of Arts degree from the University of Pennsylvania and had studied art in Europe before trying his luck in the gold fields. He soon decided that the life in the mining camps was too rough for him but before he left for home he made numerous on-the-spot sketches of Sacramento and San Francisco—17 of them were used to illustrate his book. Merle Johnson, in his *High Spots of American Literature* (N.Y., 1929) included Stewart Edward White's California trilogy: *Gold* (Garden City, N.Y., 1913), *The Gray Dawn* (Garden City, N.Y., 1915), and *The Rose Dawn* (Garden City, N.Y., 1920). *Gold* deals with the days of '49; *The Gray Dawn* with the struggle to establish law and order including the vigilantes, and *The Rose Dawn* with the widespread agricultural development of the state. All are very good, indeed.

The discovery of gold and the rush of settlers to California gave further emphasis to the need for a railroad link between the two coasts. Both the Government and the railroads had survey parties in the field to determine the most practical routes. *Reports of Explorations and Surveys to Ascertain the Most Practical and Economic Route for a Railroad from the Mississippi River to the Pacific Ocean* (commonly called *The Railroad Surveys*) was issued by the government, volume by volume, 1855 to 1861—the set with the atlas totaled 12 volumes and volume 12 was issued in two parts. In this set the whole of the West was mapped and pictured rather adequately for the first time. John Mix Stanley, a very good artist who had been west several times before, was responsible for many of the illustrations and he had competent assistants. A. B. Gray's *Survey of a Route for the Southern Pacific on 32nd Parallel* (Cincinnati, 1856) was privately issued and I chose the second edition because the plates are vastly superior—some of the best ever made of southwestern scenes.

The Civil War slowed the westward movement materially but when it was over, the rush started again. The railroads were building westward and a good many Southerners could not abide the scalawag-carpetbagger rule during Reconstruction and took their families to the West. While many of the Confederates soldiers went home to hopeless situations, such was not the case in Texas. While the Texans were away fighting, their Longhorn herds had continued to grow—the old men and boys who were left at home had been unable to brand them and only a few had reached the market. The Texans had the meat on hoof—the North wanted the meat and had the money to pay for it. Fortunately, the Longhorn was ideal for trail driving and the solution was easy—let meat and money come together at some half-way point, usually at some railroad town in Kansas. It was an exciting period—populations mushroomed at the cattle shipping centers and a huge time was had by all. The books on the trail-cowtown days are numerous and I suppose it is only fair to mention first *Historic Sketches of the Cattle Trade* (Kansas City, 1874) by Joseph G. McCoy. It was McCoy who conceived and built the shipping pens and other facilities for marketing and handling trail herds at Abilene, Kansas. Andy Adams' *The Log of a Cowboy* (Boston, 1903) is my favorite on trail driving and Dobie, in his *Guide* tells one why: "If all other books on trail driving were destroyed, a reader could still get a just and authentic conception of trail men, trail work, range cattle, cow horses, and the cow country in general from *The Log of a Cowboy*." Sam P. Riding's *The Chisholm Trail* (Guthrie, 1936) and Wayne Gard's *The Chisholm Trail* (Norman, 1954) are tops on the most important of the trails. I regard Floyd B. Streeter's *Prairie Trails & Cow Towns* (Boston, 1936) as the classic on the Kansas cow-towns and, for the critters, there is nothing that will even approach J. Frank Dobie's *The Longhorns* (Boston, 1941).

The driving of the last spike that connected the Union Pacific and the Central Pacific at Promontory, Utah, on May 10, 1869 was certainly a high spot in the westward movement. However, long before it was driven, the railroads were keenly aware of the need for freight revenues if the lines were to be made to pay. The Union Pacific also faced the problem of dealing with the myth of The Great

THE MUSTANGS

by J. Frank Dobie

ILLUSTRATED BY CHARLES BANKS WILSON

Little, Brown and Company · Boston

Courtesy of Little, Brown and Company

79

Mustangs
and
Cow Horses

Edited by

J. FRANK DOBIE

MODY C. BOATRIGHT

HARRY H. RANSOM

ILLUSTRATED

AUSTIN

TEXAS FOLK-LORE SOCIETY

1940

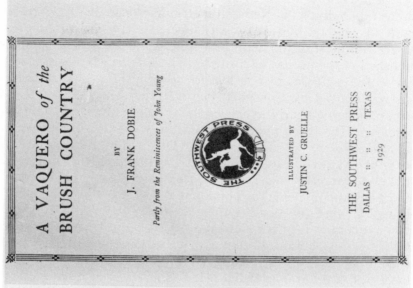

A VAQUERO *of the* BRUSH COUNTRY

BY

J. FRANK DOBIE

Partly from the Reminiscences of John Young

ILLUSTRATED BY

JUSTIN C. GRUELLE

THE SOUTHWEST PRESS
DALLAS :: :: TEXAS
1929

One of the Mossy Horns: "Old Champion," owned by J. M. Dobie, Live Oak County, Texas, 1899

American Desert. The area between the Missouri and the Rockies and as far south as the Red and its tributaries and with an average width of 500 or 600 miles was labeled "The Great American Desert" on most of the maps in histories, atlases, and geographies published in the period 1820–1850. The Stephen H. Long expedition of 1819–20 was responsible for the maps but not the myth — that was started by Coronado nearly three centuries before and perpetuated by nearly every explorer and visitor to the Plains thereafter. The story and map appear in *Account of an Expedition . . . to the Rockies* (Philadelphia, 1823) edited by Edwin James. In the book, Major Long says of the great desert at the base of the Rocky Mountains: "In regard to this extensive section of country, I do not hesitate in giving the opinion that it is almost wholly unfit for cultivation, and of course uninhabitable by a people depending upon agriculture for their subsistence." Yes, the Union Pacific had problems — and a man to deal with them. Hiram Latham was the resident doctor at the U P Hospital at Laramie and an enthusiastic rancher on the Laramie Plains. He wrote a series of letters to the *Omaha Herald* and they were published as a pamphlet with the title *Trans-Missouri Stock Raising: the Pasture Lands of North America: Winter Grazing* (Omaha, 1870) with the prediction in the sub-title, *The Sources of the Future Beef and Wool Supply of the United States.* The Union Pacific distributed thousands of copies of Dr. Latham's pamphlet to promote the growth of population along their lines. Dr. Latham's account was the first general appraisal of any important segment of our great cow country. While McCoy's *Historic Sketches of the Cattle Trade* has long been regarded as the first of the great books about the range livestock industry, it was issued three years after Latham's title. Only 12 copies of the Latham pamphlet are known today — all in institutional libraries. By 1881, the Union Pacific needed a new promotional piece and they persuaded General James S. Brisbin to lend his name to a rewrite of Latham's pamphlet. It was published by J. B. Lippincott & Co. of Philadelphia with the title *The Beef Bonanza; or, How to Get Rich on the Plains.* Brisbin's book is credited with helping promote the great cattle boom of the early 1880's and with leading the British capitalists to invest considerable sums in the cattle industry in the West.

The Indians were off their reservations in great numbers in the spring and summer of 1874 in the southern plains. They raided in Texas and southern Colorado and were beaten off when they attacked a group of buffalo hide hunters at Adobe Walls in the Texas Panhandle. As winter approached, the Comanches, Kiowas, Chey-

82

The Windmill Crew, by Peter Hurd

Guide to

LIFE AND LITERATURE

of the

SOUTHWEST

WITH A FEW OBSERVATIONS

By J. FRANK DOBIE

ILLUSTRATED

Published by

THE UNIVERSITY OF TEXAS PRESS, AUSTIN

———

Special printing for
UNIVERSITY PRESS IN DALLAS
SOUTHERN METHODIST UNIVERSITY

1 9 4 3

ennes, and Arapahoes gathered on the floor of Palo Duro Canyon, a deep gash in the Llano Estacado. This was one of the last strongholds of the Indians and a favorite spot to winter. At dawn on September 28, 1874, Colonel Ranald Mackenzie and eight troops of the Fourth Cavalry surprised and routed the Indians. It was not quite a bloodless battle as the Indians may have lost as many as 50 to 60 warriors while the Cavalry's losses were negligible. However, Mackenzie struck the Indians two fatal blows—he captured and destroyed their horse herd and chopped up and burned the lodges, buffalo robes, and the winter food supply—the Indians were forced to return to their reservations. The victory at Palo Duro opened the South Plains and the Panhandle of Texas to settlement. Within months Charles Goodnight moved a cow herd into the Palo Duro to begin ranching operations. Captain Robert G. Carter's *On The Border with Mackenzie* (Washington, D. C., 1935) is excellent on the battle. Rupert Norval Richardson's *The Comanche Barrier to South Plains Settlement* is just as good on the events leading up to the battle.

After the standoff on the Rosebud and the disaster at the Little Big Horn in 1876, the army was strongly reinforced but was unable to find the Sioux and their allies. However, General Nelson A. Miles conducted an amazing campaign in the winter of 1876–77 that brought the Sioux to their knees and sent them back to their reservations. Miles operated from a post at the mouth of the Tongue River (near the present site of Miles City, Montana) and he searched out and destroyed the winter camps of the Indians. The Indians did not like to fight in the cold and snow of winter and Miles kept the pressure on with his surprise attacks and artillery. By the summer of 1877 the fighting was all but over—Sitting Bull fled to Canada, occasionally crossing the border into Montana in search of food and loot although he was closely watched by Miles until he surrendered in 1881. The Northern Plains were finally open for settlement. General Miles' own book, *Personal Recollections and Observations* (New York, 1896), is almost surely the best evidence on the winter campaign.

Someone, perhaps J. Frank Dobie, paraphrased the old saying "Civilization follows the plow" with "Civilization follows the Longhorns" and this was certainly true in the Great Plains. The Longhorns moved into the southern plains in 1875 and into northern plains late in the summer of 1877. The great era of the open range cattle industry was beginning. Many great books were written about that period in our peopling of the West. Granville Stuart's two

84

John C. Duval and Bigfoot Wallace, by Tom Lea, from
John C. Duval: First Texas Man of Letters, by J. Frank Dobie

volume account, *Forty Years on the Frontier* (Cleveland, 1925) is great on Montana. John Clay's *My Life on the Range* (Chicago, 1924) is just as good on Wyoming. Not all the cattle that stocked the Montana and Wyoming ranges came up the trail from Texas—some herds of Oregon and Washington cattle were driven east to cross with the Longhorns. Charles J. Steedman's *Bucking the Sagebrush* (New York, 1904) is good on the eastbound drives and is enhanced with brilliant illustrations in color by Charles M. Russell. Far to the south, J. Evetts Haley memorialized the greatest range man of them all in *Charles Goodnight, Cowman and Plainsman* (Boston, 1936). In my opinion, this is the best biography of a cowman ever written and it may be the best biography ever written of any Westerner.

In addition to the books dealing with important events and significant aspects of the westward movement, a number of our competent historians, amateur and professional, have summarized and editorialized on major segments of the movement as a whole. Among those over-all books that impressed me the most are—*The Westward March of American Settlement* (Chicago, 1927) by Hamlin Garland; *The Far Western Frontier* (New York, 1956) by Ray A. Billington; *America's Frontier Story* (New York, etc., 1969) edited by Martin Ridge and Ray A. Billington; *The Early Far West* (N.Y., 1931) by W. J. Ghent; *America Moves West* (New York, 1930) by Robert E. Riegel and *The Westward Movement* (New York, 1939) by Ina Fay Woestemeyer with the editorial collaboration of J. Mongomery Gambrill. I have saved until the last three of my favorite books—each about a major area of our great West—*The Southwest, Old and New* (New York, 1961) by W. Eugene Hollon; *Frontiers of the Northwest* (New York, London, 1940) by Harold E. Briggs, and *The Great Plains* (Boston, 1931) by Walter Prescott Webb. Hollon and Briggs did beautiful jobs on their regions and, in my opinion, *The Great Plains* is the best by far of all the books on any major area of the West. Webb was my favorite historian and a good friend. However, it was another friend, Bernard De Voto, in his finely edited and interpreted *The Journals of Lewis and Clark* (Boston, 1953) who used the words that describe us best "a westering Nation." And we have the literature to prove it.

Agriculture with Hoof and Horn: An Analysis of the Historical Literature of the Cattle Industry

By
Walter Rundell, Jr. and Anne M. Butler

The range cattle industry constitutes a major element in the development of American agriculture. The organizational structure, economic components, and social implications of the cattle enterprise affected the entire agrarian experience of this nation. Spawned in a frontier environment that pulsated with economic possibilities, cattle driving evolved into a viable industry that extended far beyond the Western plains and permeated the economic and political fabric of American society.

Not only did the cattle industry itself evolve, so, too, has the historian's vision of it. A survey of thirteen prominent cattle studies, considered in order of publication, clearly illustrates this evolution. The interpretations form a sort of historical pyramid, moving from broad-based surveys to specialized monographs.

The pioneer among surveys is Ernest S. Osgood's excellent *Day of the Cattleman,* published in 1929. Osgood's intention was to elevate the cattle story from the realm of reminiscence and to focus

Dr. Rundell and Ms. Butler, Department of History, University of Maryland, College Park, Maryland.

upon the economic implications of the enterprise.[1] Masterfully re-created by Osgood is the frontier milieu prior to the emergence of the cattle industry. Here he stresses the transformation of a frontier where cattle supplanted mining as the dominant economic and social factors. In the settlements of the trans-Mississippi West, local cattle owners of the 1860's began to see that a growing transient population of migrants, miners, and railroad workers was increasing the demand for beef. Exploitation of this economic potential required utilization of the resources of the Plains and extension of the enterprise beyond the immediate locale.

As the small herd owner of Colorado, Wyoming, Nebraska, Montana, and Kansas awakened to the commercial possibilities of selling cattle at distant markets, Texans with the same idea herded thousands of mavericks, descendants of the sixteenth century Spanish imports, and started them on the long drives in search of markets. These cattle thundered out of Texas and into the economic life of the nation. Their arrival on the Great Plains marked the first contact of large herd owners with local cattle owners of the northern plains. It was a meeting replete with hostility, but, though strife temporarily dominated the encounters, the fruition of this merger would be seen in the cattle boom of the 1880's. The union of these divergent cattle holders would in itself be quite a tale, but Osgood treats the Western cattle venture in relation to Eastern capital.[2] The fever of economic promise flashed through the nation and inspired a citizenry only too recently licking the wounds of civil strife. Partially responsible for this burst of national enthusiasm was a massive publicity campaign. Disseminated through pamphlets, newspapers, and letters, the message crackled with promises of wealth and the East responded by sending men and money. The demand for movement of men, supplies, and cattle spurred the extension of railroad lines far south into Texas and north to Wyoming as the range industry sprang into national and international dimensions.

As the local cattle owners of the northern plains had learned to tolerate the large herd owners of Texas, so did Western cattlemen find they must align themselves with moneyed groups of the East. The union of Western expertise with Eastern and foreign capital instigated the organization of cattle companies that minimized individual risk and could raise vast sums of cash. In 1883, twenty such companies were incorporated in Wyoming alone.[3] Indeed, the population thrilled to the boom, but the bonanza contained the seeds of its own destruction. The potential dangers of saturating the ranges, overloading the market, wild speculation, inflation, staggering losses through disease or severe climate were all ignored as profits crested.

Whatever the fortunes of the moment, the cattle industry had obviously passed from its first days of simplicity to an era of complexity that demanded regulation and control both through local organization and federal legislation. Osgood maintains that formation of various stock growers associations—the Wyoming Stock Growers Association, the Laramie County Stock Growers Association, the Montana Stock Growers Association—was alien to the essentially individualistic nature of cattlemen who desired only to preserve herds through isolation.[4] Perhaps—but extra-legal organizations in the West have always sprung from the belief of an interest group that united community action would compensate for the lack of effective government regulation. Law, as defined by the cattlemen, required control of land, crime, and Indians. In keeping with this view, the communal activities of cattlemen included range protection, vigilante control, quarantine agitation, and political lobbying. This muscle, demonstrated through local organization and action, forced authorities to enact legislation that not only defined range privileges but also encompassed interstate transportation rates, quarantine laws, and international shipping.

Osgood marks the disastrous winter of 1886–87 as the beginning of the end for the range industry, and concludes that by 1913 the demise was complete.[5] Short on analytical interpretation, Osgood's *Day of the Cattleman* offers a wealth of material and highlights three important concepts: (1) the cattle industry shifted frontier economic concerns from mining to animal husbandry; (2) the expansion of the industry into national and international spheres tempered the regional quality of the venture; and (3) blinded by desire for quick profit, investors extended beyond the capacities of the environment and market.

Edward Everett Dale's *The Range Cattle Industry,* published in 1930, is cattle history with a Turnerian thrust. An excellently concise presentation of cattle ranching from 1865 to 1925, the text reflects both Frederick Jackson Turner's frontier thesis and the author's personal ranching experiences. Dale focuses upon those variations in the business influenced by topographical and climatic elements. According to Dale, development of the Western range industry related closely to that of the Eastern corn belt.[6] Dale separates the cattle territory into two areas: (1) the Southwest, including Texas, Indian territory, and a portion of New Mexico, and (2) the central and northern plains. The development of the indus-

THE RANGE CATTLE INDUSTRY

BY EDWARD EVERETT DALE

NORMAN
UNIVERSITY OF OKLAHOMA PRESS
1 9 3 0

Courtesy of the University of Oklahoma Press. New edition copyright 1960.

try saw the Southwest utilized as a breeding ground, while the Great Plains area provided pasture lands to fatten the beef.[7]

In the Southwest, Dale maintains ranching styles were created in response to Texas topography and water supply. The land areas involved were so overwhelmingly vast that cattlemen began to cry for a system of permanent land tenure, range enclosure, and transport accessibility. The demands for cattle breeding and land control stimulated the creation of corporate structures better able to meet the challenges of an immense range operation. This massive breeding program of the Southwest gave rise to expansion of feed supplies on the Plains and ultimately brought the prices of beef and corn into a parallel relationship. Economic ties between breeders and farmers intensified, Dale asserts, as both sought capital from the same lending institutions.[8]

Dale's book treats all the expected topics—foreign investments, stock growers associations, the winter of 1886–87, and the decline of profits. His posture through all this strongly advocates "land utilization" for capitalistic endeavor. A popular rationalization in the development of the frontier and a logical corollary of the Turner thesis, this concept is not so fashionable today. Nor is it so acceptable to justify the absorption of so-called "unused" Indian lands for Anglo business interests as "progress." Dale becomes sentimental about the misunderstood hard working cattlemen and blames their bad press on the irresponsible actions of a few renegades. Recognizing these elements as products of the era of publication and of Dale's own life on the range, they should be dismissed and the high quality of the research and writing heralded.

Dale's book is a concise presentation of the same material Osgood uses, but here is strong analysis with a rugged individualistic, Turner thesis bias. This book must be rated as an important study in the progression of cattle literature.

A third survey of cattle history is Louis Pelzer's *The Cattlemen's Frontier,* published in 1936. Pelzer's purpose is to show that motives dominating the creation of the range industry were economic and that profits and dividends were more important than adventure in the cow country.[9] With the Osgood and Dale publications having appeared in 1929 and 1930, it is unlikely many would dispute Pelzer's thesis. The question becomes, why did he publish this book? The work had already been done—and done better—by two historians before him. Perhaps Pelzer provides the answer in the preface where he states, "Certain chapters of this work have been read before various historical bodies."[10] This may well explain the

91

uneven repetitious style of the text. Neither the chronology nor the subject matter flows logically, and transitions between chapters become jarring.

The last chapter describes businessman Joseph McCoy's endeavors to establish Abilene, Kansas as a cow town. It seems strangely out of place—surely it all belonged in a sadly deficient earlier chapter entitled, "Shifting Cow Towns of Kansas," where only Dodge City received substantial consideration.

Pelzer does include discussions of the expansion of the cattle companies, the economic ups and downs of the 1880's, and the financial machinations of the investors. This being the somewhat jumbled thrust of the chapters, it is a bit startling when the summary suddenly praises the life and glory of the individual cowboy.[11] Pelzer's final statements ignore the economic interpretation he promised and bring his volume to a close on a romantic note. Pelzer concludes, "Transitory as it was the cattlemen's frontier was the most American of America's frontiers, and the horsemen who invaded this vacant empire dismounted not without regret."[12] Why the cattle frontier was the most American, indeed, even what that means, must remain a mystery, for Pelzer does not say.

To criticize a work long regarded as a classic may seem irreverent. Unfortunately, the flagrant weaknesses of the book are painfully apparent when contrasted with superior publications. The text is heavily footnoted, yet many quotations have no documentation. The content suffers from poor editing as the same information is repeatedly introduced in successive chapters, a symptom of the often disjointed nature of a work drawn from lectures. A plethora of detail can be found in the Pelzer book, but it lacks the organization of Osgood and the analysis of Dale.

Perhaps one could argue that J. Frank Dobie's 1941 publication, *The Longhorns,* does not properly belong in this assessment. It misses the specifications for inclusion as it does not deal with the structure and economics of the cattle industry. Dobie says of his book, "It is about the animal itself that generated cowboys, brought ranches into existence, gave character to the grazing world of America, and furnished material for political economy."[13] Whether he intended to or not, Dobie reveals much about range management by focusing on the main characters of the industry—the cattle themselves. Part of the vitality of the industry stemmed from adjustments cattlemen learned to make to accommodate animals to the environment.

The pace of the herd, river crossings, watering techniques,

stampede control, and weather conditions influenced the success of the drive—success measured by sales at the market. Ignorance of these range elements could only bring severe financial losses to investors. Indeed, Dobie's book is a love-song to the local range experience that made possible the realization of huge profit at the corporate level. The text is largely anecdotal and riddled with folklore, but it seems fair here to salute the author who focused on the primary ingredient of the range industry—the critters themselves.

In 1954 Wayne Gard narrowed the cattle topic further with *The Chisholm Trail*. Disturbed by fictional distortions and historical neglect, Gard offers a scholarly study of the Chisholm Trail, the cattle route from southern Texas to Abilene, Kansas.[14]

Gard begins his study with background information—a physical description of Texas cattle, a short history of their importation by the Spanish, the roundup of mavericks, the Civil War disruption, and the first schemes of a trail drive.

Gard deftly describes the post-Civil War struggles of the incipient industry. Experimentation with early routes took a heavy toll as men and cattle were lost to stampedes, river crossings, and thirst. Survivors who made it to the Kansas-Missouri borders could expect to be halted by irate local cattlemen who feared the virulent Texas tick fever. Here it would finally be Joseph McCoy, livestock entrepreneur, who would convert the Chisholm Trail from a faltering disappointment into an industry lifeline terminating at the stockyards of Abilene. McCoy, a flamboyant character given to self-aggrandizement, determined to construct the shipping center Texas drivers needed to reach the national market. McCoy's efforts encompassed construction of a stockyard, enlargement of railroad facilities, a personalized publicity campaign among the Texas cattle people, and a hard-sell local drive to convince merchants and farmers that blockage of the cattle drives retarded their own economic potential.

The extensive activities of Joseph McCoy demonstrate that cattle trails did not sprout spontaneously upon the horizon. They were part of the operational refinements where owners learned that care of the cattle, the best trail routes, and an organized sales center meant the greatest monetary return.

Gard's material must be sifted to extract that information which relates to the economic structure of the livestock industry. Much of the text focuses on personal trail experiences, daily schedules, and the bizarre social conduct of cowboys. The social history is interesting, though a bit spastic, jumping from range conditions to dance hall murders — but it is not the critical point of this book. *The Chisholm Trail* shows that the overland routes were one stage in the organizational structure of the industry and that they influenced the expansion of related endeavors such as railroad construction and town building. Wayne Gard's book, though filled with lots of folklore, accentuates the influence of the cow trail.

Lewis Atherton's 1961 publication, *The Cattle Kings,* represents another aspect of the topical pyramid. Atherton addresses the subject of the ranch owners who headed the industry and seeks to explain what they were really like and what they stood for.[15]

The book's significance lies in its examination of the cattle industry from a new viewpoint. Although relying on many of the same sources as the volumes previously discussed, the author, by asking different questions of the data, adds another important dimension to our understanding of the subject. Long before women's history came into vogue, Atherton understood that wives of cattle kings — the cattle queens, if you will — deserved analysis. His chapter on this subject constitutes the first scholarly treatment of the contributions of women to the managerial-entrepreneurial aspect of the cattle business. Similarly, a further revealing aspect of the impact of cattle kings on Western society comes in the chapter on their philanthropy. Atherton does not dodge the point that as philanthropists, these men wanted to recreate their own kind of world where their values would be enshrined.

The author obviously identifies more with his subject than with their hired hands. He makes points about the virtues of the cattle kings at the expense of the cowboys, as if the reader had to choose between them. Atherton denounces the elevation of the cowhand to the role of folk hero, asserting " . . . his career consisted of running away from life or of adjusting to it at the lowest common denominator." The characteristic he most frequently attributes to cattle kings is rugged individualism, the book's leitmotif.[16]

Atherton suggests that the foundation of the cattle society was based upon a concept of "live and let live," an outgrowth of the amalgamation of many persons of diversified backgrounds. This may have been the case among business colleagues with mutual interests, but it is hardly a philosophy typified by the Johnson County War. Here Atherton's vision of justice appears clouded, as he admits the cattle owners exceeded legal authority, but justifies it as a desperate reaction to farmers who were using agriculture as a disguise for theft. Loss of power and prestige for the cattlemen seems more serious to Atherton than loss of life for the lynch victims.[17]

When Atherton deals with the business affairs of the ranchers, he identifies with the subject. He shows that the financial activities of Richard King, Charles Goodnight, George Littlefield, and Alexander Swan reflect shrewd business acumen. But his presentation of their investment policies and banking procedures is tinged with indignation that the general populace frowned upon ranchers as an arm of big business. Then he concludes that Western ranchers were like big businessmen everywhere in the country: acquisitive, protective of their economic status, exponents of laissez-faire — wary of governmental interference, but not assistance — politically conservative, and class conscious.[18] The cattle baron becomes the frontier captain of industry, while the cowboy takes his place beside the urban factory worker. The resulting impact is two-fold: a defensive interpretation of the cattlemen's business tactics and a social posture rare in Western literature — one that is sharply class conscious. The tone is unfortunate for it hampers appreciation for a text that has been expertly researched and imaginatively conceptualized.

Many have assumed that the historically significant cattle era had ended by the start of the twentieth century. In 1963, John T. Schlebecker, in *Cattle Raising on the Plains: 1900-1961*, suggested that this idea was not accurate. Schlebecker sees the cattle industry as an on-going economic reality whose original characteristics adjusted to meet the changing demands of an urban-industrial society.[19] Schlebecker charges that we have forgotten that any major industry cannot be all bonanza, and that the normal course of economic fortunes will produce cycles of prosperity and decline.

The close of the open range did not bring the industry to a halt, but thrust it into a new era marked by continuous extension of barbed wire and federal intervention. The uneven quality of that intervention prompted cattlemen to form new protective associations and, by 1905, the American Stock Growers Association exercised sufficient lobbying power to influence the passage of legislation at the federal level.

The years prior to World War I established two characteristics for the evolving industry: (1) improved range management for protection against disease and climate, and (2) a steady increase in the activities of federal agencies. The national economy would flourish and falter and flourish again in the next fifty years, but these two characteristics would continue to dominate the cattle industry.

During World War I cattle owners accepted broader federal

controls, but enjoyed unprecedented prosperity. Struck by the postwar depression of 1919–1922, owners looked for federal aid to improve farming methods. The twenties saw an economic upswing as cattlemen turned to the federal government for assistance with credit, land control, and disease prevention. The economic and environmental depression of the thirties brought concern for price supports, direct aid, soil conservation, drought relief, and tariff protection. World War II catapulted the beef industry, along with the rest of the country, into a new era of sophistication and made the national transformation to an urban industrial society complete.

Schlebecker shows that through each one of these cycles — whether of prosperity or depression — cattlemen have traditionally expected and received government support. Stockmen, unlike many other American businessmen, have relied on close association with the federal government and have maintained a lobby to insure that relationship, despite their putative rugged individualism. Advances in range management, disease control, and the use of biochemistry in animal husbandry all flowed to the industry through federal agencies.

Schlebecker has presented a fascinating chronological narrative, not of termination but of evolution. This outstanding study shows that stock owners consistently relied on technological and economic assistance from the government, and so transformed their industry from a primitive frontier adventure of the nineteenth century into a highly sophisticated economic operation of the twentieth century. Schlebecker's *Cattle Raising on The Plains* is a brilliant contribution to cattle studies. It is as basic to an understanding of the cattle business in the twentieth century as Osgood and Dale are for the nineteenth. Like them, it forms the foundation on which more specialized monographic studies can be built.

Some attention must be directed to William M. Pearce's 1964 publication, *The Matador Land and Cattle Company*. Historical surveys make repeated references to the extensive amount of foreign capital used in the American stock industry. Pearce chooses to investigate one example of such international enterprise — the Matador Land and Cattle Company. Pearce contends that the Matador was typical of other foreign joint-stock organizations as investors sought to exploit the profits of the American West, but unique in an exceptional management that kept the company a viable business until 1951.[20]

Formed in Texas in 1879, the Matador Cattle Company affiliated with Scottish investors in 1882. The Scots knew of cattle raising from their own domestic industry and so their speculation in America was not without knowledge or experience. The operation of the Matador Company represented the blending of astute business acumen with practical cattle knowledge. Strict corporate control by the board of directors avoided local neglect, uninterest, and corruption, problems inherent in any absentee owner's business. The singular success of the Matador must be attributed to the exceptional personnel who for forty years guided the bi-national company through the tangles of land policy, market fluctuation, taxation, government regulations and political intrigue. The long-time direction of Alexander Mackay, secretary of the board of directors in Scotland, and Murdo Mackenzie, manager in America, provided stability and continuity in company affairs.

Murdo Mackenzie, a forceful and decisive personality, assumed the managerial position in 1890, and immediately extended the Matador's interest beyond Texas and onto the northern grasslands. The initial negative response from the board of directors, accustomed to making all financial decisions in Scotland, quickly turned to approval as Mackenzie's expertise in market trends, cattle care, and personnel management emerged. Not only was he knowledgeable but also his tireless efforts and diplomacy impressed the board who soon deferred to Mackenzie's opinions and recommendations. The credit for this harmonious relationship lies with Mackenzie, whose loyalty was unmatched among range managers.

At the corporate level, policy was carefully planned and cautiously implemented. Conservative action designed to promote investors' dividends protected the Matador in times of drought or market fluctuation. The wild speculation and over-expansion of some cattle companies was not a part of the Matador's program and was a critical element in its longevity.

In the twentieth century, the Matador records continued to show a profit while other companies struggled to survive fluctuations of the economy. The tradition of conservative policy, backed by an efficient business operation designed to improve herd quality, sustained the Matador profits through World War II.

Pearce's book illustrates a successful business structured upon consistent conservative policy implemented by loyal employees with various kinds of expertise. That may seem idealistic and obvious, but within the cattle industry it was unique. This book demonstrates clearly that the profitable cattle venture was not the product of a single rugged individualist. Rather it was a well blended corporate effort, cautiously guided by both Western and non-Western knowledge. Pearce's book is thoroughly researched, with a wealth of business detail. Unimaginatively, it incorporates excessively long direct quotations. It is, nevertheless, a penetrating case study of a cattle corporation.

In 1965, two UCLA English professors, Philip Durham and Everett Jones, collaborated to produce a volume entitled *The Negro Cowboys*. The popular work is an excellent example of the forces which influence topic selections. The rise of the civil rights movement of the 1960's brought with it concern about academic voids in black studies. A host of works on black literature and especially black history appeared on the market. The Durham-Jones book is part of that effort to bring the Negro-American into national consciousness.[21]

In American literature, folklore, and film of the West, blacks have rarely appeared. Yet the research of these authors reveals that black cowboys numbered in the thousands along the cattle trails. The textual content is similar to many other cattle studies, but the emphasis has been shifted. The Texas drive, life on the trail to Abilene, social life in the cattle towns, end of the open range are all included, but they furnish only background, for in the spotlight here are black westerners. This is not the presentation of a lot of heroic underdogs, but a straightforward account of people — some heroes, some villains.

The image of the Western experience evokes concepts of individual freedom and face value acceptance. In some measure black cowhands found this to be true on the trail, but it was erratic equality that could be snatched away in a sudden burst of racial hatred or drunken lunacy. It was never equality so sound that blacks could attain managerial or entrepreneurial status.

The Negro Cowboys is a bit anecdotal in its presentation. Within this format the authors unveil such a wide swath of western racial attitudes that, happily, it is impossible to depict a stereotype of black westerners. The book encompasses far more than the experiences of the black cowboys, touching on outlaws, prospectors, soldiers, mustangers, and entertainers as well. It is the story of black males in the West, for references to black women are scattered and slight.

Truly this is a study which helps to unmask the myth of the West. The authors reveal the American image of a Western society established solely by white men dedicated to the principle of equality for all as false. If Durham and Jones sound a bit idealistic when they state: "Certainly recent history has shown a continuous decline in

PHILIP DURHAM
AND
EVERETT L. JONES

The Negro Cowboys

Courtesy of Dodd, Mead & Company, Inc.

AND
CATTLEMEN

BY
GENE M. GRESSLEY

THE STOCKS-AND-BONDS, HAVANA-CIGAR,

MAHOGANY-AND-LEATHER SIDE OF THE COWBOY ERA

POLITICS, INVESTORS, OPERATORS

FROM 1870 to 1900

Reprinted from title of book by permission of the University of Nebraska Press

American bigotry,"[22] they should be excused. Many Americans of the 1960's dreamed of a new day of racial unity. If this nation later lost some of that spiritual vision, perhaps it can be regained. Studies such as *The Negro Cowboys* can aid us to find honesty for today through honesty in our history.

In 1966, Gene M. Gressley published his superb *Bankers and Cattlemen*. The purpose of Gressley's book is to "trace the main configurations of Eastern investment in the cattle industry."[23] Gressley tailors this topic to include motivations for investment, the enormity of Eastern financing, the investor, the commission firm, and responses to financial decline.

Gressley's opening descriptions of the character and mentality of the Wall Street businessman were juxtaposed with the mentality and aspirations of the Western opportunist to establish an economic atmosphere charged with exploitative potential. Nineteenth-century financial minds, aided by a helpful political, social, and philosophical climate in the East, seized the opportunity to utilize the abundant natural resources that their Western associates assumed were endless. Gressley, like others before him, seems to indicate that the story of the cattle industry was not so much the masterpiece of the rugged individualist as it was an extension of the entrepreneurship that characterized Eastern urban centers of the day.

The experiences of corporate union between East and West were typified by friction and misunderstanding. While Eastern investors watched annual profits, Western range managers wrestled with problems of land, labor, capital, and cattle. The good fortune of hiring a manager skilled in all these areas fell to only a few companies, such as the Matador, Pratt-Ferris, and the Aztec Land and Cattle companies. The affairs of others were often characterized by dishonesty and incompetence.

Financial transactions were no smoother. Eastern banks retracted their liberal loan policy when cattle fortunes faltered, while Western banks, caught in the vortex of the problem, seldom had sufficient collateral to take up the slack. As for the owner, whether tied to an Eastern bank, Western bank, or commission firm, loan payments and high interest rates kept him a debtor.

Though burdened with common financial stress, cattlemen allowed their divergent views on local issues to keep them divided politically. Unable to agree on the issues of a national cattle trail, distribution of the public domain, disease control, or relations with homesteaders, stock owners failed to develop a cohesive political front. Expectations that Eastern investors would use their political connections to aid Western cattlemen proved vain, and it became

The CATTLE TOWNS

A
Social History
of the Kansas Cattle
Trading Centers
Abilene, Ellsworth, Wichita,
Dodge City and Caldwell,
1867 to 1885

By Robert R. Dykstra

clear that Western political power would have to spring from the local level.

Thus Gressley neatly presents a summary of those problems which have traditionally hampered East-West relationships. Ignorant of the realities of the West, the East provided the vast capital that stock owners could never raise in their own section. This, Gressley concludes, temporarily inflated the cattle industry, but ultimately reinforced Western feelings of "Eastern economic exploitation and political domination."[24]

Gressley's study is a giant among books of the cattle industry, incorporating the best qualities of historical writing. Careful research of a little known topic has been blended with skillful style and thoughtful analysis to produce one of the most difficult of historical works—a truly fascinating economic study.

In 1968, Robert Dykstra published a study of the Kansas cow towns. His *The Cattle Towns* aimed to discuss the social processes of frontier communities where leaders sought to maintain commercial enterprise and to avoid financial decline.[25] Dykstra traces the birth, life, and demise of five Kansas cattle towns—Abilene, Ellsworth, Wichita, Dodge City, and Caldwell. Dykstra focuses on trans-Mississippi urban development as a by-product of the burgeoning cattle industry. The personification of that development was Abilene's Joseph McCoy and Dykstra devotes considerable discussion to the actions of this intriguing person.

More than that, Dykstra offers varied insights into the complexities of community life where economic prosperity is not only seasonal, but also dependent upon a rather bizarre transient consumer group. Local tensions intensified as town dwellers were pitted against farmers and farmers against cattle drivers. Businessmen urged minimal law enforcement in matters of crime and morality. Factionalism within the cattle towns mushroomed as residents structured the communities to accommodate migrant groups.

Dykstra's most critical observations indicate that frontier democracy did not blossom out of solidarity and peaceful agreement. Rather, frontier democracy painfully evolved through dissension, strife, and violence. Frequently, legislation benefited not the majority, but the powerful. Dykstra has stripped away our civics text vision of the democratic process and allowed it to stand as a real experience—not motivated out of some Pollyanna vision of goodness but forged in the furnace of ambition, need, and demand.

Ultimately, any major changes in the cattle operation affected the cow towns. Extension of railroads, changes in land policy, and the influx of homesteaders staggered the little centers built on a monolithic economy. Regardless of how much they had catered to the cowboy's bawdy drunkeness, once the trail drive ended, the cattle towns, without economic diversity, faced decay or oblivion.

Dykstra's significant book includes fine biographical data of cow town personalities, interesting sketches of daily life, and a valuable interpretation of the nature of political and economic factionalism in frontier town building. Perhaps his most valuable contribution is the examination of difficulties in constructing viable urban government within a rigid economy. Dykstra has written an exceptional study of the cattle enterprise as the catalyst in the growth of democracy on the urban frontier.

The year 1968 also saw the publication of W. Turrentine Jackson's *The Enterprising Scot: Investors in the American West After 1873*. Jackson investigates the financial acumen of Scots, but especially as it relates to long range entrepreneurial skills.[26] *The Enterprising Scot* surveys Scottish cattle investments, but also other endeavors in the American West including mining, land speculation, and soil usage.

Jackson chronicles the slow but steady development of Scottish investments that flowed into the American West. He emphasizes that his study should be regarded as the first stage in an investigation of the full implications of foreign speculation on the frontier. Scottish investments expanded in the 1870's with the shift of capital from land to cattle businesses. Rise of the U. S. cattle industry provided a convenient moment for the Scots to withdraw from frontier land deals where their foreign ownership of American soil was less than welcome. Cattle corporations were psychologically less visible and between 1880–82 several Scottish firms came to life. All struggled with the now familiar problems of long distance managerial conflicts, recession, and severe weather. Although Jackson maintains that the Scots' fiscal policies retained a strong flavor of conservativism, some did succumb to the lure of speculation. Ultimately, all but the Matador suffered from over-production and low prices.

Much of Jackson's text is devoted to an examination of the Scots' mining ventures and land schemes. The entire scope of the book is important for it shows the far-reaching involvement of foreign capital in Western industry. This book helps to reduce the concept of the West as the playground of the single adventurer and emphasizes the highly complex international aspects of the transformation of a frontier society to an industrial society. Jackson's book is

104

impressively researched and carefully written. If it is not always scintillating reading, it nonetheless offers deep perception into the economic aspect of western experience.

In 1973, William W. Savage's *The Cherokee Strip Live Stock Association: Federal Regulation and the Cattleman's Last Frontier* appeared. Not only is the format of this volume startlingly different — almost like those flat story books of our elementary days — but also fine research and sharp analysis characterize this study.

Savage maintains that the Cherokee Strip Live Stock Association is peculiar because it was formed in reaction to federal interference, most stock associations having organized for want of federal action.[27] Savage contends that governmental policy in the Cherokee Outlet of Oklahoma was detrimental to cattle interests because of two guiding principles: (1) Indian affairs should be totally controlled by federal agencies, and (2) the area would and should be turned over to farmers.

These two principles were largely responsible for a tenuous alliance that formed between stock owners and the Cherokee nation. The cattlemen's need for grazing land and the Cherokee's desire for economic self-sufficiency prompted the creation of a grazing lease program on the Cherokee reservation. Here are the ingredients for a local episode in the story of the cattle industry. But Savage extends his treatment to the level of federal involvement and what emerges is a concise picture of federal land and Indian policy. Without the details, the conclusion is predictable — the ranchers were forced to withdraw and the Indians were denied both monies and land. Savage's book offers a fresh slant in several areas. One more generalization of the West is undone — all stock growers' associations did not emerge for the same reasons. Although most associations acted as extra-legal organizations, the Cherokee Strip Live Stock Association conducted the majority of its affairs through a tangled series of litigations. The presentation of the federal bureaucracy as the oppressor of the Indian is not so new. What is new is Savage's presentation of the Cherokee people as entrepreneurs working to maintain economic vitality within the structure of white society. This is a volume filled with political, economic, and social implications heretofore untouched.

The historical study of the American cattle industry — our pyramid — obviously is still building. Further writings may well alter its shape. This examination can serve to remind scholars of three points.

First, we have moved away from descriptive surveys. Of course, broad surveys are needed, for they suggest a host of topics for additional research. But there is no reason for writers to recaptitulate well-worked material. Footnotes and episodes in many of the volumes discussed are distressingly repetitive. Each author, of course, would claim he was doing something different and would, therefore, justify himself in repeating anecdotes, citing the same sources. But a survey of this nature reveals that much of the conceptualization about the history of the cattle business is unimaginative and threadbare. When an author asks new questions of old material, as Atherton did, or treats an old subject from a new angle and with new sources, as Dykstra did, the reader can be grateful.

Second, topic selection and tone of presentation are so often a spin-off from the climate of the day that it is critical to look beyond the text itself and to view the attitudes of society at the time of publication. No historian is immune from the vibrations of society and the careful scholar will find this reflected in the historical text.

Third, historical investigation is never complete. That is part of the charm of the profession. With this as a guide, we can be assured that the historiographic pyramid will continue to grow and with it our understanding of the intriguing complexities of the American cattle industry. With the exciting specialized publications of recent years, the time may be near when a rewarding new synthesis may be possible.

REFERENCES

1. E. S. Osgood, *Day of the Cattleman* (Minneapolis: University of Minnesota Press, 1929), p. [ix].
2. Ibid., passim.
3. Ibid., p. 97.
4. Ibid., p. 115.
5. Ibid., p. 258.
6. E. E. Dale, *The Range Cattle Industry: Ranching on the Great Plains from 1865 to 1925* (Norman: University of Oklahoma Press, 1930), p. xiii.
7. Ibid., p. 56.
8. Ibid., pp. 166–68.
9. Louis Pelzer, *The Cattlemen's Frontier* (Glendale, Calif.: Arthur H. Clark Co., 1936), p. [15].
10. Ibid.
11. Ibid., pp. 242–48.
12. Ibid., p. 248.
13. J. Frank Dobie, *The Longhorns* (New York: Grosset and Dunlap, 1941), p. xviii.
14. Wayne Gard, *The Chisholm Trail* (Norman: University of Oklahoma Press, 1954), pp. vi–vii.
15. Lewis Atherton, *The Cattle Kings* (Bloomington: Indiana University Press, 1961), p. xi.
16. Ibid., p. 250.
17. Ibid., pp. 53–55.

18. Ibid., pp. 266–68.

19. John Schlebecker, *Cattle Raising on the Plains: 1900–1961* (Lincoln: University of Nebraska Press, 1963), p. vii.

20. William M. Pearce, *The Matador Land and Cattle Company* (Norman: University of Oklahoma Press, 1964), p. vii.

21. Philip Durham and Everett L. Jones, *The Negro Cowboys* (New York: Dodd, Mead and Co., 1965), pp. 1–2.

22. Ibid., p. 228.

23. Gene M. Gressley, *Bankers and Cattlemen* (Lincoln: University of Nebraska Press, 1966), p. viii.

24. Ibid., p. 296.

25. Robert Dykstra, *The Cattle Towns* (New York: Atheneum, 1973), p. 5.

26. W. T. Jackson, *The Enterprising Scot* (Edinburgh: Edinburgh University Publications, 1968), pp. vii–viii.

27. William W. Savage, *The Cherokee Strip Live Stock Association* (Columbia: University of Missouri Press, 1973), pp. 8–9.

Horticultural Heritage: The Influence of U. S. Nurserymen

By
Elisabeth Woodburn

It is hard to keep in mind that history is to-day. We peer back through the reversed telescope of time trying to see how it was. We see great wars, famous people, and events solemnly recorded and interpreted. In the past, as to-day, the daily round of our lives is unrecorded and lost even to ourselves. The proliferation of printed record tends to ignore rather than illumine the figure of the quiet man. It is the quiet man, however, accomplishing the round of his work and goals who provides the background for the pomp and circumstance of recorded history. His thoughts and deeds are rarely noted.

Of all quiet people, few are more lost to view than gardeners. This is not hard to understand. A garden, after all, represents Eden, or Heaven — no easy goal. With soil and sun, wind and rain, acting more often as adversaries than aids, gardeners soon learn humility.

To-day our gardens are big business, catered to, studied and advised from every angle from earthworm to acid rain. We are inoculated with the idea that someone will somehow make life easy for us. It is a shock, therefore, to find that in gardening, fundamentals of work — digging, planting, and cultivating — are as much facts of gardening for us as for our ancestors. Our headstart over our

Mrs. Woodburn, of Hopewell, New Jersey, is a bookdealer in agricultural literature.

forbears is the how-to-do-it records they have left us. These basic concepts for a green thumb have been examined, re-examined, and enlarged by new varieties. Reassuringly for our chaotic world, these basic concepts remain as Adam found them. The horticultural literature of our ancestors tells us much about the quiet men — who they were and why they left us records.

The working texts discussed here fail for the most part in qualifying for that favorite adjective of booksellers — "rare". While many are uncommon to-day, in their time they had considerable popularity. So-called editions, with no more than a change of date on the title page, were quite common. The number of the editions, and reprintings, and the fact that some covered a 50 year span shows their popularity. One does not have to be imaginative to say these books were needed, used, and had influence.

It is not surprising that our first texts dealt with agriculture. What was astonishing, however, was the late start of our indigenous literature. It is hard to understand why it took 127 years from the Pilgrim arrival until Jared Eliot wrote *Essays on Field Husbandry,* the first agricultural book published here in 1747. It must have been more fertility of the soil than the mind which kept the colonists alive. The English texts which they used were certainly no more suited to our climate then than now. But the Reverend Eliot started the presses rolling on an outpouring of agricultural books which even so large a library as the National Agricultural Library cannot hope to encompass.

It is not, fortunately, within my province to cover agricultural literature in the United States. It is my hope to touch a few highlights of one branch of agriculture in discussing the books and people who helped to develop knowledge of our horticulture.

History tantalizes us with bits and pieces. A letter, a diary, a passing allusion in a book of travel or social comment, are fascinating but isolated clues to our early flowers and gardens. Books of instruction give us visible history. They are the how and what of our forbears' gardening practices and knowledge. It takes no crystal ball to know the early settlers had time to grow only basic food and medicinal plants. Horticulture as applied to flowers and gardens was a term of the middle nineteenth century. Horticulture meant fruit trees and kitchen gardens. Flowers, if mentioned at all, were added at the end of the early garden manuals as a polite gesture for the ladies.

Nursery and seed catalogues are evidence of this practical approach to horticulture. Fruit trees were the main offerings. One of our most famous colonial nurseries, the Prince nursery of Flushing, Long Island, was established as our first commerical nursery in 1737. Four generations of the Prince family gave it a long history. Their catalogues which have survived show the early emphasis on practical plants at first and the gradual introduction of more and more ornamentals.

The National Agricultural Library has one of the largest collections of seed and nursery catalogues in the country. It contains some early Prince material including one angry broadside about an impostor posing as Prince. The impostor was going around taking orders — and payments — for plants to be delivered by the Prince Nursery, or Linnean Botanic Garden, as it was called. It appears neither orders nor payment reached Prince.

Now we regret that no serious attempt was made early in our horticultural history to keep continuous files of our seed and nursery catalogues. No better year by year history of our horticulture and the men who created it exist. The brief personal notes in some of these catalogues are real footnotes of history.

If the catalogues are ephemera, the books are not. While they have not been collected assiduously, enough have come down to us to study them. One common denominator is shared by both the books and catalogues, which has taken me twenty-five years to realize. Horticulture in this country was developed and taught by American nurserymen. They grew the plants. They issued the catalogues. They wrote the books. They wrote all but a few of the gardening books from the earliest through the middle of the nineteenth century. It was simple cause and effect. If they wanted to sell seeds and plants, they had to tell people how to grow them.

One can start with our first great botanical explorer and plantsman, John Bartram. His Botanic Garden was a nursery for growing the plants he found for his European patrons. It is also noteworthy that he grew plants from European seeds as well as sending our seeds abroad. This two way traffic was a forerunner of what has become a major transference of world flora.

Humphry Marshall, Bartram's cousin, likewise established a botanic garden. In it he grew some of the trees he described in our first indigenous work on trees, *Arbustrum(sic) Americanum*. The subtitle notes it contains "hints for their uses in medicine, dyes, and domestic economy," details of interest to his fellow citizens when it was published in Philadelphia in 1785. The book was also of enough interest to the French for a translation of it to appear in Paris in 1788.

Supplying plants for overseas demand was an incentive to nurserymen of such caliber as the Bartrams, Marshall, the Michaux, and others who gathered American plants for European buyers. This keen interest made possible the publication of Michaux' beautiful *Histoire Des Arbres Forestier de l'Amerique Septentrionale,* in Paris 1810–1813. France's greatest botanical artists of the period, Redoute and Bessa did the plates. It was four years before an English translation appeared. However, importations were two-way. Michaux and his son contributed to American gardens by importing plants here which they raised in gardens established first in New Jersey and later in South Carolina. Other examples of plant importation are shown in the Prince catalogues, previously mentioned, among others. These European novelties appealed to estate and greenhouse owners.

It may have been that South Carolina had a sufficiently different climate from England that the English books could not be "translated" into useful instructions. Whatever the cause, the first garden book of which we have record is an advertisement in the South Carolina Gazette in 1752 for Martha Logan's *The Gardener's Kalendar.* This fragile clue is all there is, alas, as no copy has yet been found. It was probably an almanac of planting operations which was the standard format for the day.

A surer cornerstone for our horticultural literature is *The Gardener's Calendar for South Carolina and North Carolina by Robert Squibb,* published in Charleston, S.C. in 1787. The author was a nurseryman who carried on the nursery tradition that John Watson had established before the Revolution. His book was illustrated by a woodcut frontispiece showing a greenhouse. The book proved useful and was apparently in demand further afield as "and Georgia" was added to the title for the later editions of 1809, 1813, and 1827. A revised version appeared as late as 1842, giving the book influence for fifty-seven years.

The American Gardener by John Gardiner and David Hepburn was our next indigenous book. It appeared in The City of Washington in 1804. While largely on kitchen gardens it had a small section on hothouses and greenhouses. The second edition of 1818 contains a reprint of another tantalizingly elusive early work, the anonymous *Treatise on Gardening* by a Gentleman of Virginia, identified as John Randolph. This was also a work on the kitchen garden. Tacked on at the end is the title's promised "A few hints on the cultivation of native vines, and directions for making domestic wines." It contains some unhappy remarks about the over indulgence in strong spirits by the citizenry. The remedy suggested is to drink wine made from native grapes. A local gentleman is quoted as the source of the suggestion of using native grapes. The wording is strongly reminiscent of John Adlum. He had a good-sized farm in Georgetown where he raised many kinds of grapes. Gardiner and Hepburn would likely have known such a prominent citizen. Adlum's own findings on grapes and wine appeared five years later as our first book on the subject, *A Memoir on the Cultivation of the Vine in America,* which was also published in Washington.

Another example of the small world aspect of the early years came into my hands. A copy of the 1804 edition of *The American Gardener* which I had was signed on the title with the unlikely signature of A. Burr. Although this hardly seemed fare for a conspirator, I checked the list of subscribers in the book. It was headed "Thos. Jefferson, President, 2 copies." The second line said "Aaron Burr, Vice-president, 1 copy."

Jefferson's name and the City of Washington are associated with our first publication on hedges. Thomas Main, said to be a nurseryman from whom Jefferson purchased plants, published a pamphlet with the weighty title of *Transplantation and Management of Young Thorn and Other Hedge Plants,* in 1807.

Finally, in 1806 a garden book appeared which set a standard for the full scale treatment of horticulture. It is still hard to find a rival for Bernard M'Mahon's *The American Gardener's Calendar,* published in Philadelphia. The lengthy subtitle, listing the subjects covered, almost filled the title page. Much of it was based on English books but it was modified for local conditions. The chapter on landscape is considered the foundation for the subject here. Linnean names as well as English were given. The 600 page book included a good index. M'Mahon, trained as a gardener in his native Ireland, reportedly came here for political refuge. Whatever his reasons, he enriched his adopted country with his Old World knowledge of gardening and books. The 11th, and last edition of his book, published in 1857, contains a description of his store and nursery. It gives the flavor of this center of botanical and horticultural life in Philadelphia. Lewis and Clark are said to have planned part of their expedition there. M'Mahon was given some of the seeds from the expedition to propagate, and helped in the introduction of plants from the western regions into the eastern part of the United States.

The David Landreths, father and son, had another famous Philadelphia nursery, established in 1784. They, too, were propagators of the Lewis and Clark seeds, as well as being growers and importers of plants. They issued many catalogues, as well as making a major contribution to our literature with *The Floral Magazine and Botanical Repository*. It lasted only from 1832 to 1835, but it was the first work devoted to flowers which had colored plates and may be considered our first floral magazine. They are quoted as having had to give it up for lack of both artists and colorists to do the plates.

The early books were the liaison between the nurseryman and the emerging middle income group. There were not enough trained gardeners to go around nor funds to employ them. The catalogues with their steadily increasing lists of "novelties," "exotics," and "new introductions," presaging the more lurid press to come, required help to sell their wares. The books provided help and instructions for new gardeners. "Horticulture," as defined by our greatest horticulturist, L. H. Bailey, is "the growing of flowers, fruits and vegetables, and of plants for ornament or fancy." The early books helped to establish our horticulture as a full member of the agricultural family.

William Coxe maintained a large orchard in Burlington, N. J. What he learned from it resulted in *A View of the Cultivation of Fruit Trees and the Management of Orchards and Cider,* published in Philadelphia in 1817. It was our first native work on fruit. This pomology, filled with outline drawings of the fruits, was the start of what many consider our most important contribution to horticultural literature during the Victorian era. It was also a milestone in being topical in approach rather than in calendar form. A proposed second edition with fine color plates by his daughters was never published. It is part of our heritage, however, and is preserved in the National Agricultural Library. The exact rendering of the coloring enables modern scientists to identify insect and disease problems of the period, giving historians a clue to the introduction of these pests. Although only one edition was published it must have been a fair sized edition, as copies are in many libraries and some appear on the market.

The succession of pomological works by nurserymen, after this first publication, show the accumulating range of knowledge and the increasing list of varieties. William Kenrick had a knowledge of fruit from having been exposed to them first in his father's nursery and then his own. He planted extensive amounts of imported varieties and observed them carefully. His *The New American Orchardist* first came out in Boston in 1833. The 8th edition, "enlarged and improved with a supplement" published in 1848, proved it had met

114

AMERICAN GARDENER'S
CALENDAR;

ADAPTED

TO THE CLIMATES AND SEASONS

OF THE

UNITED STATES.

CONTAINING

A COMPLETE ACCOUNT OF ALL THE WORK NECESSARY TO BE
DONE IN THE

KITCHEN-GARDEN,		PLEASURE-GROUND,
FRUIT-GARDEN,		FLOWER-GARDEN,
ORCHARD,		GREEN-HOUSE,
VINEYARD,		HOT-HOUSE, and
NURSERY,		FORCING FRAMES,

FOR EVERY MONTH IN THE YEAR;

WITH AMPLE PRACTICAL DIRECTIONS
FOR PERFORMING THE SAME.

ALSO,

General as well as minute instructions, for laying out, or erecting, each and
every of the above departments, according to modern taste and the most
approved plans; the ORNAMENTAL PLANTING OF PLEASURE-GROUNDS,
in the ancient and modern stile; the cultivation of THORN-QUICKS and
other plants suitable for LIVE HEDGES, with the best methods of making
them, &c.

TO WHICH ARE ANNEXED,

Extensive CATALOGUES of the different kinds of plants, which may be cultivated either for use or ornament in the several departments, or in rural
economy; divided into eighteen separate alphabetical classes, according
to their habits, duration, and modes of culture; with explanatory introductions, marginal marks, and their true *Linnean* or *Botanical*, as well as
English names; together with a copious *Index* to the body of the work.

BY BERNARD M'MAHON,

NURSERY, SEEDSMAN, AND FLORIST.

PHILADELPHIA:

PRINTED BY B. GRAVES, NO. 40, NORTH FOURTH-STREET,
FOR THE AUTHOR.

1806.

a need. Kenrick's writings also included a work on one of the great "fevers" of the time. *The American Silk-Growers' Guide,* on the culture of the Morus multicaulis, was a directive for all those who wished to grow rich rapidly. It did happen that Kenrick sold this tree in quantity before the silk-growing bubble burst, but writers of the day hasten to say that Mr. Kenrick was a true believer in the possibilities of this home industry. His enthusiasm for horticulture cannot be doubted because he was one of the sixteen founding members of the Massachusetts Horticultural Society in 1829.

Robert Manning grew over 2000 varieties of fruit—almost half of them pears—in his "Pomological Garden" in Salem, Massachusetts. This enabled him to clarify many descriptions when writing his *Book of Fruits,* First Series in 1838. The work was of help at the time because of these descriptions since nomenclature was loosely applied and frequently misleading. His testing of so many varieties was also useful. It is hard to believe that any figure even close to a thousand represented the varieties of pears grown. Manning imported many of them including the famed Van Mons developments. John M. Ives was joint author of the second edition which was called *The New England Fruit Book* when it appeared in 1844. Ives took full credit for the third edition with the third title of *The New England Book of Fruits.* Attractive frontispieces in these little books were sometimes colored, sometimes not.

The Prince nursery, in addition to its prominence as one of the oldest and finest establishments in the country, provided the background of knowledge which enabled its proprietors to publish some valuable books. William Prince, son of the founder, wrote one of our earliest horticultural treatises. *A Treatise on Fruit and Ornamental Trees and Plants* was an 81 page work issued in 1820. It was largely a catalogue of plants with their prices. In 1828 an expanded 196 page version, entitled *A Short Treatise on Horticulture Embracing Descriptions of a Great Variety of Fruit and Ornamental Trees,* was an expanded version with 196 pages. This treatise was intended to instruct people, not just tell them what was available.

William Prince joined with his son, William Robert Prince, to write the two volume *The Pomological Manual* which appeared in two editions of 1831 and 1832, and *A Treatise on the Vine* in 1830. This last had a frontispiece by W. Prince of Vitis labrusca, v. Isabella. It would have been helpful if he had illustrated the Zinfandel grape of such controversial background. In 1846, William Robert Prince issued *A Manual of Roses,* with lists of roses and good instructions for growing them. W. R. Prince also wrote a pamphlet

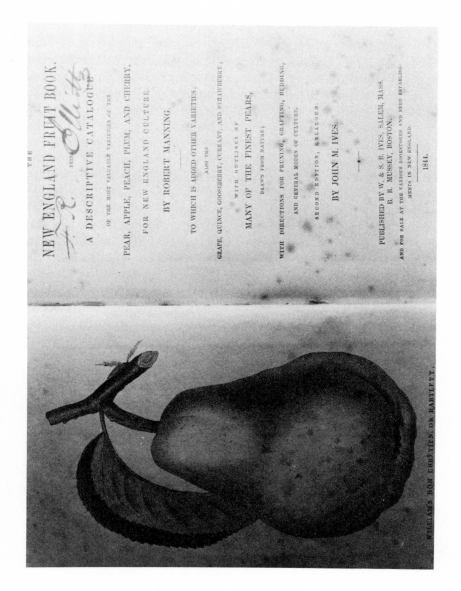

THE

NEW ENGLAND FRUIT BOOK.

BEING

A DESCRIPTIVE CATALOGUE

OF THE MOST VALUABLE VARIETIES OF THE

PEAR, APPLE, PEACH, PLUM, AND CHERRY,

FOR NEW ENGLAND CULTURE.

BY ROBERT MANNING.

TO WHICH IS ADDED OTHER VARIETIES;

ALSO THE

GRAPE, QUINCE, GOOSEBERRY, CURRANT, AND STRAWBERRY,

WITH OUTLINES OF

MANY OF THE FINEST PEARS,

DRAWN FROM NATURE;

WITH DIRECTIONS FOR PRUNING, GRAFTING, BUDDING,

AND GENERAL MODES OF CULTURE.

SECOND EDITION, ENLARGED.

BY JOHN M. IVES.

PUBLISHED BY W. & S. B. IVES, SALEM, MASS.
B. B. MUSSEY, BOSTON.
AND FOR SALE AT THE VARIOUS BOOKSTORES AND SEED ESTABLISH-
MENTS IN NEW ENGLAND.

1844.

WILLIAMS BON CHRÉTIEN, OR BARTLETT.

which sounds interesting but not one which greatly advanced horti-culture. His *A Treatise on Nature's Sovereign Remedials, Eclectic Fluid Compounds Extracted from Plants, Humanized Electricity and Magnetism, the Life Fluid and Life Food* was only 16 pages, barely long enough to list the title much less cover so involved a subject.

One man in a brief life produced two outstanding books. One of these books, in fact, is almost as well known in our own day as when it was published in 1841. Andrew Jackson Downing wrote *A Treatise on the Theory and Practice of Landscape Gardening* when he was twenty-six years old. His background of growing up in the Hudson Valley area and working in his father's nursery made him aware of both natural beauty and plant material. An innate artist's eye enabled him to correlate them into settings which appealed to a public increasingly aware of the possibilities of beautifying their grounds. As one who appealed to all for naturalistic settings he was one of the prophets of to-day's ecology. His editorship of *The Horticulturist* from its founding in 1846 until his untimely death in 1852 made it the finest source of horticultural information of that time and for us in examining records of the period. His *Fruits and Fruit Trees,* first published in 1845, revised by him subsequently, and later greatly extended by his brother Charles, was still being published in 1900. Charles Downing had his own nursery for some years in which his younger brother, Andrew, had worked. He sold it, but continued an experimental test orchard where he grew thousands of varieties. These provided the basis for his careful notes for the continuing revisions for the book. It was expanded from the original work of 594 pages to 1200 pages.

Another nurseryman-writer of a long popular work was Patrick Barry. His *Treatise on the Fruit Garden* appeared in 1851. A revised version in 1872 came out as *Barry's Fruit Garden.* By that time, it was good publishing to put Barry's name on the cover. The book was good. Copies turn up often enough to show it was kept as a work of value by succeeding generations. It was not only for this book that Barry's name was known. His partnership with George Ellwanger in creating the famous Mount Hope Nurseries in Roches-ter, New York, proved to be one of pride for all. Between them, they worked hard for their adopted city in developing parks and helping put on the magnificent floral displays that gave the nick-name of "The Flower City" to Rochester. Their nurseries and catalogues were the finest contributions to horticulture of the pe-riod. Their location enabled them to develop plants which could withstand the colder inland climates. They provided these for the

A

TREATISE

ON

THE THEORY AND PRACTICE

OF

LANDSCAPE GARDENING,

ADAPTED TO

NORTH AMERICA;

WITH A VIEW TO

THE IMPROVEMENT OF COUNTRY RESIDENCES.

COMPRISING

HISTORICAL NOTICES AND GENERAL PRINCIPLES OF THE ART,
DIRECTIONS FOR LAYING OUT GROUNDS AND ARRANGING PLANTATIONS,
THE DESCRIPTION AND CULTIVATION OF HARDY TREES,
DECORATIVE ACCOMPANIMENTS TO THE HOUSE AND GROUNDS,
THE FORMATION OF PIECES OF ARTIFICIAL WATER, FLOWER GARDENS, ETC.

WITH REMARKS ON

RURAL ARCHITECTURE.

ILLUSTRATED BY ENGRAVINGS.

By A. J. DOWNING.

"Insult not Nature with absurd expense,
Nor spoil her simple charms by vain pretence;
Weigh well the subject, be with caution bold,
Profuse of genius, not profuse of gold."

NEW-YORK & LONDON:

WILEY AND PUTNAM.

BOSTON.—C. C. LITTLE & Co.

1841.

new nurseries opening up farther west. Their example and success inspired other nurserymen in western New York to develop nursery and seed businesses as well. An interesting offshoot of all the nurseries in the area was the development of a number of agricultural presses in the Rochester area to provide all the catalogues required. One name in particular comes down to us. D. M. Dewey and Company provided a spectacular line of color plates of flowers and trees quite often found in salesmen's catalogues. These interesting publications had no text generally. Apparently, they were carried as sample books from which to take orders.

In addition to his other activities, Barry was editor of the horticultural department for *The Genesee Farmer* for eight years. In 1854 and 1855 he was the editor for *The Horticulturist* which James Vick had bought after Downing's death. Numerous addresses to horticultural and agricultural societies also kept Barry busy during the fifty year span of the firm of Ellwanger and Barry. In the period of 1840 to 1890, when Barry died, the firm's records of shipments to our steadily expanding Western territory—even a major shipment to Japan—provide a prime source of history. Even the first of the modern California orchards were started with nursery stock from the Mount Hope Nurseries. Small wonder Mr. Barry's fruit book turned up in so many places.

The second of L. H. Bailey's four branches of horticulture is that of olericulture or vegetable gardening. Everyone wrote on kitchen gardens but surprisingly little developmental work was done on vegetables until late in the nineteenth century. John Josselyn's *New England Rarities Discovered* in 1672 gave an extensive list of garden herbs which included most of the vegetables grown through the middle of the 1800s. There were essentially three noteworthy separate publications on vegetables, if one excludes the general horticultural manuals of the time. Naturally, general manuals included kitchen gardens, as the vegetables and the "sweet or pot herbs" were basic plants. In the seventeenth and eighteenth centuries, the list of herbs included the medicinal as well, since gardens had to supply health as well as nourishment. Medicinal herbs were elevated to a separate branch of science by the late Colonial period with a literature of their own. It is interesting to note that today the reawakened interest in herbs finds the various branches of herb lore —culinary, medicinal, fragrant, and dyes—is producing a new line of books on the subject.

The three B's of early vegetable books were Bridgeman, Buist, and Burr. Thomas Bridgeman's *The Kitchen Gardener's Instructor*

THE

KITCHEN GARDENER'S INSTRUCTOR,

CONTAINING A CATALOGUE OF

GARDEN AND HERB SEED,

WITH

PRACTICAL DIRECTIONS UNDER EACH HEAD

FOR THE CULTIVATION OF

CULINARY VEGETABLES AND HERBS.

WITH A CALENDAR,

SHOWING THE WORK NECESSARY TO BE DONE IN A KITCHEN GARDEN
EVERY MONTH THROUGHOUT THE SEASON.

ALSO, DIRECTIONS FOR

FORCING OR FORWARDING VEGETABLES

OUT OF THE ORDINARY SEASON.

THE WHOLE ADAPTED TO THE CLIMATE OF THE UNITED STATES.

A NEW AND IMPROVED EDITION.

BY THOMAS BRIDGEMAN,

GARDENER, SEEDSMAN, AND FLORIST.

NEW YORK:

C. M. SAXTON AND COMPANY,

AGRICULTURAL BOOK PUBLISHERS,

No. 140 FULTON STREET,

1857.

mentions in the subtitle it contains "a catalogue of garden and herb seeds" among other virtues. It was first issued in Brooklyn in 1829 as part of his *The Young Gardener's Assistant* but was issued on its own in New York in 1836. In the preface, Mr. Bridgeman states its publication was

> to enable our respectable seedsmen to afford instruction, at a trifling expense, to those of their customers whose attention may be directed wholly to that branch of Horticulture and thereby save themselves the blame of such as may not have given their seeds a fair trial, for want of knowing how to dispose of them in the ground.

As a well-known seedsman, he knew the problems. His conditions for gardening success still apply for us.

Mr. Bridgeman also gives cooking advice and the names of the culinary vegetables and herbs in English and French, as well as the Latin nomenclature. In the early editions of his book — it was still being reprinted in 1867 as *The American Kitchen-Gardener* — there are two headings under which one finds "The Tomato, Tomate, Pomme D'Amour; Solanum Lycopersicum." Under cultivation is the note that "this delicious vegetable . . may . . after being deprived of the skin, be preserved in sugar and used either as a dessert, or on the tea-table, as a substitute for Peaches or other sweetmeats. It also makes exquisite pies and tarts." Under a heading of "Forwarding Tomatoes," he notes it "has of late been highly extolled in respectable periodicals" and that "a celebrated writer observes that . . 'made into a gravy, by stewing over the fire, and used as a sauce for meat, has been known to quicken the action of the liver, and of the bowels, better than any medicine he ever made use of.'" To clinch this, the unacknowledged authority adds "When afflicted with inaction of the bowels, head-ache, a bad taste of the mouth, straitness of the chest, and a dull and painful heaviness of the region of the liver, the whole of these symptoms are removed by Tomatoe sauce, and the mind, in the course of some few hours, is put in perfect tune like a new violin." Mr. Bridgeman adds a recipe for catsup to this interesting report. As a further note on the recurring question of how early the tomato was actually used in this country, there is a final page in the 1818 edition of the aforementioned *The American Gardener* by Gardiner and Hepburn that is headed "To Make Tomato Ketchup" and proceeds to give a recipe of fairly exact measurements for ingredients and methods of preparation.

Robert Buist, in *The Family Kitchen Gardener,* gives "descriptions of all the different species and varieties of culinary vegetables

THE

FAMILY KITCHEN GARDENER,

CONTAINING

PLAIN AND ACCURATE DESCRIPTIONS

OF ALL THE

DIFFERENT SPECIES AND VARIETIES

OF

CULINARY VEGETABLES;

WITH

THEIR BOTANICAL, ENGLISH, FRENCH, AND GERMAN NAMES, ALPHABETICALLY
ARRANGED, AND THE BEST MODE OF CULTIVATING THEM, IN THE GARDEN
OR UNDER GLASS; WITH A DESCRIPTION OF IMPLEMENTS AND
MEDICINAL HERBS IN GENERAL USE.

ALSO,

DESCRIPTIONS AND CHARACTERS OF THE MOST SELECT
FRUITS, THEIR MANAGEMENT, PROPAGATION, ETC.

ILLUSTRATED WITH TWENTY-FIVE ENGRAVINGS.

BY ROBERT BUIST,

AUTHOR OF THE AMERICAN FLOWER-GARDEN DIRECTORY, ROSE MANUAL, ETC.

NEW YORK
C. M. SAXTON AND COMPANY,
AGRICULTURAL BOOK-PUBLISHERS,
No. 140 FULTON STREET,
1857.

123

with their botanical, English, French and German names, . . . implements and medicinal herbs in general use." He also adds a section on fruits. As a leading nurseryman of the Philadelphia area he knew how popular they were. His book, copyrighted in 1847, makes some further observations on that strictly American vegetable, the tomato. No mention of its earlier name of "love-apple" is made. He states

> In taking a retrospect of the past eighteen years, there is no vegetable on the catalogue that has obtained such popularity in so short a period . . . In 1828–9 it was almost detested; in ten years more every variety of pill and panacea was 'extract of tomato.' It now occupies as great a surface of ground as Cabbage, and is cultivated the length and breadth of the country. As a culinary dish it is on every table from July to October. . . It is brought to the table in an infinite variety of forms . . stewed and seasoned, stuffed and fried, roasted and raw, in nearly every form palatable to all. It is also made into pickles, catsup, and salted in barrels for Winter use so that with a few years more experience we may expect to see it as an every-day dish from January to January.

These prophetic words, followed by a list of the different types—no named varieties—are followed by planting instructions. This book was still being published twenty years later, so it is apparent the tomato was in general use and culture longer than is generally credited.

The third of our B's, Fearing Burr, Jr., wrote *Field and Garden Vegetables of America,* published in Boston in 1863. The subtitle says it contains descriptions of nearly eleven hundred species and varieties, with directions for propagation, culture, and use. It was intended as a guide to assist in the selection of varieties listed in this large 674 page work, impossible to find now if one consulted all the modern catalogues. The book is attractively illustrated by no less an artist than Isaac Sprague. An 1865 edition of it came out in a smaller format with some text changes and 40 additional drawings by Mr. Sprague. An offshoot of this was the 1866 publication of Burr's *Garden Vegetables and How To Cultivate Them.* Burr's partnership in the seed firm of M. & F. Burr not only gave him the basis for his knowledge of plants but a good incentive for writing a book about them.

It may be that Grant Thorburn's note in Hovey's *American Garden Magazine,* Volume I of 1835 is a clue to why there were not more books on vegetables. Stated briefly—as Mr. Thorburn was not likely to have done—he claims the future progress of gardening depends on two factors; the improved taste of the patrons of gardening and improved practices of gardening. He continues that part of the lack of vegetables is, to quote more directly,

> ignorance of the proper mode of cooking vegetables, and especially of dressing salads, which exists among the middling classes . . a French laborer out of a few leaves of dandelion and wild sorrel . . gathered by the hedgesides . . will produce, merely by the aid of common condiments, what the wives of the greater number of respectable American farmers and tradesmen have no idea of. There can be no great demand for a thing, of which the use is not thoroughly understood . . an improvement in the knowledge and practice of cooking must take place, among a certain class, before much can be expected . . of the gardening articles which they commonly consume.

In view of what passes as salad dressing offered in most of our markets to-day, one can only conclude sadly that Mr. Thorburn's words were never heeded. The editor's notes about Mr. Thorburn's letter make some interesting footnotes on the newer vegetables with especial praise for the tomato.

It is an interesting point to observe by inference, that flowers were of more interest to a prospering Republic than were vegetables. After the initial publications mentioned which covered fruits, vegetables, trees, shrubs with a nod at flowers, in about that order, the first separate flower books began to appear. Historic for us, as the first work entirely on flowers, is Roland Green's little book *Treatise on the Cultivation of Ornamental Flowers*. About all that is known of the author is that Grant Thorburn published his book in New York in 1828. Probably to avoid being castigated as too frivolous, the author took the precaution of adding a few vegetables and trees.

Grant Thorburn's name weaves in and out of the pages of nineteenth century horticulture. His only garden book, *The Gentleman and Gardener's Kalendar for the Middle States of North America,* was published in editions of 1812, 1817 and 1824. He opened, what he claimed, was the first succesful seed and flower shop in New York. The series of articles and books he wrote as "Lawrie Todd" (John Galt used the name as a title of one of his novels) were full of piety. He did much to publicize a knowledge of horticulture.

The American Flower Garden Directory by Hibbert and Buist had an attractive color frontispiece of a Camellia fimbriata when it was first published in Philadelphia in 1832. It was unashamedly a flower book. The lengthy subtitle has no sops for the kitchen garden

125

THE AMERICAN

FLOWER GARDEN DIRECTORY:

CONTAINING

PRACTICAL DIRECTIONS FOR THE CULTURE OF PLANTS

IN THE

FLOWER GARDEN, HOT-HOUSE, GREEN-HOUSE, ROOMS,
OR PARLOUR WINDOWS,

FOR EVERY MONTH IN THE YEAR.

WITH

A Description of the Plants most desirable in each, the Nature of the Soil, and
Situation best adapted to their Growth, the proper Season for
Transplanting, &c.

INSTRUCTIONS FOR ERECTING A

HOT-HOUSE, GREEN-HOUSE, AND LAYING OUT A
FLOWER GARDEN.

ALSO,

Table of Soils most congenial to the Plants contained in the Work.

THE WHOLE ADAPTED

To either Large or Small Gardens, with instructions for preparing the Soil,
Propagating, Planting, Pruning, Training, and Fruiting the

GRAPE VINE.

With Descriptions of the best Sorts for cultivating in the open Air.

NEW EDITION, WITH NUMEROUS ADDITIONS.

—:o:—

BY ROBERT BUIST,

NURSERYMAN AND FLORIST.

—:o:—

PHILADELPHIA:

CAREY AND HART.

1841.

126

practicality. An interesting note on the last page states the authors have purchased the "nursery grounds . . . of the late B. M'Mahon . . .," another link in the interlocking descent of our horticultural heritage. A number of subsequent editions of this book appeared but without the frontispiece, in a smaller format, and with Robert Buist as sole author, but still worth reprinting near the turn of the century by Orange Judd.

The Florist's Guide by Thomas Bridgeman was a more modest work published in New York in 1835. One of the flowers it featured was the current favorite, the double dahlia. It, too, went through a number of editions, appearing as late as 1872 as part of the volume of Bridgeman's collected works *The American Gardener's Assistant*. This, as mentioned previously, first came out in Brooklyn in 1828 as *The Young Gardener's Assistant* with only 96 pages. In its final version it contained three separately paged works on kitchen gardening, fruit, and flower gardening with a total of over 500 pages.

Edward Sayers, whose book *The American Flower Garden Companion Adapted to the Northern States,* first came out in 1838, added to the subtitle "And Middle States" when the second edition came out in 1839. The first edition published by another seedsman, Joseph Breck & Company, had five pages of ads for different nurserymen. Mr. Sayers seems to have had the wanderlust because his third edition enlarged, came out in 1846 in Cincinnati. Before he had left Boston he wrote another noteworthy title. His *Treatise on the Culture of the Dahlia and the Cactus* published in 1839 was the first monograph on a single flower (the cactus is not emphasized) written in the U.S.

Flower monographs were not numerous but Robert Buist added another with his *The Rose Manual* first published in 1844. It contained a list of varieties which Mr. Buist happened to have grown at his nursery. By the time of the fourth edition published in 1854 it had grown in both size and list of varieties. The second rose book, the *Manual of Roses* by William Robert Prince, appeared in 1846. It was a more thorough book than Buist's, but the style was not as readable. It had only one edition. An earlier work on roses than either of these was *The Queen of Flowers: or, Memoirs of the Rose,* published in 1841 in Philadelphia. It was a reissue of a book of sentimental tributes first published in London in 1824 as *Memoirs of the Rose.*

The next monograph of importance was also on the rose, showing its growing popularity. Samuel B. Parson's *The Rose: Its History, Poetry, Culture, and Classification,* was published in New York in

THE

ROSE MANUAL;

CONTAINING

ACCURATE DESCRIPTIONS OF ALL THE FINEST VARIETIES

OF

ROSES,

PROPERLY CLASSED IN THEIR RESPECTIVE FAMILIES,
THEIR CHARACTER AND MODE OF CULTURE,

WITH

DIRECTIONS FOR THEIR PROPAGATION,

AND THE DESTRUCTION OF INSECTS.

WITH ENGRAVINGS.

BY ROBERT BUIST,
NURSERYMAN AND FLORIST.

PHILADELPHIA.

FOR THE AUTHOR AND MESSRS. CAREY AND HART.

1844.

1847. This first edition had two beautiful color plates of roses by Cheirat, imported from France for this work. The author, another of the influential nurserymen from Long Island, is also credited with introducing the first Japanese maples in this country as well as being one of the first to propagate rhododendrons. Later editions, including one the same year which added the promised 36 page descriptive list not ready for the first printing, were all without the color plates. All but the two 1847 printings were smaller formats as well. *Parsons on the Rose* was still being published in 1920. Since the Parsons nursery was founded in 1838, it was a name long known to gardeners.

The Flower Garden by Joseph Breck first published in Boston in 1851 has a delightful frontispiece of a garden. It could not be said to have been influenced by Downing's naturalistic style. Despite Downing's landscape book demonstrating fairly simple landscapes, the Victorians took to bedding plants. It may have been they were so intoxicated by the wealth of flowers appearing in ever greater abundance that they were more interested in seeing the plants than in seeing the effects they could achieve in planting. Mr. Breck, as a seedsman, naturally described the wealth of blooms available.

In a desire to bring to their customers, real and potential, news of horticultural interest, a number of nursery firms over the years started horticultural journals. Most were short-lived but a few made names which are remembered. As mentioned, the Landreth's *Floral Magazine* was the first to be devoted solely to flowers and to have colored flower plates. *The Horticultural Register and Gardeners Magazine* was edited by Breck and Fessenden and ran only from 1835 to 1839. The 1839 issue was a good year for its reprint of Henry A. S. Dearborn's translation of Abbé Berlese "Monography Of The Genus Camellia" with a classified color chart. The camellia, the most popular flower of the day, was the subject of our first flower monograph. Breck first published this Berlese work the previous year as a separate volume.

Journals which had longer lives were those started by the Hoveys and the one begun by A. J. Downing. The Hoveys began in 1835 as *The American Gardener's Magazine and Register of Useful Discoveries*. With the third year it was called *Magazine of Horticulture* and continued as that until 1868. A. J. Downing's periodical, *The Horticulturist* was started in 1846. Other writers, including Patrick Barry, carried it on for 30 years. It is the most outstanding of these periodicals. As less able editors carried it on, however, its fame dimmed. Copies of the early years can still be found. As this periodical became less valuable, it was less valued. However, it is difficult to locate copies of the late years.

Thomas Meehan, another of the immigrants to Philadelphia who contributed so much to our horticulture, published an excellent magazine which began in this period and was a link to a later period. *The Gardener's Monthly* ran from 1859 to 1888. It was newsworthy for the time it covered. Meehan was another of the important links in the chain of nurserymen. When he arrived in Philadelphia, he went to work for Robert Buist and was superintendent of Bartram's Garden. *The American Handbook of Ornamental Trees,* published in 1853, records details of the trees in the Garden while he was there.

The publications issued in the East seemed to cover the requirements of the rest of the country for the opening years of expansion. One of the few early works published in the Deep South was J. F. Lelievre's *Nouveau Jardinier de la Louisiane* published in New Orleans in 1838. It is important as both our first French garden book and our first from the region. This lone French book is contrasted by a number of nurseries in France issuing catalogues in English. The Missouri Historical Society holds one from a local family that was issued by M. Ronna and Company in Lyon in 1820. The practice of issuing English catalogues continued. I have had Andre Leroy's *Descriptive Catalogue of Fruit and Ornamental Trees, Shrubs, Seedlings, etc.* from his nursery near the railroad station at Angers. It contains 119 pages of plant listings and thoughtfully provides a map of the French railway system showing all lines lead to Angers, at least in 1856.

The middle 1800's brought some publications from beyond the Appalachians. The authors had grounds and plantings which could have qualified them as professional rather than amateur nurserymen. Nicholas Longworth was an outstanding horticulturist in Cincinnati. His work with both strawberries and grapes was notable. He described this in *The Cultivation of the Grape And Manufacture of Wine; also the Character and Habits of Strawberries,* published in Cincinnati in 1846. This small work was incorporated in another Cincinnatian's book. Robert Buchanan's *The Culture of the Grape and Wine Making; with an Appendix Containing Directions for the Cultivation of the Strawberry by N. Longworth* came out in Cincinnati in 1852. Proof of its popularity is shown by an eighth 'edition' appearing as late as 1865.

E. J. Hooper's *Western Fruit Book,* published in Cincinnati in 1857, included what is certainly one of the most engaging frontis-

NOUVEAU
JARDINIER
DE LA LOUISIANE,

CONTENANT LES INSTRUCTIONS NECESSAIRES
Aux Personnes qui s'occupent de Jardinage.

PAR J. F. LELIEVRE,

Ex-Jardinier-Agriculteur du Gouvernement Français
pour les Colonies.

NOUVELLE-ORLEANS.

CHEZ J. F. LELIEVRE, LIBRAIRE,

Encoignure Royale et Ste.-Anne.

1838.

pieces in all our literature. This is a lithographed group portrait of the prominent contemporary horticulturists. This assemblage of stern-visaged, frock-coated gentlemen makes a mug shot which has much greater appeal than the four nice color plates. Two further enlarged editions appeared shortly after but, alas, without this lovely frontispiece.

Another Cincinnati author, John A. Warder, wrote *Hedges and Evergreens,* published in 1858, which had a section devoted to that important hedge plant, the Maclura or Osage orange. This was of great value for boundaries, stock control, and wind-breaks in the newer territories as it grew well and fast.

Franklin Reuben Elliott, from Cleveland, wrote *The Fruit Book or, the American Fruit-Growers Guide . . .* published in New York in 1854. Later editions had two other titles: *Elliott's Fruit Book* as well as *The Western Fruit-Book.* For further confusion, both were the 4th edition of 1859. Still later a revised edition appeared as *Hand-Book for Fruit Growers,* issued in 1876. A trifle further west, in Indiana, Henry Ward Beecher's enthusiastic columns from *The Western Farmer and Gardener* were issued as a book in 1859 and called *Plain and Pleasant Talks About Fruits, Flowers, and Farming.*

From the South at this period only one noteworthy book of lasting value appeared. William Nathaniel White wrote *Gardening in the South* which first came out in Athens, Georgia, in 1856. It must have been helpful, because a third revised and enlarged edition was published in Richmond, Virginia, in 1901.

The land beyond the Mississippi had not produced much horticultural literature by the 1860's. Although the wonders of Western plant life had been introduced and described for Easterners, texts for Western gardeners were yet to come. The process of trial and error for cultivating these plants successfully would require more years of patient effort.

By the 1860's additional sources of gardening information began to appear. While such fine nurserymen as James Vick, Peter Henderson, and others continued to publish good gardening books to encourage their patrons to know how to grow their plants and seeds to perfection, other pens were contributing to the growing body of horticultural literature. It was no longer necessary to publish or perish. Now many writers contribute ideas, facts, figures, pictures, knowledge, and history to our literature but the contribution of our past nurserymen is incalcuable. They, more than anyone, knew, grew, and studied plant material and added a steady line of new plants for our use and enjoyment. Their knowledge was shared in their books and catalogues. In reading them one catches their enthusiasm for the treasures of the green world they inhabited.

Nurserymen and seedsmen of the past have given us a marvelous horticultural heritage. Let us hope that at our Tricentennial someone can give as glowing an acknowledgement for the nurserymen of our time. It may be said of them that they developed the plants which enabled mankind to survive. It is a worthwhile goal for quiet men.

CHRONOLOGY OF AMERICAN HORTICULTURAL TEXTS MENTIONED

1785. Humphry Marshall. *Arbustrum (sic) Americanum: The American Grove or an Alphabetical Catalogue of Forest Trees & Shrubs.* Philadelphia.

1787. Robert Squibb. *The Gardener's Calender for South Carolina and North Carolina. Charleston, South Carolina.* Later editions added Georgia to title. Published in 1809, 1813, 1827.

1804. John Gardiner & David Hepburn. *The American Gardener Containing Ample Directions for Working a Kitchen Garden Every Month in the Year; & Copious Instructions for the Cultivation of Flower Gardens, Vineyards, Nurseries, Hop-yards, Green Houses and Hot Houses.* City of Washington.

1806. Bernard M'Mahon. *The American Gardener's Calendar Adapted to the Climate & Seasons of the U.S., Containing a Complete Account of all the Work to be Done in the Kitchen-garden, Fruit-garden, Orchard, Vineyard, Nursery, Pleasure Grounds, Green-house, Hot-house & Forcing Frame . . . also, General as well as Minute Instructions for Laying Out, or Erecting . . . the Above According to the Modern Taste . . . the Ornamental Planting of Pleasure Grounds in the Ancient and Modern Style . . . Plants Suitable for Live Hedges . . . Extensive Catalogue of the Different Kinds of Plants Which be Cultivated for Use or for Ornament . . . into 18 Separate Alphabetical Classes . . .* Philadelphia. 11 editions to 1857 basically unchanged to the last in 1857 which had a memoir of the author, rev & illus by J. J. Smith, Philadelphia. (2nd ed. 1818).

1807. Thomas Main. *Directions for the Transplantation & Management of Young Thorn or Other Hedge Plants.* City of Washington.

1817. William Coxe. *A View of The Cultivation of Fruit Trees & the Management of Orchards and Cider.* Philadelphia.

1818. J. Gardiner & David Hepburn. *The American Gardener . . . (see 1st ed. 1804) A New Edition Much Enlarged to Which is Added A Treatise on Gardening by a Citizen of Virginia. Also, a Few Hints on the Cultivation of Native Vines, and Directions for Making Domestic Wines.* Third ed. Georgetown, D. C. 1826, Washington City, 1826.

1820. William Prince. A *Treatise on Fruit & Ornamental Trees & Plants Cultivated at the Linnaean Botanic Garden,* Flushing, Long-Island, near New York.

1828. Roland Green. *A Treatise on The Cultivation of Ornamental Flowers.* Boston and New York.

1828. William Prince. A *Short Treatise on Horticulture Embracing Descriptions of a Great Variety of Fruit and Ornamental Trees & Shrubs, Grape Vines, Bulbous Flowers . . .* New York.

1829. Thomas Bridgeman. *The Young Gardener's Assistant Containing a Catalogue of Garden and Flower Seeds . . . Culinary Vegetables, Some of Which are not Generally Introduced into the United States* (85 of the 96 pages are on vegetables) Brooklyn. Went through 12 numbered editions, new editions, and finally appeared as *The American Gardener's Assistant* as late as 1871.

1830.   William Robert Prince aided by William Prince. *A Treatise on the Vine Embracing Its History from the Earliest Ages to the Present Day, with Descriptions of above 200 Foreign and 80 American Varieties; Together With a Complete Dissertation on the Establishment, Culture & Management of Vineyards.* frontis. New York.

1831.   ———. *The Pomological Manual; or a Treatise on Fruits: Containing Descriptions of a Great Number of the Most Valuable Varieties for the Orchard and Garden.* 2 parts 2nd edition. New York, 1832.

1832.   Hibbert & Buist. *The American Flower Garden Directory, Containing Practical Directions for the Culture of Plants in the Hot-house, Garden-house, Flower Garden & Rooms or Parlous, for Every Month of the Year. With a Description of the Plants Most Desirable in Each . . . Instructions for Erecting a Hot-house, Green-house & Laying out a Flower Garden . . . With Lists of annuals, Biennials and Ornamental Shrubs, Contents, a General Index . . .* frontis. Philadelphia. A second printing of this with frontis. issued in 1834.

1832.   *The Floral Magazine & Botanical Repository.* Philadelphia, D. & C. Landreth. Vol. I, 31 colors pls.

1833.   William Kenrick. *The New American Orchadist or an Account of the Most Valuable Varieties of Fruit, Adapted to Cultivation in the Climate of the U.S. . . . Uses, Mode of Management, Remedies; also a Brief Description of the Most Ornamental Forest Trees, Shrubs, Flowers, etc.* Boston. Editions to 1848.

1835.   Thomas Bridgeman. *The Florist's Guide: Containing Practical Directions for the Cultivation of Annual, Biennial & Perennial Flowering Plants . . . Including the Double Dahlia; with a Monthly Calender, Containing Instructions for the Management of Green-house Plants.* New York. Separate editions thru 1847. Later included in *The Young Gardener's Assistant* published thru 1865.

1835/   C. M. and P. B. Hovey, Jr. *The American Gardener's Magazine and Register of Useful*
1868.   *Discoveries & Improvements in Horticulture & Rural Affairs.* Vols. 1 & 2-1836. Vol. 3-1837 title changes to *The Magazine of Horticulture, Botany & All Useful Discoveries and Improvements in Rural Affairs.* to 1868. Boston.

1835/   Thomas G. Fessenden, Joseph Breck, J. E. Teschemacher, editors—*Horticultural*
1839.   *Register and Gardener's Magazine.* Vol. 1 had 4 color pls. Discontinued after vol. 4 because Breck, as publisher, decided material could be covered in his *New England Farmer & Gardener's Journal.*

1836.   Thomas Bridgeman. *The Kitchen Gardener's Instructor Containing a Catalogue of Garden & Herb Seeds . . . Practical Directions Under Each Head for the Cultivation of Herbs, with a Calendar Showing the Work Necessary to be Done in a Kitchen Garden in Every Month . . . also, . . . Forcing or Forwarding Vegetables Out of the Ordinary Season.* New York. Five subsequent enlarged editions. First appeared in *The Young Gardener's Assistant* (see 1829) with last publication in *The American Gardener's Assistant,* rev. & enl. by S. Edwards Todd, New York. 1871.

1838.   J. F. Lelievre. *Nouveau Jardinier De La Louisiane Contenant les Instructions Necessaires aux Personnes qui S'occupent de Jardinage.* Nouvelle-Orleans.

1838.   Robert Manning. *Book of Fruits.* First series. Salem, (Mass). Later revised editions see 1844 and 1847.

1838.   Edward Sayers. *The American Flower Garden Companion Adapted to the Northern States.* 2nd ed. Boston. Boston, 1839 edition adds "and Middle States" to title. 3rd ed. Cincinnati, Oh. 1846.

1939.   Robert Buist. *American Flower Garden Directory.* 2nd ed with Buist only as author (see 1832, Hibbert & Buist) continuing through printings to 1854. No frontispieces. Philadelphia.

1839.   William Kenrick. *The American Silk Grower's Guide; or the Art of Raising the Mulberry and Silk.* Boston.

1939.   Edward Sayers. *Treatise on the Culture of the Dahlia and Cactus.* Boston.

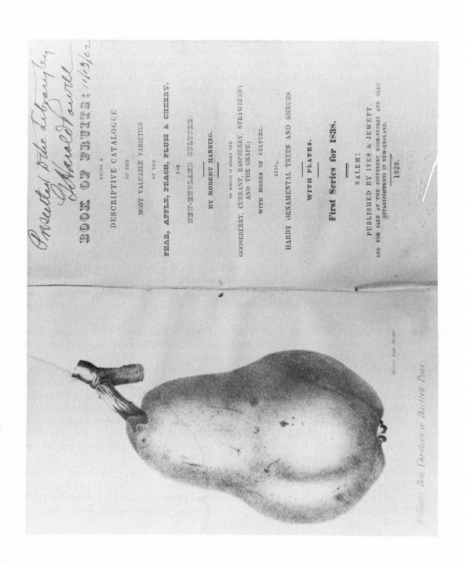

BOOK OF FRUITS:

BEING A

DESCRIPTIVE CATALOGUE

OF THE

MOST VALUABLE VARIETIES

OF THE

PEAR, APPLE, PEACH, PLUM & CHERRY,

FOR

NEW-ENGLAND CULTURE.

BY ROBERT MANNING.

TO WHICH IS ADDED THE

GOOSEBERRY, CURRANT, RASPBERRY, STRAWBERRY
AND THE GRAPE;

WITH MODES OF CULTURE.

ALSO,

HARDY ORNAMENTAL TREES AND SHRUBS

WITH PLATES.

First Series for 1838.

SALEM:

PUBLISHED BY IVES & JEWETT,

AND FOR SALE AT THE DIFFERENT BOOK-STORES AND SEED
ESTABLISHMENTS IN NEW-ENGLAND.

1838.

Williams Bon Chretien or Bartlett Pear.

1841. Andrew Jackson Downing. A *Treatise on the Theory and Practice of Landscape Gardening Adapted to North America with a View to the Improvement of Country Residence* . . . New York. Revised editions published 1853–1875.

1844. Robert Buist. The *Rose Manual Containing Accurate Descriptions of all the Finest Varieties of Roses* . . . *Their Character and Mode of Culture, with Directions for Their Propagation and the Destruction of Insects.* Philadelphia. Revised editions 1847, 1851 and 1854.

1844. Robert Manning & John Ives. *The New England Book of Fruit.* See 1838. Manning.

1845. Andrew Jackson Downing. *The Fruits & Fruit Trees of America, or the Culture, Propagation, and Management, in the Garden and Orchard, of Fruit Trees Generally; with Descriptions of the Finest Varieties of Fruit, Native & Foreign, Cultivated in this Country.* New York. 14 editions to 1853. Rev. & corrected by Charles Downing, with large editions printed thru 1900 (1847 to 1850 some issues have 66 to 70 color pls.).

1846/ ————. The *Horticulturist and Journal of Rural Art and Rural Taste.* Downing editor
1875. through 1852, succeeded by Patrick Barry, et al. Ran until 1875 when it merged with *Gardeners Monthly*.

1846. William Robert Prince. *Prince's Manual of Roses Comprising the Most Complete History of the Rose Including Every Class, & All the Most Admirable Varieties that have Appeared in Europe & America; Together with Ample Information on the Culture and Propagation.* New York.

1846. Nicholas Longworth. *The Cultivation of the Grape & Manufacture of Wine; also, Character & Habits of the Strawberry plant.* Cincinnati.

1847. John M. Ives. *The New England Book of Fruits.* Boston. See Manning, 1838 and 1844.

1847. Robert Buist. *The Family Kitchen Garden* . . . *Descriptions of All the Different Species & Varieties of Culinary Vegetables, with Their Botanical, English, French & German Names* . . . *Best Mode of Cultivating them in the Garden or under Glass, with a Description of Implements and Medicinal Herbs in General Use. Also, the most Select Fruit, Their Management, Propagation, etc.* New York. Printings through 1867.

1847. Parsons, Samuel B. *The Rose: Its History, Poetry, Culture, and Classification.* New York. Revised editions with last entitled *Parsons On The Rose* being reprinted in 1910. First edition only had two color plates.

1851. Patrick Barry. *The Fruit Garden. A Treatise Intended to Explain and Illustrate the Physiology of Fruit Trees, the Theory and Practice of all Operations Connected with the Propagation, Transplanting, Pruning & Training of Orchard & Garden Trees as Standards, Dwarfs, Pyramids, Espaliers, etc., the Laying Out and Arranging Different Kinds of Orchards & Gardens, the Selection of Suitable Varieties for Different Purposes and Localities, Gathering & Preserving, Treatment of Diseases* . . . *Insects, Implements.* . . . *with 150 figures.* New York. Last revision as Barry's *Fruit Garden* issued in 1883.

1851. Joseph Breck. *The Flower Garden or Breck's Book of Flowers in Which Are Described* . . . *Hardy Herbaceous Perennials, Annuals, Shrubby Plants, and Evergreen Trees, Desirable for Every Ornamental Purpose, with Directions for Their Cultivation.* Boston. Several revisions, last being Breck's *New Book of Flowers,* 1866.

1852. Robert Buchanan. *The Culture of The Grape & Wine Making with an Appendix on the Strawberry by N. Longworth.* Cincinnati. Reprinted a number of times to 1865.

1853. Thomas Meehan. *The American Handbook of Ornamental Trees.* Philadelphia.

1854. Franklin Reuben Elliott. *The Fruit Book, or, The American Fruitgrower's Guide in Orchard and Garden. Being a Compend of History, Modes of Propagation, Culture, etc. of Fruit Trees and Shrubs, Descriptions of Nearly all Varieties of Fruits Grown*

136

NEW ENGLAND
BOOK OF FRUIT;

CONTAINING AN ABRIDGMENT OF

MANNING'S DESCRIPTIVE CATALOGUE

OF THE MOST VALUABLE VARIETIES OF THE

PEAR, APPLE, PEACH, PLUM, AND CHERRY,

FOR NEW ENGLAND CULTURE.

TO WHICH ARE ADDED THE

GRAPE, QUINCE, GOOSEBERRY, CURRANT, AND STRAWBERRY;

WITH OUTLINES OF

MANY OF THE FINEST SORTS OF PEARS

DRAWN FROM NATURE;

WITH DIRECTIONS FOR PRUNING, GRAFTING, AND GEN-
ERAL MODES OF CULTURE.

THIRD EDITION, REVISED AND ENLARGED.

BY JOHN M. IVES.

SALEM:
W. & S. B. IVES.
BOSTON: W. J. REYNOLDS & CO., B. B. MUSSEY & CO.
AND FOR SALE AT MOST OF THE AGRICULTURAL AND SEED STORES IN
THE UNITED STATES.
1847.

ELLIOTT'S FRUIT BOOK;

OR, THE

American Fruit-Grower's Guide

IN

ORCHARD AND GARDEN.

BEING A COMPEND OF THE HISTORY, MODES OF PROPAGATION, CULTURE, &C., OF
FRUIT TREES AND SHRUBS, WITH DESCRIPTIONS OF NEARLY ALL THE
VARIETIES OF FRUITS CULTIVATED IN THIS COUNTRY: NOTES
OF THEIR ADAPTATION TO LOCALITIES AND SOILS,
AND ALSO A COMPLETE LIST OF FRUITS
WORTHY OF CULTIVATION.

BY F. R. ELLIOTT.

FOURTH EDITION—REVISED, ENLARGED, AND IMPROVED.

New York:
A. O. MOORE & CO.,
AGRICULTURAL BOOK PUBLISHERS, 140 FULTON STREET.
1859.

138

Gardening for the South;

OR,

HOW TO GROW @@@@@@@@
VEGETABLES AND FRUITS.

BY THE LATE

WILLIAM N. WHITE,

OF ATHENS, GA.

THIRD EDITION, REVISED AND ENLARGED.

...BY...

P. H. MELL, Ph. D.,

Professor of Botany and Geology, Alabama Polytechnic Institute, Director of Alabama
Agricultural Experiment Station.

WITH MANY ILLUSTRATIONS.

Wm. N. White

PLATE I.

PINUS PINASTER.

The Pinaster, or Cluster Pine.—(See Page 248.)

in this Country, Notes of Their Adaptation . . . Lists of Fruits Worthy of Cultivation. New York. Later printings came out as both Elliott's *Fruit book,* and *The Western Fruit Book,* in 1859. A final revision appeared as *Hand-Book for Fruit Growers in Rochester,* New York in 1876.

1856. William Nathaniel White. *Gardening for the South; or the Kitchen and Fruit Garden; with Best Methods for their Cultivations, . . . Hints upon Landscape and Flower-gardening. Containing Modes of Culture & Descriptions of the Species & Varieties of the Culinary Vegetables, Fruit Trees & Fruits, & a Select List of Ornamental Trees & Plants Found by Trial Adapted to the States of the Union South of Pennsylvania, with Gardening Calendars for the Same.* New York. Revised editions last published in Richmond, Virgina. in 1901.

1857. E. J. Hooper. *Hooper's Western Fruit Book. A Compendious Collection of Facts, from the Notes & Experience of Successful Fruit Culturists, Arranged for Practical Use in the Orchard and Garden.* Frontis. & 4 color pls. Cincinnati. 3rd & last ed. 1858.

1858. John A. Warder. *Hedges & Evergreens. A Complete Manual for the· Cultivation, Pruning & Management of all Plants Suitable for American hedging; Especially the Maclura or Osage Orange, Fully Illustrated with Engravings of Plants, Implements and Processes. To Which is Added a Treatise on Evergreens; Their Different Varieties; Their Propagation, Transplanting, and Culture in the United States.* New York.

1859. Thomas Meehan. *The Gardener's Monthly and Horticultural Advertiser.* Philadelphia. Vol. 1, 1859 folio, subsequent issues thru to last in Jan. 1888 in quarto.

1863. Fearing Burr, Jr. *The Field and Garden Vegetables of America Containing Full Descriptions of Nearly 1100 Species and Varieties, with Directions for Propagation & Use.* Boston Revised edition 1865. Abridged edition — *Garden Vegetables & how to Cultivate Them published 1866.*

Horticultural Heritage — The Influence of the U.S. Nurserymen: A Commentary

By
Charles van Ravenswaay

Elisabeth Woodburn's survey of American horticultural literature published before 1860 reflects her deep interest in the subject, and her complete familiarity with it. For many years, she has collected, studied, compared, and physically handled the books that she describes. To her, the authors are old friends whose practical knowledge she respects and whose foibles she understands. Few could have her patience with the pious self-esteem of the canny Scot, Grant Thorburn, or more respect for his contributions as "the father of the plant and seed business in the United States." He and other immigrants from Scotland, Ireland, England, France, Germany, and Belgium were among the pioneer nurserymen and seedsmen instrumental in developing American horticulture.

Woodburn has called attention to some aspects of our horticultural history which have been overlooked. Answers to some of these matters and many others may require an exchange of expertise between plant historians and cultural and social historians. For example, as mentioned by early writers, more needs to be known about the use of the tomato in both Spanish Florida and the French and Spanish colonial settlements in the Mississippi Valley. Why did

Mr. Van Ravenswaay is Director of the Winterthur Museum, Winterthur, Delaware.

the cultivation of vegetables hold such little interest in the early Republic? Was it because the English settlers and their descendants along the east coast preferred the traditional British diet with its accent on meat, fowl, and fish? Was the raising of vegetables stimulated by a preference for them by the Germans in Pennsylvania and the French in the Mississippi Valley and later nineteenth-century European immigrants?

Woodburn also suggests that many aspects of our horticultural history and its relationship to our national history remain to be explored. Few other major segments of the American past have received so little attention. Collections are limited to relatively few libraries. To my knowledge, no one has provided the bibliographical data on these imprints which are so essential to the specialist, the collector, and the librarian.

Perhaps, as so often happens, it may be the pressure of public interest rather than the leadership of specialists, that will bring a change. The current interest in gardening, inclusive of the reintroduction of early species and varieties of plant material and the restoration of period gardens and landscapes, has created a climate that should encourage studies in many unexplored aspects of our horticultural past. This meeting and other similar stirrings of interest, such as the recent formation of the Chapter for Landscape Architecture and the Allied Arts of the Society of Architectural Historians, are good beginnings.

The most neglected segment of our horticultural literature is the gardening catalogue published by the seed houses and nurseries. (For convenience here I use the word *catalogue* to refer to plant material offered for sale in the form of printed or manuscript lists, broadsides, circulars, pamphlets, or any of the many other forms used.) I have not been able to discover when the first gardening catalogue was published in America. Presumably, it was issued in 1771 by the Prince Nursery of Flushing, New York. Before 1800 a small number of other catalogues had been produced by the few firms along the east coast. Generally, however, advertisements in local papers sufficed. Many individuals continued to order their seeds from Europe. Budded or grafted fruit stock was also imported, although most farmers were satisfied with growing fruit trees from seed because the bulk of their apples and pears were used in making cider. With such a limited trade, the number of American seed houses and nurseries increased very slowly. Jesse Buel of Albany, New York, a pioneer agricultural journalist and author, stated that there were only "four or five public nurseries of any note that he could recollect in 1810, and these by no means profitable."

Beginning in the 1820's, the nurseries and seed houses began to proliferate. By 1850, there were hundreds of these firms, many of them very small, serving the needs of immediate communities. In Boston, New York, Philadelphia, and other centers, larger firms were operating; others appeared in the years before and after the Civil War. The latter included Ellwanger & Barry, and, later, Burpee, Childs, Henderson, Storrs & Harrison, and Vick. All of these were headed by men who sensed the national market potential and who had the drive and promotional skills to carry through their objectives. Their advent, along with hundreds of smaller firms from coast to coast, made the years from the 1850s into the 1880s the golden years of American gardening catalogues.

The reasons were not accidental. The growth in sales of horticultural material followed the increase in population and general prosperity. As the nation expanded westward, there was a growing need for plant material to sustain new homesteads. Transportation and postal services improved. Printing became cheaper and faster. With these aids the larger firms could reach a national market and, through skillful promotion, the firm name or, more generally, the name of the owner or senior partner, became familiar to households throughout America.

In the 1870's, hundreds of thousands of catalogues were being issued each year but only a very small percentage of these have survived. Many were modest productions and are particularly important as records of pioneering firms, especially those issued by firms in small towns in the new states and territories. Interesting, too, are the catalogues issued by firms owned and managed by women who were active during the 1880's and 1890's, such as C. H. Lippincott, of Minneapolis, and Ella V. Baines, of Springfield, Ohio. Whatever the size or content of these catalogues may be, they are our best source of information about what type of plant material was available, the location and the date. And, as we shall see, the catalogues offer considerably more information on other matters of historical interest.

It is surprising how skillful the major firms were in being all things to all people. Many of them sought a national market but professional pride led them to make their catalogues scientifically accurate. At the same time, they developed their catalogues into handbooks of plant cultivation and perfected a style of writing which intrigued the average reader and stimulated sales.

With their constant efforts to develop new ways of attracting attention and customers, it was inevitable that the major firms should have turned to illustrations. Wood engravings first appeared in the 1840's. At about the same time some publishers of gardening books and periodicals began using colored illustrations. As these were usually printed from English or French plates that required hand coloring, the process was too expensive and too slow to be practical for the mass production of catalogues. A first step in the use of such prints for the selling of garden material was made by nurserymen who found it helpful to have their traveling agents, generally called tree peddlers, armed with glamorous colored prints of their wares. These albums were relatively expensive but their use was so profitable that the investment was justified. This specialized kind of work for the nursery trade is said to have been originated by Joseph Prestele of Amana Society, located in Homestead, Iowa. According to his son, William H., Joseph made the first lithographed colored fruit and flower plates for the use of nurserymen in the United States about 1849. After Joseph's death in 1867, William carried on the business, first in Bloomington, Illinois, and later in Iowa City where he was still working in 1879. Meanwhile, the concentration of nurseries in Rochester, New York, there encouraged a number of firms to enter that field. Among the earliest of these were E. A. Kellogg, D. M. Dewey, the book and stationery merchant, and others, including George Frauenberger, who advertised that he "engraved on wood and printed in colors." Firms in other cities soon followed.

The middle of the 19th century was a period of innovation in many areas of technology, including the mass production of inexpensive colored pictures. Many different techniques were developed and older ones were refined so that by 1860, a number of possibilities existed for use in gardening catalogues. None met all the requirements until the chromolithographic process was developed to its greatest potential, making it possible to produce exceedingly beautiful prints in many colors at a reasonable price. The earliest gardening catalogue with a colored plate that I know of was issued in 1864 by James Vick, the aggressive journalist turned seedsman and the innovative pace setter for the trade. Interestingly enough, the subject chosen was the double zinnia. Vick's innovation was quickly imitated. The public was enthusiastic but reacted in ways that had not been anticipated. Americans, it seemed, particularly farm families and those living in small towns, were hungry for colored pictures. Since many of them ordered the catalogues only for the colored plates, it became necessary for the firms to counter by charging for their catalogues. Some firms also issued de luxe catalogues, heavily illustrated, and bound in hard covers while many

146

offered individual prints for sale. Large prints either framed or unframed were sold in great numbers. In these various ways the seed- and the nurserymen inadvertently found themselves in the art business for the millions. Their success provides a fascinating chapter in the history of American popular art.

Meanwhile, the catalogues themselves grew in size and lavishness. In addition to the plant material offered for sale many firms increased their stocks of various farm and garden supplies, including lawn mowers which came into use during the 1850's and which did more to stimulate lawn beautification than almost any other single innovation. The practical advantages of raising vegetables continued to be stressed along with the moral and esthetic values of raising flowers. Every conceivable way of attracting public interest and sales was attempted, for instance, catalogues were combined with almanacs or with gardening periodicals. Beginning in the 1850s, some firms issued four catalogues a year, in addition to circulars and other mailing pieces designed to stimulate trade, as well as foreign language editions to capture the trade of immigrants. In 1873, for example, Kern, Steber & Co., of St. Louis issued catalogues in German, English, and French. The smaller firms often used the same catalogue for several years, creating dating problems for us today.

Most of the larger firms aimed at a mass market but, as the interest in horticulture grew and the number of specialized and moneyed plant collectors increased, some firms devoted their efforts to supplying the more affluent customers. In 1861, the nursery of historian Francis Parkman was the first to receive a shipment of plant material sent directly from Japan to the United States. In 1874, George Such of South Amboy, New Jersey, priced exotic specimens from his collection for as much as $500 each, which, as one writer commented, "marked an era in American horticulture." Later in the century, A. Blanc of Philadelphia, specialized in cacti while the Royal Palm Nurseries of Manatee, Florida, specialized in tropical specimens. Although many catalogues were edited by knowledgeable horticulturists, few could equal the one of 1883 produced by Bush & Son & Meissner of Bushberg, Mo., specialists in grapes. It included contributions by the distinguished botanist, Dr. George Engelmann, and other authorities in various aspects of grape culture.

As I have suggested, these catalogues are not only a major source of information about the history of horticultural material used in America, but also they present an interesting record of other historical developments. They represent the first successful development of the mail-order business in the nation, as well as the creation of advertising and promotional techniques later used by other types of businesses. Publishers of catalogues invented the mail-order blank, and vigorously badgered the "lunatics" in the postal department (as James Vick referred to them) to clarify the postal regulations relating to their type of business. Through their informative explanations of plant culture, catalogues taught the average American how to garden and how to beautify both his home and his community.

The cresendo of excitement, experimental promotion, and all the other innovative work carried on by the trade, however, could not be sustained indefinitely. The lavish catalogues became too expensive. By the late 1880's, the market had changed and many of the most vigorous leaders in the field were aged or deceased. Farmers and home gardeners grew fewer fruits and berries than in the earlier days and they wanted fewer and better varieties of vegetables. It was chiefly in the ornamental material that the housewife was still intrigued by novelties as well as by the larger and more colorful flowers. By the beginning of this century, old firms were disappearing. Catalogues shrank in size and gradually evolved into the publications that we know today. The pioneering years had ended but during their years of innovation and education for millions of Americans, horticultural catalogues filled an important need.

Past and New Directions in Agricultural Education

By
John B. Holden

In discussing the past as well as the new directions in agricultural education, I wish to comment on rural America and about the great success that our farmers have had in the production of food and fiber. I would like to make the case for research and education through the Department of Agriculture, the land-grant colleges, and the county agents. May I point out that the Cooperative Extension Service is the largest adult education program in the world. It has more full time people, and more volunteers, and perhaps more participants than any other program. It is this large, extensive, and effective program that has played an important part in our rural America and in helping to make America the greatest country in the world as well as the greatest producer of food and fiber. Along with this broad and effective educational program, the U.S. Department of Agriculture has created the Graduate School of the USDA which has not only served Agriculture, but also has been a government-wide continuing education program for the entire federal government.

I am frequently asked why should this government-wide program be in the Department of Agriculture. Why not the Department of

Dr. Holden is Director, Graduate School, U.S. Department of Agriculture, Washington, D.C.

Health, Education, and Welfare, the Office of Education or the Civil Service Commission? A partial answer to this lies in the fact that there was no Department of Health, Education, and Welfare 55 years ago; the Office of Education was small and simply collected facts and trends; the Civil Service Commission never got around to training until the Eisenhower administration, when it was required by an act of Congress.

The Graduate School started in the U.S. Department of Agriculture because the employees felt the need for it, had experience in education, and organized a program so attractive that it continues to grow and serve — adjusting to the changing needs of our government and our society. The Cooperative Extension and the Graduate School are now looking to the future and they will continue to adjust, to cope, and to help enrich the lives of those with whom they serve and work. Not only will they do this, but also they will work with other continuing education programs in other major segments of our society to help us improve our performance on the job, in the marketplace, and in the home.

The development of agricultural education and the United States of America has gone hand in hand over the years. The first society for the promotion of agriculture in the United States was organized in Philadelphia in 1785, with George Washington and Benjamin Franklin as members. Two years later in the same city, the same two men were key members of the Constitutional Convention which brought forth our unique form of government. And, in the climate of freedom that followed, both agriculture and the Nation have flourished. I do not believe this was coincidental. The same factors which favor agricultural development also favor the development of our people and our Nation.

Peter Drucker has said that development of people is our most wealth-producing resource. So, too, agricultural research and education have been the key factors in the amazing productivity of our Nation's agriculture. The greatest success story of the world is the ability and know-how of the eight million American farmers to produce the most and best food and fiber in the world — to feed our own 200 million people and to produce enough to sell to our friends, to give a substantial amount to starving people in other countries and, also, to sell wheat, corn, and barley to some of the communistic countries.

In tracing some of that development, following the establishment of that first agricultural society in 1785, there followed the formation of agricultural societies in other parts of the country and these, in turn, led to the establishment of agricultural fairs and exhibitions in the early 1800's. The Columbian Agricultural Society, formed in 1809 by citizens of Maryland, Virginia, and the District of Columbia, for example, for many years carried out programs of educating farmers by means of fairs for many years. Agricultural fairs have proliferated and, to this day, continue to serve as an effective agency for disseminating information on new crops, implements, stock, and other improvements in agriculture.

The Philadelphia Society for the Promotion of Agriculture was appointed in 1794 to plan for the teaching of agriculture. This group submitted a report which presented several propositions for incorporating agricultural education into the universities and seminaries of learning as well as in the common schools. This is the first known effort of a formal nature to promote agricultural education. Although the U.S. Department of Agriculture grew out of the recommendation of President Washington for a national board of agriculture, it developed directly out of the seed distribution program by the Department of State under John Quincy Adams. Seeds were collected by the consuls in various parts of the world and delivered to the U.S. Patent Office, then under the Department of State, for distribution in this country.

The Act of 1862 set up an independent Department of Agriculture headed by a Commissioner of Agriculture with the duties of acquiring and diffusing "useful information on subjects connected with agriculture in the most general sense of the word, and to procure and propagate among the people new and valuable seeds and plants." An act of Congress in 1889 finally created the U.S. Department of Agriculture as an executive department elevating its administrator to cabinet rank. From the beginning, employees of the Department were educators. The U.S. Department of Agriculture built a reputation as one of the foremost institutions of scientific research in the country, drawing outstanding scientists who, in turn, attracted younger men to work with them. The combined activities of these colleagues — the teachers and the taught — marked the Department as a place of learning as well as one of public service.

The year 1862 was a significant one for farmers in America. Not only was the Department of Agriculture created, but also the Morrill Act was passed by Congress. This law provided generous grants of public land to each state to establish a college for the primary purpose of teaching agriculture and the mechanic arts. Thus, in 1862, new directions for agricultural education were established through the land-grant colleges, and the U.S. Department of Agriculture. Later, through the Hatch Act of 1887, an agricultural experiment station was established at each land-grant college. Thus, throughout the nation, a problem-solving system was established to deal with varying climates, soils, and people.

The development of new institutions is always a slow and often a painful process. The four decades leading up to the turn of the century were especially difficult. Farmers, for the most part, were on their own and little or no exchange of information or experience occurred, especially between states and regions. Scientific farming was entering its experimental years. Farmers faced a seemingly endless number of difficulties such as cold winters, scorching summers, high winds and, in some cases, an inadequate water supply. They faced many other calamities such as the grasshopper plague of 1874. There was no one who could explain to the farmer the shortcomings of his methods. In addition to this, when yields were unusually high, farm prices fell to a very low figure. For example, soon after the War Between the States, a bushel of wheat selling for only 76 cents dropped as low as 28 cents in 1889. The sad truth was that it was cheaper to use corn for fuel than to sell it and buy fuel. A farmer could not meet his expenses no matter how hard he worked; and, on top of all this, he was usually charged 10 percent or more interest when he had to borrow money. One observer of these difficult times expressed the following:

> there are three great crops raised in Nebraska, One is the crop of corn, one a crop of freight rates, and one a crop of interest. One is produced by farmers who by sweat and toil, farm the land. The other two are produced by men who sit in their offices and behind their bank counters and farm the farmer.[1]

These and other conditions led farmers to organize. The first important step was taken by Oliver H. Kelly who organized the "Patrons of Husbandry," with local units called "granges." The granges grew by leaps and bounds and, by 1875, had a membership of three quarters of a million men. They were organized primarily in an effort to improve not only conditions for farmers but also their economic and political position; their members were able to cooperate on purchases of equipment and supplies, on building factories, operating banks, retail stores, etc. Although these cooperative efforts were relatively unsuccessful due to opposition of bankers and other businessmen, nevertheless they were forerunners of many educational enterprises, businesses, and industries which were to come later in the 20th century. Before the turn of the century, the grange had accumulated more than a million members who became a powerful political force and were able to influence many state legislatures to raise the prices on farm products and lower the interest rate.

In the apparent losses and defeats enumerated above, the farmers discovered a dormant strength. They had learned to cooperate and to work together for special causes and to build on their new political strength. Much credit must be given to these pioneers for initiating movements which later were to play important roles in the development of education in agriculture.

The current multi-million bushels of grain sales and the 1973 and 1975 Russian "wheat deals," in particular, would have seemed beyond belief at the turn of the century save perhaps to people like Mark Carleton and Luther Burbank. The quiet researcher, Mark Carleton, worked arduously for years to find a wheat that would grow and produce with little rainfall. Carleton's contemporary, Luther Burbank, eventually gained world-wide fame, due largely to his early experimentation with seeds and flowers. His motivation is best expressed in his own words: "I shall be contented if, because of me, there shall be better fruits and fairer flowers."[2] He went on to experiment with many thousands of plants, through many plant generations, in this search for better varieties of fruits, vegetables, and flowers. His practical research led him to the development of the thornless cactus which provided new sources of food for livestock. Through the efforts of great men such as these and countless others who have followed, Congress passed important acts in the support of agricultural education in the early part of the 20th century. Among these were the Smith-Lever Act (1914) and the Smith-Hughes Act (1917).

How are farmers to learn and use new scientific methods of farming? To answer this and numerous other questions, the Extension Service of the U.S. Department of Agriculture was formed. An event that led to its creation was the fact that agents had been sent to the southern states to help farmers fight the boll weevil and the success of this endeavor so impressed Congress that the Smith-Lever Act was passed. The work of county agents in spreading agricultural information grew in leaps and bounds over the years and often is credited as the source of our agricultural abundances. Some of the essential features of the Extension Service are the assessment of needs, the development of programs, demonstration of successful practices, and evaluation of results. How are children to learn about the new scientific methods while in school? Congress found it necessary and important to pass the Smith-Hughes Act in order to answer the question. It made possible the teaching of vocational education in the secondary schools, including agricultural education, home economics, and other vocational fields. The federal government now could pay for part of the cost of instruction.

Three significant informational organizations were soon to follow: 4-H clubs, Future Farmers of America, and Future Homemakers of America. Today, there are about 128,450 of these clubs for boys and girls, ranging in age from 9 to 19, in the United States and in nearly every country in the world. Here at home the total number of members exceeds seven million. These organizations were a great help to rural young people for they stressed the importance of agriculture and the roles played by the young in improving both farming and home living.

The foundation stone of the Cooperative Extension Service is found in the first sentence of the Smith-Lever Act: " . . . to aid in diffusing among the people of the United States useful and practical information on subjects relating to agriculture and home economics, and to encourage the application of the same . . . " The phenomenal growth of land-grant colleges and extension services is due to careful adherence of these institutions to the basic philosophy expressed above and to the subsequent enabling state legislation.

The Cooperative Extension Service transmits information from the research scientist to the public. It is an agency for the conducting of interdisciplinary programs as we experience them. Individual problem solving can lead to group problem solving and growth. These, in turn, can be further strengthened by organizations, institutions, and legislative support.

Let us now digress a moment to discuss how the Graduate School of the U.S. Department of Agriculture came into being. While education was being increased in the farm communities by the U.S. Department of Agriculture, it was only natural that the employees within the Department would be concerned with their own continuing education.

As early as 1898, the Secretary of Agriculture expressed the need for a form of post-graduate training in the Department. There was a special need for continuing education for young scientists doing research in the Department of Agriculture. However, no action was taken at that time. Shortly after the First World War, when the demand for qualified personnel became acute throughout the Federal Government, the Congressional Joint Committee on the Reclassification of Salaries recommended that the governmental departments give more attention to the development of opportunities within the Federal Service for the continuing education of their employees. About a year after the joint committee's report, Assistant Secretary E. D. Ball wrote to Secretary Henry C. Wallace to propose

> a system of graduate training within the Department . . . supplemented by liberal arrangements for cooperating with the Universities and agricultural colleges of this country in furthering and completing this training leading to advanced degrees.[3]

The Department's educational deficiencies were discovered at about this time by Henry C. Taylor who had been charged with the job of organizing the Bureau of Agricultural Economics. He found that many people assigned to him simply could not apply their education to agricultural problems without further training. That unhappy situation — soon remedied by a series of in-service lectures — was just one additional goal in a process that was already moving, for by then, Henry C. Wallace had endorsed the proposed graduate school.

During the summer of 1921, Dr. Ball headed a committee that established six fundamental guidelines for the Graduate School. First, the School was to give training to scientists to help them advance within the Department. Second, instruction was to be carried on after office hours. Third, the School was to be supported by student fees. Fourth, arrangements were to be made for the acceptance of these credits by the graduate departments of leading universities. Fifth, there was to be cooperation with other institutions in Washington. Sixth, the Department was to modify its administrative regulations so as to encourage student participation in the Graduate School and in other universities.

By 1935, the Graduate School enrollment had reached 700, and nearly one-half of that number came from outside the Department. By 1940, enrollment was up to 3,000 students and the number of courses hit 130. The School had obviously gone far beyond its original intention of supplying advanced training to U.S. Department of Agriculture scientists. It served students throughout Government and, occasionally, in nongovernment establishments; its courses ranged from serious to recreational.

In the late 1950's, the Graduate School complemented its evening and correspondence programs with "Special Courses," normally taught during working hours and designed to meet the specific needs of any agency or group of agencies. The Special Programs has had its greatest success in providing management development training for Federal executives and university leaders. In addition, the Independent Study Programs has 30 courses offered to students all over the world, and the International Programs offers training in Agro-Industrial Management for government officials from developing countries.

In my opinion, some of the same forces and factors that led to our national and agricultural growth are also critical to the growth and development of the Graduate School, U.S. Department of Agriculture. Freedom is number one in importance, freedom to analyze the ever-changing needs of adults in government and the needs of their agencies. Next in importance is flexibility — flexibility to experiment and to try new ways of meeting these needs without the restraint of academic departmentalization and administrative red tape.

Both in the classrooms of the Graduate School and in its administration, we work hard to create and maintain a healthy climate for adults to learn from each other. Widespread involvement and participation in the process of problem-identification and problem-solving are vital ingredients. Both the Cooperative Extension Service and the Graduate School are looking to the future in order to help adults continue their education. The adult continuing learner of tomorrow will be a more demanding, critical, and impatient consumer of educational programs and activities. He will demand and get more flexible, practical, relevant, and realistic results. More continuing education will be outside both the classroom and the school. The adult learner of tomorrow will be more skilled in knowing how to unlearn, how to learn, and how to keep learning. The more we learn and keep learning, the more we will be intrinsically motivated.

Increasingly, the adult learner of tomorrow will be a more equal partner in the learning process. The line between teacher and student will practically disappear, and adults will more effectively learn from and with each other in a continuing learning community where the curriculum will be prescribed by the rapidly changing needs of the individual and society. All of us will need to work and learn together in order to cope with our environment, our work situations, our communities, and our families.

In doing this, we need to further research the real needs of adults, the most effective teaching and learning experiences, and the most accurate means of communication. This research must also take into consideration attitudes, emotions, and effective learning as well as learning skills and knowledge.

In the belief that we learn from each other and from others, we are now trying to broaden our scope to include other segments of our society and other countries. All of us need to work and to learn together in order to improve the quality of life. We should do no less, and I am sure that working together we can all do more.

REFERENCES

1. Leon H. Canfield and Howard B. Wilder, *The Making of Modern America* (Cambridge, Mass.: Houghton-Mifflin Company, 1952), p. 402.
2. *Ibid.,* p. 551.
3. David E. Brewster, *USDA's Graduate School: The Growth of an Educational Institution* (Washington, D. C.: Graduate School Press, U. S. Department of Agriculture, 1973), p. 94.

Bibliography

American Vocational Association. Curriculum Materials Committee. Agricultural Education. *New Instructional Materials for Agricultural Education, 1974–75.* Urbana, Ill.: University of Illinois Vocational Agriculture Service.

Beard, Charles A. and Beard, Mary R. *Basic History of the United States.* New York: Doubleday, Doran and Company, 1944.

Bedford, Henry F. and Colburn, Trevor. *The Americans, A Brief History to 1887.* New York: Harcourt, Brace Jovanovich, 1971.

Bender, Ralph E., *et al. Adult Education in Agriculture.* Columbus, Ohio: Charles E. Merrill, 1972.

Brewster, David E. *USDA's Graduate School: The Growth of an Educational Institution.* Washington, D. C.: Graduate School Press, U. S. Department of Agriculture, 1973.

Canfield, Leon H. and Wilder, Howard B. *The Making of Modern America.* Cambridge, Mass.: Houghton-Mifflin Company, 1952.

Collings, Mary L., ed. *The Concept Approach to Programming in Adult Education With Special Application to Extension Education.* Washington, D. C.: Department of Agriculture Extension Service, National Technical Information Service, U. S. Department of Commerce, 1974.

Halcrow, Howard G. *Agricultural Policy of the United States.* New York: Prentice-Hall, 1953.

Mays, Arthur B. *Principles and Practices of Vocational Education.* New York: McGraw-Hill, 1948.

Report of the Joint USDA-NASULGC Study Committee on Cooperative Extension. *A People and A Spirit,* 1968.

Stimson, Rufus W. and Lathrop, Frank W. *History of Agricultural Education of Less Than College Grade in the United States.* Vocational Division Bulletin No. 217. Agricultural Series No. 55. Washington, D. C.: Federal Security Agency, U. S. Office of Education, 1942.

Swanson, J. Chester, comp. *Development of Federal Legislation for Vocational Education.* Prepared for the Panel of Consultants on Vocational Education. Washington, D. C.: U. S. Department of Health, Education and Welfare, 1962.

Leadership in American Agriculture: The Published Documentary Heritage

By
Harold T. Pinkett

Leadership in American agriculture has been credited to a great number of individuals who have contributed in varying ways to the improvement of agricultural activities and rural life in the nation. The first leaders were often men of political affairs, like Washington and Jefferson, who undertook agricultural experimentation on their vast estates and gave the benefit of their farm observations to friends. In the later vanguard, there has been a long line of agricultural editors and writers, inventors, scientists, educators, leaders of farm organizations, and government officials, whose contributions to American agriculture have been more varied but often less publicized. This paper seeks to identify some representative agricultural leaders of the nation whose contributions are documented importantly in their published writings and speeches. It briefly describes the nature of these contributions and the relevant documentary sources. Because of its wide range in chronology and subject matter, it can only be illustrative of the contributions and the leaders.

The early and continued interest of Americans in publishing papers of famous political leaders, who had significant interest in

Dr. Pinkett is Chief, Natural Resources Branch of the National Archives and Records Service, U.S. General Services Administration, Washington, D.C.

agricultural matters, has produced a rich heritage of documentation concerning some facets of agricultural leadership. In the forefront of these leaders was George Washington. His advanced ideas and innovative methods for the improvement of agriculture are set forth significantly in four volumes of *Diaries* edited by J. C. Fitzpatrick and 39 volumes of *Writings* by the same editor.[1] Earlier multi-volume but less complete editions of his writings produced by Jared Sparks and Worthington C. Ford also attest to Washington's preeminence as an agriculturist.[2] Then, too, there are useful publications containing selected examples of his agricultural writings edited by Franklin Knight, Moncure D. Conway, Walter E. Brooks, and others.[3] In these compilations there is revealed a deep, abiding interest in farming that once evoked this famous encomium on agriculture:

> The more I am acquainted with agricultural affairs, the better I am pleased with them . . . I am led to reflect how much more delightful to an undebauched mind is the task of making improvements on the earth, than all the vain glory which can be acquired from ravaging it, by the most uninterrupted career of conquests.[4]

This acquaintance with agriculture, so fondly cherished and eagerly pursued by Washington, was attested importantly by his correspondence with the noted English agriculturists, Arthur Young and Sir John Sinclair; his experiments with fertilizers and improved agricultural machinery, and his advocacy of agricultural societies and a Federal board of agriculture.

Also in the vanguard of early political leaders, who helped to share American agricultural thought and practice, was Thomas Jefferson. His contributions in this connection are documented importantly in the voluminous compilations of his writings by Paul L. Ford and A. A. Lipscomb and A. E. Bergh and, especially, by Julian P. Boyd's monumental edition of his papers that began to be published in 1950.[5] These documents offer extensive testimony of Jefferson's eminence as an agriculturist. They reveal his impressive efforts to make Monticello a progressive experimental farm where new agricultural machinery and methods and various types of fertilizers were tried out and new crops, plants, and animals were introduced. They also disclose his wide interest in education, which included advocacy of the teaching of agriculture in all colleges and universities of the nation. More importantly, perhaps, they set forth his concept of agrarianism that has persisted in American thought with vitality in spite of changing national conditions. This concept

160

put stress upon an agrarian ideal resting on the following tenets: (1) that agriculture is the fundamental enterprise of mankind; (2) that agricultural life is the natural life for man and, hence, city life is artificial and essentially bad; and (3) that the United States ought, therefore, to become and remain a nation of relatively small farmers, with families owning the farms that they operate.

Although leadership in early American agriculture tends to be dominated by the shadow of Washington and Jefferson, it was also characterized by contributions of other figures. Indeed, the innovative efforts of these leaders were in some instances preceded or accompanied by the novel agricultural activities of men like Jared Eliot, Samuel Deane, John Beale Bordley, Elkanah Watson, and John Taylor. The earliest of these, Eliot, for many years carried on experiments in soil conservation and crop improvement and, in 1748, began to present his ideas in a series of essays, which formed the first American book devoted exclusively to agriculture.[6] Deane suggested new methods of preventing soil erosion and of rotating crops and, in 1790, published the first encyclopedic work on American agriculture.[7] The writings of Bordley at the close of the 18th century were influential in disseminating useful information concerning improved agricultural methods in England and American experiments in animal husbandry and crop rotation.[8] The memoirs of Watson reveal his pioneering efforts in conducting agricultural fairs and promoting agricultural societies.[9] Taylor has been acclaimed as the most influential southern agricultural reformer of his time. This esteem rises mainly from a series of essays on deep plowing, soil fertility, and planting that were first published as a book in 1813 and ran through eight editions. These essays, in the opinion of John Adams, Thomas Jefferson, and James Madison, established Taylor as the final authority on agricultural subjects.[10]

During the first half of the 19th century improved methods in American agriculture began to be given an important stimulus by the efforts of several journalists. The most famous and influential person in this group was John S. Skinner who was a prolific contributor to the agricultural literature of the United States for 32 years and is credited with establishing the nation's first successful farm journal, the *American Farmer*. Prominent among the broad subjects that found their way to the columns of this journal were the introduction of new crops; improvements in tillage, fertilization, and drainage; and advances in the breeding of livestock. Among the distinguished agriculturists whose views appeared on the pages of the *American Farmer* were Thomas Jefferson, John Taylor, and

161

Edmund Ruffin. [11] Another important agricultural publicist in the early and middle years of the last century was Solon Robinson, whose extensive travel notes, articles, and editorials in agricultural and other journals provide critical and illuminating commentary on agricultural practices and rural life of his time. Everett E. Edwards called Robinson a "veritable Arthur Young of mid-nineteenth century America" and appraised his writings as "a treasure chest of historical data."[12] Also in the vanguard of 19th century agricultural publicists was Thomas Affleck who helped to advance southern agriculture through his writings and example as a successful planter and commercial nurseryman. [13] Meanwhile, in the northeastern United States, agricultural improvement was being encouraged by still another leading journalist, Jesse Buel. His literary labors for agricultural reform included editing of *The Cultivator*, one of the most popular farm journals of the 1830's, and the writing of more than 100 articles on farm practices and rural life for other agricultural magazines such as the *New England Farmer* and the *American Farmer*.[14]

A contemporary of these publicists was Edmund Ruffin whom Lewis C. Gray has characterized as the "most influential leader of southern agriculture and one of the greatest agricultural figures America has produced." This acclaim has rested mainly on his pioneering experiments in soil conservation and his discussion of them in books and articles that were among the most widely read agricultural publications of 19th century America. His famous *Essay on Calcareous Manures*, first appearing as a book in 1832, the less familiar but significant *Essays and Notes on Agriculture* published in 1852, and numerous articles and editorials in the *American Farmer*, and his own journal, the *Farmer's Register*, were landmark contributions to the struggle for agricultural improvement in the pre-Civil War era.[15]

Agricultural leadership of the Civil War period is notable for the thrust that it gave to historic Federal legislation. Prominent in this development were Abraham Lincoln and Justin S. Morrill. In his first annual message to Congress in 1861, President Lincoln expressed the regret that "Agriculture, confessedly the largest interest of the nation" was without proper representation in the Federal government. He, therefore, suggested that an "agricultural and statistical bureau" should be organized for the promotion of agricultural interests. Along with other influences, notably the rising demand of farmers for greater recognition of their activities and the trend toward greater Federal authority accelerated by the war, Lincoln's suggestion helped to usher in a new era of American public policy toward agriculture. On May 15, 1862, he signed an act to establish the U. S. Department of Agriculture and on May 20 and July 2, respectively, two other epoch-making agricultural acts: The Homestead Act and Land Grant College Act. The documentary evidence of Lincoln's concern for agriculture is provided not only by these legislative measures but also by several editions of his writings, including a nine-volume edition prepared by Roy P. Basler during the 1950's.[16] The Land Grant College Act signed by Lincoln was largely the result of the persistent advocacy of Senator Justin S. Morrill of Vermont who, in 1857, began to work for legislation enabling the establishment of colleges that would emphasize research and instruction especially beneficial to agricultural production and that could be attended at minimum cost by a larger number of American youths. Senator Morrill's efforts for land-grant colleges achieved further success in 1890 with the enactment of a measure providing more substantial support of the colleges. Documentation of these activities of Morrill is offered importantly in many of the more than 100 speeches that he delivered in Congress.

Improvements in agriculture and rural life, stimulated by leadership in the U. S. Department of Agriculture since 1862, are significantly shown in voluminous publications of the Department. Monthly reports issued from 1863 to 1876, annual reports since 1862, and treatises on every aspect of agriculture and rural life for more than a century attest to the zeal with which Secretaries of Agriculture, scientists, and administrators have striven to carry out the Department's original mandate — to acquire and widely diffuse information concerning agriculture. In recent years, these publications mirror the response of the Department to a great variety of conditions such as economic depressions, agrarian protest, and utilization and population changes, fluctuating markets, and environmental distress.

The eminence attained by leaders of the Department of Agriculture is suggested by the fact that more than 100 of them have been accorded sketches in the *Dictionary of American Biography*. Among them are persons whose ideas and actions have greatly influenced the course of agricultural research, farm policies and methods, natural resource protection and development, and rural life. In this category, there inevitably come to mind such noteworthy figures as Townend Glover, first Federal entomologist; Jacob R.

Dodge, early statistician; Harvey W. Wiley, pure food reformer; Seaman A. Knapp, inaugurator of the Farmer's Cooperative Demonstration Work; James Wilson, Secretary of Agriculture for 16 years and very successful promoter of scientific work; Gifford Pinchot, famous apostle of the early crusade for conservation; Leland O. Howard, leader in the development of insect control; Alfred C. True, ardent advocate of agricultural education; Daniel E. Salmon, noted veterinarian; William J. Spillman, innovative agricultural economist; Erwin F. Smith, distinguished plant pathologist; Marion Dorset, pioneer biochemist; and Curtis F. Marbut, expert in the study and mapping of soils. In editions of the *Dictionary of American Biography* that will appear during the next few years, there will undoubtedly appear accounts of the achievements of such Department leaders as Henry C. Taylor, spearhead in the profession of agricultural economics; David Fairchild, famous world explorer for new seeds and plants; Hugh H. Bennett, father of the soil conservation movement; Aldo Leopold, influential environmental conservationist; Louise Stanley, director of the first national survey of farm housing and inaugurator of major studies of home economics and human nutrition; Morris Cooke, leader in the movement for rural electrification; and Henry A. Wallace, first administrator of New Deal farm programs. For many of these personages, Department of Agriculture publications constitute a principal source of information concerning their views and activities. The increasing use of microfilming as a method of publication seems likely to add to the published documentary heritage of these and other agricultural leaders. There are, for example, useful microfilm editions of the papers of two Secretaries of Agriculture, J. Sterling Morton and Henry A. Wallace, prepared by the Nebraska State Historical Society and the University of Iowa, respectively.

Meanwhile during the past century the published papers of presidents of the United States sometimes have mirrored their role in agricultural affairs. It is easy, however, to exaggerate this role, since until recent years most presidents, with or without justification, have striven to be regarded as products of a rustic environment and champions of rural values. This tendency was noted early by Josiah Quincy, Jr. who in 1845 declared:

> Our chief magistrates have differed in many points, but they have generally agreed in this; that before, and in many cases after the election, they have been farmers . . . So that it may well be urged, that though all farmers can't be presidents, all presidents must be farmers.[17]

Despite this tradition, however, it may be cautiously suggested that a few presidents did in fact exert significant agricultural leadership that may be noted in their published papers. Thus, the writings of Theodore Roosevelt, for example, reveal what has generally been conceded to be an important publicity effort on behalf of forest protection and the welfare of rural America. Symbols of this effort were his White House Conference on Conservation in 1908 and his Country Life Commission of the same year. Similarly, the public papers of Woodrow Wilson document serious and constructive presidential attention to basic problems of agricultural credit and marketing; and those of Franklin D. Roosevelt disclose innovative approaches to crop production adjustment and environmental conservation.[18]

Even more traditional than presidential reverence for rurality has been major congressional advocacy and action for agrarian causes. The published documentation resulting from this effort is contained mainly in voluminous congressional publications. Any roster of leaders of the effort would be long but would probably include certain stalwarts. For the first half of the 20th century, there would perhaps be listed such figures as Henry C. Adams, Asbury F. Lever, Charles L. McNary, Arthur Capper, George W. Norris, John H. Bankhead, II, and Marvin Jones. Printed records of debates in Congress and reports of congressional committees document extensively pivotal roles of these and other legislators in protecting and advancing agricultural interests. The role of these and other champions of agricultural measures in Congress seems likely to become known better through the inclusion of their papers in the expanding field of microfilm publications.

At the state level, for more than a century, significant leadership in agricultural affairs has been provided by colleges of agriculture, boards, departments, or commissions of agriculture, and agricultural societies. From the colleges, there has emanated leadership in agricultural research, study of rural life, and extension work. In the annals of their achievements are names of famous agriculturists such as Eugene W. Hilgard, eminent soil scientist of California; Wilbur O. Atwater of Connecticut, pioneer investigator of the calorific value of foodstuffs; Liberty H. Bailey of New York, prolific writer and editor of agricultural books; Stephen M. Babcock of Wisconsin, developer of a famous milk-fat test; Louis H. Pammel of Iowa, noted botanist; and George W. Carver of Alabama, searcher for new uses of southern crops. The work of these and other leaders in the agricultural colleges is shown in thousands of bulletins and reports published by experiment stations and extension service offices. Other work for agricultural improvement in the states since the middle of the last century has been carried on by state boards, departments, or commissions of agriculture. Annual and other reports of these organizations describe their activities in gathering and disseminating information concerning crop and livestock conditions and conducting state fairs and other locally oriented agricultural programs. Often closely associated with these state organizations, especially during the 19th century, were agricultural societies led by planters and agricultural journalists of the type mentioned earlier in this paper. The pioneering work of these societies in agricultural education was often narrated in farm periodicals and compilations of proceedings of meetings.

Efforts for agricultural betterment by Federal and state government officials, which have just been noted, have been prodded often by action of leaders of farm organizations during the past century. In general, the organizations have striven to secure economic equality for agriculture primarily with government intervention. Two of such groups, prominent during the 1880's, were the Northern Farmers Alliance and the Southern Alliance led by Milton George and C. W. Macune, respectively. Objectives of their leadership are mainly documented in organizational periodicals. In the 20th century, the largest of these organizations have been the National Grange, National Farmers Union, and American Farm Bureau Federation. With a combined membership of approximately three million farmers these groups in recent decades have constituted a powerful force in pressing for legislation and other benefits in behalf of farm operators. In this effort, the Grange was long led by Louis J. Taber, the National Farmers Union by Charles S. Barrett, and the American Farm Bureau Federation by Edward A. O'Neal. The record of their strivings unfolds to a great extent in major periodicals of their organizations published in recent years under such titles as the *National Grange Monthly*, *National Union Farmer*, and *Nation's Agriculture*. Supplementing these sources, there are statements of leaders of the organizations in periodicals of their state units and in leading privately owned journals throughout the country. Less well known and available is the documentation of the leadership of smaller and short-lived farm organizations, many of which were concerned with the plight of the most economically and socially disadvantaged farmers. One of such organizations in recent years was the Southern Tenant Farmers Union led by H. L. Mitchell. The efforts of Mitchell and his associates in behalf of sharecroppers and tenants during the 1930's have been revealed to some extent in oral history interviews, magazine articles, and published proceedings of meetings of the union.

The work of farm organizations for improvement of agricultural conditions has been aided significantly by the efforts of some agricultural editors who have had much influence in the formulation of national farm policies. Two outstanding examples of such editors in the 20th century are Clifford V. Gregory and Clarence Poe. Gregory, editor of the *Prairie Farmer* for more than a quarter of a century, was the founder of the "Master Farmer Movement," which sought to give public awards to successful farmers beginning with a Master Farmers banquet in Chicago in 1925. His paper was an important voice in the campaign for the McNary-Haugen bill and the enactment of farm relief legislation during the early years of the New Deal. Also influential in regional and national agricultural affairs during this era was Clarence Poe, long-term editor of the *Progressive Farmer*. This journal, long read widely in the South and eventually throughout the United States, constantly stressed the need for improved rural schools and social services; advocated balanced farm operations in the south, with less dependence on cotton and tobacco; and called for equitable treatment of small farmers under New Deal programs. The ideas and interests of Poe are also recorded in an autobiography with the naturally progressive title, *My First 80 Years*. It is a tribute to the stature of both Gregory and Poe and, perhaps, also a mark of their wisdom, that both of them were highly recommended to be U. S. Secretary of Agriculture and both respectfully withdrew their names from presidential consideration.

It is evident, therefore, that leadership in American agriculture is revealed in a vast and varied array of published documentary materials. These materials range in historical and sentimental significance from that possessed by the letters of the nation's founding fathers to that of writings of obscure farm journal editors. They vary in quantity from thousands of reports and bulletins of Federal and state government agencies to single books of innovative agriculturists. In passing, it should be noted that in many instances these published materials are only small portions of related large accumulations of unpublished documents relating to American agriculture that are preserved in archival and manuscript repositories.[19] They constitute, nevertheless, a valuable reservoir of information concerning leadership in what has always been a major area of American life and history.

REFERENCES

1. George Washington, *The Diaries of George Washington, 1748–1799*, ed. J. C. Fitzpatrick, 4 vols., illus. (Boston and New York: Houghton Mifflin Co., 1925). *The Writings of George Washington from the Original Manuscript Sources, 1745–1799*, ed. Fitzpatrick, 39 vols. (Washington: U. S. Govt. Print. Off., 1931–1944).

2. ———, *The Writings of George Washington; Being His Correspondence, Addresses, and Other Papers, Official and Private*, ed. Jared Sparks, 12 vols. (New York: 1847–1848). *The Writings of George Washington*, ed. Worthington C. Ford, 14 vols. (New York: G. P. Putnam's Sons, 1889–1893).

3. See Everett E. Edwards, *George Washington and Agriculture*. Bibliographical Contribution No. 22, U. S. Department of Agriculture Library (Washington, September 1931), pp. 1–5.

4. George Washington, *Letters on Agriculture from His Excellency George Washington*, ed. Franklin Knight (Washington, D. C., 1847), p. 24.

5. Thomas Jefferson, *Writings of Thomas Jefferson*, ed. Paul L. Ford, 10 vols. (New York: G. P. Putnam's Sons, 1892–1899); *Writings*, ed. A. A. Lipscomb and A. E. Bergh, 10 vols. (Washington: Thomas Jefferson Memorial Assn., 1903–04); *Papers*, ed. Julian P. Boyd, 19 vols. (Princeton, N. J.: Princeton Univ. Press, 1950–74).

6. See U. S. Department of Agriculture, *Early American Soil Conservationists*. Miscellaneous Publication No. 449. (Washington: U. S. Govt. Print. Off., 1941), pp. 3–7.

7. *Ibid.*, pp. 7–11.

8. See Lewis C. Gray, *History of Agriculture in the Southern United States to 1860* (New York: Peter Smith, 1941), pp. 612–613, 779, 845.

9. See Percy W. Bidwell and John Falconer, *History of Agriculture in the Northern United States, 1620–1860*. (Washington: Carnegie Institution of Washington, 1925), pp. 187–188.

10. *Early American Soil Conservationists, op. cit.*, p. 21.

11. Harold T. Pinkett, "The American Farmer, A Pioneer Agricultural Journal, 1819–1834," *Agricultural History*, 24 (July 1950): 146–151.

12. Everett E. Edwards, "Agricultural Records; Their Nature and Value for Research," *Agricultural History*, 13 (January 1939): 10.

13. *History of Agriculture in the Southern United States to 1860, op. cit.*, p. 782.

14. Harry J. Carman, *Jesse Buel, Agricultural Reformer* (New York: Columbia Univ. Press, 1947), pp. xxxii–xxxiii.

15. *History of Agriculture in the Southern United States to 1860, op. cit.*, pp. 780–781.

16. Lincoln, Abraham, *Collected Works*, ed. Roy P. Basler, 9 vols. (New Brunswick, N. J.: Rutgers Univ. Press, 1953–1955).

17. Cited from Earle D. Ross, "The Agricultural Backgrounds and Attitudes of American Presidents," *Social Forces*, 13 (October 1934):37.

18. See Theodore Roosevelt, *Letters*, ed. Eltinge E. Morison et al. 8 vols., (Cambridge, Mass.: Harvard Univ. Press, 1951–54); Woodrow Wilson, *Public Papers*, ed. R. S. Baker and W. E. Dodds. 6 vols. (New York: Harper & Brothers, 1925–27); Franklin D. Roosevelt, *Conservation*, 1911–1945, ed. Edgar B. Nixon. 2 vols. (Hyde Park, N. Y.: Franklin D. Roosevelt Library, 1957).

19. See Edwards, "Agricultural Records; Their Nature and Value for Research," *op. cit.*; and Harold T. Pinkett, "The Archival Product of a Century of Federal Assistance to Agriculture," *American Historical Review*, 69 (April 1964):689–706.

Who's a leader? The Published Documents: A Commentary

By
John T. Schlebecker

Dr. Pinkett's delightful account probably should have been entitled: "Prominent Leaders in American Agriculture." A slight error in the title, however, does not mar a most excellent discourse, and the mistake does give a commentator something to say.

Since about 1620, American farmers have been independent adventurers. Of course, indentured servants, slaves, some tenants, and most sharecroppers have farmed at the will of others. Nevertheless, the vast bulk of American farmers have been managers of their own affairs.

Agriculture, in contrast to other industries, is in the hands of a multitude of managers. Each farmer personally decides what he will do. A small group of corporation executives can decide to introduce computers into their business and, behold, computers are introduced. A small group of agricultural leaders can decide that farmers should grow a new variety of hybrid corn and, behold, the farmers do as they think best. In short, each farmer is the leader of his own enterprise. The glory of American farming resides, and has always resided, in the managerial skills and educational attainments of millions of entrepreneurs.

Dr. Schlebecker is Curator, Division of Agriculture, U. S. Smithsonian Institution, Washington, D.C.

When discussing leaders in agriculture, therefore, the published documents under consideration ought to include the vernacular as well as the literary. Furthermore, the concept of literature might profitably be expanded to include more than the records of the mighty.

Probably, we should not altogether ignore the poets like Vachel Lindsay, Robert Frost, or even Edgar Guest. The line, "We force nature with harrow and plow" defines farming in a way that we seldom think about but should. Who but a poet would have thought about it?

Novels of farm life by authors who knew something about it are part of the record and should be used. On the other hand, TV shows and movies based on the *Little House on the Prairie* or *The Grapes of Wrath* should be viewed with some scepticism. The trouble with using fiction and poetry lies in the fact that it is so hard to keep up with this literature. It is also difficult to assess its accuracy. Most historians solve the problem by ignoring or denigrating this part of the record.

Another often ignored part of the record consists of the printed autobiographies, diaries, and journals. There are a good many of these and they are only moderately difficult to find. Historians, economists, and the like, seem to encounter trouble in using this literature because so much of the material appears to be irrelevant agriculturally. The real trouble may rest in a constricted, possibly myopic, definition of agriculture. As Dr. Pinkett has so elegantly shown, agriculture properly includes all aspects of farm life. If a person had any agrarian experience at all, the autobiography is a prime, if sometimes limited, source of information on farm leadership.

Which brings up another question. Why should the farm leadership of the conspicuous be seen only through the eyes of those prominent barons? The plowman also sees what is going on and, sometimes, more clearly than the observers we usually choose. Inconspicuous American farmers have also left their literary remains which can and should be exploited. Unlike their Old World brethren, American farmers have always been remarkably literate.

Finally, there is the statistical record. If we leave no other trace, we at least usually manage to have witnesses to our arrival and departure. Oftimes, someone also officially notes our existence and activities between cradle and coffin. We may appear only as a number, but such notice is a part of the printed documentary record. Not that we need make much of this. Agriculturists, practical or literary, make altogether too much use of statistics. Dr. Pinkett is probably right in intentionally ignoring the *U. S. Census*.

Still, the records of the prominent invariably throw light on the lives of the less prominent. Those seeking to know about the less prominent can profitably use the documents which Dr. Pinkett has so ably and charmingly called to our attention.

The Making of an Agricultural Publisher: Edwin T. Meredith and the Development of *Successful Farming* Magazine

By
Peter L. Petersen

On January 26, 1920, President Woodrow Wilson named Edwin T. Meredith, a 43 year-old Iowa publisher, to be the new Secretary of Agriculture. The Cabinet position was the culmination of a rapid succession of appointments for Meredith, beginning with service on the Treasury Department's Advisory Committee on Excessive Profits in 1917, then as a member of the America Labor Mission which visited England and France in 1918, and followed by a position as a representative of the public at the October, 1919, National Industrial Conference. Meredith's unwavering support of Wilsonian policies, especially after the nation entered World War I; his energy and relative youth; and a developing friendship with William Gibbs McAdoo, Wilson's son-in-law and the wartime Secretary of the Treasury, were major contributing factors in these appointments. But the overriding factor was Meredith's identification with *Successful Farming,* one of the nation's most prosperous and widely read farm magazines.[1]

Dr. Petersen is Associate Professor of History. West Texas State University, Canyon, Texas. A grant from the West Texas State University Committee on Organized Research assisted in the preparation of this paper.

Edwin T. Meredith, center, watches as his friendly rival publisher, Henry Cantwell Wallace, right, succeeds him as Secretary of Agriculture in March, 1921. R. M. Reece, Chief Clerk of the Department of Agriculture, administers the oath. (*Courtesy of Annals of Iowa*)

Meredith's brief tenure as Secretary of Agriculture[2]—there were only thirteen months remaining in the Wilson Administration when he was appointed—marks a dividing line in his distinguished publishing career. After his return to Iowa in 1921 he continued to be active in both politics and agricultural journalism. The following year he bought *Dairy Farmer*. However, much of his energy was now devoted to the creation of a new magazine. The first issues of *Fruit, Garden and Home* rolled off the Meredith presses in October, 1922. Renamed *Better Homes and Gardens* in 1924, it soon became, and remains today, one of the nation's major publications in terms of circulation and advertising revenue.[3] *Better Homes and Gardens* is eloquent testimony to Meredith's publishing genius, but the national renown associated with this publication has often overshadowed his earlier achievements in agricultural journalism. Accordingly, the focus of this paper will be on the beginnings of Meredith's career as a publisher, particularly his development of *Successful Farming* magazine which, by 1920, only 18 years after its founding, had over 800,000 subscribers, a circulation exceeded only by that of the *Farm Journal*.[4]

Edwin T. Meredith was born in the little western Iowa town of Avoca on December 23 in the Centennial year of the United States. He was the eldest of the seven children of Thomas Oliver and Minerva J. (Marsh) Meredith. His father was a farm implement dealer who, in the early 1880s, sold his store and moved to a farm near Marne, in Cass County, Iowa. Here the Meredith children attended the local four-room school and helped with the field work and chores. For the most part, the adolesence of Edwin T. Meredith followed the normal or typical pattern of an Iowa farm boy. Yet, there were differences, especially as he reached his mid-teens. Unlike most of his boyhood friends, he finished high school and prepared to enter college, and, more important, he had an influential grandfather. In combination, these two factors were destined to launch him on the career that would bring him national prominence.

In the fall of 1892, having reached the age of 16 and receiving one of the two Marne high school diplomas granted that year, young Ed took the train to Des Moines and enrolled at Highland Park College where he took courses in business and didactics, and waited tables to earn "extra spending money."[6] One of his instructors remembered him as a big farm boy, often wide-eyed, but eager to learn.[7] His college career, however, proved short-lived. After a few months he left school, not because of finances or scholarship, but because his grandfather had offered him a job on a newspaper.

175

Edwin's grandfather, Thomas Meredith or "Uncle Tommy," as everyone in town called him, was an English immigrant who had prospered in the buying and selling of land in western Iowa. After his retirement from farming, "Uncle Tommy" had moved to Des Moines where, by the early 1890's, he had become, largely by default, the principal financial sponsor of the *Farmers' Tribune,* the major voice in Iowa of the People's or "Populist" party.[8] Originally called the *Iowa Tribune,* this paper had been founded at Atlantic in 1878 and had soon become the personal organ of General James B. Weaver who eventually moved it to the state capital and renamed it.[9] It had come into the elder Meredith's hands as partial repayment for his heavy contributions to the Weaver presidential campaign of 1892. Since the paper was not a paying proposition, the exchange was something less than munificent. "Uncle Tommy," though, could afford the loss, and was determined to keep publishing until the "masses" triumphed over "monopoly." And, accordingly, in early 1893, he asked his young grandson to come work for him.

Edwin accepted without hesitation. As he was to remark later, he had then viewed the *Farmers' Tribune* as "about the biggest thing on earth."[10] And it was undoubtedly exciting for a boy of 17, who only months before had left the farm to work on a paper edited by a man of General Weaver's stature. Through the small offices of the paper poured not only the leaders of the state party, but also correspondence from reformers with a national reputation as well.

At first, young Meredith worked in the mailroom, ran errands, and did odd jobs around the office. Not unexpectedly, his grandfather soon promoted him. In the issue for April 11, 1894, he was listed as one of the paper's general managers. A few weeks later, his name appeared alone and, by September, he had acquired the additional title of company treasurer. With these new responsibilities came a more active role in politics. During the campaign of 1895, 18 year old Edwin Meredith served as the Secretary of the "People's" Party State Central Committee as organizer and coordinator of tours by such "imported" speakers as Jacob Coxey and Ralph Beaumont, and, most discouragingly, as semi-official fund raiser. Addressing the readers of the *Farmers' Tribune* as "Dear brothers in the cause of humanity,"[11] he made repeated appeals for money but apparently to little avail, since his financial report in mid-September revealed a woeful lack of cash. The State Central Committee, he was forced to acknowledge, had collected only $66.09! Subsequently, the *Farmers' Tribune* lamented that the Populists

176

were "getting just as discouraged as the money power wants us to be."[12]

Nor did the election returns do much to lift their spirits. Far from achieving the anticipated doubling of strength, Iowa Populists lost ground and, in the wake of the setback, "Uncle Tommy" conceded that he had the "blues." By this time, in fact, as he neared his 72nd birthday, the elder Meredith was ready to give up on a newspaper that was being published at a loss of fifty dollars per week.[13] Instead of letting the *Farmers' Tribune* fold, however, he decided merely to withdraw. In December, 1895, as a wedding present, he gave a half interest in it to his newly-married grandson and, at the same time, sold the other half to Sylvanus B. Crane, the recently defeated Populist candidate for governor.

For young Edwin, who had been courting his future wife, Edna C. Elliot, and giving considerably more thought to marriage than to becoming a newspaper publisher, the gift came as a surprise. Asked years later to explain how he became a publisher, he replied simply that he had "drifted" into it.[14] Yet, having done so, he was ready to work with his new business partner to develop "the *Tribune's* power for good . . . and make it the best reform paper in the United States."[15] Under the new dispensation, Crane became managing editor while Meredith handled the business end of the enterprise.

The campaign and election of 1896 marked the climax of Populism in Iowa. Its following there, which was never large tended, in the words of a later historian, "to disappear with the return of prosperity."[16] But, as Populism waned, Edwin T. Meredith tried to remain a reformer, pledging that "the *Tribune* will always be fighting for . . . every interest of the common people." Yet, he also warned, in ever more plaintive appeals to those who were allowing their subscriptions to expire, that he could not continue the fight without the financial support of the very same "common people."[17] Indeed, the precarious financial condition of the paper had caused Crane to turn over his share in the venture to his "boy partner," and Meredith was, by late 1896, the sole proprietor of the *Farmers' Tribune*. Financially insecure to begin with, his enterprise could not hope to avoid bankruptcy unless it could revive the political and economic ferment out of which it had grown or could develop some new way of holding existing subscribers and attracting new ones. This was reality, and 20 year old Edwin T. Meredith obviously understood it far better than many other publishers caught in the same dilemma.[18]

Accordingly, while he appealed for the support of reform-minded elements, he also set out to make the paper more attractive, both in design and content. Beginning in January, 1897, he adopted a new format of 16 quarto pages and, while avowing that the paper would maintain its political policy, he announced that it would "curtail the amount of political matter to some extent" and devote more space to other matters, particularly to "market reports and the agricultural department."[19] The change, moreover, was soon readily apparent. One summer issue featured pictures of the fusion candidates for office; another, only three weeks later, gave the cover spot to a large black sow with the distinguished-sounding name of Woodburn Medium 2nd Sister. And similarly, on November 3, the preliminary reports of the state election and the obituary of Henry George, "a great Man," shared equal billing with a balanced ration for hogs.

In the years that followed, the emphasis upon agricultural news and service became more pronounced than ever. Lead articles discussed such subjects as "Stud Books of Great Britain" and "the Art of Feeding Fine Stock," inside material was now subdivided into departments and arranged under the headings of Horticulture, Livestock, Poultry, Young People, Family Reading, "Our Bee Department," and the work of the Experiment Stations. Periodically, Meredith restated his intentions and objectives. Writing in late 1899, for example, he said that his policy would be "push" and the information printed in the *Farmers' Tribune* would be "practical" His aim was

> to get close to the farmer who raises his crops under ordinary conditions and by suggestions couched in such language that he does not need a Latin dictionary to guide him, assist him in growing better crops, keep his soil in better condition, sell to better advantage or feed with greater economy. If he is a stock raiser we propose to make the paper a medium through which he might glean better methods of breeding, and caring for his stock.[20]

By his 25th birthday, Meredith was well along the road toward realizing his ambition of publishing a "first rate farm paper." Unlike scores of publishers with far more maturity and experience, he had succeeded in tailoring his offerings to the changing nature of agriculture. He had profited from the fact that much of rural America had now embarked on a period of prolonged prosperity (what historians have called its "golden age"). Farmers wanted information about the production of corn and the breeding, raising, and feeding of livestock and these concerns were reflected in the content of the *Tribune*. Of equal importance, Meredith's readers were financially able to respond to the offerings of advertisers.[21] From all of this, some of it probably fortuitous, Meredith benefited and, driven by a keen ambition, accompanied by industry, business sense, imagination, and occasional grants from his grandfather, he managed to push the weekly circulation of his paper to about 33,000, and in his words, to make "a small profit each year."[22]

This success, moreover, seemed to convince the young publisher that he could conquer still larger fields, particularly if he could break out of the restraining limits imposed by the nature of his current publishing enterprise. The *Farmers' Tribune*, after all, was by tradition a weekly, limited in readership to the state of Iowa, beyond this, it still suffered from the stigma of its reformist origins and previous championship of lost causes. Real success, it appeared, would require a new vehicle. Consequently, in early 1902, Meredith began preparations for a new monthly journal, to be entitled *Successful Farming* which would appear in October of that year. Asked about the title, Meredith explained that he had tried to think of "the thing I wanted most to do, to be" and, since he "wanted most of all" to be "successful," this had become the title of the new magazine.[23]

The turn of the century was an auspicious time for American journalism and this was certainly to Meredith's advantage. As Homer E. Socolofsky has pointed out in his study of the development of the Capper farm press, new printing techniques "better links with the news agencies and governmental agencies such as the Department of Agriculture" — and the evolution of rural free delivery, greatly increased the opportunities for agricultural publishers.[24] And although the concept of the farmer as a consumer as well as a producer was far from being well established, agricultural publishers found manufacturers increasingly willing to purchase advertising in the pages of farm magazines.

Nevertheless, the early years of *Successful Farming* were difficult ones. Meredith served in the triple capacity of publisher, advertising manager, and production manager of both *Successful Farming* and the *Farmers' Tribune*. E. E. Faville was editor of both the new magazine and the paper. Beyond this, Meredith employed only a bookkeeper, a stenographer, three printers to set type, and one man to handle the mailing and subscription lists. Nor were the quarters in which *Successful Farming* was born very spacious ones. They consisted of three second-floor rooms, an office, a mail room, and an unplastered composing room where printers carried kerosene lamps from case to case to illuminate their work. Since Meredith did not have a press that could handle even the few thousand initial copies,

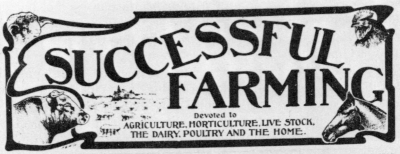

SUCCESSFUL FARMING

Devoted to
AGRICULTURE, HORTICULTURE, LIVE STOCK,
THE DAIRY, POULTRY AND THE HOME.

MONTHLY.   DES MOINES, IOWA. OCTOBER. 1902.   50 CENTS A YEAR
Single N s. 5 Cts

OUR BEST FARMERS

The question, "Who are your best farmers?" is a query often heard expressed by the stranger on visiting a farming district for the first time. The answer is pretty sure to come with a touch of pride, when the successful farmers are pointed out, as they may be in any farming community in our country.

We find the homeseeker striving, above all else, to locate as near as possible to those farmers classed as best. By best we mean the ones who are making the most of their chances and are taking advantage of their opportunities— the fellows who are pushing to the front and making records for themselves in their chosen occupation.

Our best farmers are those who get at the bottom of things and keep posted on the up-to-date methods employed in general farm work. You will find them carrying on their farm operations with none but the best implements known to the trade; a keen interest is taken in the work that is being carried on by our experiment stations, an agricultural journal makes its regular visits to the home the doings of the outside world are noted, crop and market reports are watched, a word our best farmers are thoughtful. They think, reason, plan and out of it all is developed strict attention to business rules and methods and to the applying of them with courage and persistance. From the work that our best farmers are doing has come a healthy growth in our great agricultural industry. The list of successful farmers is being rapidly increased as the years go by, until no farmer can afford to be found anywhere but in the van of the procession of the BEST FARMERS.

* * * * *

A most wonderful exodus of farmers and investors from the United States has been made into Northwestern Canada during the year. The out-

The Canadian Northwest.

look for next spring, points to a still larger exodus of our young farmers into that country. The cause of this movement may be attributed chiefly to three reasons: First, cheaper farm lands; second, inducements held out by the Canadian government to actual settlers; third, the wonderful yield of grain during the past three years.

The provinces, which on account of their agricultural resources are attracting settlers and investors, are

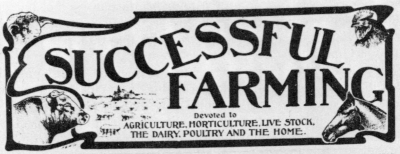
Two Profitable Guernsey Cows, selected with Care.

Manitoba, Assiniboia, Alberta and Saskatchewan. The area of these provinces would easily sustain a population of 50,000,000 people. Laws governing the taking of homesteads are broad and the terms most liberal. Wheat raising is the chief industry, although large yields of oats, flax and barley are reported. Excellent ranching facilities may be found in the provinces of Alberta and Saskatchewan. The tide of immigration to this entire district of Canada is rapidly increasing. The railway facilities are rapidly spreading and an era of prosperity has come to our Canadian neighbors.

The "hit and miss" method won't work to a profit in the selection of farm stock for specific purposes. Most noticeable is this fact in reference to

Care in Selection.

the dairy cow. The economical production of large quantities of milk high in percentage of butter fat indicates the value of the dairy cow along practical lines, and in selecting dairy cows for the home herd this first consideration should be uppermost. The points of importance indicating production of milk, may be said to consist: 1st, of a good constitution, by the means of which the dairy cow is enabled to stand long service in feeding and milking. The indications of a proper constitution are, deep chest, good heart girth and general appearance of vigor and good health; added to this in order to bring about the production of a large yield. There should be a wide muzzle, a comparatively open backbone which readily distinguishes the dairy from the beef type, the latter being close and compact (necessary for proper beef production). The dairy cow should have a large barrel or belly for the proper digestion of feed, and a well shaped udder, wide from side to side, extending well forward, well backward also and high up between the thighs, with prominent milk veins leading forward into large so-called wells." In the breeding of a dairy herd aim to breed from cows of known capacity and from bulls whose dams have been tested and their value as dairy cows fully established.

* * * * *

Between the many who are poor and the few who are rich stands the American farmer. The Census Bureau in reporting on the value of farming property show conclusively that after all, so far as the actual wealth is concerned the farmers are capitalists. The estimate given is as follows: 5,339,657 farms of the United States are worth $16,674,690,247. Of this amount $3,560,198,191, or 21.4 per cent, represents the value of buildings, and $13,114,492,056, or 87.6 per cent, the value of land and improvements.

An Important Census Report.

The front page of *Successful Farming's* initial issue October, 1902. (Courtesy of Meredith Corporation)

he engaged the machinery of the Western Newspaper Union which had its shop downstairs.

The shortage of finances during these days is borne out by the recollections of several early employees. On one occasion, for example, Mrs. Meredith came to the office, asked her husband for money to buy a mouse trap, and received the reply, "Why you know, Edna, I don't have any money." Only when she became insistent did Meredith go through the incoming mail and, locating a quarter from a subscriber, was able to supply the necessary funds. And on more than one occasion, the publisher found himself in such financial straits that he was unable to pay the postage necessary to send his magazine on its way. In these cases, Meredith often hurried about Des Moines attempting to sell an ad in the forthcoming issue so that he could get the current one in the mail. And, at times, he was forced to ask his employees to forego part of their salaries until funds could be secured.[25]

One obvious reason, however, for this seemingly perennial shortage of cash was Meredith's policy of plowing almost every cent earned back into the magazine, including the meager proceeds from his sale of the *Farmers' Tribune* in 1904. [26] Although Meredith had little cash, one employee recalls that the publisher did have credit with other publishers. Thus he was able to place a $1,300 ad soliciting subscribers in the *Cincinnati Inquirer* "when he did not have 13¢." But the ad brought in over $2,600 and he discounted his bill, took the rest, and advertised widely. Many of these ads consisted of a "count the dots" contest whereby for each $0.50 annual subscription to *Successful Farming* an individual was entitled to two guesses at the number of dots in a picture. Cash and merchandise, usually pianos, were offered as prizes. Although it is impossible to tell how many subscribers were gained through these contests, they apparently worked well and the claim of one employee that Meredith took in over $25,000 from dot contests in 1903 is probably not far off. [27] In any case, *Successful Farming's* circulation soon climbed past the 100,000 mark and Meredith began soliciting advertising at the rate of $0.50 an agate line.

During the next few years Meredith employed a variety of means to further increase circulation. One of the most popular of these was the offering of prizes such as rifles, shotguns, magic lanterns, telescopes, model steam engines, pocket knives, and watches to boys who sold a certain number of subscriptions, usually between six and twelve, at the special rate of $0.25 per year. Similarly, girls could win "solid gold" rings for signing up six new subscribers while

Staff of *Successful Farming* publishing company, Circa 1909. Edwin T. Meredith is the hatless gentleman with a mustache at the far right of the second row. (Courtesy of Meredith Corporation)

mother had the opportunity of gaining a complete set of dinnerware for her family. Nor were fathers ignored. In 1909, *Successful Farming* purchased much of the prizewinning corn at the National Corn Exhibition held at Omaha, paying $75 for the first prize ear, $280 for the best ten ears, and $265 for the best bushel of corn. Farmers were then offered 25 kernels of this corn in return for four subscriptions.[28] The response to this offer was so overwhelming that the next year Meredith bid a record $160 for the grand champion ear of the Iowa corn show. It is little wonder, then, that one of *Successful Farming's* editors would describe the publisher as "a wizard on circulation schemes."[29]

Yet it would be a mistake to attribute Meredith's eventual success solely to circulation gimmicks. More to the point, certainly, was the content of *Successful Farming* itself. The direction the magazine would take was set forth in the lead editorial of the initial issue. There was "plenty of room," declared Meredith, "for a live up to date farm paper," whose object was

> the discussion of farm matters employed in making farming a success. We intend to live up to the title of our paper by sending to our readers each month such information as will be helpful to them in carrying on the many duties, on the farm and about the home. We want our paper to stand for *successful farming* in the truest sense of the word and shall strive in the different departments, to discuss in concise and practical manner, the various subjects under consideration.[30]

The magazine was to be non-partisan; from the beginning, however, it was anything but non-political. In addition to prohibition and women's suffrage, *Successful Farming* supported such rural-oriented reforms as parcel post, good roads, postal savings banks, mutual rural telephone companies, equitable interstate freight rates, and improved educational facilities. Editorials constantly called for the elevation of farming to "a position on a par with that of banking, manufacturing, merchandising, or any of the professions," and for the practical employment in agriculture of science and technology because only through "the proper application of energy" could the farmer hope to keep up in this "busy age of keen competition . . . ."[31]

Greater agricultural efficiency was a recurrent theme in *Successful Farming* as its publisher filled column after column with practical information about profitable and labor-saving farming methods. Articles by faculty members at the agricultural colleges appeared regularly. Along this line, perhaps the most popular thing ever published in *Successful Farming* was a six-part series beginning in October, 1905, on "corn culture" written by "the corn evangelist," Professor Perry G. Holden, then Head of the Department of Agronomy at Iowa State College. Holden argued that farmers could not hope to improve their yields until they took more care in selecting seed corn and used some method of determining the likelihood of germination. Meredith ran thousands of extra copies of Holden's writings and offered them as subscription premiums.[32] Thus, through *Successful Farming*, Holden's "corn gospel" was spread far beyond the borders of the Hawkeye state.

Holden's efforts to improve corn production by a careful process of seed selection coincided with Meredith's enthusiasm for science and its application to agricultural improvement through education. The two men became friends and seldom did an issue of *Successful Farming* pass without some favorable mention of the work being done at the agricultural colleges. Repeatedly, farm youth were urged to seek higher education.[33] Nor was the work of the Department of Agriculture and the Experiment Stations ignored. Farmers were urged "to go and see" what was being done. Not surprisingly, *Successful Farming* enthusiastically supported the work of the Iowa State College Extension Service which was founded in 1906 with Holden as its first director. In fact, Meredith soon hired one of Holden's top assistants, Professor Addison H. Synder to be associate-editor of *Successful Farming*.[34] Synder teamed with Alson Secor, a liberally-educated farmer turned writer whom Meredith prized as having the "common touch," to give the magazine talented editorial direction. Secor devoted himself to politics, reform, and everyday farm life, while Synder wrote on scientific and technical matters and strengthened the already strong ties with various agricultural institutions.

The arrival of Secor and Synder allowed Meredith to concentrate on other matters, particularly advertising. Aware that farmers were often victimized by fraudulent advertising, from the first issue, he sought to protect his readers by promising to "make good any loss to paid subscribers sustained by trusting any deliberate swindler advertising in our columns . . . ."[35] By 1906 the magazine had largely purged itself of patent medicine ads as well. Advertisements for liquor and tobacco were forbidden and the "clean" nature of *Successful Farming* was seen as a selling point. When an advertising agency representing a well-known pipe tobacco approached Meredith in 1925, the publisher explained that *Successful Farming* had been conceived as a family magazine, to be read not only by the head of the house, but also by his wife and children as well. And since there were "tens of thousands" of mothers who did not want their sons encouraged to use tobacco and "would resent anyone calling who would urge tobacco," he felt that "these same mothers would resent their favorite paper doing the same thing when it came into their home."[36]

Although important in giving a certain image to *Successful Farming,* Meredith's efforts to protect his subscribers from swindlers and his refusal to accept patent medicine, liquor, and tobacco ads were not quite as unique as some members of the Meredith Publishing Company were to claim later.[37] Yet, in at least two areas, Meredith's advertising policies were truly innovative.

Very early he recognized that the regional nature of agriculture had implications for advertising. Thus he set out to promote the image of *Successful Farming* as a journal with a circulation superior to the many state-oriented farm magazines, yet one deliberately limited to the corn belt, or the "Heartland," as the magazine's staff liked to call it. By stressing that his publication reached more homes than any other journal in this, the richest agricultural region in the United States, Meredith had a powerful selling point when he sought advertisers.[38] Concentrating on one type of agriculture, more-over, had certain editorial advantages and gave added appeal to articles such as those by Holden on corn.

In 1911, as *Successful Farming's* circulation passed the half million mark, Meredith began construction of a permanent home for his magazine and his staff which now numbered more than three hundred employees. Located in downtown Des Moines, the building was designed to house both administrative offices and printing equipment. Completed the following year, the five-story building was an impressive structure, well-lighted, well-ventilated, and fireproof. One source estimated the cost at somewhere between $150,000 and $175,000, all of which Meredith had to borrow.[39]

In completing the building, which today still houses the headquarters of the Meredith Corporation, the publisher had stretched his financial resources to the limit. Yet, once it was done, he called in his general manager and asked him to borrow additional money, this time to finance the bringing of eastern advertising men to Des Moines to show them the new plant and to introduce them to midwestern agriculture. When the latter protested that the company was already overextended with its creditors, Meredith is supposed to have replied, "Well, tell them that unless we can show these people what we have we are 'broke' and they are 'broke' with us. If

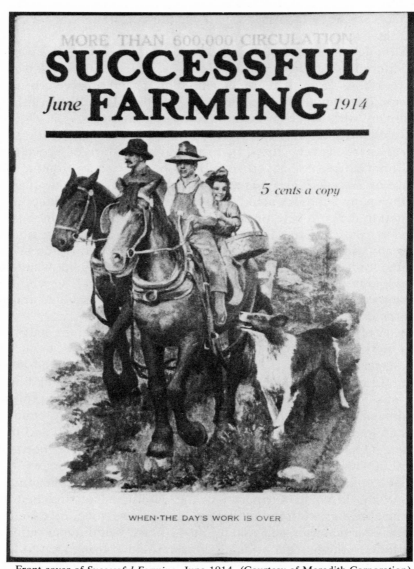

MORE THAN 600,000 CIRCULATION

SUCCESSFUL
June FARMING *1914*

5 cents a copy

WHEN·THE DAY'S WORK IS OVER

Front cover of *Successful Farming*, June 1914. (Courtesy of Meredith Corporation)

they put up an additional $10,000 to finance this trip, then we are sure to make good on the investment in this building and equipment."[40] In the end, he had his way. In May and November, 1913, and again in June of the next year, a total of nearly one hundred advertising and business men were given an all expense paid trip to Des Moines, and most were thoroughly impressed by what they saw.

From the standpoint of securing advertisers, the tour was a success. One example was the reaction of Otto E. Sovereign of the North American Construction Company of Bay City, Michigan, who, upon returning home, dashed off a letter to Meredith recalling the chorus line to a little ditty passed out with other sheet music at a banquet in the new plant. "I will take a page . . . " he wrote, "That's about the shortest way I can express to you the result of my trip." Meredith replied in the same spirit. "I believe that 'I will take a page' song is the most beautiful piece I ever heard. There is something about it that appeals to me. On the other hand, I suppose it is quite 'touching' to you." Touching indeed! The March 1915 issue of *Successful Farming* has four full pages advertising Sovereign's products.[41]

These tours, described by Nelson A. Crawford and Charles E. Rogers as the first effort to "bring advertising experts into direct personal contact with farming and farmers in order to show farm purchasing power,"[42] mark a turning point in the development of *Successful Farming*. Advertising income, already substantial, now began to soar. In early 1922 Meredith confided to his friend Bernard Baruch that *Successful Farming,* for a number of years, had not "paid less than two hundred thousand dollars and from that up to four hundred and fifty thousand dollars."[43]

By his early forties, then, Edwin T. Meredith had achieved much of the success he had longed for as a young publisher and, upon those who met him, he generally left a lasting impression. Physically, to be sure, there was nothing really unusual about his broad-shouldered, six-foot frame, his dark hair now graying at the edges, or the narrow, close-clipped dark bristle that had replaced the broad bushy mustache of his youth. Physical appearances, however, were deceptive. Beginning with a "firm" handshake and speaking with "frankness" in a voice revealing a slight touch of his grandfather's British up-bringing but, above all, generating an infectious enthusiasm and warmth of character, he quickly established himself as a dominant and highly attractive personality. Those who knew him best spoke often of the "warmth and genuineness of his friendship," of his energy, vision, and concept of service.[44]

It is this last characteristic — Meredith's concept of service — that several scholars find as the key ingredient in the phenomenal success of his publishing ventures. Indeed, a recent study of *Better Homes and Gardens* suggests that the continued success of this magazine can be explained by its adherence to principles of service set forth by Meredith at the time of its founding.[45] This is not surprising, for Meredith always saw his magazines as more than mere publications. "We are building here," he said of *Successful Farming* in 1919, "an Institution for the service of Agriculture, and for the people engaged in or interested in agriculture and the problems of farm life, in this Great Food Production Heart of the Nation."[46] His motives, of course, were a mixture of altruism and self-interest. He obviously stood to benefit financially from increased rural productivity; yet he also believed in the superiority of rural life and was attempting to solve the problems of agriculture within the larger context of an increasingly industrialized economy.

As his business prospered and word of his financial success spread, numerous individuals and organizations sought Meredith's advice and assistance. And since the publisher shared with his fellow Iowan, Herbert Hoover, the belief that successful businessmen had an obligation to lend their talents to public service, more often than not he accepted these requests. He played a major role in the development of Farm Boys' and Girls' Clubs, forerunners of the 4-H, by serving as president of the National Committee on Boys' and Girls' Club work, and by establishing and endowing a $200,000 loan fund from which farm children could borrow enough money to purchase pigs, calves, lambs, chickens, or whatever would make them property owners.[47] He became a director of the Chamber of Commerce of the United States and his efforts to convince businessmen of the importance of a healthy rural economy eventually won him the title of "agriculture is fundamental" Meredith.[48] In addition to his role in the Wilson Administration mentioned at the beginning of this paper, he served as president of both the Associated Advertising Clubs of the World and the Agricultural Publishers' Association.

Many of those who knew him saw in Meredith the potential for political leadership. Though a reluctant candidate, he twice made unsuccessful bids for office in heavily Republican Iowa. In 1920, he was that state's "favorite-son" presidential candidate at the Democratic National Convention. Four years later, party elder statesman

William Jennings Bryan endorsed Meredith for the presidency; and John W. Davis, after securing the nomination, attempted to get the publisher to be his vice-presidential running mate. Meredith declined. "I may have an exaggerated idea of the matter," he told a press conference upon his return to Des Moines, "but I feel that in giving my attention to publications going into the homes of 1,500,000 families, doing what we can for the progressive thought of the country, right living and better methods, I am rendering a greater service than I could possibly render by presiding over the Senate of the United States."[49] Numerous Democrats hoped Meredith would challenge Al Smith for the presidential nomination in 1928. Again the Iowan held back, partly because he found politics increasingly distasteful, and partly because of the precarious nature of his health.[50] For years he had suffered from acute hypertension and the prolonged strain had weakened his heart. On June 17, 1928, Edwin T. Meredith died at his home in Des Moines. He was fifty-one years of age.

For such a short life, he had accomplished much and those who eulogized him often noted his many honors and awards. Yet these meant less to him, his associates believed, than did a letter of appreciation from some farm child whom he had helped or the knowledge that because of his magazines the quality of American life, especially rural life, had been improved.[51] It is fitting, then, that as we use this symposium on agricultural literature to commemorate the 200th birthday of the United States, we also note that 1976 marks the 100th anniversary of Edwin T. Meredith's birth.

REFERENCES

1. Woodrow Wilson to Edwin T. Merdith, January 26, 1920, copy in the Edwin T. *Meredith Papers,* Special Collections Department, University of Iowa Libraries, Iowa City, Iowa; Meredith to Wilson, January 26, 1920, *Woodrow Wilson Papers,* Manuscript Division, Library of Congress; William Gibbs McAdoo to Gary T. Grayson, January 28, 1920, *Willaim Gibbs McAdoo Papers,* Manuscript Divison, Library of Congress.
2. See Peter L. Petersen, "Edwin T. Meredith: Iowa's Other Secretary of Agriculture," *The Iowan* 21 (Spring 1973): 39–41.
3. Frank Luther Mott, *A History of American Magazines,* vol. 5: *Sketches of 21 Magazines* (Cambridge: Harvard University Press, 1968), pp. 36–48; Theodore Peterson, *Magazines in the Twentieth Century,* 2d ed. (Urbana, University of Illinois Press, 1964), pp. 382–384; Carol Reuss, "Edwin T. Meredith: Founder of *Better Homes & Gardens,*" *Annals of Iowa* 42 (Spring 1975): 609–619. For a brief sketch of the *Dairy Farmer,* see John T. Schlebecker and Andrew W. Hopkins, *A History of Dairy Journalism in the United States, 1810–1950* (Madison: University of Wisconsin Press, 1957), pp. 285–287.
4. *Ayer's American Newspaper Annual and Directory* (Philadelphia: N.W. Ayer & Son, 1920), pp.1206,1210.
5. Richard M. Winans, "An Interview with Secretary Meredith," June 12, 1920, copy in the *Meredith Papers.*

6. Letter from Meredith to Alson Secor, n.d., *Meredith Papers*.

7. Chesla C. Sherlock, "Being a Personality," (unpublished manuscript, 1926): 12. Sherlock was a Meredith employee who conceived the idea of preparing a biography of his "chief" as a gift for Meredith's fiftieth birthday. As one would expect, the result was highly laudatory, but "Being a Personality" remains a valuable source of information about the development of Meredith's publishing career. A bound ribbon typescript copy and an unbound carbon copy are in the *Meredith Papers*.

8. Thomas Meredith, "Personal Recollections of a Pioneer," *History of Cass County Iowa* (Springfield, Illinois: Continental Historical Company, 1884), pp. 282–287; C.A. Meredith to J.S. McCluen, August 3, 1926, *Meredith Papers*. Fred Emory Haynes quotes an unidentified source claiming that Thomas Meredith contributed $25,000.00 to the populist movement in Iowa. See Haynes, *Third Party Movements since the Civil War with Special Reference to Iowa* (Iowa City: State Historical Society of Iowa, 1916), pp. 355.

9. Frank Luther Mott, "Iowa Magazines—Series 2,"*Palimpset* 44 (August 1963): 351.

10. Meredith to Alson Secor, n.d., *Meredith Papers*.

11. *Farmers' Tribune*, August 7, October 9, 1895.

12. *Ibid.*, September 18, November 13, 20, 1895.

13. *Ibid.*, November 13, December 4, 1895.

14. Meredith to Alson Secor, n.d., *Meredith Papers*.

15. *Farmers' Tribune*, January 8, 1896.

16. Herman Clarence Nixon, "The Populist Movement in Iowa," *Iowa Journal of History and Politics* 24 (January 1926): 100.

17. *Farmers' Tribune*, January 6, 27, June 30, 1897.

18. Seymour Lutsky, "The Reform Editors and Their Press," (unpublished Ph.D. Thesis, University of Iowa, 1951), pp. 26–27

19. *Farmers' Tribune*, January 27, 1897.

20. *Ibid.*, December 13, 1899.

21. See Earle D. Ross, *Iowa Agriculture: An Historical Survey* (Iowa City: State Historical Society of Iowa, 1951), pp. 118

22. Meredith to Alson Secor, n.d., *Meredith Papers*.

23. *Successful Farming* Staff, "Edwin T. Meredith," *Annals of Iowa* 29 (April 1949): 572–573.

24. Homer E. Socolofsky, "Development of the Capper Farm Press," *Agricultural History* 31 (October 1957): 34. See also Wayne E. Fuller, *RFD: The Changing Face of Rural America* (Bloomington: Indiana University Press, 1964), pp. 298–314.

25. In the 1960s several members of the Meredith Corporation realized the shortage of information about the origins of their firm and set out to secure interviews with some of the surviving early Meredith employees. One of the most valuable of these interview sessions occurred on April 28, 1965, when Lester H. Mugge recorded a conversation with Carol Preston. Preston went to work for Meredith in 1902 and was, by the following year, in charge of the mail room. Mugge generously furnished the author with a typescript copy of this lenghty interview. He also supplied copies of several interviews conducted by Alson Secor in early 1926. Mugge, himself, was a valuable source of information, for he served as Meredith's personal secretary from 1921 until 1928. Lester H. Mugge to the author, July 18, 1969.

26. Meredith to H.C. McMillan, July 10, 1907, Meredith Papers. The new owners of the *Farmers' Tribune* moved it to Sioux City where it became the *Farmer and Breeder* in 1911.

27. Carol Preston, interview with L. H. Mugge, April 28, 1965. For a good example of the dot contests, see *Successful Farming* 2 (August 1903): 18.

28. *Successful Farming* 8 (January 1909): 47.

29. Alson Secor, "A History of Successful Farming," (unpublished manuscript in files of Meredith Corporation, Des Moines). Secor interviewed several long-time Meredith employees in 1926 with the intent of preparing a brief history of the magazine. The project was never completed and all that remains are a few of the interviews and a copy of a March 26, 1926 speech by Secor "outlining" the results of his research.

30. *Successful Farming* 1 (October 1902): 2.

31. *Ibid.*, 6 (November 1907): 2

32. *Ibid.*, 4 (March 1906): 2-3. For a good account of Holden's work with corn, see Martin L. Mosher, *Early Iowa Corn Yield Tests and Related Later Programs* (Ames: Iowa State University Press, 1962).

33. See, for example, *Successful Farming* 6 (November 1907): 2.

34. Ralph K. Bliss, *History of Cooperative Agriculture and Home Economics Extension in Iowa — The First Fifty Years* (Ames: Iowa State University of Science and Technology, 1960), pp. 59, 83.

35. *Successful Farming* 1 (October 1902): 2.

36. Meredith to F. L. Swigert, October 27, 1925, Meredith Papers. See "With Successful Farming Publishers," *Successful Farming* 2 (March 1904): 18.

37. *Successful Farming* Staff, "Edwin T. Meredith," *Annals of Iowa* 29 (April 1949): 578. Some twenty years before *Successful Farming* began publication, Wilmer Atkinson had made a similar statement in the pages of the *Farm Journal*. See Nora C. Quebral, "Wilmer Atkinson and the Early *Farm Journal*," *Journalism Quarterly* 47 (Spring 1970): 66. Even earlier, Orange Judd, editor of the *American Agriculturist,* had used his "Humbug Column" to expose many frauds. See Earl W. Hayter, *The Troubled Farmer 1850-1900: Rural Adjustment to Industrialism* (DeKalb: Northern Illinois University Press, 1968), pp. 221-222.

38. Peterson, *Magazines,* p. 72. Out of a total circulation of 821,091 at the end of 1918, 549,912 subscribers to *Successful Farming* were listed as residents of the 13 "Heartland" states of Illinois, Indiana, Iowa, Kansas, Michigan, Minnesota, Missouri, Nebraska, North Dakota, Ohio, Oklahoma, South Dakota, and Wisconsin. Figures based on an Audit Bureau of Circulations' Report, December 31, 1918, printed in Edwin T. Meredith, *An Agricultural Institution for the Service of the Farm People of the Great Middle West* (Des Moines: *Successful Farming* Publishing Company, [1919]), pp. 62.

39. *Des Moines Register and Leader,* September 8, 1912; Tim W. LeQuatte to Editors, *Associated Advertising,* February 5, 1920, copy in the *Meredith Papers*.

40. Tim W. LeQuatte to Editors, *Associated Advertising,* February 5, 1920, copy in the Meredith Papers; Sherlock, "Being a Personality," 16.

41. Otto E. Sovereign to Meredith, November 6, 1913; Meredith to Sovereign, November 8, 1913, both in *Meredith Papers; Successful Farming* 14 (March 1915): 63-66.

42. Nelson Antrim Crawford and Charles Elkins Rogers, *Agricultural Journalism* (New York: F.S. Crofts, 1931), pp. 243-244.

43. Meredith to Bernard M. Baruch, February 25th, 1922, copy in Meredith Papers. By 1920 *Successful Farming* had an advertising rate of $2,700.00 a page with many issues containing more than 200 pages.

44. Newton D. Baker to Harry C. Evans, March 18, 1929; Arthur Capper to Evans, March 19, 1929; William H. Rankin to Evans, March 20, 1929, all in an unpublished collection of "Letters and Manuscripts Commemorating the Life and Services of Mr. Meredith," now in the possession of Edwin T. Meredith, III.

45. Carol Reuss, "*Better Homes and Gardens*: Consistent Concern Key to Long Life," *Journalism Quarterly* 51 (Summer 1974): 292-296.

46. Meredith, *An Agricultural Institution*, pp. 3.

47. *Successful Farming* 16 (April 1917): 40; Theodore A. Erickson, *My Sixty Years with Rural Youth* (Minneapolis: The University of Minnesota Press, 1956), pp. 82-83.

48. Charles C. Youngreen to Meredith, June 6, 1927, Meredith Papers.

49. *Des Moines Sunday Register*, July 13, 1924.

50. For an account of Meredith's political career, see Peter L. Petersen, "A Publisher in Politics: Edwin T. Meredith, Progressive Reform, and the Democratic Party, 1912-1928" (unpublished Ph.D. Thesis, University of Iowa, 1971).

51. See *Edwin T. Meredith, 1876-1928: A Memorial Volume* (Des Moines, Meredith Publishing Company, 1931).

Great Men and Enduring Farm Magazines: A Commentary

By
Earl W. McMunn

Writing about a man in such a way that he is comfortable when he sees the story in print is one measure of journalistic excellence. Measured by that standard, Petersen's paper is outstanding.

There is a strong spirit of loyalty and deep understanding between those of us who have spent most of our lives in the farm magazine business. We are few enough in number that we get to know each other on a first-name basis. We have shared successes and failures. Upon occasion, we may disagree. But we have the utmost respect for each other and admiration for the giants of our profession.

In preparing for this assignment, I looked to my editor friends for help. I asked about their most distinguished editors and publishers. Also, about the accomplishments which contributed most to the success of their magazines. The information was many times greater than I could possibly condense into this paper. Most important were the parallels between the information received from my friends, and that contained in Petersen's paper. Certain key words and phrases stand out. "Dedication," "involvement," "understanding," "concern for the common man," are examples.

It is also true that most of the great editors and publishers had a humble beginning. They were willing to work. They persisted in the

Mr. McMunn formerly editor of *The Ohio Farmer,* is now Director of Public Affairs, The Harvest Publishing Company, Columbus Ohio.

face of difficulty. Now we honor them as great men. And, rightly so. The honors they have won are richly deserved. The giants of our business have had ability, dedication, and understanding. It is also true that the business offers unusual opportunity for the development of talent. Involvement in agriculture and the issues of the day permits every man to go as far as his ambition and his ability will allow. The pages of a farm magazine are an excellent "launching pad" for ideas. Some have comprehended and taken full advantage. Those associated with viable magazines which lived were also practical men. They understood the need for making a profit. They were idealists and reformers. But they knew that staying in business is fundamental to everything else.

Public opinion polls are a popular exercise of our time. Farm magazines have been conducting polls from their very beginning. A vote of confidence is recorded with every order accompanied by a check from subscriber or advertiser. When those orders stop coming in it is a vote of "no confidence."

This grueling test of survival is probably the truest measure of the worth of a farm magazine. Readers and advertisers make critical judgments. They are not swayed for long by sympathy or emotion. And the size of the check is some measure of the extent of their sincerity. Credibility shows through in the magazines which survive. Once lost, a magazine can't live long enough to gain it back.

Petersen has written a truly outstanding paper about the life and times of one great publisher. He linked this with the development of one magazine. He painted an in-depth picture. I'd like to add breadth to the picture by telling about other great men in the farm magazine business and magazines they helped develop to their present level of leadership. I'll talk about a couple of regional magazines, one which is national, two that are "specialized" and about several serving individual states.

The first issue of *American Agriculturist* was published at 36 Park Row, New York City, in April of 1842. It was a monthly magazine with A. B. Allen and R. L. Allen as editors. The publisher was George A. Peters. In explaining the purpose of the magazine the editors said:

> It is but a few years since the first agricultural periodical issued from an American press, to flicker for a short period before the listless gaze of public apathy, and then expire for want of adequate support. . . . In accordance with the public demand, several useful and well sustained papers have sprung into existence within the last few years, which from the intelligence they have imparted on

AMERICAN AGRICULTURIST

FOR THE

Farm, Garden, and Household.

"AGRICULTURE IS THE MOST HEALTHFUL, MOST USEFUL, AND MOST NOBLE EMPLOYMENT OF MAN."—Washington.

ORANGE JUDD & CO.,
PUBLISHERS AND PROPRIETORS.
Office, 245 BROADWAY.

ESTABLISHED IN 1842.
Published also in German at $1.50 a Year.

$1.50 PER ANNUM, IN ADVANCE.
SINGLE NUMBER, 15 CENTS.
4 Copies for $5; 10 for $12; 20 or more, $1 each.

Entered according to Act of Congress in November, 1867, by ORANGE JUDD & Co., in the Clerk's Office of the District Court of the United States for the Southern District of New-York.

VOLUME XXVI—No. 12.   NEW-YORK, DECEMBER, 1867.   NEW SERIES—No. 251

THE INTERRUPTED SUPPER.—AFTER A PAINTING BY LUDWIG BECKMAN, DUSSELDORF.—*Engraved for the American Agriculturist.*

One of the pests of European agriculture is the rabbit, which breeds seven times in a year, and as it produces eight at a birth, it is estimated that the progeny of a single pair would in four years amount to the enormous number of 1,274,480. It is fortunate that they have so many enemies, besides man, to keep them in check. Rabbits and hares are much alike, but differ in their habits—the hare is a solitary animal, and makes its nest or "form" on the ground, while the rabbit burrows and lives in large colonies. Naturalists place all our animals that are usually called rabbits among the the hares, of which we have in our entire territory some twenty species. Our common species is the *Lepus sylvaticus*, found throughout the greater part of the United States. It retains its brown color all winter, while the Northern Hare, *Lepus Americanus*, which has a more northern range, is brown in summer, and white in winter. Both hares and rabbits are exceedingly timid, and for their safety from their enemies rely upon their fleetness. Our domestic rabbits are supposed to be varieties of the European *L. cuniculus*. The above group admirably represents characteristics common to these animals—contentment when no danger is suspected, and great timidity when alarmed,

195

agricultural subjects throughout the country, have added millions to our national wealth and prosperity.

They went on to explain:

> The pursuit of agriculture, in its broadest sense, it need hardly be observed, constitutes the basis of our national virtue and national wealth. . . . The pecuniary troubles, which, within the last few years, have so extensively visited our country, have been produced *almost exclusively* by the neglect of this indispensable basis, on which all other pursuits should rest.[1]

These and other statements in the first issue indicate the dedication of editors to improvement of public understanding and their awareness that the job would not be easy.

From its very first issue, the editor of *American Agriculturist* showed that he understood the need for fiscal responsibility in government by observing:

> That shrewd observer of men and things, Baron Rothschild, foresaw with a noon-day clearness, the tendency of our system in the recent heyday of our fictitious prosperity, when he refused the tempting offer of an American loan at a large premium, for says the sagacious banker, 'a nation that ought from its pursuits, to furnish a surplus of produce, can find money neither for principal or interest while it has to buy its bread from Europe.[2]

The *American Agriculturist* has endured through the years because of dedicated leadership by a succession of able editors and publishers. Perhaps most famous was Edward R. Eastman who occupied the editor's chair for a period of 35 years. He was a teacher, county agricultural agent, and editor of the *Dairymen's League News* before becoming editor of *American Agriculturist* in 1922. The publication at that time was owned by Henry Morganthau, Jr. Later, Eastman became president of the corporation.

Eastman's record of public service is typical of others who have been privileged to edit major farm magazines. However, he possessed that happy combination of ability, common sense, and dedication which permitted him to attain a level of distinction reached by few others in the farm magazine field. For 17 years he was a director of the Federal Land Bank's District No. 1. He was a member of the National Citizens Commission for the Public Schools, and a member of the 1955 White House Conference on Education. He was elected a trustee of Cornell University and served from 1921 to 1928, and again from 1934 to 1946, when he resigned because of his appointment as a member of the New York

State Board of Regents. He then became a trustee of Ithaca College. "Eastman's Chestnuts," a feature of his *American Agriculturist* editorial page, reflected his dry wit and humor. He wrote a number of books—several dealing with agriculture in "horse-and-buggy" days. *Journey to Day Before Yesterday*, is perhaps his best known and best loved book. Helping readers to make a better living at farming and to have a better life in their homes and communities has been a guiding principle of *American Agriculturist* through the years. "This has come about not by spectacular journalism, but rather by sawing a little wood every day in terms of finding and printing the kinds of information that they need."[3]

Progressive Farmer is an outstanding example of a farm magazine published on a regional basis. The result of merging three publications, one in the Southeast, one in the Mid-South, and another in the Southwest, it now serves more than a million subscribers. But, like many other farm publications, the road to success was not an easy one. The oldest branch was started in 1886 at Winston, North Carolina, by L. L. Polk. A confederate veteran, this prominent farm leader campaigned for agricultural equality. He also campaigned for better schools and better farming as well as a state agricultural college. Backed by farm clubs, Polk in five years was able to get a land-grant agricultural college, a state railroad commission, and reorganize the State Department of Agriculture. Polk died in 1892 and, for 10 years thereafter, the publication was edited by J. L. Ramsey while Polk's son-in-law handled the business affairs.

Shortly after Polk's death and nine years after the founding of *Progressive Farmer* in North Carolina, Tait Butler established the *Southern Farm Magazine* at Starkville, Mississippi. At that time, he was professor of veterinary medicine at Mississippi A&M College. Three years later, in 1898, he was forced to sell the publication. The same year Butler sold the *Southern Farm Magazine*, Clarence Poe joined *Progressive Farmer* as assistant editor. He was 16 years old at the time. In a year, he was its editor, and four years later, in 1903, he purchased the publication, which had a circulation of 5,800 for $7,500.

With Poe as president and editor, *Progressive Farmer* grew from a circulation of 5,800 with a $4,000 income to a circulation of 22,000 with a $24,000 gross income by 1908. At that time, Tait Butler, who was State Veterinarian in North Carolina, and John S. Pearson bought stock in *Progressive Farmer*. Butler became vice-president and Pearson became secretary-treasurer and business manager. These three men—Poe, Butler, and Pearson—are credited with

197

setting the publication on the sound editorial and business course that has led to its outstanding success. Clarence Poe was editor of the publication for 67 years, and president of the company for 50 years. Butler continued with the company as vice-president and editor until his death in 1939 and Pearson was a *Progressive Farmer* official for 49 years.

Probably the most distinctive contribution *Progressive Farmer* has made to American magazine publishing is its separate edition structure with its localized editorial, advertising, and circulation services. It is only in comparatively recent years that some other magazines have broken out circulation into separate editions to provide readers with localized editorial and advertising service. The separate edition structure of the *Progressive Farmer* dates back 65 years to 1908 when an Eastern edition was established covering North Carolina, South Carolina, Virginia, Georgia, and Florida and a Western edition for Alabama, Mississippi, Louisiana, Arkansas, and Tennessee. Over the years, *Progressive Farmer* has been a magazine for the farm family. It has given attention to policies and practices that would improve farming and family income. *Progressive Farmer* has also been a crusading magazine. "It has been willing to support aggressively the causes it conceived to be for the welfare of Southern Agriculture."[4]

Farm Journal is a magazine with a national circulation of more than 1.6 million, which will soon reach its hundredth year of publication. It was founded in March, 1877, by Wilmer Atkinson who was a native of Montgomery County, Pennsylvania. He was a crusading type. Being a Quaker, he campaigned hard for women's suffrage, also for rural free delivery. Perhaps Atkinson's most unique contribution to agricultural publishing was what came to be known as his "fair play statement." In the magazine, he guaranteed to his readers that he would stand behind the integrity and dependability of his advertisers. He promised to make good any fraud or deception that an advertiser perpetrated upon a reader. The publication continued to run the statement until about 10 years ago when the penchant for litigation began sweeping the country.[5] Atkinson had a talent for simple and direct writing. He announced in his prospectus that he intended to keep the articles short. This has served as a commendable goal for each succeeding editor.

Carroll P. Streeter made a major contribution to the magazine when he reoriented it from a strictly rural publication of general interest, to a business-oriented publication. In the process, editors began paying extra attention to the specialized interests of major commodity producers—first, with geographic editions beginning in 1952 and demographic inserts (the livestock extras) beginning 10 years later.

California Farmer goes back in history for 121 years. The original editor was a Colonel Warren who came from a botanical arboretum in England. Early historians credit him with introducing the tomato to the United States. Warren put on the first California State Fair and paid for it out of his own pocket. It cost about $10,000. Warren was active in promoting a wide range of crops in the state at a time when miners were becoming disillusioned with that industry and were turning to agriculture. At one time, opium was a legal crop and opium prices were quoted as part of the market news coverage.

Four editors have served the publication for most of its history with a few interim editors for short periods of time. An outstanding editor was Wickson who was head of all the University of California Experiment Stations, editor of *California Farmer*, and the author of many books, particularly on deciduous fruits. Wickson was called upon to locate property for an agricultural college. Using a horse and buggy, he rode up and down the great Central Valley until he found a piece of land—some 3,000 acres—which he chose as the site for the college. He had a good eye. It turned out to be some of the best land in the state. Another outstanding editor was John E. Pickett, father of the present editor. The elder Pickett at one time was editor of *Country Gentleman* and the *Ladies Home Journal*. Pickett went West to buy into the paper which was then called the *Pacific Rural Press*. He served as editor from 1924 to 1952. During the formative years of the state, *California Farmer* was a strong influence in establishing a State Department of Agriculture, starting the University of California, and a strong influence on legislation throughout its 121 years. The most recent legislative effort was to get a proposition on the ballot to have a public vote on a farm labor bill. The present editor called three state-wide meetings that were the largest meetings of influential men ever called in the state. A budget of more than a million dollars was raised, but the bill did not pass. Recently, with prodding from the governor, a farm labor bill was passed.[6]

Nebraska Farmer was established in 1859 and is now publishing Volume 117. The founder was Robert W. Furnas, second governor of Nebraska. He took office in 1873. Sam McKelvie became editor in 1905 and owner and publisher in 1908 until his death in 1956. He was governor of Nebraska for two terms beginning in 1919. It was he who built the publication to prominence as an influence for progress in Nebraska agriculture. In addition to his accomplishments in the publishing and political fields, Sam McKelvie was also one of the great leaders in the cattle business. His "By The Way" ranch was known to Hereford breeders everywhere. It also provided the title for his column in *Nebraska Farmer*. McKelvie served for several terms as the president of the Board of the American Hereford Association. During his tenure, the Association established a $4 million trust fund and built a half-million-dollar headquarters in Kansas City. They also launched a research program to make Hereford cattle the best source of beef in the nation. Falling cattle prices in 1938 led to formation of the Sandhills Cattle Association. Again, McKelvie was a leader. The Association was formed to let everyone know the merits of Sandhill cattle and to maintain a code of ethics between buyers and sellers.[7]

Tom Leadley, fresh out of Kansas State, joined the editorial staff in 1913. He became managing editor in 1918, then was editor for 25 years from 1930 until his retirement at the end of 1955. Marvin Russell became managing editor of *Colorado Rancher and Farmer* when the *Nebraska Farmer* established that publication in 1947. He became editor of *Colorado Rancher and Farmer* in 1956, then editor of both publications in 1957. He retired in July of 1975 after 18 years as editor of *Nebraska Farmer*.

Marvin Russell says:

> Tom Leadley had the 'touch' to produce a family magazine which became trusted and even beloved by Nebraska farm families. He left an editorial heritage which makes strong demands on the people who follow him—demands for accuracy, honesty, sincerity and credibility. *Nebraska Farmer* readers expect nothing less from their state farm magazine, because that's the way it was under the long-time guidance of Tom Leadley.[8]

Kansas Farmer was founded in 1863 by the Kansas Department of Agriculture. Over the years it has changed ownership a number of times and has had mergers with other publications. One merger was with *Mail and Breeze*, but the name *Kansas Farmer* has always been used. One of the most prominent figures associated with the publication was the late Arthur Capper who was owner and publisher for many years. Capper was a distinguished United States Senator from Kansas and was responsible for many pieces of important legislation, including the Capper-Volstead Act which provided the basis for the development of agricultural cooperatives in America. Other farm publications which Capper owned in whole or in part were *Capper's Farmer, Missouri Ruralist, Ohio Farmer, Michigan Farmer,* and *Pennsylvania Farmer.*

Kansas Farmer was instrumental in founding the Kansas Livestock Association. In turn, this Association is credited with founding the National Livestock and Meat Board. The editor saw the need for a stockman's organization and promoted it through the magazine. Today, the Kansas Livestock Association is one of the state's important and influential farm groups. *Kansas Farmer* was the leader in organizing Kansas Flying Farmers. In cooperation with Kansas State University, the magazine was also the original promoter of the Master Farmer-Master Homemaker organization in the state. The magazine, in the early 1960's, was the only supporter of the state's first bull testing station. Progress was slow during the first few years before some leading cattlemen backed the idea. Later came support from the Kansas Livestock Association and from Kansas State University. Today, the livestock association and the university operate a fine bull testing station at one of the state's better feedlots. Also in the 1960's, the magazine launched an editorial effort to increase and improve the swine industry in Kansas. A succession of articles pointed out that Kansas has the feed, land, water, and markets. The Extension Service expanded its educational efforts. New vigor was infused in the state producer organization. Swine production is now a major enterprise on many farms.[9]

Missouri Ruralist under that name goes back "only" to 1902. However, it emerged from other publications going back to about 1848. One of these was *Colman's Rural World* published in St. Louis. The founder of that magazine, Norman J. Colman, was later the first Secretary of Agriculture. Founder and first editor of *Missouri Ruralist* was Boyd Carroll who was a crusader and started the long-time boosting of the Missouri State Fair. He was also able to bring about appointment of a Missouri state dairy commissioner and campaigned for more sheep in Missouri.

John Case was editor from 1913 to 1955 and became a prominent figure in agriculture. In the early 1920's, he served as president of the State Board of Agriculture. Later he was a member of the conservation commission which took conservation out of politics and served as a model for many other states. He was succeeded by Cordell Tindall who continues the tradition of service to readers.

Missouri Ruralist has always promoted good seed. The publication pushed hybrid corn at a time when many agricultural leaders

201

COLMAN'S RURAL WORLD

Established 1848.   ST. LOUIS, THURSDAY, JANUARY 11, 1883.   No. 2, Vol. XXXVI.

Sorgo Department.

The widow of the late Isaac A. Hedges will continue the seed department of his business, under the management of his business.

This proved to not so how too seen to advertise our seeds' preparation and all the prompt registeration for the prompt of Northern sugarcane. We have already not application.

Those who have good, well-ripened cane seed, will find plenty of customers for it by advertising it in the RURAL WORLD, and now is the time to do it. We will insert a half-inch card sixteen weeks for $10.

Those offering seed for sale should have it thoroughly cleaned of all dirt, staff and trash over grains, and be sure that it has been so cured as to insure a good amount and clean.

...

Clydesdale Mare, Darling XII. and her Foal, Property of Moffatt & Bro., Paw Paw, Ills.

were opposed to the use of "the new foreign seed." Editors also served as superintendent of the Missouri State Corn Shucking Contests. These corn husking contests were popular during the days before mechanical harvesting and drew large crowds. The publication has conducted quiet crusades for many changes in farm practices. Editors encouraged raising soybeans as a grain crop. Today, Missouri ranks number four among the states in soybean production, and the acreage is double that in corn.

The magazine has also promoted lespedeza and year-around pasture for cattle production. In cooperation with the Farmers Home Administration, they conducted winter pasture tours to show what fescue would do for winter grazing. *Missouri Ruralist* also promoted more beef cattle and the state is now number 2 in beef cows. "Right now, I am not so proud of that," says editor Tindall.[10]

The Farmer, started in 1882 by Edward A. Webb, serves readers in two editions, one going to Minnesota and the other to North and South Dakota. One editor who exerted great influence was Dan A. Wallace who joined *The Farmer* in 1905 and was directing editor from the 1920's to the early 1940's. Dan was the son of the late Henry Wallace who founded *Wallace's Farmer* and a brother of Henry C. Wallace, Secretary of Agriculture in the Harding administration. Dan Wallace was an uncle of Henry A. Wallace, Secretary of Agriculture, Secretary of Commerce, and Vice-President in the Roosevelt era. Dan had such skill with the pen that he was often asked to help with speeches and important letters as well as writing for *The Farmer*. Once he wrote a letter to the governor of Minnesota for a livestock group, blistering the governor's hide for not supporting some action of vital concern to the stockmen. Upon receiving the letter, the governor called Dan, demanding that he come to the State Capitol immediately. When Dan arrived, the governor handed him the letter (which Dan had written but which carried someone else's signature) asking that he immediately draft a reply in kind. This Dan did — writing a blistering letter back to the livestock group without ever revealing, either to the governor or to the stockmen, that he had been the author of both letters. This bit of nostalgia makes the point that farm magazine editors have been influential, through their writing and their thinking, in molding agricultural policy. Dan Wallace, for example, was involved in early development of the old AAA program.

Farm magazine editors are also perceptive. For example, Norman Borlaug was given a Distinguished Man of Agriculture award by the American Agricultural Editors Association in 1967. This was four years before he was singled out for international recognition as a Nobel Prize winner. At the time, Robert Rupp, editor of *The Farmer* and president of AAEA, made the presentation to Borlaug. Four years later, he saw the award hanging in Borlaug's office outside Mexico City. [11]

Wallace's Farmer, and its predecessor, *Iowa Homestead*, spans some 115 years of American history. Mark Miller first started his farm paper at Racine, Wisconsin, then moved it to Dubuque, Iowa. Prices were good in those days with July wheat priced at $1.06 at Iowa points. After Civil War inflation came the slump. Hogs sold for $3.40 in 1871. Wheat was $0.74 in 1874. Farmers had bought farms, machinery, and livestock at high prices. Now they were in trouble. W. P. Wilson, then editor of the *Homestead*, felt that the new Granger movement would help farmers get lower freight rates. In 1872, with *Homestead's* help, there were 652 new Granges organized in Iowa. Times were a little better in 1883 when J. H. Duffus bought the paper and hired "Uncle Henry" Wallace as editor. In 1885, James M. Pierce became publisher and majority stockholder while Wallace continued as editor. Wallace had an inquiring mind, pumping information out of both farmers and scientists. He took hold of new ideas in farming and urged that they be tried out. Farmers read him and believed in him and the *Homestead*. "Uncle Henry" Wallace died in 1916. His old associate, J. M. Pierce, died in 1920 and was followed by his son, Dante Pierce, who pulled the *Iowa Homestead* through post-war difficulties. In the meantime, Henry C. Wallace had gone to Washington as Secretary of Agriculture and *Wallace's Farmer* was campaigning for the McNary-Haugen farm bill. In 1929, the Wallaces bought *Iowa Homestead* and the combined publications began a new career.

In 1938, editor Donald R. Murphy started the Wallace-Homestead Poll. This was a survey conducted through personal interviews which aimed to find out what farm people read as well as their attitudes on various questions. The editors, for the first time, began to have measures of how they were getting along with subscribers. With this early start, *Wallace's Farmer* and its associated publications became national leaders in measuring farm readership and making farm opinion polls.

In 1957, The Prairie Farmer Publishing Company bought *Wallace's Farmer* and *Iowa Homestead* along with *Wisconsin Agriculturist*. All three publications are more than 100 years old.[12] Originated in 1841, *Prairie Farmer* is now the nation's oldest farm magazine. The first editor and publisher was John Steven Wright who took a

THE IOWA HOMESTEAD

ESTABLISHED 1855.   ONLY AGRICULTURAL WEEKLY IN THE STATE. $1.50 PER YEAR.

VOL. XXX. NO. 14.   DES MOINES, IOWA, FRIDAY, APRIL 3, 1885.   WHOLE NO. 1,526.

Garden Crops on the Farm—Farm Gardening

PRINCE IMPERIAL 2d, 6054. Bred by G. S. Burleigh, Mechanicsville, Iowa.

Don't Sell Tops.

A Successful Poultry Keeper.

Try It.

Prince Imperial 2d 6054.

Bred by G. S. Burleigh, Mechanicsville, Iowa. Sire 1d Duke of Manchester 1961 Dam Princess 5 1777. Princess Imperial 2d 6054, won first prize at Chicago, 1851; State Fair; and at Des Moines, (Iowa) State Fair, and first prize and in sweepstakes herd.

Good Roads.

Mind Your Own Business.

Cooking Schools for Farmers' Daughters.

Frozen Apples.

leading part in founding the University of Illinois. He was appalled at the illiteracy on the farms in that day and lack of schools in the state. He used *Prairie Farmer* as a vehicle to bring schools to the people. He also encouraged teaching of mechanics and agriculture at the University of Illinois, rather than the classics in which he had been trained. In the panic of 1856, Wright lost *Prairie Farmer* to his printers. Between 1856 and 1909, the magazine changed hands several times and was published with varying degrees of success. It was then purchased by Burridge D. Butler for about $20,000. Butler looked around for an editor who could help him make the magazine a success.

In 1911, he found Clifford V. Gregory, a 27-year-old graduate of Iowa State College. For the next 26 years he worked with Butler in revitalizing *Prairie Farmer*. In about 20 years it became the outstanding Illinois farm magazine. Butler's basic philosophy was to continually express interest in the common man. Gregory was active in the organization and beginning of the Farm Bureau. He counseled with men like Earl Smith and Ed O'Neal, vice-president and president of the American Farm Bureau Federation, during the depression years when every scheme imaginable was being proposed to help farmers. Gregory started the Master Farmer program which spread throughout the United States. It was devised to honor and build the self-esteem of farmers as important contributors to the economy of the nation.[13]

Another farm publication with a proud heritage going back more than 100 years is *Ohio Farmer* which was founded in 1848 by Thomas Brown of Cleveland. In his first issue, the editor-publisher declared his purpose to "do all we may be able to do for the gratification, enlightenment and advancement" of subscribers. This concern for readers seems to be a common goal running through the minds of those who have guided the destinies of the publications which have survived. John F. Cunningham joined the editorial staff in 1899 and became editor in 1910. He served until 1922 when he purchased the *Wisconsin Agriculturist* and later the *Florida Grower*. In 1932, he left the farm paper field to become dean of the College of Agriculture at The Ohio State University from which post he retired in 1947. Cunningham was succeeded as dean of the College of Agriculture by another former staff member of *Ohio Farmer*, L. L. Rummell, who was field editor for 20 years and then spent several years with the Kroger Company before moving on to become the college dean.

Ever since its early days, *Ohio Farmer* has taken an active interest in agricultural matters. In many it has taken the lead. In the 1880's it helped pioneer the use of the silo and called a silo convention in 1889 attended by 350 farmers. That was the first boost the silo received in the state. *Ohio Farmer* also campaigned for improved highways which were linked closely with the establishment of a rural free delivery mail. It also gave stalwart support in the fight to protect butter from the unfair competition of substitutes. It was also a leader in campaigns to eradicate such livestock diseases as tuberculosis and brucellosis. The publication was the first farm magazine to arrange and conduct vacation tours for readers. It was the first to publish regularly a Farmers' Sermon. George D. Black, former president of Antioch College, was the author for many years and a sermon is still a regular feature under the title of "The Country Parson Ponders."[14] The editorial content of the magazine has changed over the years to keep pace with changing times. More attention is given to public issues of the day which affect the well being of the agricultural community. They include such things as overregulation by government, federal spending which feeds the fires of inflation, environmental demands, and other questions of public policy.

Pennsylvania Farmer has served agricultural interests of that state for more than 95 years. For countless Pennsylvania farmers it has been a source of needed information and also a trusted friend. E. S. Bayard served for 60 years as a member of the editorial staff. He was editor for many of those years. *Pennsylvania Farmer* was a major force in bringing the Pennsylvania Farm Show into being. Bayard, then editor, was chairman of the first Farm Show Committee. In the early days it was a private show, but eventually was taken over by the state. Today, the show draws 600,000 and the Farm Show building houses 100 other events annually. Bayard was also chairman of the board at Penn State during his tenure as editor. In recent years, *Pennsylvania Farmer* editors have been actively involved in legislative matters. They have supported such acts as the Clean and Green and Interim Appointment amendments to the state constitution.[15]

Founded 90 years ago, *Hoard's Dairyman* has had but three editors of whom W. D. Hoard was the first serving until his death in 1918. He was succeeded by A. J. Glover who was editor until his demise in 1949. At that time he was followed by W. D. Knox who is now president of the company. William Dempster Hoard was also

HOARD'S DAIRYMAN.

Weekly Dairy Edition of the JEFFERSON COUNTY UNION, Devoted to Dairying and Dairy Stock Interests.

VOLUME XVI.   FORT ATKINSON, WISCONSIN, MARCH 13, 1885.   NUMBER 2

HOARD'S DAIRYMAN.

W. D. HOARD,

Please Read This.

A NOTABLE GROUP OF HOLSTEINS.

THE FRAUD.

COLORING BUTTER.

THE FARMERS AND THE TIMES.

INDIVIDUAL DIFFERENCES IN DAIRY COWS.

governor of his state. Press comment at the time of his death indicated the high esteem in which he was held. A few quotes follow:

> Soldier, statesman, journalist, educator, farmer — advisedly we give the last word climatic place — William Dempster Hoard served the people and the state with patriotism, ability and high purpose.
>
> Governor W. D. Hoard's work for advancement of agriculture brought him world distinction and recognition, but some of his greatest efforts were made in behalf of better citizenship.
>
> No man living has done more for the farming interests of Wisconsin and America than Governor Hoard, and because of his efforts for many years as a leader, Wisconsin stands first in the nation today as a dairy state.
>
> Governor Hoard was a strong, convincing speaker, possessed an analytical mind and a clear vision of the future needs of agriculture. He wanted his brother farmers to read, to study, and to think, and to master the problems of the farm.[16]

These qualities, possessed in such unusual degree by Governor Hoard, are also to be found in the biographies of other leaders in the farm magazine field. All were endowed with ability to serve in a variety of ways.

A later editor, William D. Knox, has continued the tradition for service. He has been a member of many national boards and commissions. He was founding chairman, secretary, and president of the National Brucellosis Committee. He was appointed by President Kennedy to a bipartisan National Agricultural Advisory Commission in 1961 and served on committees on departmental administration, ASCS investigations, strategic food reserves, and liaison with the Dairy Stabilization Advisory Committee.

American Fruit Grower's family tree was planted in 1880 by Charles A. Green, editor, fruit grower and nurseryman of Rochester, New York. He wrote about his experiences in *Green's Fruit Grower*, later to be called *American Fruit Grower*. Green was so successful that he absorbed other publications and lists of subscribers grew. A new era for *American Fruit Grower* began when E. G. K. Meister took over as editor-publisher. His faith and conviction led the publication through the difficult days of the thirties. He breathed new life into the publication, broadened coverage, and built circulation. Meister took the magazine into the era of scientific fruit production. Fruit growers were coached in use of the new organic insecticides and growth regulator sprays which performed miracles in the orchard.

Leading horticulturists also took part in editorial planning. They included J. H. Gourley, head of the Department of Horticulture at Ohio State University, who was associate editor from 1936 to 1946; and Harold B. Tukey, head of the Horticulture Department at Michigan State University, who was associate editor from 1946 to 1973. To fill the needs of subscribers for in-depth reporting of important subjects Meister developed the "special issue" idea with a whole issue devoted to one subject. These special issues were well received by growers. The "Buyer's Guide" issue, first produced in 1936, is still one of the most popular issues published.[17]

These are only a handful of the nation's great farm magazines. They were not selected as "greatest." They were chosen to represent various geographical areas of the country and illustrate some of the enduring qualities in farm magazine publishing. All have long records of success. It is impossible to measure the full impact of farm magazines upon the development of American agriculture and changing patterns of rural living. The record proves they played a leading role. Turn through old volumes of your favorite farm magazine and you will find a running account of every change. The reading columns recorded history in the making. Every commercial input that "caught on" with farmers was advertised in farm magazines. Thousands of farm magazines have come and gone. Those that survive endure a grueling selection process. There is a new challenge with each new issue. A major slip in judgment or in understanding may be fatal. But challenge and excitement lives on. Opportunities abound as never before. Backed by a proud heritage, farm magazine editors and publishers look with confidence to even greater days ahead.

REFERENCES

1. *The American Agriculturist*, Volume 1, No. 2, published at 36 Park Row, New York City, (April, 1842.)
2. Ibid.
3. Letter to the author from Gordon Conklin, Editor, *American Agriculturist*, dated June 23, 1975.
4. Letter to the author from C. G. Scruggs, vice-president and editorial director of *Progressive Farmer*.
5. Letter to the author from Lane Palmer, Editor, *Farm Journal*, dated July 1, 1975.
6. Letter to the author from Jack T. Pickett, Editor, *California Farmer*, dated June 24, 1975.
7. Sam McKelvie, *Son of The Soil* (Lincoln, Nebraska: Johnson Publishing Company, 1954).

8. Letter to the author from Marvin Russell, Editor, *Nebraska Farmer,* dated July 1, 1975.
9. Letter to the author from George L. Smith, Editor, *Kansas Farmer*, dated June 30, 1975.
10. Letter to the author from Cordell Tindall, Editor of *Missouri Ruralist*, dated July 8, 1975.

11. Letter to the author from Robert G. Rupp, Editor, *The Farmer*, dated July 1, 1975.

12. *A Brief History of Wallaces Farmer* (Des Moines, Iowa: Wallace-Homestead Company).

13. Letter to the author from James C. Thomson, Editor, *Prairie Farmer*, dated June 27, 1975.

14. *The Ohio Farmer*, (January 3, 1948).

15. Letter to the author from Robert H. Williams, Editor, *Pennsylvania Farmer*, dated July 15, 1975.

16. George William Rankin, *William Dempster Hoard* ([Wisconsin]: W. D. Hoard and Sons Co., [1925])

17 Letter to the author from Richard T. Meister, Editor, *American Fruit Grower*, dated June 30, 1975.

Agricultural People

By
John J. McKelvey, Jr.

My topic, "Agricultural People" has enormous scope because it defines agricultural literature. Without agricultural people there would be no agriculture; no agricultural literature. For today's purposes, I will consider agricultural people to include — in addition to farmers, dairymen, and others who work directly in agricultural pursuits — all those who care enough about agriculture to do something about it, those who write about it, and those who from other walks of life work with agriculturists to help to create agricultural literature. First, I want to tell you about some of those people of the past who have imparted agricultural knowledge to me through literature, then about people of the present whom I have come to know personally.

Agricultural people cropped up everywhere among the men and women who lived long ago when I searched for information about the tsetse fly of Africa which transmits sleeping sickness to people and a similar disease, nagana or trypanosomiasis, to cattle. Doctor-explorers, a woman entrepreneur, missionaries, scientists, environmentalists, writers, and poets figured among them. What did they do? Why? How did their experiences relate to my agricultural interests?

Dr. McKelvey, Jr., is Associate Director, the Rockefeller Foundation, New York, New York.

Mungo Park, for example, a doctor-explorer who in 1792 sustained incredible hardships as he traversed the area we now know as the Sahel from west to east looking for the mouth of the Niger River, knew little, if anything, about agriculture *per se*. He was simply a poorly paid man with a wanderlust doing what he was asked to do by the Royal Geographical Society. He picked his way by horseback and by foot across the region where Peace Corps members and USAID workers have gone so easily in the last few years by jeep and by plane to help the 25 million inhabitants who live there cope with a seven-years drought.

But, for me at least, Mungo Park, who drowned when his canoe was upset on the Niger River, became an agricultural person. He pressed on with the explorer's drive to meet his objectives even when it meant giving away his saddle, his horse, the brass buttons off of his coat as peace offerings to the tribal chieftains of the area to assure himself a welcome from one village to the next. Mungo Park imparted to me an agricultural curiosity about the Sahel, its aridity, its insect population, and the crops grown there. In his diary, he reported mosquito populations so intense that he had to sleep through the daytime when the mosquitoes were not out and to walk through the night when they were, for, by walking he could keep ahead of them. He gave me a new slant on slavery, that invidious agricultural "institution" that followed the sugar cane and cotton planting cultures to the New World. But he did not answer my most urgent question — whether or not he encountered the dreaded tsetse fly — nor did he write of riverblindness which is transmitted by black flies, nor of the debilitating disease common in the area today, schistosomiasis — all of which influence agriculture and the agricultural productivity of the people of Africa.

In my search through the available literature for information on who brought sleeping sickness to Prince's Island on the west coast of Africa near Gabon, I fell madly in love with a young Portuguese woman, Dona Maria Correia, who owned virtually the whole of that tropical island, lived on it, and managed her extensive sugar cane and cacao plantations there. I spent two years tracking her down to find out why she lived there in days, the early eighteen hundreds, when women rarely went of their own accord to tropical isles, much less owned them, and I conjured up all sorts of fanciful dreams about her which I hoped would come true. Alas, bits and pieces of gossip and hearsay, from the literature and from personal communication with my friends in Portugal, dashed it all. She turned out to be an unsavory woman who dealt in slaves and in other evil business. To push my inquiry further would have taken me out of agricultural literature and her away from being an agricultural person.

David Livingstone, the missionary doctor, told me much more than of the hardships he endured in travelling through the southern part of Africa, when he lost his beasts of burden — when tsetse flies bit his oxen and they died of nagana. He also told of his efforts to introduce cotton as an economic crop to that part of Africa. David Bruce, an army doctor, in working out the association of the fly with the disease organisms it carried — trypanosomes — paved the way for others to control them and to open up areas of the continent previously closed to cattle production.

And Charles Swynnerton, a farmer-naturalist, through his actions and writings, demonstrated all too clearly that one can overdo it in trying to manipulate an environment to control an insect. He taught us a lesson we would do well to remember in our day when we work so hard to devise measures of insect control alternative to the use of pesticides.

With his vivid prose, the writer Joseph Conrad also became involved as an agricultural person; in *Heart of Darkness* he describes men dying from sleeping sickness.

My search for information brought me to the writings of the African poet, Archibald Campbell Jordan, a Zulu from South Africa, whose poetry conveys the earthy, agricultural imagery of Zululand.

These and many others whose interests were not strictly agricultural helped me to understand what impeded or advanced agricultural development in Africa.

Surely each of us has his favorite literary companions who also are agricultural people for the ideas they express and the agricultural settings they use. Robert Burns can take me to a field to plow and make me enjoy it (figuratively). Similarly, a walk through a cow pasture gives me more pleasure than I would derive from it otherwise because of Robert Frost's poem "You Come Too." For me Walter D. Edmond's *Drums along the Mohawk* is primarily an agricultural novel, dealing as it does with the vagaries of getting started in farming in upstate New York during the Revolutionary War years. *Anna Karenina*, after all, is an excellent treatise on the agricultural stresses in Russia during the mid-nineteenth century.

We may widen our circle of agricultural people as we please; our concept of agricultural literature correspondingly will diffuse into that of the literature of everyday life. The cartoonist has an impor-

215

tant message for us when he depicts two insects discussing their respective stations in life — one saying to the other "I am an insect, you are a pest." He tells us to consider what *is* an insect pest in the first place. The salesmen and the sign painters of rural America have fixed in our minds indelibly Mail Pouch Tobacco and Lydia Pinkham's compound, the former an agricultural product and the latter derived from agricultural products, not in books but just as effectively on weathered barn siding. A coiner of place names in a word or two can characterize a region or a condition for us as dramatically as can an author who chooses a title for his book. A farmer who had many daughters but no sons lived where the Delaware Lackawanna Railroad crossed a farm road in central New York a generation ago and that place still carries the name Petticoat Junction, and with it the image of young suitors congregated at that junction.

Farmers themselves display a great span of talent and capability in reporting their thoughts and actions in the trade journals. Consider the challenge they present to the editors of those journals to assist these men and women in recognizing and developing such skills.

Given the breadth and the depth of agricultural literature stemming from people, just people, its quality and worth, we must also remember the vital sector of that literature which we owe to those keen observant professionals who devote their lives to soil improvement, insect and plant disease control, raising the yields of our plant and animal stocks to supply adequate amounts of food to meet our needs.

A number of the agricultural people I know best personally built their agricultural careers as members of the Rockefeller Foundation's Mexican Agricultural Program. Constraints to food crop production were particularly acute in Mexico, birthplace of the Green Revolution in the early 1940's; the Mexican government had requested that the Rockefeller Foundation initiate a program to assist Mexico to increase its production of basic food crops — beans, corn, and wheat. I shall draw your attention to six members of that group; they and their colleagues generated the wave of agricultural literature about the Revolution which we read today.

J. George Harrar, a plant pathologist, co-author of *Guide to Southern Trees* and *Principles of Plant Pathology,* and the Foundation's Field Director for Agriculture, at that time, recruited the staff and gave the program scientific direction. He had remarkable administrative and executive capacity. We had a minimum of bureauc-

216

racy, no individual program budgets, but all the flexibility and freedom we needed to get on with our respective jobs. One could always depend on his help if one was in trouble. When recruiting staff for a foreign post, he always insisted on interviewing the wives as well as the men to make certain both would be happy and could work effectively in a foreign country.

E. J. Wellhausen, trained at Iowa and West Virginia State Universities, our plant breeder, was in charge of the corn improvement work. He had an easy going, philosophical, but determined turn of mind. Well trained in agronomy, he was the one among us best equipped to take care of the experiment station and did so. Somehow, it usually turned out that the best land on the grounds was planted to his experiments. When we became concerned that we were long on effort, short on accomplishment, Wellhausen used to remark, "If among my Mexican students I can turn out one good plant breeder each year, think what I will have achieved in ten years." And this is to say nothing of the actual research leading to greatly improved varieties of corn.

Dorothy Parker, trained as a botanist and one of the original "persistant pioneers," as E. C. Stakman termed the first comers to the program in his *Campaigns Against Hunger,* built the working library. Sandwiches from home and Coca-Cola in the librarian's office constituted our daily noontime fare if we were in town, a time and a place to exchange points of view. Stak, as everyone calls him, then and now, was and is the elder statesman of the group.

Norman Borlaug, who was graduated from the University of Minnesota as a forester, joined the Mexican Program as a plant pathologist, but he soon became a wheat breeder in response to the need to develop wheat varieties resistant to their diseases. An indefatigable worker, he was always in the field, rarely at home. Good students gravitated to his program; he knew them well, inspired them, and rarely was he wrong in his evaluations of the people he knew when he recommended them to others.

Robert Chandler, who co-authored the book, *Forest Soils,* took charge of the soils program. An inveterate mountaineer, he climbed the two snowcapped mountains, Ixtacihautl and Popocatepetl, near Mexico City several times. He demonstrated similar physical drive and stamina in setting out field experiments throughout Mexico.

One of the first buildings on our experimental grounds was the insectary at Chapingo, our field station—the only screened building on the experiment station grounds. It became the luncheon counter

217

and the meeting place for visiting dignitaries who came to the station — Nelson Rockefeller, John D. Rockefeller III, W. I. Myers, then Dean of the College of Agriculture of Cornell University.

Over the years the group dispersed. Harrar became President and subsequently President-Emeritus of the Rockefeller Foundation. Dr. Wellhausen became Director of the International Corn and Wheat Improvement Center in Mexico and now serves as a consultant in agriculture to the World Bank. Borlaug is Director of the Wheat Improvement Program of the Center; as we all know he received the Nobel Prize for his work on high yielding dwarf wheats. Robert Chandler went on to head up the International Rice Research Institute, in the Philippines, then the Asian Vegetable Research and Development Center, in Taiwan, and now serves as consultant for the West African Rice Development Association on problems of rice production in Africa. Parker, as an Associate Director in New York, became the Foundation's expert in librarianship. Now emeritus, she travels widely and consults on matters that concern agricultural libraries.

The men and women who started the Green Revolution continue to devote their energies to ways and means of easing the lot of the world's agricultural people. Does the wealth of agricultural literature, which stems from their efforts and those of their colleagues reach the most important agricultural person, the farmer? Can the farmer separate fact from fiction?

The farmers, whom these people have been trying to help, have themselves been extremely hard working too. For example, my Uncle Ethan, an Ohio farmer, never had time to read the daily newspaper during the summer months. But he carefully stacked the papers away chronologically and, come winter time, started at the beginning to read those papers in order one by one. He would have scorned the "hop, skip and jump" method some readers use today to scan a book, the bane of any writer who tries to make every word he sets on paper count. And he could have exasperated any newspaper reporter bent on a scoop. But he got his reading done.

We may hope that the force of the Green Revolution, in carrying the farmer way beyond the present exigencies he faces in earning a living, will expand his opportunities to read and to write and thus to become better acquainted with agricultural literature and with agricultural people for both business and for pleasure.

218

The History of Agricultural Libraries in the United States

By
J. Richard Blanchard

THE ORIGINS

As one would expect, the history of agricultural libraries parallels the development of agricultural literature and the advance of agricultural techniques. Cuneiform inscriptions concerning agricultural matters have been found on the clay tablets assembled in Babylonian libraries. The great library of Alexandria undoubtedly had many treatises on agriculture inscribed on papyrus. Writing on agriculture was a Roman tradition fostered by Cato, Vergil, Varro, Columnella, and others. This literature was kept in private collections as well as in large public libraries in Rome and other great cities of the Empire. Monks transferred much of the classical literature on agriculture to vellum during the Middle Ages and protected it in closely guarded libraries where books were often chained for better protection.

The introduction of paper from China and the invention of printing with moveable type in the 15th century permitted a great expansion in literature with a resulting growth of libraries which were, however, usually regarded as museums for the exclusive use of the small number of educated elite rather than as service agencies

Dr. Blanchard is Librarian Emeritus, University of California, Davis, California.

which would further the extension of public education. Specialized agricultural libraries hardly existed until the 18th century when agricultural techniques were greatly improved through the stimulus provided by the period of the Enlightenment and the Industrial Revolution in Western Europe. The formation of scientific societies and academies interested in agriculture reflected the fervid interest in all aspects of science. The Academia Economico-Agraria dei Georgifili, founded in Florence, Italy, in 1753, established one of the earliest modern agricultural libraries. Another early agricultural library, still flourishing, was started in 1761 by the Academie d'Agriculture of France. Other libraries were started in the late 18th century by the Royal Hanoverian Agricultural Society in Germany (between 1765 and 1770), the Highlands and Agricultural Society of Scotland (1784), and the Royal Veterinary and Agricultural College of Copenhagen (1783).[1]

Men such as Arthur Young and Coke of England and the physiocrats of France who wrote of the need to improve agriculture, often with much literary flair, usually had excellent private libraries. Arthur Young stated that during one of his journeys on horseback through France, he found at least one gentleman of culture who had nearly as good a library on agriculture as his own.[2]

Early Development in the United States

These trends in Europe were also evident in the United States and the first agricultural libraries were established by agricultural societies shortly after the end of the Revolutionary War. The societies assembled and published papers and other publications on agriculture and exchanged them for similar publications issued by other organizations in this country and abroad, thus forming the basis for collections which eventually became the first publicly available agricultural libraries in the new nation. They also made plans for systems of agricultural libraries. For instance, the Philadelphia Society for the Promotion of Agriculture, established in 1785 with Washington and Franklin as members, in 1794 proposed the founding of libraries throughout Pennsylvania in connection with a new statewide agricultural society. Country schoolmasters were to be secretaries of the various branches and libraries were to be founded in the schoolhouses. The New York Society for the Promotion of Agriculture proposed a similar plan. Neither came to fruition although small libraries were maintained at headquarters in both Philadelphia and New York. The Massachusetts Society for Promoting Agriculture also started a collection in 1797. These libraries were apparently small, probably having no more than 50 to 100 volumes, and contained a few books by European authorities, some classical literature, pamphlets, and papers. A survey of the library of the Massachusetts Society indicated that as late as 1815 it had only 125 volumes. Agricultural books were also to be found in the small college libraries. The Harvard College library catalog of 1790 lists only about 18 books specifically on agriculture, but there were undoubtedly many others in the 12,000 volume library of the time dealing with botany, chemistry, and other subjects related to agriculture. One must also remember that very few printed books were then available on the subject of agriculture, for the bulk of printed literature was largely concerned with theology, law, and the classical languages.[3]

In considering early libraries in the United States, one should not forget the private libraries, particularly those of Washington and Jefferson. Washington's library of about 900 volumes had over 50 titles on agriculture.[4] Millicent Sowerby's catalog of Thomas Jefferson's library[5] lists 133 titles in the agriculture section. These books, many of which were presentation copies, were sold by Jefferson in 1815 to Congress for its library which had been devastated by fire in 1814. Jefferson also made lists of agricultural works which he recommended to friends as required readings. The list which he sent to George W. Jeffreys in 1817, for instance, contained 54 titles including the usual classical writers, a few books from Italy and France, and the remainder from England and America. It included the *Memoirs* of the Philadelphia Society for Promoting Agriculture and the *Transactions* of the New York Society. He lists four books by Young, but does not include his *Annals of Agriculture* which Jefferson stated was written merely for monetary purposes and was scarcely worth buying.[6] Jefferson's general interest in libraries was expressed in a letter to John Wyche in 1809 in which he wrote: ". . . nothing would do more extensive good at small expense than the establishment of a small circulating library in every county, to consist of a few well-chosen books, to be lent to the people of the county . . . ".[7]

The Massachusetts and Pennsylvania Horticultural Societies, formed in 1829 and 1827 respectively, established libraries. The most notable was the library of the Massachusetts Horticultural Society which had grown to 10,000 volumes by July of 1899 and which included one of the most complete collections of botanical works available in the United States. The New York Agricultural Society founded in 1832 had 2,097 volumes by 1857 including 76

Library of the Department of Agriculture (east half shown), Plate XL from *Yearbook U. S. Department of Agriculture*, published in 1899. (Courtesy, National Agricultural Library, General Collection)

Library Staff, 1912. (Courtesy, National Agricultural Library, Archives Collection)

agricultural journals of which 18 were received from abroad. In addition, libraries were started by the boards of agriculture of Massachusetts and Illinois in the middle of the 19th century. Public libraries were established as the century wore on, the largest ones located in Boston, New York, Philadelphia, and Chicago. Some of them had useful collections on agriculture.

The most significant events in the history of agricultural libraries in the United States occurred in 1862 with the passage of the Federal Land Grant Act (the Morrill Act), the establishment of the U. S. Department of Agriculture Library, and the transfer to it of the books collected by the agricultural section of the Patent Office. Although growth was quite slow in the early 1800's, some strong collections and specialized libraries in agriculture had been developed by the end of the century, inclusive of the U. S. Department of Agriculture Library as well as those at state colleges and universities which were mostly started between 1850 and 1900. Greathouse's survey of agricultural libraries which was published in 1899[8] listed 80 libraries, the majority of which belonged to state universities and colleges but also included libraries of societies, state boards, and experiment stations separate from the state academic institutions. U. S. governmental libraries were not included in the survey, although in 1899 the U.S. Department of Agriculture Library had 68,000 volumes and the Library of Congress had 10,000 volumes related to agriculture. The largest collections specifically relating to agriculture listed by Greathouse were housed at Cornell University (15,000 volumes), Rutgers College (12,855 volumes), the Massachusetts Historical Society (10,000 volumes), and the Michigan State Agricultural College (9,000 volumes). Many of the newer institutions, particularly some of those in the West, still had pathetically small collections of 100 volumes or less. Nevertheless, by the end of the 19th century, a very respectable development had occurred and the stage was set for the rapid growth of both great research libraries and networks of libraries in the following century.

Later Development

As agricultural education was extended and scientific research in the field of agriculture broadened, there was a natural increase in the literature which usually fell into one of three broad categories: trade publications (usually agricultural papers and journals for the farmer and agricultural industry); extension type publications distributed by experiment stations and extension services for the use of the farmer and the agents who work with him; and, most important of all, the research literature published in journals, experiment station bulletins and, occasionally in books. The number of publications in all of these fields grew rapidly after 1900, but the quantity in some of the related subject areas such as chemistry literally exploded after World War II. Naturally this rapid development of literature had a profound effect upon both the growth and the proliferation of libraries. For instance, an international survey of agricultural libraries conducted in 1934/35 by S. von Frauendorfer, Librarian of the International Institute of Agriculture, listed a total of 944 libraries. The United States, with 125, had the largest number of any country, an increase of 48 since the Greathouse survey was conducted in 1899.[9] According to an international directory published in 1960,[10] agricultural libraries had increased to 2,531 by 1959 of that number, 215 were in the United States.

TYPES OF AGRICULTURAL LIBRARIES

The majority of agricultural libraries in the United States and elsewhere can be divided into four categories: those associated with governmental agencies such as the United States Department of Agriculture or state departments of agriculture; those serving agricultural colleges and/or experiment stations; those serving scientific societies; and document centers or special libraries, designed to support the research work of industrial firms or privately supported research agencies. In addition, there are a few libraries serving international organizations. It may be useful to discuss briefly the development in each of these categories with special attention given to certain key or representative libraries.

GOVERNMENT LIBRARIES

The history of the National Agricultural Library, one of the great research libraries of the world, has been well covered in a series of scholarly studies.[11-15] To capitulate: The U.S. Department of Agriculture Library, founded in 1862, was based on a nucleus of 1,000 volumes transferred from the Agricultural Division of the Patent Office which was created in 1839. By 1871 the library had 8,000 volumes and by 1898 it was considered the most complete agricultural library in the world. It now has over 1,500,000 volumes. During the period of 1893 to 1939 and under the guidance of William Parker Cutter, Josephine A. Clark, and Claribel Barnett, the library developed from a small organization largely serving the U.S. Department of Agriculture to a national institution providing loans of material and reference services to libraries and research

225

workers throughout the country, particularly those in the land-grant colleges. Close relations were established with the Library of Congress and the National Library of Medicine in connection with the production of catalog cards and the avoidance of unnecessary duplication. The Copyright Office of the Library of Congress automatically sent one copy of each book received on agriculture to the U.S. Department of Agriculture Library for deposit. An international system of exchange plus gifts and purchases made possible the development of strong collections, notable examples being apiculture and horticultural trade catalog collections. Excellent collections were also developed in chemistry, botany, economics, and microbiology. In 1934, at the request of the American Documentation Institute, the Library became the first experimental center for supplying microfilm and photocopies of material on a large scale to scientific workers. This service has been continued and extended. Extensive bibliographic services were provided by various staff members of the main library and the bureau libraries. Notable examples are the *Plant Science Catalog* developed by Alice C. Atwood and the *Index . . . to the Literature of American Economic Entomology* by Mabel Colcord. Numerous special bibliographies were prepared by such meticulous bibliographers as Mary Goodwin Lacey and Louise O. Bercaw. An extensive system of field libraries, consisting at one time of ten branches and 11 sub-branches, was set up to serve U.S. Department of Agriculture workers in the various regions.

Major advances were also made during the tenure of Ralph R. Shaw, Librarian from 1940 to 1954. Before 1942, library services were provided by the main library and a system of bureau libraries. There was some coordination but a lack of strong centralized direction of the library services. In 1942, on the order of President Roosevelt and the Secretary of Agriculture, the library system was completely centralized under the Librarian of the U.S. Department of Agriculture; all bureau collections were shifted to the main library. Another major step initiated in 1942 was the publication of the *Bibliography of Agriculture,* the world's most comprehensive indexing service for agriculture.

From 1954 to date, under librarians Foster Mohrhardt, John Sherrod and Richard Farley, NAL has continued to make advances. Officially designated the National Agricultural Library on its centennial birthday in 1962, it moved from horribly cramped quarters to a splendid new building in Beltsville. Among its publications have been the *Dictionary Catalog of the National Agricultural Library,*

Secretary of Agriculture Orville L. Freeman, left, with Foster E. Mohrhardt, marks the 100th anniversary of the U. S. Department of Agriculture's Library, March 23, 1962, by signing papers designating it as the National Agricultural Library. (Courtesy, National Agricultural Library, Archives Collection)

1862–1965 and its supplement, the *National Agricultural Library Catalog*. The Library's enormous indexing output was put into machine readable form and made available to the scientific community.

Throughout its history NAL has participated and led the way in national and international cooperative efforts. Of special note has been the effort to establish a national agricultural library network consisting largely of input from NAL and land-grant college libraries. A beginning was made in 1950 through a contract with the University of Nebraska library providing for the provision of library services to agricultural workers in that region. Comparable contracts were signed in 1953 with the University of Rhode Island, the Florida Experiment Station, Oklahoma A & M College, and the University of California at Davis. These proved successful, particularly since most of the field libraries had been closed because of restricted funds. In spite of strong urgings by a committee of land-grant college librarians[16] to continue this system, the contracts were terminated, due largely to the inadequate funding provided by Secretary Ezra Taft Benson's administration. Plans for a national network were resurrected as a result of both Project ABLE[17] and a study conducted by EDUCOM.[18] Cooperative services, therefore, are once again available through contracts with land-grant colleges in various regions of the country. Cooperative projects involving online service for CAIN, and intensive regional collecting of agricultural literature have also been undertaken with the land-grant college libraries in recent years.[19–20] Staff members of NAL have long been active in the Agricultural and Biological Sciences Section of the Association of College and Research Libraries resulting in a continuing coordination which prevents unnecessary overlapping of collections and strengthens services throughout the country.

NAL has also been active and influential in international cooperative efforts for many years. Before World War II it worked with Dr. S. von Frauendorfer of the International Institute of Agriculture to sponsor an international meeting of agricultural librarians in 1935.[21] In 1955 Foster Mohrhardt assisted in the formation of the International Association of Agricultural Librarians and Documentalists in Brussels. In addition, NAL is assisting FAO in the development of the International Information System for Agricultural Libraries and Technology (AGRIS) which began in March 1973.[22] This current awareness service will include input from NAL's *Bibliography of Agriculture* plus the world's other major agricultural indexing services. The resulting publication entitled *AGRINDEX* has already been issued.

Another recent and promising experiment in the field of agricultural documentation is called AGLINET (Agricultural Libraries Network).[23] AGLINET's international center is located in FAO's David Lubin Memorial Library in Rome. Regional centers include NAL, the Ministry of Agriculture, Fisheries and Food Library in London, the International Institute of Tropical Agriculture in Ibadan, Nigeria, and the Centro Tropical in Cali, Colombia. It is hoped that AGLINET will promote efficient and effective delivery of library materials through a network of regional centers.

Other government libraries of importance to agriculture include the National Library of Medicine, particularly valuable for its veterinary medicine collection, and the Library of Congress for its national cataloging efforts and magnificent general collection. Special collections of importance are also available in such libraries as those at the U.S. Geological Survey and the Bureau of Standards.

LAND GRANT COLLEGE LIBRARIES

Agricultural colleges were a natural outgrowth of the educational work attempted by the agricultural societies. A few schools were started with state aid in New York, Maine, Connecticut, and Massachusetts. Soon, not only did a few private schools join in the effort but also agricultural courses began to be established in existing college curricula.[24] It was not until 1857, however, that the first official state agricultural college was started in Michigan. In the same year, Congressman Justin S. Morrill introduced his first bill for federal assistance to agricultural education. Although his initial bill failed, it was finally passed in 1862. By the end of the century, land-grant colleges were spread across the country and all of them had libraries varying in both size and quality of materials. In some institutions such as Cornell University and the University of Minnesota, the agricultural collections were kept in separate libraries near both the agricultural academic departments and the experiment station headquarters. In others, such as Iowa State College at Ames, they were maintained in the main library.

The few histories of individual land-grant college libraries which exist show a generally uniform pattern of development.[25-27] In the East, they were often based on collections formerly owned by societies. For instance, in New Jersey, books formerly belonging to the Agricultural Society of New Brunswick which existed in the early 19th century, were passed on to student literary and debating societies and a few of these books eventually ended up in the possession of Rutgers College.

In the early years, libraries were usually located in a classroom and often consisted of only a few bulletins and a handful of books with a professor usually acting as librarian in his spare time. Not only were hours of service very limited but also funds available were pitifully small, usually well under $1,000 a year. Much material was received on deposit or exchange from the U.S. Government, other state institutions, and foreign organizations. Many of the collections included personal libraries donated by dedicated faculty members.

At first, the permanent staff who took over from the part-time professors were non-professionals with varying degrees of education and capabilities. In the early 1900's, as library schools gradually developed, a greater number of trained personnel were employed, thus permitting more consistent and intelligent use of cataloging and classification systems. As a result, collections became better organized and reference and interlibrary loan services were established. At some institutions, according to a questionnaire sent out in 1947, 25 out of 40 departmental libraries were developed and maintained.[28] As noted earlier, a few universities had separate agricultural libraries, sometimes under the direction of a dean. Such branch and departmental libraries still exist, although the trend, in recent years, has been to centralize library services under a library director and to inhibit the development of branch collections.

In the early period, most instruction in the land-grant colleges was handled by the lecture and textbook method which required little use of the library — a method adhered to even to this day by some professors. In general, however, professors now encourage students to read widely in order to broaden their horizons. This movement is reflected in the efforts of John W. Crist of Michigan State College who, in the 1930's, prepared a list of general recommended readings for graduate students in the agricultural sciences. Alarmed about the limited and narrow knowledge of students, he wrote: "They revealed that they have read too little, too narrowly, too superficially, too dependently, too much as a means to the ends of class grades and the attainment of various kinds of practical and professional ability."[29] Such students still exist in the 1970's but the parochial attitude towards knowledge has largely changed and as a result, land-grant libraries are now used more extensively by students and the library itself has become a more important educational instrument.

Greatly accelerated research as well as a vast increase in literature have also stimulated library development. Students and professors demand large collections, not only in agricultural specialities, but also in the broader fields of the natural and social sciences. Generally, land-grant university libraries now have collections numbering into the millions of volumes. Even more specialized college branch libraries specifically tailored for agriculture, such as the Albert R. Mann Library at Cornell University, have hundreds of thousands of volumes.

EXPERIMENT STATION LIBRARIES

Probably the first experiment station was established in Alsace in 1834 by Jean Baptiste Boussingault. The oldest experiment station still in use is at Rothamsted, England and was also started in 1834. In Germany, the first station was started in 1851. The Hatch Act of 1887 gave great emphasis to the experiment station movement in the United States, although a few stations—Connecticut, North Carolina, New Jersey, New York, Ohio, Massachusetts—were established before 1887.[30]

Today, the majority of agricultural experiment stations are located at or near the campuses of the land-grant universities which they serve. A few, however, such as those in Ohio, Connecticut, and New York are situated quite apart from the main campuses. All experiment stations at separate locations have established libraries. Stations located at land-grant university campuses usually depend upon the main library or the agricultural college branch library although there may be a small branch specifically for experiment station staff. According to a survey made in 1932, 25 agricultural experiment station libraries on college campuses were housed separately from the main library—two were in the main library but shelved separately and 16 were assimilated into the main library collection.[31] At that time, the college librarian's authority extended over 29 station libraries, but not over 14. In most cases some financial support was provided for library service by the experiment station director. If a survey were to be made at the present time, however, it would probably indicate an increase in centralization with much more service being provided exclusively by the main library or one of its branches. This change was partly initiated no doubt by a study of land-grant college and university libraries which was made in 1931; this study strongly criticized the quality and fragmentation of library service and recommended increased centralization.[32]

231

Historical studies have been prepared for the three aforementioned agricultural experiment station libraries[33-35] which are housed separately from their central libraries. The Connecticut Agricultural Experiment Station was established in 1875 and was the first of its kind in the country. Samuel W. Johnson of Yale, who had studied under Liebig in Germany, was principally responsible for its establishment and the station's library was based initially upon his collection in the field of chemistry. The agricultural experiment station library at Geneva, founded in 1882, also was much indebted to private collections and received many valuable books from two of the directors who were noted scientists — E. Lewis Sturtevant and Ulysses Prentice Hedrick. Developmental problems for the station libraries in the early days were comparable to those faced by the college libraries: the staffs in each case usually either lacked training or were part-time; the funds with which they had to operate were very meager; physical facilities were inadequate. The urge, to develop separate departmental libraries in Connecticut and Ohio also caused fragmentation of materials. In any case, these difficulties were largely overcome and these separate experiment station libraries having good but basic collections now collaborate not only with libraries at the academic institutions but also with NAL to provide improved service.

OTHER LIBRARIES

Some of the society libraries mentioned earlier still exist. For instance, the Massachusetts Horticultural Society Library and the Pennsylvania Horticultural Society Library, founded in 1829 and 1827 respectively, continue to thrive. The agricultural society collections, however, seem to have been generally dispersed to colleges and other institutions. Many libraries also serve industrial concerns, institutes, and laboratories such as the American Meat Institution Foundation Library in Chicago, the John Deere Company Library in Moline, Illinois, the Central Research Library of the General Foods Corporation in Hoboken, New Jersey, and the Boyce Thompson Institute for Plant Research, Inc. Library in Yonkers, New York. As far as can be determined, all libraries of this type were started after World War I. A fairly recent movement has been the development of documentation centers for laboratories and industries. Although basically functioning as libraries, they also are capable of providing more extensive services, such as translations, surveys of the literature and automated data collection. However, many of the older libraries initially based on more conventional patterns, such as NAL, are also attempting to provide this type of service.

Rural library service for farmers was first proposed shortly after the Revolution by both the Philadelphia and New York Societies for the Promotion of Agriculture although nothing was done at that time. Late in the 19th century, however, farmers' reading clubs which distributed books were started in Pennsylvania, New York, Connecticut, Michigan, and other states. The traveling library movement started in 1892 by Melvil Dewey, Librarian of the New York State Library at Albany, was a boon to farm families and the idea spread rapidly to other states. In Illinois, the traveling libraries were an adjunct to farmers' institutes. Libraries were also started by some of the granges.[36] As late as 1938, it was reported that home demonstration clubs in North Carolina were providing book stations where rural people could obtain a large variety of reading material.[37] Library service for rural people is now being handled in most states by county libraries working in connection with state libraries. The books provided, which are usually more general than agricultural in nature, are distributed through bookmobiles or placed in small deposit or branch collections.

Summary

Library service for agriculture in this country has developed from very small collections serving the literate elite in the 18th century to a network of large libraries in the 20th century which use modern technology for the organization and dissemination of information and which serve all classes of individuals from the farm child to the most sophisticated scientist. The future will no doubt see further advances and change through the use of data processing machinery, the transmittal of information by satellite and other means, and the storage of information in forms other than the book. Because agriculture must draw knowledge from all disciplines, libraries serving agriculture must continue to develop more comprehensive and general collections.

REFERENCES

1. Sigmund von Frauendorfer, "Agricultural Libraries," *International Review of Agriculture,* 31 (August 1940): 255–264.
2. Norman Scott Brien Gras, *A History of Agriculture in Europe and America* (New York: F. S. Crofts & Co., 1940), p. 245.
3. Charles H. Greathouse, "Development of Agricultural Libraries," *U.S. Department of Agriculture Yearbook* (1899): 491–512.
4. *Catalogue of the Washington Collection in the Boston Athenaeum,* compiled and annotated by P. C. Griffin (1897).

5. U.S. Library of Congress, *Catalogue of the Library of Thomas Jefferson,* compiled with annotations by E. Millicent Sowerby (Washington, D.C.: Library of Congress, 1952), vols. 1–5.

6. Jefferson to George W. Jeffreys, from Monticello, March 3, 1817 in *American Farmer* 2 (1820): 93–94 as quoted in Everett E. Edwards, *Jefferson and Agriculture.* U.S. Bureau of Agricultural Economics, Agricultural History Series, No. 7 (1943): 79–80.

7. Jefferson to John Wyche, from Monticello, May 19, 1809, as quoted in Edwards, *ibid.,* pp. 7, 8.

8. Greathouse, *ibid.,* pp. 757–8.

9. Frauendorfer, *ibid.*

10. D. H. Boalch, ed., *World Directory of Agricultural Libraries and Documentation Centers* (Harpenden, Herts.: International Association of Agricultural Libraries and Documentalists, 1960).

11. Foster E. Mohrhardt, "The Library of the United States Department of Agriculture," *Library Quarterly* 27 (April 1957): 61–82.

12. Ralph R. Shaw, "Distinguished Agricultural Librarians," *College and Research Libraries* 4 (June 1973): 239–244

13. Shaw, Ibid., "The Department of Agriculture Library and Its Services," *College and Research Libraries* 9 (April 1948): 133–135.

14. Angelina J. Carabelli, ed., "Centennary of the National Agricultural Library, U.S.D.A. 1862–1962. Papers in Celebration of the Occasion," *Quarterly Bulletin of the International Association of Agricultural Librarians and Documentalists* 7 (1962): 97–137.

15. Mildred B. Buhler, "Field Library Services of the US Department of Agriculture Library," *College and Research Libraries* 4 (December 1942): 35–40

16. Association of College and Research Libraries, Agricultural Libraries Section, *Report on the Policies and Programs of the United States Department of Agriculture Library* (1951).

17. U.S. Department of Agriculture. Task Force ABLE, *Agricultural-Biological Literature Exploitation: A Systems Study of the National Agricultural Library and its Users* (Washington, D.C.:U.S. National Agricultural Library, 1965).

18. *EDUCOM. Agricultural Sciences Information Network Development Plan,* EDUCOM Research Report 169 (Boston, 1969).

19. Kirby Payne, "Agricultural Library Network," *Library Journal* 88 (November 1, 1963): 4143–4148.

20. Foster E. Mohrhardt and Blanche L. Oliveri, "A National Network of Biological-Agricultural Libraries," *College and Research Libraries* 28 (January 1967): 9–16.

21. Sigmund von Frauendorfer, "International Collaboration of the Agricultural Libraries of Different Countries," *Agricultural Library Notes* 10 (August 1935): 344–347.

22. G. DuBois, "Un Système Internationale d'Information pour les Sciences et la Technologie Agricoles (AGRIS)," *Quarterly Bulletin of the International Association of Agricultural Librarians and Documentalists* 17 (1972): 55–64.

23. "AGLINET News – 1," *Quarterly Bulletin of the International Association of Agricultural Librarians and Documentalists* 19 (1974): 116–120.

24. Evangeline Thurber, "American Agricultural College Libraries," *College and Research Libraries* 6 (September 1945): 346–352.

25. J. G. Lipman, "Library of the College of Agriculture," *Rutgers University Library Journal* 2 (December 1938): 11–13

26. S. C. Currell, "Aspects of Organization of a Library for the Agricultural College and the Experiment Station," *American Library Association Bulletin* 34 (August 1940): 51–54.

27. W. R. Collings, "College of Agriculture Library at the University of Nebraska," *Mountain Plains Library Quarterly,* 8 (Winter 1964): 7–10.

28. Stephen A. McCarthy, "Administrative Organization and Financial Support of Land Grant College and University Libraries," *College and Research Libraries,* 9 (October 1948): 327–331.

29. John W. Crist, "Readings for Graduate Students in Agricultural Science," *Agricultural Library Notes* 8 (November 1933): 143–155.

234

30. Alfred Charles True, *A History of Agricultural Experimentation and Research in the United States, 1607–1925,* U.S. Department of Agriculture, Miscellaneous Publication 251 (Washington, 1937).

31. J. E. Towne, "Books, Their Deposition and Administrative Control in State Agricultural Experiment Stations," *Agricultural Library Notes* 8 (November 1933): 138–142.

32. George A. Works, "The Survey of the Land Grant College and University Libraries," *Agricultural Library Notes,* 6 (December, 1931): 175–179 (address given at the convention of the Association of Land Grant Colleges and Universities, Chicago, November 17, 1931).

33. Ruth H. Giandonato, "An Agricultural Research Library," *Special Libraries* 36 (April 1947): 111–113.

34. Norma North, "O.A.E.S.L., A History of the Library of the Ohio Agricultural Experiment Station at Wooster, Ohio," MS dissertation, School of Library Science, *Western Reserve University, 1953* (typewritten).

35. Pauline Jennings, "The Library of the New York State Agricultural Experiment Station at Geneva, New York," *Quarterly Bulletin of the International Association of Agricultural Librarians and Documentalists* 2 (January 1957): 137–139.

36. Greathouse, *ibid,* pp 508–512.

37. "Increase in Rural Book Station," *Agricultural Library Notes,* 13 (July 1938): 425 (quoted from *Extension Service Review,* 7, July, 1938).

The Development of Agricultural Libraries in the United States: A Commentary

By
Richard A. Farley

In my comments I propose to expand on several aspects of Blanchard's excellent review of the history of agricultural libraries, paying special attention to conditions, trends, and the human factors that brought agricultural libraries to what they are today.

Last year, in the summer issue of *Daedalus* Andre and Jean Mayer wrote the very provocative article entitled "Agriculture, the Island Empire." They pointed out that "intellectually, and institutionally, agriculture has been and remains an island . . . " As it developed into an intellectual discipline in the 19th century, it did so in academic divisions which were isolated from the liberal arts center of the university, and which have grown no less isolated as they developed into massive schools, experiment stations, and far-flung extension centers.

It was inevitable that the agricultural libraries would reflect this isolation. But, even more interesting is the development of isolated

Dr. Farley is Director, National Agricultural Library, U.S. Department of Agriculture, Beltsville, Maryland.

branch libraries within this island empire. Nowhere was this more evident than in the U.S. Department of Agriculture.

Shortly after J. Sterling Morton assumed duties as the third Secretary of Agriculture, it was noted that he took a special interest in the Department's library. In 1893, he contacted Colonel Lowdermilk, a well-known Washington book dealer, to undertake a monetary appraisal of the library's holdings and estimate the cost of preparing a catalog. In cooperation with the Civil Service Commission, Secretary Morton also made plans for a meeting to be held at Colonel Lowdermilk's home for the purpose of preparing the first Civil Service examination for applicants for the position of Librarian of the Department. At the same time, he directed a letter to Melville Dewey asking that he prepare appropriate questions for the examination to be administered to the applicants for the library position. Out of the 30 applicants, only one was certified for appointment. He was William P. Cutter, a graduate of Cornell University and a member of the faculty of the Utah Agricultural College. Cutter and his newly appointed assistant, Josephine Clark, set about immediately to organize the Department's library.

Cutter set the stage with a letter to Secretary Morton dated May 10, 1895:

> The Honorable,
>   The Secretary of Agriculture.
> Sir:
>   I have the honor to call your attention to the following facts, with reference to the so-called division libraries in the Department.
>   More than one-half of all the books which are the property of the Department are deposited with the several scientific divisions of the Department, forming so-called division libraries. The number of books in each of these libraries will vary from fifty to five thousand.
>   Many of these books are of interest only to the division workers in the branch where they are deposited, while others are of general interest. As a result of the previous management of the library, it became the policy of each division to retain every book to which the employees ever might want to refer, in order to have them accessible, many of the men believing that if any of the books were returned to the main library, they would become lost in the general confusion. Many of the books have been duplicated, as a result of this policy.
>   There seems to be an impression in the minds of several of the division chiefs that these books are the property of the division, and are not subject to recall by the Department library, except for a very limited time.
>   An example of this condition may be cited in the Division of

238

Experiment Stations, where it is nearly impossible to get a book returned, even if only loaned temporarily from the main library.

In order to arrive at an understanding in the matter, I have the honor to request an order, defining the powers of the Librarian in this direction, stating whether he has the power to recall books for permanent file in the main library. No half-way or compromise will be of any value. Such a power given to the Librarian will be intelligibly and equitably used, for the good of the greatest number of the employees of the Department.

Were the several divisions not located in separate building, [sic] I believe that the best interests of all concerned would call for the return of all books to the main library, except those so purely relating to the work in any one division as to be useless to any other. All bound volumes of general periodicals should, in my judgment, be kept in the library, and a time limit put on them. I shall in a short time recommend that all numbers of periodicals be kept in the library and not allowed to go out until bound. I cannot see any great objection to this plan, and it would result in a saving of a large amount of money spent in procuring numbers carelessly lost in the divisions. Lack of accommodations for a reading-room to accommodate all has prevented this plan being tried before.

In a number of divisions, clerks are employed to take charge of the books in the division, in some instances devoting all their time to this work. If the greater part of the books were returned, there need be none of this money being spent. I doubt if a great good would not result from such action. The main library, however, has not enough shelf-room for all these books. But it would be possible to accommodate all by building more cases, or better, by erecting steel stacks, that might be used in a new building. A portion of the money spent on the salaries of division librarians would erect such stacks, and pay the salary of one more assistant, rendered necessary by the increased number of books. There would be probably a great amount of opposition to such action, until it was seen that the books were really more accessible in the main library. There is hardly a day that I am not called on to find a book in one of the division libraries, which is lost, on account of the careless manner in which the books are taken care of.

Very respectfully
W. P. Cutter, Librarian

Thus began the great battle of centralization versus decentralization of libraries. In November of that year, Cutter was given the authority to recall all books for cataloging and storage in the main library, the only exceptions being the books in the Weather Bureau and divisions of the Department. One can only guess at the pulling and tugging and the gnashing of teeth that went on during this move. And the cries of "over my dead body, you will move those books!" But, the move was accomplished and at the beginning of the 20th century there was a consolidated collection of some 60,000 volumes.

In the 1940's, 45 years later, like mushrooms in the morning, 20 branch U.S. Department of Agriculture libraries were scattered and flourishing throughout the Washington area. In the Washington, D.C., area, there were, to the best of my knowledge, 20 libraries scattered throughout. They were:

Agricultural Chemistry & Engineering
Agricultural Economics
   Cotton Marketing
   Land Economics
Animal Husbandry
Commodity Exchange Administration
Dairy Industry
Entomology & Plant Quarantine
   Bee Culture – at Beltsville
Experiment Stations
Fertilizer Research
Forest Service
Home Economics
Plant Industry
Soil Conservation Service
Solicitors Office
Weather Bureau
Farm Credit Administration
Rural Electrification Administration

And again, with a Secretarial order in hand, Ralph Shaw[1], who was then Director of the Library, brought them into the central building in the District. This consolidation was really not accomplished until 1970 when the present National Agricultural Library building was completed, and the Animal Husbandry and Bee branches were amalgamated in 1970. I am certain that Ralph Shaw would be highly amused to know that I am still being scolded for that time when "that fellow Shaw took our books away from us."

In retrospect, we must surely ask ourselves, "Did the centralization of the library do real harm to the U.S. Department of Agriculture research effort?" Until some bright young Ph.D. candidate researches this for us, we can only speculate. As a librarian, I am deeply concerned when a scientist says to me, "Since you moved my books, I never use the library any more." At the same time, I see the central collection being used more and more each year. Nevertheless, I suffer a twinge at the loss of even one of my flock.

As Blanchard has pointed out, this trend to centralization developed along similar lines in the land-grant universities. There is hardly an agricultural library in the country that is not centralized administratively in the university library system. I underlined that word administratively because physically many of the libraries have moved into fine new separate buildings. There is a bit of truth in the fact that this kind of separation was not very difficult to maintain since a good number of our humanities colleagues didn't want those "agriculture" books in the central library anyway.

In these days of affirmative action it is important to point out that a second important factor in the development of agricultural libraries was the role of women in building those libraries. In the field of agriculture, males dominate the leadership roles but, in agricultural librarianship females played a dominant role. No one can sit at my desk today without recognizing that the things that count in libraries, the collections and the catalogs, were created largely by women. Some of my more militant female colleagues would scold me for that statement and assure me that these were only menial tasks. But if one examines the record, however, it would be found that women shared a good part of the administrative direction of this Library.

A third factor, which has come upon us during the past two or three years like a bolt of lightning, is everything that goes under the general heading of automation. Perhaps, here at last, we are going to be able to return the library to the scientist at his desk and in his laboratory. We have just passed the first budget hurdle that will permit us to provide online bibliographic service to a few of our field stations, essentially, taking the library's catalogs and periodical indexes to the users.

Now, if Ralph Shaw and Foster Mohrhardt[2] thought that they had troubles with branch libraries, think of the present director who must control the growth of automated data bases. Everyone is getting into this act. With branch libraries, we worried about spending thousands of dollars. With data bases we worry about millions. This morning a note came to my desk telling me that we had lost the documentation to the INTREDIS data base. I use to worry about lost books, now I worry about these things.

Finally, Foster Mohrhardt and John Sherrod[3] took the steps that made this library world-renown. Wherever I go outside this country their names are mentioned, and I am asked to carry greetings to them. To put it simply, the agricultural library world looks to the United States for leadership. I do not mean by this the sending of a few interlibrary loans through the mails. I speak rather of the exchange of data bases with other nations of the world. I hope that at some future meeting, such as this, the director of the National Agricultural Library might say of me, he was the man who struck a balance between the national and international demands on this great library.

REFERENCES

1. Ralph R. Shaw, Director of Libraries, U.S. Department of Agriculture, 1940–1954.
2. Foster E. Mohrhardt, Director, National Agricultural Library, 1955–1968.
3. John Sherrod, Director, Agricultural Library, 1968–1973.

Historical Research within the College of Agriculture

By
Irvin M. May, Jr.

Colleges of agriculture have contributed profoundly to the well-being of state land-grant universities and to the life of their state's inhabitants.[1] Since their inception, these colleges have responded to a multiplicity of problems, encompassing the educational needs of their students, producers, and consumers, as well as the limiting factors of their state's soil and climate. Yet a deeper perceptive appreciation of the important goals, complexities and creativity of agricultural colleges has failed to materialize in the minds of agriculturists, of college professors, or the urban-oriented public.

In the college of agriculture, itself, attempts have been made in the past to educate the public by agricultural scientists, county agents, and departments of agricultural communications. However, in 1974, Sylvan H. Wittwer, Director of the Michigan Agricultural Experiment Station, concluded that "the real message of the needs of agricultural research have not been reported to the nation. There is little appreciation by the American public for what agriculture is doing or could do."[2] To this interpretation, one might add the following question: Is the public fully aware of the technological and social revolution in which local agricultural colleges have contributed to the total development of their state, region, and nation?

Dr. May is Research Historian, Department of Agricultural Economics, Texas Agricultural Experiment Station, Texas A & M University, College Station, Texas.

Operating within colleges of liberal arts, historians followed traditional approaches to solving the challenges confronting agriculture. Gilbert C. Fite saw clearly the lack of appreciation and interest by the historians of mankind for America's agricultural achievements and heritage. Agricultural historians were few in number and woefully weak in financial resources. These ragged orphans of Clio could not effectively meet their professional responsibilities alone.

In 1961, Fite's presidential address at the Agricultural History Society called for expanded frontiers in agricultural history.[3] At colleges of agriculture, the means to venture forth remained for the future. Facing this challenge in 1974, Texas A & M University created an office for agri-historical research to solve the current crisis that both disciplines shared together. Appropriately, the Office of Research Historian of the Texas Agricultural Experiment Station united historians and agricultural scientists in name, purpose, dedication, and administration.

This paper proposes to stimulate thought and share ideas on how professional agricultural historians, working independently or as an integral part of an inter-disciplinary team, can effectively communicate the achievements of agricultural research to consumers, producers, and the agricultural academic community. The paper shall not analyze agricultural literature written about agricultural colleges or other projects of other agriculturists. Rather, the focus of the paper is centered upon the Texas A & M experiment.[4] Clearly, the challenge facing the college of agriculture offers agricultural historians vast opportunities for service.

Recently, the educational leadership at land-grant universities has increased their explanations of experiment station, extension services, and agricultural educational programs whose existence is crucial to meeting the increasing needs and demands of a consumer-oriented society. Coming to the heart of the matter, H. O. Kunkel, College of Agriculture at Texas A & M University, called for a "view of agricultural research and education with as much honesty and sense of reality as we can muster." He believed that if agricultural contributions were honestly presented to the public by modern techniques, then the public would become conscious of its proud agricultural heritage and insure agriculture's future progress. Kunkel made the following statement:

> "Agricultural research without basic research or the diversity of disciplines that researches for fundamental understandings of the biologic, ecologic, physical or behavioral basis of agricultural or related socio-economic phenomena leaves itself vulnerable — vul-

nerable to insufficent understandings of the meanings of the data obtained or to inaccurate and perhaps unfortunate, extrapolation of data to the production or use of the agricultural process, and its products or the natural resources. Agricultural research without that mix of disciplines can be indeed stale and less fully productive. For we now need the broadest vision that we can to develop the agriculture and the life style we want tomorrow."[5]

In response to this appeal for a team approach to solve these problems, agricultural leaders at Texas A & M wondered if an agricultural historian could serve on a team with others engaged in agricultural literary activities.[6] This seemed a new departure from traditional communications. Logically the question arose as to why either the agricultural college or experiment station needed an agricultural historian? Could a historian with a broad liberal arts background work effectively with agricultural scientists? With the Bicentennial near at hand, the need for projects and contributions from agricultural historians became both apparent and necessary.

Realistically speaking, agriculture has benefited from the study of history. The accomplishments and future promise of the Agricultural History Branch of the United States Department of Agriculture, the National Agricultural Library, and the Agricultural History Center at the University of California at Davis served as precedents for action that Texas A & M was soon to take. Other factors included the abundance of agriculturally historically related literature and the promise of additional works during the Bicentennial.[7] In 1974, agricultural officials created the Office of Research Historian within the Texas Agricultural Experiment Station and employed the author of this paper to determine the feasibility of adapting policies and procedures of nationally-oriented agricultural historical agencies at the state level.

In facing problem areas for service to the college of agriculture, the new Office of Research Historian realized self-evident ideas shared by others who had ventured forth into the field. At a state land-grant institution the phrase — the heritage of the past is the seed that brings forth the harvest of the future — now contained new possibilities of state and national significance. Previously, history had shaped the decisions of agricultural leaders, and obviously the agrarian heritage lived in speeches, books, articles, television programs, and other forms of mass media.

As agricultural colleges moved into the rapidly changing, consumer-urban complex, the situation demanded that agriculturists gain a glimpse of events in their proper perspective, not as isolated acts. Equally significant, with the rise of agricultural specialists, agricultural administrators sought to fill a void created by the decline of the general agricultural scientist. If this proved impossible, then some publication must provide the specialist with an overall picture of agricultural development. At the same time, the innovations of natural and social scientists had to be clearly recognized as valid components in solving state problems. Upon the Office of Research Historian rested the responsibility of continuing to separate myth from reality in agricultural life and of assessing the impact of agriculture itself.

A sense of urgency accompanied the creation of this new office emphasizing the need for a scholarly or popularly written book to inform the general public, agricultural scholars, and laymen of the contributions made by the Texas Agricultural Experiment Station. As a potential reference tool, this publication would examine the origins, progress, development, significant contributions, current status, and future goals of the state's most important agricultural research agency. In the words of Jarvis E. Miller, Director of the Texas Agricultural Experiment Station, "the contributions of agricultural research to the growth and development of the state's economy must be better understood."[8] Ironically, Director Bonney Youngblood had encountered a similar problem in 1924. At that time, Youngblood wrote that information of agricultural achievements "enables the men of the city to appreciate the importance of agriculture to other industries, and possibly to become more considerate of the farmers' and the stockmen's problems than otherwise would be the case."[9] But Youngblood had relied upon journalists and extension personnel in conjunction with the scientists to solve the problem. The immense progress made since World War II necessitated that an agricultural historian serve as part of a team effort along with agricultural administrators, journalists, and scientists. The historian and his associates could complement previous work, prepare new projects, and also make a distinct contribution to agricultural development.

Within the Office of Research Historian, the team effort moved well, for a full-time agricultural historian was employed to supervise research and eventually write the history. But the agricultural policy makers realized that the historian needed the services of one who understood the complexities of agricultural science and technology and who was well-known within the agricultural community. At that point, R. D. Lewis, former head of the Agronomy Department of Ohio State and Director Emeritus of the Texas Agricultural Experiment Station, consented to serve as consultant to the Research Historian in regard to the more technical matters.

An agri-historical team emerged, combining knowledge of the problems of historical research and knowledge of daily agricultural operations to best possible advantage of both natural science and agricultural history. Sometimes, however, it was difficult to reconcile the approaches of both natural science and agricultural history.[10] But patience, frank discussions, understanding, and dedication to research mingled with sleepless nights created a common bond shared by the research historian and the consultant alike. Two graduate students were hired as research assistants to aid the Office of Research Historian. Like their senior colleagues, one was an agricultural historian while the other was a specialist from within a department of the college of agriculture. Can one identify problem areas for historical accomplishment within the framework of a state college of agriculture? What historical goals are immediately attainable or have a reasonable chance of success? What will be the future of this program? Where is the place of an Office of Research Historian within a university framework? Lastly, using the Texas A & M University System as an infant model, what may be the future of such a team effort?

The method of serving agriculture will differ because of each state's needs, administrative policies and characteristics. But the underlying answer to these issues lies in how the agricultural historian and his team can render their professional services to agriculture at the state level. Within each state, many unexplored and obscure areas remain as frontiers for independent or joint historical research projects. The scope, progress, and service will depend upon a number of factors including the priorities of the agricultural administration, funding, the talents and interests of the research team, and the availability of materials. For this reason, the list of potential projects will never remain constant.

What remains foremost is the urgent need for public understanding and appreciation of the college of agriculture and its associates — the state agricultural experiment station and state extension service. Many contributions of agricultural colleges have been revealed in university histories. For example, Gould Colman presented an in depth analysis in *Education & Agriculture* regarding Cornell.[11] Unfortunately, many agricultural college histories have been written by a chronologically-oriented writer who failed to convey the depth of his college's impact on state agriculture. Most individuals have read the latter type, wishing for footnotes to soothe curiosity for a human interest story, or even for a controversial interpretation to breathe some life into the author's manuscript.

For example, the modern reader needs to know specific agricultural achievements and what forces have been actively at work on present agricultural problems. Within a particular state, how did the college of agriculture determine and meet its responsibilities? Honestly admitting some mistakes along the road to progress, the agricultural historian must point out the scientific achievements resulting from the determined relentless work of agricultural scientists and teachers. A case in point for Texas might be the Brazos Blackberry which resulted from a team of agricultural scientists producing 85 varieties and then carefully selecting the best one for introduction into their state's agricultural program. Supported by their college and by the TAES, Sid Yarnell, Homer Blackhurst, Harry Morris, and Benton Storey aided significantly in their state's food production by carrying on a tradition founded by the late Helge Ness. Following in the footsteps of Louis Pasteur and Theobald Smith, Mark Francis's experiments in Texas tick fever eradication were among the first significant contributions made by the college of agriculture to Texas. Now, Raymond Reiser's current studies of cholesterol enrich the understanding of agriculture and the American Heart Association.

Within the college of agriculture itself, what are the significant departments which contributed to the growth of the state's agricultural development? Recently at Texas A & M, the Department of Animal Science funded an M.A. thesis in history describing the development of agricultural science at TAMU. Similarly but with greater complexity, some universities are preparing scholarly histories to accompany their own centennials. The future promises to produce scholarly histories showing the college of agriculture in its proper relationship within academic life as well as separate publications containing more human interest stories and pictures. Both methods offer promise for effective communication.[12]

As previously mentioned, the area of agricultural experimental research and extension needs further explanation and interpretation.[13] Each state has made its own unique contributions to improving the quality of life. Highpoints in the life of the TAES include "the development of hybrid sorghum; short-statured wheats and rices; stormproof cotton; vitamins for domesticated livestock; methods to overcome the phosphorous deficiency in cattle; mechanization of farming; the cotton stripper; performance testing and crossbreeding in livestock; . . . irrigation system design and development."[14] Agricultural research achievements differ in Georgia, New York, and California, and greater awareness of agricultural progress can be obtained from books and articles regarding the broad role of the specific research and extension centers.

Another area involves the effect of cooperative federalism on state agricultural programs. State agricultural scientists work together with their federal counterparts, often at the same location. How have these joint efforts combined towards solving the state's agricultural needs? What state contributions have had an impact at the national level? The historian can also help describe the responses of these scientists to international agriculture and provide background insights on problems like the food crisis.[15] The relationships of cooperative federalism are not unique to one state for their responses vary with geographical regions and circumstances.

Agricultural historians have documented the significant achievement of successful agriculturists; for instance, one can turn to bibliographies prepared by the Agricultural History Center and John T. Schlebecker. Also, paths lighted by biographers such as C. Vann Woodward and Avery Craven can be followed by the agri-historian's team in researching lives of administrators, teachers, and scientists. Because of the historian's responsibilities to his state, the Office of Research Historian can present biographical sketches of state agricultural leaders not directly associated with the college of agriculture. For example, *Men and Milestones* and *Titans of the Soil* exemplify biographical approaches which could apply in each state. [16]

Have state agricultural legislators received proper attention in biographies? The studies of agricultural congressmen and administrators who contributed to state and national legislation remain valid opportunities for historical investigation. While state legislators appear neglected, national leaders seemed to have captured the spotlight. Edward and Frederick Schapsmeir's two-volume biography of Henry A. Wallace, William Rowley's study of M. L. Wilson, and Roy Scott's and James Shoalmire's analysis of Cully Cobb have provided worthy examples. The promising field of agri-political history could be strengthened by studies on Clifford Hope, John Bankhead, other U.S. congressional leaders and the activities and impact of state agriculture committees.

In the research process, the agricultural historian should acquire manuscripts and conduct interviews with retired scientists. Because the historian and his associates need specific information and human interest stories that are omitted from annual reports, their participation in an ambitious oral history program enhances the success of future publications. During the interview, the scientist may offer his manuscripts to the representative of the college of agriculture. The common bond of agriculture facilitates easy acquisition but in these policies, the university archivist has final authority. Whenever possible, the university archivist must be the collecting agent.

In Texas, mini-archival practices are a daily activity in the current program. For example, both the Research Historian and the Consultant serve on the University Archives and Historical Committee which reviews archival policies. The Office of Research Historian collects data in accord with these policies, keeps some records for immediate research priorities but, eventually, transfers all materials to the university archives. Acting with the consent of the university archivist, the Research Historian's office supervises all interviews for historical purposes concerning the history of the Texas Agricultural Experiment Station. Similiar procedures could be initiated for the college of agriculture in order to prevent needless duplication. Within the agri-historical office, the interviews are transcribed into the form desired by the university archivist, but their transcription never acquires priority over the preparation of manuscripts.

Agricultural leaders seek information from their agri-historians on issues ranging from oral history to the number of historical materials in a certain subject held by the library. When asked for an opinion the historical office gladly responds, although these requests have been of a minor nature in Texas. Once an effective and productive historical program is clearly established, the Office of Research Historian will take full advantage of this opportunity. The team will be aided by significant document collections which Texas A & M agricultural officials have deposited with the university archives.

Lastly, the state agricultural commodity programs provide an area for historical consideration. Wayne Rasmussen called for greater historical understanding of the problems faced by farmers as well as their immediate interests relating to the production of crops, livestock, or services.[18] The gradual evolution of ideas regarding the state's production, distribution, and consumption of commodities provides an opportunity for joint or independent research. The correlation of these developments within a specific age and the prospects of projecting future trends will confront a well-established program of historical research. In addition to previously mentioned opportunities, a few of the interesting questions will involve the role and development of technology,[19] the shifting patterns of farm labor,[20] and the development of new varieties of farm products for consumers. An important consideration is the relationship between the geographical movement of various commodities and the human element. For example, in Texas, cotton moved west. While Texans concentrated on cattle feeding operations in the areas of grain sorghum production, the state's pasture-cattle kingdom turned from the Great Plains toward the lush grasslands of East Texas. A review of the state's definable geographical areas reveals historically determinable ages and trends, but what impact and significance did the college of agriculture have in this regard?

The place of the Office of Research Historian within the university will vary depending upon the circumstances. Currently,this process is unfolding at Texas A&M, but our experiences may suggest some logical administrative areas. As an historian, trained in the traditional methodology of a university history department, a logical solution would be the housing and joint-funding of the agrihistorical team within the department of history. The attractiveness of association with fellow historians and opportunities for teaching and recruiting talented agricultural history students are obvious advantages. For research historians who love teaching and research, this location seems the best choice. Yet, does this location meet the needs of the college of agriculture? The agricultural historian needs identification and association with agricultural scientists. If the historian is to write effectively of agricultural accomplishments, he needs to learn and appreciate ideas, concepts, methodology and past accomplishments which come to him in daily conversations with agriculturists. Through these means, the research historian and his associates can share a better understanding of agriculture's present and future.

If the agricultural research historian operates within his traditional department, his colleagues must possess a favorable attitude towards interdisciplinary projects. In comparison to agricultural departments which have a long tradition of inter-disciplinary research and cooperation, some history departments lack the necessary experience and appreciation of these projects. Also, agricultural research in the history department creates inter-college administration problems.

On the other hand, relations with the history department provide opportunities to recruit talented graduate assistants. This involves the popularity of the professor's individual courses and the degree of salesmanship to attract students. In the history department of some land-grant universities students have enrolled to prepare their lives for teaching; if they preferred research, they would have entered the history departments of more prestigious research-oriented institutions. Inevitably, during the first years, the historian encounters the reluctance of graduate students to stake their future on a trial experiment.

For the research historian, independent recruitment of graduate students outside Texas A & M remains a problem. Close cooperation between the research historian and the department of history can provide continual replenishment of graduate research assistants for the agri-historical team. Hence, the research historian works closely and in harmony with the department's graduate advisor, because the degree of success in graduate assistance is proportionately related to the degree of support furnished by the history department.

Can a research historian and his staff operate within the organization of a university library? Within this neutral arena, opportunities exist for recruiting graduate assistants trained in the acquisition and cataloging of manuscripts and preparation of oral history transcripts. One of the prime limitations of this arrangement is the danger of the historian becoming involved with the secondary priority — that of collecting manuscripts instead of pursuing his primary research of these documents. Yet the careers of some distinguished agricultural historians reveal that one can master the arts and responsibilities of both the library and historical writing and research.

Promising areas for the research historian's staff exist within the college of agriculture. Traditionally, historical achievements have resulted from the research of agricultural economists; one example of which was Walter Wilcox's *The Farmer in the Second World War*.[21] Many contributions of agricultural economists responded to immediate needs and their appreciation of history varied widely from outright skepticism to an excellent appreciation of agricultural achievements. For the research historian, problems associated with teaching and recruitment of graduate students are similar but of greater intensity than those in the history department. Within the college, the department of agricultural economics, however, remains the traditional department for agricultural historical studies, combining inter-disciplinary research with the inherent team approach.

Another alternative with vast potential exists within the departments of agricultural journalism and communications; the former oriented to teaching and the latter primarily oriented towards informing the public of agricultural research and extension procedures and accomplishments. In their presentation of information, the agricultural journalists and agricultural historians share common bonds with opportunities for joint or independent action.

Applied historical research is easily facilitated through association with the department of agricultural communications. For example, experts from agricultural journalism and agricultural communications participate in seminars and workshops with agricultural historians concerning effective interviewing techniques and gathering of information. The agri-historians serve as research associates and supply information requests from the department of agricultural communications for material regarding state agricultural developments and progress. Radio and television specialists are assured of accurate, interesting accounts for scripts on historical developments. Interesting comparisons between past and present practices may be prepared to dramatize the progress of agriculture.

The agri-historical team will publish both scholarly and popularly written articles using the experience and expertise of agricultural communications. In popular articles, the historical team should cooperate with popular science writers. The historical team can also prepare articles for the *Texas Agricultural Progress* or for various commodity journals. The potentialities of this vast unexplored area in agricultural literature remain unrealized as does the significant role which state agricultural historians can play in the process. Of the departments within the college of agriculture, the department of agricultural communications offers attractive advantages.

Should the research historian be identified directly with the administration of the college of agriculture rather than with a department? The inter-disciplinary approach of the agri-historical staff is vital to a greater realization that yesterday's research is today's progress and the only hope of tomorrow's future. Agri-historians at the main university campus and at research and extension centers throughout the state can effectively meet this challenge. Their assignment to the state's regional centers can increase more effective communications of agricultural research and extension accomplishments. By working under the direct supervision and sanction of the college of agriculture, the agri-historians can be more responsive to the multi-disciplinary needs of the college. In addition, research assistants can be recruited from the college of agriculture and research and extension centers based upon the needs of the agri-historical office. For example, one year an agricultural education specialist may be needed to explore the impact of research on

253

education or an economist may be called upon to interpret highly technical information. A member of a research center may be used to aid in assessing the impact of agriculture upon one area of the state. Later, the agri-historical team may need an agricultural journalist to help write or edit the published article or book.

To adjust to the dynamic goals of a progressive administration, the research historian must have security which will correspondingly increase his innovation and service. As a hybrid, the agri-historical team remains particularly vulnerable to administrative pressures. Whether real or imagined, there is always a temptation for the team to devote too much attention to articles, speeches, participation on national and regional programs and specialized studies, all of which can deter from the basic goal of completing a long-range major book or article with greater lasting results. The means to achieve goals should be flexible; however, a bright future for agricultural historical literature will result from permanent agri-historical offices. The freedom from financial worry, except at periodic budget reviews, will assist the agri-historians in meeting the specific needs of their state and college effectively.

At a land-grant university, the agri-historical team will encounter a vast amount of materials ranging from manuscripts to published reports, articles and bulletins. Careful selection of potential sources and their historical value is essential to avoid superficial analyses or presentation of complex subjects. Although research investigations will center upon the library for past agricultural achievements, valuable information on current subjects is always available in the busy offices of agricultural administrators on the main campus and at research and extension centers. These materials are often inconvenient sources of historical materials, and the agri-historical team may encounter unfamiliar conflicting methods of arrangement. In all instances, good manners are especially appropriate and, in pursuing their own research, the agri-historical team should remember that administrators are using their files for important daily decisions.

As part of an agricultural team, the agri-historian submits manuscripts for approval by appropriate editorial systems. This group reviews the tentative publications for content, style, and interpretation, prior to being officially submitted for printing by a state-funded or privately financed press. In revealing the contributions and problems of agricultural research and education, the agri-historian must accept criticism from his colleagues and solve any problems before eventual publication of the manuscript. The positive aspects of accuracy and perfection in writing outweigh minimal negative considerations which usually involve time. If at all possible, the editorial body must have the proposed manuscript weeks before the author's deadline with his publisher. Responsible agricultural research administration requires the historian's cooperation, for each publication represents, directly or indirectly, a product of the academic system as well as the creative contribution of the agri-historical team.

At Texas A&M, the agri-historical project is presently financed through August of 1977. During the coming year, the team will complete preliminary research on the complex history of the Texas Agricultural Experiment Station and contribute articles regarding the experiment station and related college activities. The consultant and the research historian, operating as an agri-historical team, shall continue their search for positive solutions to problems raised in this paper.

In 1974, Arnold Toynbee observed that the agricultural revolution has been the most beneficent of mankind's technological advances so far.[22] That same year came Andre and Jean Mayer's thought-provoking article which termed agriculture the first science — the mother of sciences; the science which made human life possible. Suggesting future coordination of all sciences, they envisioned agriculture at the center of a broader system integrating human society and its physical environment.[23] Agri-historians face the responsibility of insuring that all corners of American society understand this vital center, agriculture, with as much accuracy and objectivity as possible. The pressures accompanying serious world-wide food shortages interact upon the world's largest food producer and her states. If America remains in this historical production trend, agriculture must benefit from interpretation by the farmer, the housewife, and the nation's social, academic, and political leaders. Agriculturists can use historians.

But what will be the future for properly funded and supported agri-historical team projects within a state university system? In the spirit of the Bicentennial, the approaching centennial of agricultural experiment stations in 1987, and increasing public awareness of history, deans of the colleges of agriculture and directors of agricultural experiment stations and extension services watch to see if an agri-historical oriented team can provide a logical, internally consistent, self-contained answer to the challenges that bind all parties together. Each land-grant college must solve this relationship to provide maximum agri-historical contributions. Perhaps possibilities exist for a close relationship between agri-historians based within colleges of liberal arts. Will the probable solution result in an ancilliary discipline paralleling the course previously traveled by agricultural economics and rural sociology? Or, rather, will the result be the creation of offices of research historian at agricultural experiment station, agricultural extension centers, or in the college of agriculture?

At Texas A&M,[24] the Office of Research Historian, Texas Agricultural Experiment Station, continues its infant experiment, with the goals of service to the historical profession and to the scientific agricultural community.

REFERENCES

1. The college of agriculture may be a departmental structure on the main campus of a university specializing in teaching, but also an organization containing interrelations and interactions of research and extension with a complementary team approach rather than specific subsidiary agencies. Agricultural history research can be conducted at the main university campus and also at research and extension centers located throughout the state.

2. S. H. Wittwer, "Communication Goals for a Research Organization," paper presented at the Annual Texas Agricultural Experiment Station Staff Conference, College Station, Texas, January 9, 1974; see also University of Illinois, *Research Progress at the Illinois Agricultural Experiment Station: Report for 1972–1974*. (Champaign-Urbana: University of Illinois, 1975), pp. 1–5; H. C. Knoblauch, E. M. Law and W. P. Meyer, *State Agricultural Experiment Stations: A History of Research Policy and Procedures* (Washington: Government Printing Office, 1962), pp. 213–215.

3. Gilbert C. Fite, "Expanded Frontiers in Agricultural History," *Agricultural History* 35 (October, 1961): 175–181.

4. The current Texas A&M model is a development of the project of Irvin May, Jr. Agricultural History Research: Texas Agricultural Development-Significant People and Events, Texas Agricultural Experiment Station and Department of Agricultural Economics, Texas A&M University, College Station, Texas. In 1975 other projects included: S.S. Hoos, Cooperative Marketing Activities in California, Department of Agricultural Economics, University of California, Berkeley, California; A. B. Mackie, Foreign Economic Growth and United States Agricultural Trade, United States Department of Agriculture, Development and Trade Program Area, Washington, D.C.; R. H. Kirby, World Agricultural Production, U.S. Department of Agriculture, Statistics Program Area, Washington, D.C.; W. L. Bateman, Food and Feed Grains Subsector: An Analysis of the Distribution and Storage System, Department of Agricultural Economics and Georgia Agricultural Experiment Station, Athens, Georgia; D. E. Ray, Oklahoma Agriculture: Past Experience and Projected Future Changes, Department of Agricultural Economics, Oklahoma State University, Stillwater, Oklahoma; C. E. Olson, A. Vanvig and R. R. Fletcher, Agricultural Sector Study of Wyoming's Economy, Department of Agricultural Economics, University of Wyoming, Laramie, Wyoming; W. W. Cochrane, American Farm Policy: An Historical Analysis, Department of Agricultural Economics, University of Minnesota, St. Paul, Minnesota; H. K. Cordell, L. W. Moncrief and J. G. Kincaid, The Evolution of Outdoor Recreation Policy Among Federal Land Managing Agencies, Department of Recreation Resources, North Carolina State University, Raleigh, North Carolina; J. W. Whitaker, History of Midwestern Agriculture, Agricultural History-NEA Division-ERS, Iowa State University, Ames, Iowa; Vivian Wiser, Farm History Research, Agricultural History, NEA Division-ERS, U.S. Department of Agriculture, Washington, D.C.; J. T. Schlebecker, Farm History Research, NEA Division-ERS, U.S. Department of Agriculture, Washington, D.C.; James H. Shideler,

History of Far Western Agriculture and Cooperative Work on the Bibliographic Index of American Agricultural History (2 projects), Agricultural History, NEA Division-ERS, University of California, Davis, California; Gladys L. Baker, Program and Policy Research, Agricultural History, NEA Division-ERS, U.S. Department of Agriculture, Washington, D.C.

5. H. O. Kunkel, "The Climate for Agricultural Research and Education," paper presented at the Annual Texas Agricultural Experiment Staff Conference, College Station, Texas, January 11, 1974.

6. R. D. Lewis, "Today's Research — Tomorrow's Progress." Administrative Memorandum, December 6, 1967. Personal papers of Robert Donald Lewis, Bryan, Texas; Irvin May, Application for Research Support, July 30, 1971; Letter from Jarvis E. Miller, Director, TAES, to William E. Tedrick, Head, TAMU Department of Agricultural Communications, August 13, 1971; Irvin May to Dean H. O. Kunkel, Memorandum: Agriculture and History, February 1, 1973, Office of Research Historian — Texas Agricultural Experiment Station, Department of Agricultural Economics, Texas A&M University, College Station, Texas.

7. See Roy V. Scott, "Science for the Farmer," *Agricultural History* 48 (January, 1974): 215–220; John T. Schlebecker, *Bibliography of Books and Pamphlets on the History of Agriculture in the United States . . . 1607–1967,* (Santa Barbara, California: American Bibliographical Center — Clio Press, 1969); J. Richard Blanchard and Harald Ostvold, *Literature of Agricultural Research,* (Berkeley and Los Angeles: University of California Press, 1958); Special issues already in print include: University of Wisconsin. *A Century of Progress: Your College of Agricultural and Life Sciences Serves Wisconsin,* (Madison: University of Wisconsin College of Agriculture and Life Sciences, 1975); Paul Gough, "The Connecticut Agricultural Experiment Station," *League Bulletin* 26 (July, 1974): 52–55. Special issues devoted to agricultural history by agricultural journals include *Agroborealis* (University of Alaska Institute of Agricultural Sciences) 6 (December, 1974), *Ohio Report* (Ohio Agricultural Research and Development Center) 59 (September–October, 1974), and *Minnesota Science* (University of Minnesota Agricultural Experiment Station) 31 (Spring, 1975). We may look forward to future publication emphasizing historical contributions made by agriculture, which include a special issue of *Texas Agricultural Progress* (Texas A&M University) 21 (Fall, 1975), *Journal of the West* 14 (July, 1975), *Agricultural History* 50 (January, 1976) and United States Department of Agriculture, *Yearbook of Agriculture: 1975.* See also: *Journal of the West* 14 (July, 1975).

8. Jarvis E. Miller, "Guidelines for Effective Communications in the Texas Agricultural Experiment Station," paper presented at the Annual Texas Agricultural Experiment Station Staff Conference, College Station, Texas, January 10, 1974.

9. B. Youngblood, "Texas Agricultural Experiment Station System," in A&M College of Texas, Texas Agricultural Experiment Station Circular No. 33 (College Station, Texas: A&M College of Texas, 1924), p. 3. For insights into problems agricultural scientists face see R. D. Lewis, "Integrating Research and Extension in Agronomy," *Journal of the American Society of Agronomy* 30 (March, 1938): pp. 179–188.

10. See R. G. Collingwood, *The Idea of History,* ed. R. M. Knox (New York: Oxford University Press, 1945), pp. xi–xiii; 302–334.

11. George H. Callcott, *A History of the University of Maryland* (Baltimore: Maryland Historical Society, 1966); Gould P. Colman, *Education & Agriculture: A History of the New York State College of Agriculture at Cornell University,* (Ithaca, New York: Cornell University, 1963).

12. Henry C. Dethloff. *A Centennial History of Texas A&M University, 1876–1976,* 2 vols. (College Station: Texas A&M University Press, 1975); Henry C. Dethloff, *A Pictorial History of Texas A&M University,* 1876–1976, (College Station: Texas A&M University Press, 1975).

13. Tad Moses. *Agricultural Research in Texas Since 1888* (College Station, Texas: Texas Agricultural Experiment Station, 1956). At present, this brief pamphlet is the best single account of the history of the Texas Agricultural Experiment Station.

14. Texas Agricultural Experiment Station. *Texagreport: Annual Report — Texas Agricultural Station — 1973-1974* (College Station, Texas, 1974), p. 1. See also James Fallows, "The Last Aggie Joke," *Texas Monthly* 3 (August, 1975): 57-61, 77-80.

15. See Robert G. Dunbar, "The Role of Agricultural History in Economic Development," *Agricultural History* 36 (June, 1966): 329-344.

16. U.S. House. Committee on Agriculture. *Men and Milestones in American Agriculture.* 89th Congress. 2d Session. (Washington: Government Printing Office, 1966), 59 pp.; Edward Jerome Dies. *Titans of the Soil* (Chapel Hill: University of North Carolina Press, 1949); John T. Schlebecker, *Bibliography of Books and Pamphlets on the History of Agriculture in the United States . . . 1607-1967,* (Santa Barbara, California: American Bibliographical Center — Clio Press, 1969); see also Richard J. Orsi, *A History of References for the History of Agriculture in California,* (Davis, California: Agricultural History Center, University of California at Davis, 1974).

17. Edward and Frederick Schapsmeier, *Henry A. Wallace of Iowa* (Ames: The Iowa State University Press, 1968); Edward and Frederick Schapsmeier, *Prophet in Politics* (Ames: The Iowa State University Press, 1970); William D. Rowley, *M. L. Wilson and the Campaign for the Domestic Allotment* (Lincoln: University of Nebraska Press, 1970); Roy V. Scott and J. G. Shoalmire, *The Public Career of Cully A. Cobb: A Study in Agricultural Leadership* (Jackson: University and College Press of Mississippi, 1973). We also need recent studies of developments like Theodore Saloutos, *Farmer Movements in the South,* 1865-1933 (Berkeley and Los Angeles: University of California Press, 1960) and Theodore Saloutos and John D. Hicks. *Agricultural Discontent in the Middle West, 1900-1939,* (Madison: University of Wisconsin Press, 1951).

18. Wayne D. Rasmussen, "Forty Years of Agricultural History," *Agricultural History* 33 (October, 1959): 177-194.

19. See Carroll W. Pursell, Jr., and Earl M. Rogers. *A Preliminary List of References for the History of Agricultural Science and Technology in the United States* (Davis: Agricultural History Center, University of California at Davis, 1966).

20. For example see Louis Cantor, *A Prologue to the Protest Movement,* (Durham, N.C.: Duke University Press, 1969).

21. Walter W. Wilcox, *The Farmer in the Second World War,* (Ames: The Iowa State College Press, 1947).

22. Arnold Toynbee, "Inheritors of the Earth?" *Horizon* 16 (Summer, 1974): 18.

23. Andre Mayer and Jean Mayer, "Agriculture, The Island Empire," *Daedalus* 103 (Summer, 1974): 83-95.

24. The author acknowledges the value of conversations during July, 1975, with H. O. Kunkel, College of Agriculture, Texas A&M University; Jarvis E. Miller, Texas Agricultural Experiment Station; Henry C. Dethloff; and the discussions held with other members of the Office of Research Historian, Texas Agricultural Experiment Station: R. D. Lewis, James Cozine, Jr., Jean Pfluger, and Miss Adrienne Rosson. However, the author accepts the responsibility for views stated in his paper.

Historical Research within the College of Agriculture: A Commentary

By
Vivian Wiser

Irvin May has focused his attention on his part in the team approach to research at the Experiment Station of Texas A & M University. He has analyzed the various elements of the program and how he, as an historian, fits into it as an integral part. Then he has discussed how the idea can be extended. The Director of the Station is to be commended for his interest in including historical research within the scope of its activities.

Having said this, I would like to supply some background for May's paper. My initial reaction was "What precedent has there been for such a development? What historical work has been done within the colleges of agriculture and by whom?"

Under the system that has evolved in over a century, activity within the colleges of agriculture has revolved around teaching, extension, and research. Through the years the relative weight of these areas has been a subject of bitter controversy. The dean of the college frequently has general jurisdiction over the teaching, the State Extension Service, and the State Experiment Station, and an individual staff member may have his time divided three ways. But this all began long ago.

Dr. Wiser is an historian with the Economic Research Service, U.S. Department of Agriculture, Washington, D.C.

To pinpoint the beginning of agricultural research would be as futile as the medieval monks counting the angels on the point of a needle. Individuals, then both agricultural societies and agricultural journals, promoted experimentation; state geological and agricultural surveys were made; and some urged the establishment of colleges with laboratories and experimental farms. In fact, it was suggested in the early 1840's that the Smithson bequest be used to establish a national experimental farm at Mount Vernon. Some states appointed chemists who spent much of their time testing fertilizers. The publication of Justin von Leibig's work on chemistry inclusive of its application to agriculture in 1840 and its translation into English, experiments in England, and similar developments on the continent, increased interest in agricultural improvements. Some read about the advancements. Others, like John Pitkin Norton, Samuel W. Johnson, Evan Pugh, and William Smith Clark, went to Europe for further training and came back to the United States and joined others advocating experimental research by the establishment of agricultural colleges, experiment stations, and a federal department of agriculture with an experimental farm.

Legislation in 1862 provided land grants for the colleges and for the United States Department of Agriculture. In 1872, Frederick Watts, head of the Department, called a meeting in Washington to discuss agricultural education and the experiment station movement. Three years later, the Connecticut legislature set up an experiment station at Middletown which has subsequently moved to New Haven. This was soon followed by stations in other states.

A succession of meetings, some called by the Department, were held in Washington. Bills were introduced in Congress to establish a system of experiment stations and, from the beginning there was a question about their relationship to the Department in Washington. President Cleveland signed the Hatch Act on March 2, 1887 which granted money to the states for the stations. Also in 1887, the American Association of Agricultural Colleges and Experiment Stations was established. Under authority of the next U.S. Department of Agriculture Appropriation Act, the Office of Experiment Stations was established in the Department to publish results of the research in the states. Eight years later the Office was making annual visits to the stations to determine fiscal accountability and review work. The Adams Act of 1906 gave more funds to the state stations for research and, at the same time, strengthened the federal control over them. Other legislation particularly significant to the development of research in the experiment stations includes the

Purnell Act of 1925, the Bankhead-Jones Act of 1935, the Agricultural Marketing Act of 1946, and an act in 1955 consolidating laws relating to state experiment stations.

In the course of time, research in the state stations has developed primarily along local lines. More recently, especially since the Research and Marketing Act was passed, regional research has been conducted with a number of states cooperating.

The conduct of research in the state stations has been a three-sided product affected by the Office in the U.S. Department of Agriculture under varying names, the land grant college association, and the state experiment station, a part of the college of agriculture.

We are well aware of changes that are taking place within our country and in our way of life. When the colleges of agriculture were established the name described their curriculum and scope. Now the picture has changed and we find that some of the New England colleges are called College of Life Sciences and Agriculture. In New York and North Carolina, they are designated as the College of Agriculture and Life Sciences while in Connecticut and Michigan, they are called College of Agriculture and Natural Resources. Rhode Island has dropped the word "agriculture" in its College of Resource Development. In Massachusetts, the name has been changed to College of Food and Natural Resources. The California College at Davis is now referred to as the College of Agriculture and Environmental Science. Florida has a College of Agriculture in its Institute of Food and Agricultural Science. Naturally, Hawaii is named the College of Tropical Agriculture.

These changing functions are also shown in the scope of their publications with some institutions setting up series for rural sociology, economics, home economics, natural resources and the like. A cursory examination of some of these circulars or bulletins shows that scientists, economists, sociologists and the like frequently compile and include historical data or background information in their bulletins.

Articles in the 1975 *Yearbook of Agriculture* deal with the work of the experiment station system and have been prepared primarily by people from the state stations. Paul Waggoner's paper on "Research and Education in American Agriculture," presented at the Bicentennial Symposium at the Smithsonian Institution and published in the January 1976 issue of *Agricultural History,* is another timely review. He looks at the subject from the viewpoint of the state and is quite critical of the Department of Agriculture.

A. C. True's long career with the Office of Experiment Stations is

261

well known. However, it is not generally recognized that one of his first duties in the Office of Experiment Stations was to prepare an article on the experiment station movement and the history of agricultural education and research in the United States for use in connection with the Paris Exposition of 1889. Furthermore, the first bulletin of the Office, *Organization of Agricultural Experiment Stations in the United States,* had a section credited to True entitled "A Brief Account of the Experiment Stations in the United States." During the ensuing years, many bulletins and articles were published, culminating in his famous trilogy on education, extension, and research.

I would like to point out that, of course, research—historical or otherwise—is carried on by some advanced undergraduate as well as graduate students, professors, and others. And since various disciplines are represented in the experiment stations, why not include at least one historian in each state station and at the same time, develop or maintain a liaison with the history department and, of course, the agricultural history staff in the U.S. Department of Agriculture.

Agriculture in Communist China

By
Gilbert C. Fite

I feel especially fortunate to have had an opportunity to visit the People's Republic of China. We were told that not more than 6,000 to 8,000 Americans have entered China since the bamboo curtain was raised following former President Nixon's visit there in 1972. I have traveled in many parts of the world, including South Asia and the Soviet Union, but no previous trip provided the thrill and excitement as did my excursion to China.

My observations of Chinese agriculture are based on a three-week trip which began in the southeast at Canton in Kwantung Province. We then moved northward to Shanghai, Soochow, Wusih, Nanking and finally to Peking between April 1 and 21, 1975. Our party visited two communes, one near Shanghai and another on the outskirts of Wusih. We also spent a half-day at the Institute of Agricultural Scientific Research near Nanking. Besides visiting communes and traveling through the countryside by bus and train, flights over parts of China provided a larger view of some agriculturally related activities such as irrigation. In addition, I have studied the reports of other Americans who have visited China during the last two years. This has permitted me to test my conclusions against those of others. While my observations are admittedly restricted by time and place, I believe they are essentially accurate.

Dr. Fite was formerly President of Eastern Illinois University, Charleston, Illinois. and is now Richard B. Russell Professor of History, University of Georgia

One of the most fundamental changes that has occurred in the People's Republic of China since 1949 has been the reorganization of agricultural production. The concentration of land ownership and farm production for the profit of landowners has been replaced by a system of common landholding and cooperative production and distribution. The organization of rural life and farm output centers in the communes.

Approximately 80 percent, or some 650 million individuals, of China's estimated 800 million to 850 million people live in rural areas. The great majority of Chinese are directly associated with agriculture, compared to not more than five percent in the United States. The total land area of China is about 970 million hectares (2.3 billion acres) which exceeds the area of the United States if Hawaii and Alaska are excluded. While China is a large country, it has extensive regions of mountains and desert that are not agriculturally productive. The great portion of agricultural production occurs in the eastern one-third of the country.

The most startling statistic regarding farming in China is that the Chinese produce their food and fiber on only about 15 percent of the land. They not only utilize all of their arable land, they also use it more than once. One American authority has calculated that the Chinese use nearly 150 percent of their arable land each year. Such utilization is possible because of multicropping, a system in which the Chinese clearly have come to excel.

China produces a wide variety of crops. In the north and northeast, wheat, sorghum, soybeans, corn, and millet are the principal products. In the east central part of the country, rice and wheat predominate, and in the south the main crop is rice. Overall, rice is the most important grain crop in terms of both hectares planted and production achieved. Among other crops grown in China are cotton, barley, oats, rye, and a wide variety of vegetables and fruits.

Hogs are the main livestock and pork is the principal meat, other than fish, eaten by the people of China. Scarcity of land makes grazing of cattle and sheep uneconomical in the eastern part of the country. Dairying has become a specialized activity under confined conditions. We saw several large dairies. One such operation near Peking appeared to have several hundred milk cows. Another, observed in a commune where we visited, has around sixty cows.

Before describing the life and work in a commune, I would like to summarize the major agricultural developments as they appeared to this foreign visitor to the People's Republic. In the first place, agricultural production in China is carried on in a most intensive manner; both land and labor are used to the fullest extent. Multiple cropping, especially in southern and central China, is typical. In the area around Canton, producers grow three crops a year on the same land. Usually this includes two crops of rice and a crop of barley, wheat, or some other small grain. In the Shanghai area, rice and wheat are grown on the same land annually. Most rice is transplanted which saves approximately one month in the planting-harvesting cycle of each crop. Every bit of ground is farmed. Crops are even grown on the dikes that are a part of the irrigation system. Where multiple cropping cannot be carried on, there is intercropping and mixed cropping.

Secondly, the system of irrigation is expanding and both old and new methods are reaching higher levels of efficiency. As one travels by train from Nanking to Peking or flies from Peking toward Shanghai over that great plain, one cannot help being impressed with the construction and extensiveness of canals, ditches, and catchment basins, all used in irrigation. North of Peking, I saw irrigation wells with electric power pumps belching out eight-inch streams to water the young wheat. The situation is not unlike that found in west Texas or other semi-arid parts of the United States. While, historically, agricultural production in China has depended upon irrigation, progress in this area since 1949 has been rather remarkable. One estimate placed the increased land brought under irrigation since 1965 at five million hectares.

In the third place, the Chinese are increasing their output and use of commercial fertilizer. Always heavy users of human and animal waste to maintain soil productivity, they are now adding chemical fertilizers in increasing quantities. China has begun to produce chemical fertilizers in its own plants, but it is still a heavy importer. Despite the fact that China has contracted for ten or more anhydrous ammonia and urea plants, the country is still a long way from self sufficiency in the production of chemical fertilizers. A Canadian visitor in Peking told me that she had talked with an American technician who was on his way to China to help solve some of the technical problems associated with the construction and operation of the new plants. But China, at this point in time, still depends mainly on human and animal wastes to meet its fertilizer needs. Probably no society has historically, or at present, been so efficient in the use of such fertilizer. Fertilizer pits or compost holes can be found everywhere; 10 or 15 feet in diameter, several feet deep, they are located near the fields. Just before plowing and planting, the compost is carried to the fields by hand, dumped in piles, and then scattered over the land. It is a time honored process but one that still succeeds. At the Ho Lei People's Commune, we were told that the majority of producers were still using natural fertilizer, although the use of chemical nutrients was on the increase.

Mechanization of agricultural production has made little headway. Most of the field work is still done by people and animals. The most common scene as one passes through the countryside is that of groups of people, perhaps as many as 30 or 40, preparing the soil, planting, harvesting, or performing other tasks all by hand. Water buffaloes are common beasts of burden in the south, while around Peking many small horses are used. In the latter case, these animals range in size somewhere between a pony and a full-sized horse.

The most common tractor is a two-wheel vehicle which has the motor sitting above and just in front of the wheels. Having fairly large rubber tires, these tractors can operate in wet, muddy ground, although they can not pull implements more than about three feet wide. When not used in the fields, these tractors are hitched to wagons and trailers to move goods and people. I saw only one tractor of any size, which was a small Caterpillar-type machine operating in a field north of Peking.

As mentioned earlier, agricultural life and production are centered in the communes. Scattered throughout China are some 70,000 communes which vary in land area, population, and kinds of production. Our group visited the Mei Lung People's Commune some 10 or 15 miles outside of Shanghai on April 6 and the Ho Lei People's Commune near Wusih on April 10. These were showplaces and certainly were not typical of rural life in all of China. This could be verified by observing the physical appearance of some of the villages within easy sight of the railroad tracks during train trips through the countryside. The buildings in the communes we visited were, for the most part, constructed of concrete, plaster, or bricks, while houses in the poorer communes were nothing but mud huts. Nevertheless, a visit to Mei Lung and Ho Lei communes gave me some idea of the organization, operation, and achievements of agriculture in China.

We arrived at the Mei Lung People's Commune about 2:30 p.m. Scores of children, as well as officials of the commune, greeted us. Both children and adults appeared adequately dressed, well fed, and healthy. As we approached the headquarters, we could see people working in the fields, others were tending livestock, while some were just working around the buildings; everyone was busy.

Chickens and ducks wandered around the premises. No barking dogs greeted us. In fact, there seem to be very few dogs in China.

Following the exchange of pleasantries, we were ushered into a comfortable conference room. The table was covered with a blue table cloth and white tea cups and packs of cigarettes had been carefully arranged. We were scarcely seated before our hosts filled our cups with boiling hot tea. It was a damp, chilly afternoon and the tea was doubly appreciated. At one end of the room were the usual large pictures of Marx, Engels, Lenin, and Stalin and at the other end, a portrait of Chairman Mao alone and dominating.

After we were seated around the table, Wei Yeng Shan, Vice Chairman of the Revolutionary Committee, extended a warm welcome to "our American friends." Vice Chairman Wei then went into an explanation of the Commune's development. It was obvious that he had been through this exercise many times before. He spilled out statistics on crop and livestock production, the use of machinery, and irrigation without the slightest hesitation or reference to notes. Mr. Wei declared that under the guidance and inspiration of Chairman Mao's "revolutionary line," harvests had increased for 13 consecutive years. Grain output per hectare in 1974, he said, was 116 percent above that of 1957. Production of cotton, rape seeds, fish, and livestock also had experienced dramatic gains over the 1950's before the formation of the commune. He boasted that the commune had raised 30,724 hogs, 135,400 chickens, and had 63 cows in 1974. Wei added that mechanization was expanding and that the commune owned 23 large tractors and 102 walking tractors. However, if there were large tractors, none were in sight. Mr. Wei's claim that these accomplishments were directly associated with Chairman Mao's "revolutionary line" was echoed at the Ho Lei People's Commune by Lu Wei-Ping, Chairman of the Revolutionary Committee there. Lu stressed how peasant understanding of socialism, and especially Chairman Mao's thoughts, helped them to cultivate the land better and produce other products more efficiently. It was because of Chairman Mao's thoughts and wise leadership, Lu said, that the masses enjoyed their present happy condition. This, he emphasized, could only remind them of their bitter past.

The Mei Lung People's Commune covers 1,787 hectares (4,413 acres) and contains 5,400 households with a total of 23,000 people. Like other communes, Mei Lung is divided into brigades and production teams. A village or group of villages usually make up a

267

brigade and each brigade consists of production teams of 30 or 40 households. The number varies considerably. At Ho Lei there are 4,355 households in the commune, organized into seven brigades and 82 production teams. The commune is administered by a revolutionary committee with lesser revolutionary committees running the brigades and production teams. There is a close tie between the local Communist Party committee, which transmits basic policy from the central and provincial governments to the local level, and the revolutionary committees which are responsible for implementing state policy.

Each brigade and production team have production quotas set by what they call "higher authority," which means a planning committee of the government. Once the quotas are set, however, the production teams determine to a large extent how best to meet the goals. Mr. Wei said that the opinions of the masses were very important in making plans and establishing output targets. Products, other than a portion held back for seed, feed, and human consumption, are sold to the state at a price established by government order. While most brigades and production teams produce grain, some specialize in other kinds of agricultural products. We saw excellent hogs being raised in confinement, some good dairy cows, silk production, and fish raising. Officials at Ho Lei said that the commune had 152 fishponds. A seining operation at Mei Lung demonstrated most successful results as thousands of fish were trapped and easily caught. One brigade at Ho Lei comprised 1,210 households with a work force of 2,200. It was subdivided into eighteen production teams. Eight produced grain, three fish, one silk cocoons and six silk cocoons and grain combined. The brigade also had a piggery. While grain production was the most important farm activity, spokesmen at both Ho Lei and Mei Lung boasted of their balance and diversity. One of the most interesting activities we observed was the effort to raise pearls from fresh water oysters. A young lady at Ho Lei demonstrated the results when she pried open an oyster and removed a good-sized pearl. A member of our party bought the pearl for about 50 cents as a memento.

The production team is the basic work and accounting unit in the commune. Therefore, it is the production team that most directly affects the life and living standard of China's rural masses. Contrary to strict Marxism, income is not distributed according to need. This is the situation both in the country and in the city. Rather than "from each according to his ability, to each according to his need," as Marx stated the principle, Mao Tse-Tung has modified the slogan to say, "to each according to his work." Consequently, in all of Chinese society, including the communes, a person's income is determined by his or her work. Indeed, our puritan forebears would heartily agree with the strong work ethic in Chinese society. As a member of the production team, income is received on the basis of work points. These are determined by members of the team after considering the labor intensity of the task, the skill required for the job, and the person's attitude toward his or her labor — that is, the correct ideology. There is equal pay for equal work, a principle that would receive plaudits from the Wage and Hour Division of the U.S. Department of Labor. In some cases, such as rice planting, women make more than men because they are more proficient at that task.

In the Mei Lung People's Commune in 1974, each household got 798 Yuan. At the exchange rate of 56 cents per Yuan, that was a family income of $446. At Ho Lei, we were told that every able-bodied working person received 650 Yuan, which included the value of gardens, poultry and any other sidelines. Senator Mike Mansfield (Dem., Missoula, Montana) visited several communes in 1974, and he reported annual incomes per family of $234 in one and $265 in another. These figures seem very low, but families have additional economic benefits which effectively increase their incomes. For example, each family has not only a small garden plot on which it can grow vegetables that can be sold or eaten at the family table but also some poultry. Furthermore, there is practically no outlay for housing. While the quality of housing is low — many families live in one room with a kitchen nearby — it is virtually free. In the rural households that have electricity, the cost is insignificant and fuel for cooking is very cheap. Families in the communes also have what amounts to free medical and educational benefits. The old, sick, and disabled have their basic needs provided for by the commune.

Communes are more than just economic units. They run primary and secondary schools, provide medical service, and carry on propaganda activities designed to commit people to the Socialist Revolution. Elementary medical care is given by the so-called barefoot doctors. Ting Mao Sien, a barefoot doctor in Ho Lei, told us that he had taken six months training in the Wusih hospital and then began practicing among his former friends and neighbors. He could take blood pressures, dispense antibiotics — he had penicillin — and sew

269

up minor wounds. More seriously ill patients are sent to the hospital. The communes also maintain small factories. At Ho Lei we observed 27 women working in a brigade shoe factory, and 26 women were employed in an embroidery factory. The wife of barefoot doctor Ting was busy at one of the sewing machines in the embroidery factory.

At every commune, visitors are told that productivitiy has been greatly increased as a result of raising the political consciousness of the peasants, that great agricultural progress has followed a full understanding of, and commitment to, the principles of Marx, Lenin, and Chairman Mao. The credit for increased production may be given to Chairman Mao, but practical improvements in farm operations come mainly from the work done in the agricultural research institutes. We visited the Kiangsu Provincial Institute of Agricultural Scientific Research and met several scientists who were doing research in a number of aspects of agriculture. The results achieved in the Agricultural Research Institute are transmitted to the farmers through the commune organization by scientists or technicians from the Institute. The Chinese believe that it is highly important to get their agricultural scientists out of the laboratory and away from the experimental plot and place them for a period during the year in the commune where they can talk and work directly with the peasants. As our host told us at Mei Lung, the task of improving agriculture is threefold-experimentation, demonstration, and popularization. The experimentation is going on mainly in the agricultural research institutes. The demonstrations are then carried to the communes where better practices are popularized with the help of local peasants. The evidence that we saw at the agricultural institute and the improved practices observed in the communes indicate that the Chinese are achieving good results in combining scientific research and practical application. As they put it, the Chinese stress the linking of theory and practice.

In summary, it seems clear that the infrastructure of agriculture has been greatly strengthened in the last 25 years. This has been achieved through more intensive cultivation, the greater use of commercial fertilizer, the construction of irrigation ditches and dikes, the use of better plant and animal strains, and the cooperative organization of production. While the Chinese have made substantial gains in agriculture, they have not achieved as much as they claim. For example, their repeated statement that China has had 13 successive good crops and that the country is self-sufficient in food is

270

not true. China has had to import grain in several recent years and is still some time away from complete self-sufficiency. Nevertheless, they have gone a long way to produce the needed food and fiber, and the changes that have occurred in Chinese agriculture in the last quarter century have undoubtedly improved the life of rural people in the People's Republic.

Oral History as Agricultural Literature: Creativity and the Labormanagement Resource

By
Gould P. Colman

Creativity, often said to be a fundamental characteristic of literature, is certainly a fundamental feature of oral history. Oral history
and literature, then, have something in common. Creativity flour-
ishes in the oral history process as stimuli interact, stimuli as apparent as the sponsoring organization, as evident as a question, and as
secret as the respondent's self-image which forms and filters responses. "A tape recorder," says Studs Terkel, "can transform the
visitor and the host."[1]

Tuned to a sense of need and opportunity, interviewer and respondent engage each other in manifold signals, signals outside the
experience of the other being missed unless revised, signals inconsistent with needs ignored or dismissed. Sometimes signals involve
creative deception, for example, when a respondent signals for a
question which will make him appear a reluctant supplier of information he is anxious to volunteer.

Recording is also creative. Behind what the tape records is somebody's judgement about what is appropriate to document. Loss by

Dr. Colman is the University Archivist, Cornell University Libraries, Ithaca, New York.

selectivity is inevitable in documentation and this loss is supplemented by inadvertence and innocence. Even when a tape recording is extended by means of photographs, still or motion pictures, and interviewer notes, the recording process is one of reduction-distortion, distortion because all elements are not reduced proportionately.

However, taped recordings are subjected to additional reduction-distortion as oral history is made acceptable to historians, journalists, and other consumers who read rather than listen. To this end, oral history has been repackaged by means of transcription, the improved package holding less than the original because the spoken language cannot be confined within the written form. Current notions about professional propriety have led to additional refinements by editing. Caught up in enthusiasm for factor analysis but never identified by that alien term, information is pulled together in subject matter categories calculated to appeal to users while information outside these categories is eliminated. In this fractional distillation, creativity inconsistent with the utilization pattern is considered superfluous, the distillate being valued for "facts" sometimes referred to as historical truth.

Fortunately for those interested in oral history as literature, matters are not as bad as many in the emerging profession of oral history would have them. Following the launching of oral history by Allan Nevins in 1948, the transcript was the product until the mid-1960's when values were found in the oral record which justified preservation. Yet, to this date, the oral record has received little attention, in part because production and marketing capabilities of the microprint industry and the *New York Times* have focused attention on transcripts. However, the cost of transcribing, something in the neighborhood of 40 dollars per hour of interview, give or take 10 dollars depending on what support costs are covered, has saved many tapes from transcription, a salutary situation in that researchers must use the original record unpoliced by creativity.

Those who have discovered Studs Terkel's *Working: People Talk About What They Do All Day And How They Feel About What They Do,* and Theodore Rosengarten's *All God's Dangers: The Life of Nate Shaw,* may conclude that I bad-mouth oral history transcripts as literature. If so, these unusual selections, the first organized by a master journalist, the second told by a master story teller, should not be confused with the 704,543 pages of transcript reported by the Oral History Association in 1971.[2] The commercial success of these books indicates that the public wants literature which is creative and, at the same time deals with real people external to the author—that is to say, non-fiction. In 1974, the Notable Books Council of the American Library Association listed 30 titles using as principal criteria "wide general appeal and literary merit." Of the 30, 23 titles are non-fiction. Three of these 23 books were generated by means of oral history, the Studs Terkel and Theodore Rosengarten books just mentioned, and *Plain Speaking: An Oral Biography of Harry S. Truman*, by Merle Miller.[3]

As usually practiced, and the above titles reflect the usual practice, oral history is camera-like in that the record is taken quickly. Oral history interviews may require hours and even days, vast time when compared with the fraction of a second required for photography, but virtually a click when compared with the experience which justifies the record, and presumably is captured in the interview. This time frame is associated with the creativity already described: shaping experience by opportunities perceived in the interview situation.

I turn now from oral history in general to agriculture in particular. And there are many particulars, agriculture not being among oral history's neglected subjects. Within agriculture, there is a decided disproportion between numbers of people engaged in occupations constituting agriculture and occupations of people selected for interviews. It seems that people engaged in oral history are attracted to people like themselves. Although the farm population has been declining for thirty years, it still constitutes about 5 percent of the U.S. population, by far the largest identifiable occupational grouping in agriculture, and many times as large as the total staff of agriculture colleges and the U.S. Department of Agriculture. Yet oral history interviews with professors outnumber those with farmers. At the Regional Oral History Program at the University of California, Berkeley, the ratio was six professors to one farmer as of June, 1974, and one of the farmers, a secretary and director of the National Chamber of Commerce, is probably atypical of his occupation. Cornell, with an exception I will describe henceforth, is in the same pattern. Between 1963 and 1965 when oral history source material produced there dealt almost entirely with agricultural subjects, professors were preferred to farmers in about the same ratio. At Berkeley and Cornell interviews with businessmen, while falling behind the number with professors, substantially outnumbered those with farm people. Best documented are the occupations involved in food processing; Berkeley has a series on wine-making and Cornell has one on food-processing in the northeastern United

States. Politics of agriculture at the national level with particular attention to the New Deal period have been documented by Columbia University's Oral History Research Office. Aside from education (and artificial insemination, where Cornell has a series of interviews) the agricultural input industry—machinery, chemicals, credit, real estate, insurance, fuel and so forth fall somewhere between farming and food processing on a scale of underdevelopment by oral history documentation.[4]

Farming is the agricultural occupation least adequately documented by oral history and, for that matter, in the 20th century, by any other form of documentation. Three obvious considerations bear on this situation. Divided among nearly three million families in 1969, farming lacked the organizational mass required to hire recorders while occupational tasks made heavy demands on the energy of farmers having the inclination to record their experiences. Unlike the 19th century when some farmers kept diaries for personal satisfaction, documentation became an occupational necessity as society proceeded to tax the productivity of farmers while promoting greater productivity by means of rapid depreciation schedules for machinery and equipment. Energy remaining after task-related documentation is completed has not gone into other categories of documentation. Perhaps farmers have been at a loss to select items of compelling interest among the daily run of activities after the principal items in the 19th century diaries were taken over by the TV weatherman.

Another problem underlying documentation of farming is identifying the unit of production. In the United States farming is organized around families. Since World War II about 95 percent of farms have been family operated and in 1969 about 87 percent of the produce of American farms, calculated on a value basis, came from family operated farms.[5] But what constitutes a farm? Land owned, land controlled, the labor and management of family members, other capital resources, some constant combination or shifting combination of these? Obviously the answer is a shifting combination. Farm resources are organized around the skills and energy of family members and these skills and this energy vary with the stage in the family cycle. A newly formed family unit has different organizing and energizing capabilities than a family with teenagers who have mastered tasks involved in farm family operations.

Because documentation of farming varies with stages in the family cycle, documentation depends on timing. Such variations are concealed by aggregated data about farming reported by the U.S.

Bureau of the Census and U.S. Department of Agriculture. However, oral history reports at the individual level so the family cycle is a critical consideration when farming is documented by this means.

Nine years ago with four Cornell colleagues, Harold Capener and Jerry Stockdale in Rural Sociology, Howard Conklin and Arthur Bratton in Agricultural Economics, I set out to accommodate the documentation of farming to stages in the family cycle. To this end we enlisted the help of 20 farm families living in New York State.[6] The families were selected to give a range in the farm family cycle from a newly formed family unit to a family with adult children. When forming the panel we introduced other variations: type of farming, which has a significant bearing on the collection and ordering of resources, particularly labor; and level of economic success, which we expected to reflect variations unknown to us which would emerge in the course of documentation. We asked our sources for patience, explaining why it is necessary to extend the documentation process over many years. Fifteen is the number we had in mind.

Every other year we have interviewed each member of the family living at home who is over seven years old, using, until this year, a male interviewer for male members of the family and a female interviewer for female members. We have also interviewed families as a group using a game and other instruments designed to get at values and other personal characteristics and relationships which may not emerge in a question-answer context. We have also collected information about family finances and the consumption of technology by means of structured interviews.

Initially, our interest centered on decision-making in farm families. Starting with a narrative account of family development, we proceeded as if decision-making were a rational process, an assumption underlying research in farm management. However, by the second round of interviews it became evident that we could not isolate decision-making processes and structures from values and needs of family members, the resources available to the family, and the goal setting procedures followed in families, a situation which led us to conceptualize the farm family as a system of needs and resources. This, I am glad to note, has led to research which will be reported elsewhere.

Limiting to two years the time between experience and recording experience and reducing the selectivity of content attributable to interviewer characteristics by changing interviewers—eleven have now worked on the project—has brought us closer to records which

277

approximate life outside the interview. This approach is no less creative but creativity in the family is now documented more than creativity in the interview. This, I should add, is a pattern not without exception.

Farming is a relatively complex occupation, management and labor of family members being continually integrated in a variety of tasks through which farm people cope with diversity in their environment—diversity in soils and weather during the course of crop cycles, animal cycles, and people cycles, all of which are occurring simultaneously. Management in farm families is integrated with labor. The concepts of labor and management, therefore, are inappropriate when applied to farm families. The phenomenon is singular, labormanagement. Labormanagement is the central resource by which other resources in the farm family system are organized. As the essence of a life style associated with farming, labormanagement is a direct source of satisfaction to farm people. In contrast to the job alienation widely reported in industry, farm people get many satisfactions from performing occupational tasks. In part a product of socialization—learning the content of occupational tasks and the management of personal relationships—labormanagement may also involve individual and family creativity.

The remainder of this report, a paper by reason of my charge, deals with the development of labormanagement in one farm family. This is a success story involving an educational strategy directed towards enabling the family to continue on the farm over generations which, according to a recent *Successful Farming* poll, is among the most compelling concerns of farm families in the United States.[7] It is a success story because every member of both generations— both parents and children—are developing a labormanagement resource which supports intergenerational continuity. This is being accomplished through an apprenticeship in farming, where individual needs and family needs are consciously related. There is no evidence that any family member is neglected or exploited in the interest of others.

In the following interviews personal and place names are changed in accord with the agreement between Cornell University and the farm family involved.

In every system, whether a mechanical system like an engine or a social system like a family, some parts are more vital than others. One ready measure of the adequacy of labormanagement in the farm family is its command of the critical points. The Neirikers-the parents, Franz and Ellen, and the children, Karen, John and Peter-operate a nursery concentrating on the production of apple trees in conjunction with a fruit and vegetable farm. Franz Neiriker, age 40 at the time of the interview in 1968, speaks about budding, the key operation in a nursery.

> *Franz:* The most complicated thing in the nursery – what I refer to as precision work is budding, when you set a bud from the variety you want to put on that rootstock into the rootstock, that's the most complicated. It isn't really complicated, you have to work clean and you have to work fast. That's the most . . . I would say maybe the crucial point of the nursery . . . when you . . . if you do that job right, you have it made.
>
> *Colman:* Now is this work you do yourself?
>
> *Franz:* Some. But mostly I have it hired. . . I hire a man to do it. There's a specialist. Well, you might call him a specialist, they do this kind of work, and that's an older man. And I'm a little bit concerned about . . . he's an older man and I don't know how long he's able to do this work. And once he wouldn't come back I might be . . . have difficulties to get the job done.
>
> *Colman:* Um hmm.
>
> *Franz:* But we . . . I don't plan to go into the nursery business in a big way, so even if he wouldn't come back I . . . I could get it done myself on . . . It would be a certain hardship for me, but I am quite sure I would be able to get it done one way or the other.

In many of our interviews with farm families, the husband describes labormanagement in the family. In a few cases this information is confirmed by the wife and the children. Here Ellen Neiriker, age 43 in 1968, describes the development of labormanagement capability.

> *Durland:* Um. I noticed that your kids seem to be pretty much up on what happens on the farm.
>
> *Ellen:* Oh yes, goodness gracious. [laugh] Well, I guess . . . well, if you lived on a farm – you said you did not – but if you lived on a farm, I think this would be more understandable, and anyone who lives on a farm realizes that the whole family knows what's going on. You buy a tractor, everybody kn . . . everybody knows, it's a big event and everybody troops out and sees the tractor and the kids get up on it and try it and pretend that they're this and that. And you get a new truck, they went with us when we were looking at used trucks and . . . and of course it's a big stuff son-father type of situation and he consults them and says, you know, "Well, what do you think?" you know, and he brings them into it. "What do you think on this?" and, "Shall we get this?" type of thing, you know, playfully but yet a . . . challenging them to think . . .
>
> *Durland:* I see.
>
> *Ellen:* . . . on this. He does it more than I do.
>
> *Durland:* Uh huh.

279

Ellen: And of course they get . . . and they go up to International and he'll take one of them along. He's very good at taking them along. Usually one at a time. He has the advantage over . . . over me, I usually have to take all three. [laugh] But he will take one at a time and . . .

Durland: Yes, I can see you asking, "What do you think?" as you go into a grocery store. [both laugh]

Ellen: Well yes, three of them is quite different all together than when you have just one. But he has always, even from the time they were wee little ones, he would take them along with him, and the boys when they to up to International, they'll . . . so often will pick up little brochures on this and that and bring them home and big stuff, you know, and that's theirs. And then when he gets the catalogues from International or something, as it becomes outdated and he gets new ones, he says, "Well boys, do you want this one?" and they'll get it and they'll put their names on it.

Here is John, eight years old in 1968, mastering occupational tasks and developing a sphere of responsibility.

Bjergo: What kind of a, things do you do on the farm here now when summer will come?

John: Oh, plant beans. Drive the tractor. Mow the grass — other things like that. Ride the bike.

Bjergo: Do you have to mow the grass yourself?

John: Yeah. We've got a tractor with a mower mounted on the bottom and you drive right over the grass, it cuts it.

Bjergo: What make is it?

John: International

Bjergo: How long have you had that?

John: About one year, I guess right now.

Bjergo: Oh. When your dad went to buy that did you go along with him or did you have any say in how . . . which one you got?

John: No. Dad . . . Well, we . . . They seemed all alike to me, but the . . . but I had some say-so about that tractor too because there's two kinds you can get. A, a . . . Some . . . What do you call . . . I don't know what you call it but like a car, or like you have a handle up by the steering wheel, or like a car down . . .

Bjergo: A clutch, you mean?

John: Ya, without the brake in.

Although concentrating hope for intergenerational continuity on male children is the dominant pattern, farm families such as the Neirikers, looking to marriage or nonfarming careers for daughters, have not made this distinction. In 1971, Franz speaks about his daughter Karen.

Franz: Oh yes, all . . . as a matter of fact, all of them work. They work in the nursery. They don't like it, but they still . . . they still

280

work quite a bit. I'm quite pleased how . . . how they work, and especially the older girl, I was . . . the girl, I was kidding her . . . kidding her about a speech I heard in Rochester this last week at the Hort [Horticultural] Show. I guess out in Washington they use quite a few girls to train young trees, and I told her I have her going to help me, too.

Responsibility for task performance is not blurred. Mrs. Neiriker speaks in 1971.

> *Ellen:* And Franz has tried to interest them in . . . in watching, watching, or observing their own work and assigning rows to them and saying, 'Well now, you can get a certain percentage back from this, you know, and these will be your trees and you have to do . . .,' you know, all the steps that they possibly can do with them, and so that they're always doing their own row so that if one goofs off in one row and then somebody else doesn't have to do that row the next time, they don't . . . you know, each one's responsible for a certain row. It makes for a better setup, I think.

Here is the task reported from Karen's perspective. Notice the details which indicate mastery of tasks. Although the children did not report satisfactions from the performance of tasks during the early stages of apprenticeship, the absence of reported satisfaction did not cause the parents to terminate or unrealistically modify the apprenticeship.

> *Karen:* Oh boy! Changes, you should see them. Well, we have to . . . all of sudden, you know, we had to . . . First we had to work out in the nursery. That's where you have to take and on the main part of the tree you have to rub all . . . off the side things, the side little branches so there isn't any branches left, and then . . . then you have to clip the tops so there's only one top growing and . . . oh. Then we have to do root-stocks. That's where you take and trim back the roots so they can be planted without the roots going all over. And then we have to do sticks. That's where you take a . . . put two nails in these little . . . machine and then you put a stick and then you press down with your foot and the nails are forced into the stick, and we use those to separate branches on trees. And then we have to help mom do the dishes and clean the house and . . .
> *Benson:* You . . . you sound like you don't like the work very well, huh?
> *Karen:* Ho-ho, no, I don't like it at all.
> *Benson:* Do you like . . . do you like doing the nursery work better than the housework or . . .?
> *Karen:* I hate it all. No, I think I like the housework better. You get done after a while, 'cause it takes an hour . . . about an hour to do each row, but . . .

Here is Peter, age eight. Again, note the combination of task mastery, specific responsibility, and lack of satisfaction—at least at the conscious level when asked in that way. The year is 1971.

> *Cole:* You think you're going to want to stay on with it and be a Scout for quite a while?
> *Peter:* I don't think so, no, because most of the time when we get home we have to do some things over in the barn, make . . . we have to put sticks in the boards.
> *Cole:* Oh, yeah. What's that for?
> *Peter:* Oh, to hold trees up. You know those things . . . things which hold the branches down?
> *Cole:* Yeah.
> *Peter:* That's what we have to put in.
> *Cole:* Oh, you have to get . . . that's your job to get those ready, huh?
> *Peter:* Yeah.
> *Cole:* You really . . . you really enjoy doing things like that around the farm though?
> *Peter:* No.

John, now 12 years old, is extending his environment with imported plants. He is performing a range of tasks including operating a variety of equipment, maintaining equipment, and working in the nursery.

> *Colman:* So what's happened in the last two years?
> *John:* Nothing much. We went to California last year and I got those cactuses that are out in the window, and we did some . . . We haven't done very much skiing like . . . like we wanted to this year because there wasn't enough cold weather and enough snow. I fixed a few engines, got them running. I worked in the nursery a lot, helped on the farm quite a bit during the . . . summer, and I've worked on . . . on the . . . on machinery.
> *Colman:* Um-hmm. Now, when you say you worked on machinery, what . . . what kind of work did you . . . what kind of work have you done?
> *John:* Like working . . . working the ground, working with machinery, fitting the ground, planting beans, planting trees . . . and cultivating. . . . And during the winter, when it's been nice weather out, when it's been real warm, we can do a lot of trimming with the . . . this wish ba . . . wish basket we got. It's a basket that raises up and down and swings so you can get over the tree and trim them with the . . . the air guns. They're air-clippers actually. They're quite hea . . . they're not very heavy, but they . . . they're very strong, they could snap off your fingers easy, and you have to be quite care . . . careful with them.
> *Colman:* Now, do you use those now, get up in that basket?
> *John:* Yes, I do. And just this last . . . last week I worked after school most of the time, and then I helped my father working on a

282

mower which he's rebuilding where it's worn out from the grass and the rocks when you hit some rocks, and he's been teaching me how to weld.

John's recreation also contributes to labormanagement development.

> *John:* Well . . . And we haven't done very much snowmobiling because there hasn't been very much snow. And I've worked on a few engines and I got a go-cart, I'm trying to get it running.

Peter, at age 10, is well on the way to labormanagement skills concerning a vital element in the farm family system, the operation and maintenance of engines.

> *Colman:* I see. These are all hand-powered boats, or do you have a motor for them?
> *Peter:* Well . . . well, we got three motors down in the basement. In all now, engines, counting the motor boats, too, we've got fifteen.
> *Colman:* Um-hmm.
> *Peter:* Only one . . . no, none of them really work. My brother has to get a gas line for his. Five-horse he got. I got a half a horse and then two and a half.
> *Colman:* Um-hmm. You take some of the motors apart, do you?
> *Peter:* Got to, got to fix them. We got problems with the carburetors, they're always got . . . leaky and something, the gas is leaking. We got a brand new one and it's leaking already, doesn't even work.
> *Colman:* Um-hmm. You know about how engines run, do you, and about the compression cycle and this sort . . .
> *Peter:* Yeah, we got a whole manual down there of all . . . all the little engines.

Dividing system tasks among the available workers, establishing priorities, and obtaining commitment to task completion is a basic aspect of labormanagement. Here, in 1973, the Neirikers talk about this aspect of labormanagement.

> *Ellen:* A lot of times I'll say there are three jobs and I'll name the three jobs and . . .
> *Peter:* And everybody . . . we lunge for the dog job.
> *Ellen:* Then they rush like mad to get the . . . feed the dog.
> *Franz:* I . . . I do it dif . . . I do it different. I just tell them go do the whole thing and then let them decide it.
> *Karen:* Yeah. Yeah.
> *Peter:* And we have to do it until . . . everybody's got to work until everything's done.

Now, in 1975, parental expectations and apprentice satisfactions are converging. Mr. and Mrs. Neiriker speak first, then Karen.

> *Berkowitz:* Now, do you have any particular things that you would expect from them . . . to do?
>
> *Franz:* Yes, for instance, now right now, today, we start the grafting and they usually have to help an hour or so after school, or two. That's maybe a month or so. And, then in summertime they work quite a bit. They have to do some work at home. We expect them to do some things. Sometimes they don't like it but they still do it without too much arguing about . . . I mean, one thing I think they realize, work has to be done and . . . they really pitch in.
>
> *Berkowitz:* Okay. Now, do you think the fact that they are living on a farm and have this extra responsibilities, would affect their normal growing up in any way?
>
> *Franz:* I think it does, because they have to make decision. I am gone quite often and they . . . at home do some work, in nursery and . . . They have to make decision and . . . sometime they make decisions I might not like, the way they made it, but I'm glad they made the decision.
>
> *Ellen:* And so with refinements in that we have been able to expand more in our nursery than we had before which has been a very good thing, a thing that my husband has been enjoying. The children have on one hand, I think, resent the work in there, in that it's . . . it's . . . takes of their time and yet on the other hand they have the satisfaction of knowing that they know how to do something. So that's been a family operation that's been fulfilling, and interesting and has expanded and has been very profitable.
>
> *Karen:* I'm on the swim team or . . . it hasn't started yet, but I'm going to be, and we're grafting and bud . . . grafting up at the barn now every night, so I can't stay after all the times that I want to, but when swim season starts, then I won't be working up there at all, so I have to work, you know, I do paper work for Dad after supper . . .
>
> *Berkowitz:* Uh-huh.
>
> *Karen:* . . . to compensate.
>
> *Berkowitz:* I see. And how do you feel about that?
>
> *Karen:* I don't really mind it. You know, it's just a challenge.
> [laughter]

John, at age 14 also finds satisfaction from task performance.

> *Berkowitz:* Okay. Now, what do you feel you're supposed to do as . . . as a child? Like is there any responsibilities or things that you have to have?
>
> *John:* You mean have to do, or . . . Well, we have to always help around the house, clean up our own rooms, et cetera, et cetera. Help on the farm. If there's anything goes wrong, we gotta . . . when a worker doesn't show up, we gotta take his place, sometimes, if we can. And well, mainly . . . that's mainly during the summer and we have to work budding because our budding man that used to

284

come had a stroke and he can't come, so we have to take his place. And . . . we have to work quick — do quite a bit of work.

Berkowitz: How do you feel about having to do all that?

John: Well, it's not really that hard. We got plenty of free time, but . . . I think it's pretty good.

Now, for the future. Note the consistency in expectation. Having worked toward developing labormanagement skills, Franz Neiriker hopes to give his children the opportunity to use them — in contrast to many farm parents who destroy their hopes for integenerational continuity by restricting their children's opportunities to exercise labormanagement.

Berkowitz: Now, how about the children? How do you see them fitting in in the future.

Franz: Well, I hope they can take over fairly soon. I don't know if they're going to or not, but . . . they seem to be interested in farming, and if the three of them, if they could work together, I think it would be an excellent future for them.

Berkowitz: Now, do you think that they could work together?

Franz: I . . . I think so . . I certainly think so. They . . . they have some squabbles once in a while, but those are whole life. I think that really . . . I think it will work.

Karen, now 16 years old, speaks to the subject.

Karen: And then I'd like to go on and maybe get my doctorate. I don't know. I don't know what that involves, really. [laughter] And well, get out of college and I don't know, maybe work in an experiment station or something like that. Then I'd like to work on my own, because if I got married, I wouldn't want to . . . work, if I had kids. Well, let's phrase that different. If I got married, and when I had kids, after I had kids, I wouldn't want to work . . . full-time, at least, because I feel I have a responsibility to stay home. So I'd like to get into some kind of research where I could work, you know, work at home or something.

Berkowitz: Now, how about working here? Have you ever thought of doin' that?

Karen: Yeah. [laughter] I was talking with [John] about that, and he wants to become an engineer and we were thinking that we could work the farm part-time. We could take turns working it. [laughter] . . . You know, like every month somebody else would work the farm. But I . . . I would like to work here on the farm, but I don't know if I ever would.

Here is John, age 14.

Berkowitz: Uh-huh. Okay. Now if I met you in ten years, what do you think you'd be doin'?

John: In ten years . . . Probably back on the farm again after

285

college. If I'm out of college. [laughter] I don't know if I would be.

Berkowitz: Are you plannin' on goin' to college?

John: Yes.

Berkowitz: Uh-huh. You know what you want to study or anything?

John: Agriculture and mechanics.

Berkowitz: Mechanics? And why do you want to study those two?

John: Well, agriculture so I can run the farm and mechanics so I can fix things, and design things, you know, like . . . certain things like apple shakers or somethin' like that.

Berkowitz: Uh-huh. Do you ever think you'll be runnin' the farm?

John: Yeah.

Berkowitz: You do?

John: Not personally, myself. My brother and my sister also want to run the farm too, so . . .

Berkowtiz: You think that you three would be able to run it together?

John: I think so.

Berkowitz: Now, if you had your choice, would you rather be able to run the farm alone, yourself, or together, or what?

John: Well, it'd be a better farm if we run it together, but see, if I ran it myself, I'd have my own way. [laughter] . . . So . . . the farm . . . I think it'd be . . . would probably be better off with all three of us running it.

Berkowitz: And why do you say that?

John: Well, we got different opinions and if you get . . . one person gets an idea on something, usually got to tell the other person — the other two people, and then talk it out and they finally come out with the best decision, usually.

Peter, age 12 in 1975, is developing an interest in the economic aspects of labormanagement.

Berkowitz: What do you plan to be doin' when you get older?

Peter: Mm-mmmm, probably work on a nursery . . . nursery and orchard.

Berkowitz: Which one? This one?

Peter: Oh . . . yeah, but . . . see what I was planning on doin' about a year ago is havin' corn and wheat. Just growing corn and wheat, you know, I'll have one of the big operation things. Then I decided it wouldn't probably be good, I'll have to . . . I keep watching the corn rate — a bushel of corn, you know, it's been . . . it went down a fourth, just on Sunday, I guess. So I don't know, but nursery, it seems to be doin' real good, a real good nursery. Could do that real good and I like that too.

Berkowitz: Mm-hm. Do you think you want to take over this place?

Peter: Yeah, maybe, but I think my brother, he . . . he wants to take this place over too, probably.

Collectively, the Neiriker children constitute a powerful labor-management resource, a situation which their parents have recognized. Paul, too, contemplates his future on the farm. As the youngest, and, perhaps, the most fascinated with competition, he does not stress farming in cooperation with family members, although the final passage indicates a readiness to work with brother and sister and, when tension becomes too great, a device has been developed for its relief.

Berkowitz: When you work on the farm, do you usually work with your brother and your sister?

Peter: Yeah, most of the time. Most of the time when we're working, like on weekends and Saturday, we all have to work, you know? In summer, sometimes, it's busy, well, everybody doesn't do the same job. Like my sister might be workin' in somethin' in the barn and my brother is fixin' the tractor and I might be out in the nursery or out in the orchard or somethin'. Very occasionally, we're all, all together doing the same thing, except for in the winter and in the middle of the summer when we bud.

Berkowitz: And how does it work out when you're all together doin' the same thing?

Peter: It works out good but, sometimes, [John], he's always thinking he's a big shot, sometimes. He says he knows all this stuff, you know, and he talks big, so we start, when we're out in the field, we start throwin' dirt clods and that gets out to a big war, then. [laughter]

In concluding, here is retrospective comment. Looking backward from age 14, Karen testifies to the extra-monetary rewards of task performance.

Karen: I think I was maybe about eleven or so, and I was playing outside the house here and my father called me out to the nursery, we had it just down the road, and then he wanted me to do this work for him. So I came out and then he showed me how to do it and, you know, I thought it was only for that night. [both laugh] And I've been doing it ever since.

Diamant: You've been doing it ever since. [laugh] That should have told you. Do you get paid for it?

Karen: Yes.

Diamant: You do, uh-huh. Do you get a regular minimum wage per hour or . . .

Karen: No, I get paid, let's see. Well, we get paid by the row, I'm not sure how much it is.

287

In conclusion, viewing labormanagement as a continuum between great creativity and complete reliance on conventions, the Neirikers, with two other families in our panel of twenty, are at the creative extremity. They seem to recognize that public education is not adapted to the survival of the farm family. Their solution to long term survival is compensatory education provided at home.

REFERENCES

1. Terkel, Studs, *Working: People Talk About What They Do and How They Feel About What They Do,* Pantheon Books, N.Y., 1974. p. xix.
2. Shumway, Gary L., compiler, *Oral History in the United States,* The Oral History Association, N.Y., 1971, p. 3.
3. "Notable Books, 1974," Handout of the Notable Books Council, Reference and Adult Services Division, American Library Association.
4. "Interviews on Agriculture, Water Resources, and Land Use," May 1974, "California Wine Industry Interviews," June 1974, Regional Oral History Office, University of California, Berkeley, mimeo; the *Oral History Collection of Columbia University,* Oral History Research Office, New York, 1973; "Oral History Project" Report for 1962–63, 1963–64, 1964–65, New York State College of Agriculture, mimeo.
5. Calculated from data in the *1969 Census of Agriculture* and USDA ERS Reports "Corporations Having Agricultural Operations" by William Scofeld and George Coffman, No. 142 (1968) and 156 (1969). Details concerning the calculation can be obtained from the author.
6. Walter Coward replaced Jerry Stockdale in 1973. The farm family study has been supported by Cornell University Agricultural Experiment Station as a Hatch Act Project.
7. *Successful Farming,* February 1975, p. 28–29.

A Folklorist, not a Farmer: A Commentary

By
George G. Carey

Let me say at the outset that I am a folklorist not a farmer. I scarcely think I could distinguish between a harrow and a hoe, a furze and a furrow. And if you could witness the meagre returns this fall from the garden I planted last spring, I think you would understand why I am a lot better off wandering aimlessly around in the groves of the academe. Nonetheless, if my strengths do not run to working the land, my interests in seeing traditional farm methods collected, preserved, and studied run deep indeed. That is why Colman's paper intrigues me.

Quite simply, I am pleased to know that oral historians are out securing history from the bottom up as well as interviewing the Harry Trumans, Dean Achesons and close associates of John Kennedy. From the folklorist's point of view, it is this listening to the inarticulate which is so germane to field oriented research. But, I must confess, I was appalled by Colman's remark that oral history interviews with professors outnumbered interviews with farmers by six to one. In my discipline that would be analogous to taking a student interested in, let us say, the folk medicine of the Micmac

Dr. Carey is an associate professor in the Department of English, University of Massachusetts, Amherst, Massachusetts.

Indians, and sending him out to interview an anthropologist who had studied and written about the tribe. I have no idea of the kind of information the oral historians were eliciting from these professors, but it must have been data filtered through a very highly honed mind and far different from the raw data received from an actual farmer or his family.

So, from my point of view, Colman's attempt to gather his material from first hand sources is a move in the right direction. And I am much impressed with the thoroughness and persistence of his methods. His approach of returning every other year to interview members of the Neiriker family reveals a constantly swelling knowledge of labormanagement among the children. Far too often folklorists in their fieldwork employ a one shot method. They select their target for research, move into the area or among the group they intend to collect from, gather their material and then retreat to their lairs to write up their finds. In certain instances it is a gross example of what we might call cultural rip-off, particularly when widely sold books or records are the results of their research. Folklorists, I believe could learn a lot from the oral historian whose procedures seem more measured and orderly, less impressionistic. Folklorists need to return to their areas of research from time to time if, for no other reason, than to see what effects their work has had on the individual lives of their informants.

It would also appear from Colman's work that there were a number of shifts in approach that took place during the course of his interviewing, and that the interviews were never so structured that they could not accommodate those shifts. Folklorists constantly find themselves in this same sort of a situation where the initial idea which motivated the research alters as the student begins to discover that the raw materials collected differ considerably from what was expected initially. Different folk groups emphasize different things in regard to the expressive nature of their culture. Chesapeake Bay watermen, for instance, tell and enjoy humorous oral narratives and, by studying their accounts, we can find out a great deal about their attitudes towards government and the church as well as something about their entire system of values. On the other hand, the farmers of the Pennsylvannia Dutch country in southern Pennsylvania and northern Maryland seem to put more stress on their material culture, the artifactual handiwork as expressed in their fractur paintings, their furniture, their food — their crafts in general. Even the very arrangement of their farms tells us something about their sense of values. Unlike our urban-suburban cultures which mark

290

achievement by a large house, a two car garage stuffed with appropriate vehicles, or a large green sward reaching down to the curb, the Pennsylvania Dutch farmer rests his case for having made it on the size and attractiveness of his barn. These large bank barns which grace the landscape around Lancaster, Pennsylvania, virtually dwarf the farmhouse, in most cases, and attest to a farmer's industriousness; presumably, they are full come harvest time and not of cars.

As I suggest, then, it is really up to the folklorist to discover and study the most expressive facets of a group's culture and, often, he must find this by trial and error. I am really quite embarrassed to admit however, that trained folklorists have not given the agricultural community in this country the attention it deserves. In the past half century or more, what folklorists have tended to do was to venture into the field and compile large compendiums of weather lore or planting beliefs. Often in so doing, they discovered that many of the rituals or customs associated with these beliefs dated back to ancient practices connected with fertility magic. Vance Randolph, for example, who culled the Ozark Mountains in the 1920's and 1930's discovered a curious rite for sowing flax where the farmer and his wife appeared in the field at sun-up, both naked. She walked ahead, he sowed the seeds. "They chanted or sang a rhyme with the line 'Up to my ass an' higher too!' Every few steps the man threw some seeds against the woman's buttocks. Up and down the field they went, singing and scattering seed, until the planting was done. Then . . . they just laid down on the ground and had a good time." Likewise with some turnip growers from the same region, four grown girls and a boy were observed at sunrise one July morning: "The boy throwed all the seed, and the gals kept a-hollering 'Pecker deep, pecker deep!' And when they got done, the whole bunch would roll in the dust like some kind of wild animals. There ain't no sense to it, but them folks always raise the best turnips on the creek."[1]

Now, I submit, it is curiously quaint that as late as the 20th century survivals of old fertility rites were being practiced by American hill farmers, yet this does not tell us much about the modern farmer or how aspects of folklore are threaded into the fabric of his existence. To date, it has been English scholars of folklife who have been foremost in attempting to pull together the traditional aspects of farm life. Their work has been a combination of oral history and folklife studies. I hardly need mention Ronald Blythe's classic *Akenfield* for a sensitive look at village life. More to the folklorist's taste perhaps are the works of George Evans, *The Pattern Under the*

291

Plow and *Ask the Fellows Who Cut the Hay*. Yet, even here, the people interviewed for these books are older men and women and the farm life they recall is one that documents the technological revolution on the farm during the past century. Theirs was a parochial existence — some of Evan's informants lived out their very long lives never traveling more than eight miles from the house in which they were born — and consequently it was not so much that they resisted change, but simply that new ways and ideas seeped through slowly and these old farmers hung onto what they knew. As Evans writes: ". . . the farmer and farm-worker of the old pre-machine era in East Anglia had an attitude to the land that is characteristic of the primitive husbandman all over the world. It was enshrined in the proverb: 'A farmer should live as though he were going to die tomorrow; but he should farm as though he were going to live forever.'"[2] Between the farmer and the soil there was a bond that amounted, on his part, almost to veneration: the soil was something to be nursed and treated with the utmost consideration.

Unfortunately, few American scholars have undertaken studies similar to those of Blythe and Evans. One thinks perhaps of Agee's *Let Us Now Praise Famous Men* but that has always seemed to me more a long beautiful story-poem about a whole social order, albeit primarily rural and agricultural. A more detailed, if less readable accounting is Amos Long's *The Pennsylvania German Farm Family*. Though Long is not a folklorist, he does attempt to blend aspects of folklore into chapters explicitly titled "The Farmhouse," "The Barn," "The Pigeon," "The Privy." For instance, Pennsylvania German farmers believed that if the flow of milk in cows was scant, one should get up early in the morning and, before saying a word to anyone, milk the cows and pour the milk into the privy. Then one's problem would be solved.

If Long's book really fails to integrate the folklore on the farm with the rest of daily life — once more the folklore is seen as a curious attendant — it does detail for us the function of farm buildings in this daily life, and the book is valuable from this perspective. But little of this material has been elicited through actual oral interviews, though the author certainly has been a firsthand observer.

What I see facing us, then, is the question of where the oral historian's and folklorist's areas of interest overlap and when, if at all, their research can be mutually beneficial. Aside from the relatively common methods of gathering raw data which I have touched on, one area of common concern appears to be the educational process within a family structure. Colman's paper reveals to me as much about the Neiriker children's farming education as it does about the process of labormanagement itself. We are dealing here, it seems, with the whole matter of how effective knowledge is imparted, a procedure in which folklorists are becoming more and more interested. To wit, recent studies have been undertaken among Newfoundland fishermen to ascertain exactly how the young acquire good fishing techniques and ultimate success in their work. What has been discovered is that a great deal of practical knowledge is absorbed simply by listening to older men's short accounts of their day to day experiences at sea. Built into many of these personal narratives is a lesson of some kind, implied of course, but never stated.

Might not the same kind of examination be undertaken among farmers or the extended farm family in order to explore the educational factor within the traditional process? I am convinced our finds, like Colman's, would bring us in close touch not only with effective learning procedures, but also with family values and how they are subconsciously passed along.

Still, I do feel that it is equally important for both folklorist and oral historian to press their interviews with the "inarticulate" farmer for information and insight into the past as well as the present for, as one scholar has put it, "Nothing less than the whole of the past is needed to explain the future."

REFERENCES

1. *New York Review of Books* (March 28, 1968), p. 16.
2. George Ewart Evans, *The Pattern under the Plow* (London, 1966), p. 126.

Bibliography

Agee, James and Evans, Walker. *Let Us Now Praise Famous Men.* Boston: Houghton Middlin Co., 1941.

Blythe, Ronald. *Akenfield: Portrait of an English Village.* London: Allen Lane, The Penguin Press; New York: Pantheon Books, 1969.

Evans, George Ewart. *Ask the Fellows Who Cut the Hay.* With decorations by Thomas Bewick. 1st edition. London: Faber & Faber, 1956. 2nd edition, 1962.

———. *The Pattern Under the Plow: Aspects of the Folklife of East Anglia.* Illustrated by David Gentleman. London; Faber, 1966.

Long, Amos, Jr. *The Pennsylvania German Farm Family: A Regional Architectural and Folk Cultural Study of an American Agricultural Community.* Publications of the Pennsylvania German Society. Volume 6. Breinigsville, Pa.: Pennsylvania German Society, 1972.

The Mechanization of American Agriculture

By
Wayne D. Rasmussen

In 1970, one of America's foremost agricultural scientists wrote: "Continuing development and application of technology in production of food, fiber, and forest products can supply the next generation abundantly. It can enable them to take the actions necessary to have clean air, sparkling water, and a green and pleasant world in which to live."[1] Two years later, a critic of agricultural research stated: ". . .in terms of wasted lives, depleted rural areas, choked cities, poisoned land and maybe poisoned people, mechanization research has been a bad investment."[2]

Perhaps some of the contrast lies in the emphasis given, for the scientist also stated: "Our newly applied technology has brought indirect and sometimes unforeseen costs. Pesticides have been dispersed throughout our environment. Crop adjustments have left people without work or means of self-support. Our abundance has cost the taxpayer in funds for supply management and the producer in depressed prices."[3] The critic said: ". . .this focus on scientific and business efficiency has led to production (and over-production) of a bounty of food and fiber products. . . ."[4]

Dr. Rasmussen is an historian with the Economic Research Service, U.S. Department of Agriculture, Washington, D.C.

Earlier, Rachel Carson, in her book *Silent Spring,* had been critical of the use of insecticides in agriculture.[5] While this is part of our technical package, it differs from the questions which might be raised about mechanization.

In considering the past two hundred years, it must be remembered that land for farming has always been plentiful and less costly, comparatively speaking, than labor. Thus, any device permitting the use of more of the available land with the same amount of labor was usually welcomed.

At the time of the American Revolution, most of the tools used on the farm differed little from those known for the previous 2,000 years. Grain was cut almost universally with a sickle, a curved blade with a short handle, swung from a stooped position. It was not until about the time of the Revolution that first, the long-bladed and long-handled scythe, and then the cradle, a wicker frame attached to the scythe blade, catching the cut grain so that it could be laid down in windrows, came into use. In general, agriculture was in a bad way as to field work at the end of the war.[6]

American leaders were looking for new implements and for more productive methods of farming. George Washington, for example, asked Arthur Young, British advocate of agricultural change, to secure agricultural implements for him.[7]

The interest of Thomas Jefferson in the mechanical improvement of farm tools is nearly as well known as his devotion to agrarianism. He developed a seed drill, a hemp brake, an improved threshing machine, a sidehill plow, and a design for a moldboard for a plow that would turn the soil efficiently.[8] His work tended to be theoretical rather than practical, and apparently had little influence on other farmers.

The most dramatic breakthrough in farm production in the years after the Revolution occurred with the invention of the cotton gin. Upland cotton grew well throughout the South. However, the lint clung tenaciously to the seed. In 1793, Eli Whitney, a young graduate of Yale University who had accepted a teaching job in South Carolina, invented a practical machine for separating the seeds from the lint. The device dramatically changed Southern agriculture. Production of cotton increased from an estimated 10,500 bales in 1793 to 4,486,000 bales in 1861. This extensive commercial production of cotton led to the expansion of the plantation system, with its use of slave labor.[9] The dependence of the South upon a major export crop, produced largely on slave-operated plantations, set several forces in motion which led to the Civil

War. If it had not been for Eli Whitney or someone like him, cotton growing would not have become profitable, slavery would have declined and disappeared, and the Civil War would never have taken place.

The availability of low-cost cotton, together with the new spinning and weaving machinery adopted from England, led to the rapid industrialization of the New England economy. The demands of the mill towns offered New England and other farmers an expanding demand for their products. This provided a stimulus to Northern farming, heretofore lacking, which, in turn, encouraged experiments with new tools, implements, and methods.[10]

Unlike cotton production, where the new gin made almost unlimited production possible, grain farmers were faced with one bottleneck after another, demanding a whole series of inventions and improvements in labor-saving machinery.

Plowing claimed the attention of many inventors. The first patent issued for a plow went to Charles Newbold of New Jersey. His plow, except for handles and beam, was of solid cast iron. The story goes that farmers would not buy it, fearing that the iron poisoned the land and made the weeds grow. In 1814, Jethro Wood patented a cast iron plow, and improved it in 1819. The moldboard, share, and landside were cast in three interchangeable parts. Wood's plow was widely adopted.[11]

Neither the wooden nor cast iron plows were adapted to the sticky soils of the prairies. The soil would stick to the plow instead of sliding by and turning over. In 1833, John Lane, a blacksmith at Lockport, Illinois, began fastening strips of saw steel over wooden moldboards. These plows turned furrows in the Illinois prairie loam, but Lane did not patent his idea. In 1837, another Illinois blacksmith, John Deere, began using saw steel and smooth wrought iron for shares and moldboards. He went into partnership with a businessman, Leonard Andrus, and by 1846 was producing 1,000 plows a year.[12]

Harvesting was the crucial point in grain production. Thus, the mechanical reaper was probably the most significant single invention introduced into farming between 1830 and 1860. In 1833, Obed Hussey patented a practical, horse-drawn reaper. Meanwhile, Cyrus H. McCormick of Virginia had completed a machine in 1831, continuing work along lines begun by his father. McCormick patented his machine in 1834. In the 20 years that followed, McCormick obtained a dominant position in the business. By 1851, he was making 1,000 machines a year in his Chicago plant.[13] Various

Constance McL. Green

Eli Whitney
and the
Birth of American
Technology

Edited by Oscar Handlin

Little, Brown and Company · *Boston* · *Toronto*

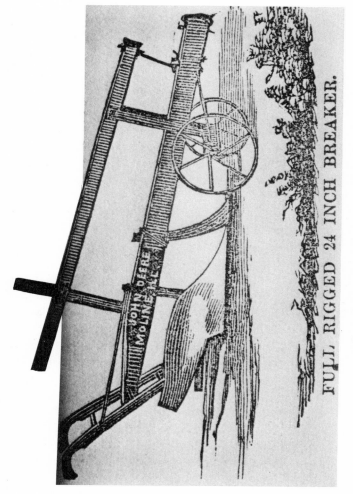

FULL RIGGED 24 INCH BREAKER.

From Country Gentleman, 10 (1857): 129.

improvements were made in the harvester over several decades. One of the most important was the twine-knotter, which was perfected by John F. Appleby in 1878 and permitted the automatic tying of the grain into bundles for quick and easy handling.[14]

The success of the reaper encouraged the development and adoption of other horse-powered equipment. Some machines, the corn cultivator for example, preceded the reaper. It was in limited use as early as the 1820's.[15] The revolving horse rake was available at about the same time.[16] In 1837, John and Hiram Pitts patented a widely-used threshing machine. A mower which was to achieve wide use was patented by W. F. Ketchum in 1844 and 1847. Other horse-powered machines developed before the Civil War included grain drills, corn shellers, hay-baling presses, cultivators of various types, and a large number of other implements.[17]

The agricultural magazines of the 1840's and 1850's urged that farmers adopt the new machines. They went even further in reporting that some machines had been "generally" or "universally" adopted.[18] Their pages were filled with advertisements extolling the new devices.

By 1860, a man's labor had become more productive if he had adopted the new horse-drawn machinery. But, as Paul W. Gates has pointed out, there were social costs. The capital needs of establishing a farm had increased, making it more difficult for laborers, tenants, and young people to become farm operators. Increased production was already leading to surpluses and periods of low prices for farm products. Farmers were becoming more dependent upon bankers and merchants. Although the South continued to rely upon slave labor rather than machines to produce its crops, the cotton gin, particularly, had tied the region to monoculture and an economy dependent upon exports.[19]

Nevertheless, many farmers had not adopted the new horse-drawn machinery, hesitating to invest in the implements until they felt that it would be profitable. The Civil War stimulated the change and resulted in the first American agricultural revolution—the change from hand power to horse power. Each farmer, on the average, invested $7 in constant dollars (adjusted to reflect changes in the economy) in new machinery and equipment in 1850, $11 in 1860, $20 in 1870, and $26 in 1880. The war-induced labor shortage, high prices, and a seemingly unlimited demand encouraged farmers to spend their savings or to go into debt to acquire the labor saving machines. And once that was done, the farmer, ready or not, found himself committed to commercial production.[20]

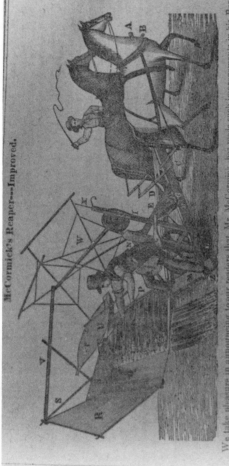

McCormick's Reaper—Improved,

We take pleasure in announcing to our readers that Mr. McCormick has made such improvements in his Reaper, as are found to greatly facilitate its operation, especially in the work of raking the cut grain from the platform, and that he is now engaged in manufacturing a large number of the machines at Cincinnati, for the supply of the south-western country. He assures us also, that the utmost attention will be paid to the character of the workmanship in constructing the machines, so that no fault shall hereafter exist on that score.

From what we have seen of the operation of this machine, and the high testimonials from those who have used it extensively, we are confident that it will do first rate work in good hands; and it will be seen from the advertisement in this paper that the terms of sale offer the fullest possible guaranty to purchasers. The need of machines for reaping grain was greatly felt by the farmers of Ohio last year, and we doubt not that a large number will be used at the coming harvest. Handbills giving fuller information, and testimonials of the character of the machine, can be obtained of Mr. McCormick, Cincinnati, or at the office of this paper. We will also, if desired order the machines for any of our readers who may wish to obtain them.

From Ohio Cultivator, 3 (1847): 57.

Pitt's Grain Thrasher and Separator.

The machine represented above, is one of much importance to the wheat growing farmers of Ohio. In the great wheat regions of New York, it has for some years been in very general use, and is more universally approved than any other machine for thrashing and cleaning grain. The "Separator" can be attached to any ordinary thrasher, if desired. It carries the straw from the thrasher, separates the wheat therefrom completely, winnows the grain and deposites it in bags, fit for market, at one operation. Large numbers of these machines are annually manufactured and sold at Rochester, our former residence, and from having frequently witnessed the perfection of their work, we feel confidence in commending them to the farmers of Ohio.

It will be seen by an advertisement on the last page of this paper, that Mr. H. D. Jamesen has procured the right of this State, and is largely engaged in the manufacture of the machines at Massillon. We are assured that they will be made in the best manner, and give satisfaction to purchasers.

From Ohio Cultivator, 3 (1847): 57.

302

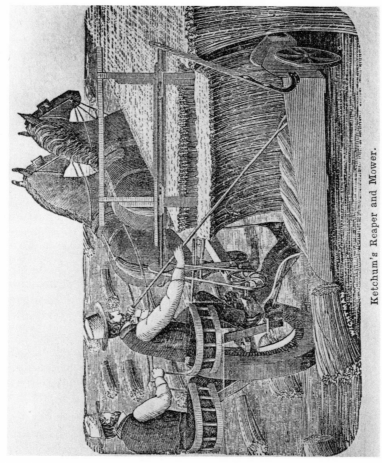

Ketchum's Reaper and Mower.

From Country Gentleman, 13 (1859): 301.

During the period from 1870 to 1900, farmers had to grow more to pay for the machines, but recurrent surpluses kept prices low. Food was cheap, but the farmer stayed poor as the opening of new land and widespread mechanization permitting a man to cultivate more acres sent floods of grain to market. He was advised to cut production, but no single farmer could influence the market, whatever he did.[21] Cooperatives helped, but, as the results of the first agricultural revolution died away, the rate of increase in production declined, and, from the Spanish-American War to World War I, production and consumption were in relative balance.

Even though many farmers faced economic difficulties between the Civil and Spanish-American wars, mechanization was almost invariably regarded as helpful. A spokesman for the Department of Agriculture wrote in 1898: "Mechanical contrivances have largely supplanted human labor in many respects, or have improved the application of labor and increased the product of agriculture, reduced the cost of production, augmented the farmer's gross income, and made his life an easier one than it was before the machine period."[22]

An historian of the period from 1860 to 1897 has pointed out that mechanization led to a reduction in spirit-breaking toil. This helped the able farmer to acquire prosperity and leisure and to educate his children. The number of people needed to feed and clothe the population of the United States and to supply its agricultural exports declined. These displaced persons sometimes found it difficult to make a living in the city. The expense of machinery, along with other factors, reduced the number of owners and added to the numbers of tenants and hired workers. And while production per manyear often more than doubled, yield per acre rarely increased. The tendency was to wear out the soil rather than improve it.[23]

In the most searching examination of farm life made before World War I, however, the Country Life Commission, in its report of 1909, made no particular reference to mechanization, although several pages are devoted to farm labor. The only mention of machines comes in a discussion of labor difficulties, where, in an effort to overcome them, it is said: "In many States the more difficult lands are being given up and machinery farming is extending."[24]

Meanwhile, new sources of power were being developed for the farm. Steam engines, first stationary and then self-propelled, were used for many operations on large farms, particularly in the West. Their greatest use came in operating threshing machines. They

304

proved to be too heavy and cumbersome for most other farm work. The peak in their manufacture came in 1913 with the production of 10,000 machines. Thereafter, production declined rapidly, as more gasoline tractors came on the market.[25]

The first practical, self-propelled gasoline tractor was built in 1892 by John Froelich of Iowa. He mounted a gasoline engine, built in Cincinnati, on a running gear equipped with a traction arrangement of his own manufacture, and completed a fifty-day threshing run with it.[26] The Froelich was the forerunner of the John Deere tractors.

The first business devoted exclusively to making tractors was established in Iowa City, Iowa in 1905, by C. W. Hart and C. H. Parr. The founders had started working on internal combustion engines after they met as students at the University of Wisconsin in 1893. Their first tractor was completed in 1901. Crude as it was, it remained in operation for about 20 years. The Hart-Parr Company later became part of the Oliver Corporation. Many tractor-manufacturing companies were formed in the next decades and many failed. A large percentage of the machines manufactured today are made by the International Harvester Co., John Deere Co., J. I. Case Co., Massey-Ferguson, Oliver Farm Equipment Co., Minneapolis—Moline Power Implement Co., Allis—Chalmers Manufacturing Co., Caterpillar Tractor Co., and Ford Motor Co.[27]

Internal-combustion engine tractors were gradually adopted up to World War I, when high prices for farm products, government appeals for increased production, and some labor shortages encouraged their wider use. In July, 1920, farm prices dropped sharply. Although there were ups-and-downs during the 1920's, farmers were nearly always in, at best, a marginal economic situation, which meant that they were reluctant to convert from proven horse-drawn equipment to tractor power, and its additional cash costs. Nevertheless, the number of horses and mules declined rather steadily and the number of tractors increased.

One machine, the combine, sometimes self-propelled, sometimes tractor drawn, had come into its own. The first successful combine, which cut and threshed the grain in one operation, was built in 1836 in Michigan. This horse-powered machine was shipped to California in 1854 and harvested several hundred acres of wheat. In the mid-1880's, steam engines were used as power sources for the numerous combines being manufactured in California.[28] The gasoline engine began to replace steam for pulling the combine and operating its mechanism about 1912. Big combines powered by gasoline engines were widely available during the 1920's and 1930's. The development of a one-man combine powered by a two-plow tractor in 1935 was another milestone. More than a million grain combines were in use by 1956, and the 1.5 million grain binders that had been in use in the decade before World War II had virtually disappeared.[29]

And not only did the binders disappear. The threshing crew was usually three men: the separator man, the engine man, and the water man. But, if the threshing was done from shocks in the field, there were two or three men to pitch bundles of grain onto the horsedrawn hayracks, each with a driver, and often one or two men to help pitch bundles into the separator. A modest-sized crew would run to about a dozen men. Those not in the family or not living nearby could sleep in the barn, but they all had to be fed. Cooking for threshers was the ultimate test of the farm housewife. Sometimes, there would be something of a competition between households as to who served the best meals but, nevertheless, threshing and feeding threshers were the hardest jobs of the year. Since the big machines have disappeared as practical tools, some farmers operate them as a hobby. In *Ohio Farm,* Wheeler McMillan writes of threshing as "the glamor job," but I remember threshing as hard, dirty work.[30]

Virtually complete transition to mechanization, marked by the change from animal power to mechanical power, was triggered by World War II. During the 1930's, the New Deal farm programs had obtained enough money for farmers so that some could replace wornout machines with current models. The rural electrification program had brought a new major power source to many, and eventually to nearly all, farms. However, it took World War II, with its farm labor shortages, its high prices for farm products, and its seemingly unlimited demand to convince nearly all American farmers to turn to tractors and related machines.

Mechanization was one part of the second American agricultural revolution. It, together with greater use of lime and fertilizer, widespread use of cover crops and other conservation practices, irrigation whenever necessary, use of improved varieties and breeds, adoption of hybrid corn, a better balanced feeding of livestock, the more effective control of insects and disease, and the use of chemicals for such purposes as weed killers and defoliants, made up a package of practices. Actually, this was a systems approach to the problems of increasing agricultural productivity. The effects were revolutionary so far as production was concerned. And, in many respects, rural life was affected just as much.

Sugar-beet production is an outstanding example of labor saving through mechanization and the development of a different seed type. Before World War II, horse-drawn drills, cultivators, lifters, and wagons were used in beet production, but hand operations dominated thinning in the spring and harvesting in the fall. In the 1930's the California Agricultural Experiment Station and the Bureau of Agricultural Engineering began cooperative research to develop a combine, that is, a machine which would lift, top, and load the sugar beets in one trip down the row. Over a period of years, several devices were developed to do one part or another of the job and were released to private manufacturers who continued the research and development work. By 1958, two major types of harvesters were being manufactured. In that year, 100 percent of the crop was harvested mechanically as compared with almost none before 1941 and seven percent in 1944.

The problem of thinning the plants was tackled both mechanically and through modification of the seed. In 1941, some multigerm seeds were sheared into segments and planted, and many of the seeds produced only one plant. The sheared seeds were adopted by many growers. However, in 1954 a much more satisfactory solution came when the first commercial mono-germ seed was released to the industry. Presently, with precision planting of mono-germ seeds and the use of a synchronous thinner, sugar-beet production is completely mechanized through the nation.[31] The growers' goal of becoming independent of migrant labor has been achieved. What has happened to the migrant workers?

The migrant worker question was back of the research leading to the mechanical tomato harvester. Its rapid adoption was a result of a shortage of experienced migrant workers following the termination of Public Law 78 on December 31, 1964, and the drastic reduction in the importation of foreign labor.

The development of the machine by researchers at the University of California, Davis, has been traced in detail elsewhere. It is of interest because it exemplifies the systems approach to an agricultural problem. A plant breeder, G. C. Hanna, developed a tomato plant whose fruit could withstand machine handling and, given the appropriate amounts of fertilizer and water, set an abundant crop of fruit ripening over a very short period. An agricultural engineer, Coby Lorenzen, devised a machine that cut the plants at ground level, elevated them into the machine, and removed the fruit by shaking the vines. A belt then moved the fruit to a crew of hand sorters standing on the machine who removed green fruit and clods.

A crew of twelve, according to Roy Bainer, handles about the same amount of fruit normally picked by sixty hand workers. The machine capacity varies from 8 to 12 tons per hour. In 1963, about 1.5 percent of California tomatoes grown for processing were harvested by machine. By 1968, the figure was 95 percent.[32]

If a mechanical tomato harvester had not been perfected, processors would have shifted their operations to Mexico, where efficient labor was plentiful. This is based upon an assumption which is probably correct—that most picking of tomatoes to be processed was done by Mexican nationals rather than by United States citizens. I have been told by growers that it is impossible to recruit Californians for this type of labor. Some labor leaders have testified otherwise. The question is a difficult one, and the answer is not readily evident.

The effects of the adoption of another invention, the mechanical cotton harvester, are more obvious, perhaps because many more people have been affected. The first device, the cotton stripper, which removed all bolls from the plant, came into widespread used in Texas in 1926. It was reasonably satisfactory only in limited areas.[33] At about the same time, John D. and Mack Rust of Texas invented a spindle picker upon which they filed a patent in January, 1928.

The spindle picker developed slowly but World War II, with its demand for cotton and its high prices, stimulated manufacturers to build more machines. In 1949, less than 10 percent of the cotton crop was machine harvested, but by 1969 the total was at least 96 percent. In that same period, improvements in land preparation, water control, planting techniques, weed control by machines and chemicals, use of fertilizer, and pest control, coupled with improved varieties, increased average yields of upland cotton from about 300 pounds of lint to over 500 pounds per acre. Most of the human drudgery had disappeared form the cotton farms. In 1948, about 140 man-hours were required to produce a bale of cotton in the United States. In 1968, only about 25 man-hours were required. With more complete mechanization, several hundred thousand fewer workers were required to produce the crop. This brought America face-to-face with a key problem, as expressed by two authors of an article in the 1970 *Yearbook of Agriculture:* "A number of these people had limited skills and limited opportunities to obtain alternative employment in other economic sectors."[34]

Mechanization of cotton production meant the virtual end of share cropping, long regarded as detrimental to the croppers, the owners, and the land itself. But there were no real alternatives within farming for the displaced share croppers.

Not long after inventing their spindle machine, the Rust brothers recognized that it would throw "75 percent of the labor population out of employment." They were unwilling to see this happen and resorted to one plan after another to prevent it. Their ideas included adapting the machine to small farms, marketing it with restrictions on how it was used, selling it only to community farming projects organized as cooperatives, and using their profits to assist displaced cotton farmers. However, none of these proved practical and all were swept aside with World War II and the entrance of several firms into the business of manufacturing cotton harvesters.

The interest of the Rust brothers in preventing social and economic disorganization in the cotton-growing areas of the nation, their failure, and the problems which arose as cotton growing was mechanized are detailed in *The New Revolution in the Cotton Economy* by James H. Street. This pioneering study by an economist who did his research at the University of Texas, the Bureau of Agricultural Economics of the U.S. Department of Agriculture, and other institutions, carries the analysis into the early 1950's. He concludes from the economic viewpoint that the mechanization process is unlikely to be reversed once it gets underway, that mechanization demands better management for efficient farming, that there will be widening disparities among farms in production, size, and income, and that it will be necessary to continue adjustments in land use. Socially, mechanization, according to Street, means continued pressure on the farm population, a rise in the rural standard of living, and, so far as the cotton areas are concerned, a lessening of racial discrimination.[35] Oddly enough, though its importance was widely recognized, this study is virtually unique in the research and scholarly literature of American agriculture.

In 1967, the President's National Advisory Commission on Rural Poverty in its report, *The People Left Behind,* stated that Federal programs for rural America, partly because of mechanization, were woefully out of date. According to the Commission, they were developed without anticipating the vast changes in technology and the consequences of this technology to rural people. The report continues: "We have not adjusted to the fact that in the brief period of 15 years, from 1950 to 1965, new machines and new methods increased farm output in the United States by 45 percent—and reduced farm employment by 45 percent. Nor is there adequate awareness that during the next 15 years the need for farm labor will decline by another 45 percent." The Commission did not suggest any attempt to do the impossible — that is, to reverse the process of mechanization. Rather, it recommended that programs to help small farmers enlarge their farms be set up, and that supervisory or management advisory services be made available.[36]

These problems have been the hidden costs, seldom mentioned, of farm mechanization and related changes. The decline in farm population and in the number of farms, the increase in size and in capital requirements for a farm to survive, the disappearance of many small towns, and the decline in rural social institutions have been recognized. It is rarely, however, that one finds a statement such as that made by Otha D. Wearin in 1971, in a volume appealing to a farm audience:

> The productive capacity of power machinery has greatly reduced the farm population. Occupied farming units have become fewer and fewer, and farther and farther apart, as producers with power machinery reach out for more and more land to justify their investment. Country churches, country schools, country society, and small country towns have suffered. In fact, many of them have completely disappeared.
>
> More and more we see the development of corporation farming that absorbs small units into larger, more profitable enterprises. The country life we once knew in the Middle West has "gone with the wind." [37]

There is at least one serious attempt to anticipate problems. The Economic Research Service of the U.S. Department of Agriculture, North Carolina State University, and the U.S. Department of Labor are studying the possible effects of the pending mechanization of tobacco production. By 1978, farmers will use mechanical harvesters to harvest an estimated 23 to 36 percent of the flue-cured tobacco acreage and will use labor-saving bulk barns to cure 65 to 80 percent of the crop. If these changes occur, labor needed during the harvest will fall as much as 50 percent between 1972 and 1978.

The studies made in the flue-cured tobacco states indicate that technological change will continue to take place and that many agricultural workers, particularly the younger (18–24 years old) and older (45–64 years old) wage earners, will have to make changes in the way they earn their livings. This is an area where we may be able to determine if research and planning can ease the human problems resulting from farm mechanization.[38]

In this brief survey of the mechanization of American agriculture and its consequences, several points stand out. Farmers have made changes on a large scale primarily when a new technology has been developed and tested and when the economic climate encouraged the new adoption. The first such period in American history came with the Civil War which triggered the first American agricultural revolution and the change from hand power to horse power. Similarly, the second agricultural revolution resulted from World War II and the change from horse power to the internal combustion engine and the adoption of a package of farm practices.

The first inventions which made mechanization possible often began in the shops of farmer-mechanics. But the testing, improving, and selling was done by new farm implement manufacturing concerns. Later, engineers at many of the land-grant universities and at the Department of Agriculture built the prototypes of new machines but, again, the farm implement manufacturers did the testing, perfecting, and distributing as well as some of the inventing. Although not directly a part of this survey, we should note that the land-grant universities, agricultural experiment stations, and extension services educated American farmers so that they could adopt and use the new machines while at the same time adjusting their farm operations to the equipment and to economic conditions.

Mechanization has been the key — not the only reason, but the key — to the increase in total production and the increased productivity per manyear of labor that has characterized American agriculture. In 1875, the United States produced 313.7 million bushels of wheat, in 1925, 668.7 million bushels and, in 1975, 2.2 billion bushels. Since 1950, wheat yields have risen from 16.5 to 32 bushels an acre, corn from 38 to 90, and soybeans from 22 to 28. Cotton yields have gone from 269 to 520 pounds an acre. The output per manhour in agriculture has increased at a rate of nearly 6 percent a year compared with 2.5 percent for all other industries.

The subsistance farmer, except from choice as a way of life, has almost disappeared from the countryside. Today's farmer produces for market rather than for home consumption. Many believe that farming as an optional way of life should be preserved but, whether it is or not, the food needed by the nation and the world will be produced by America's commercial farmers.

The number of farms in the United States has declined from 6.5 million in 1920 to 5.6 million in 1950 and to 2.8 million in 1975. The drop has resulted primarily from the machinery and other technology that permit a farmworker to handle a much larger acreage than he could before. In 1950, there were 9.9 million persons working on farms, compared with 4.3 million in 1973. Looking at it another way, in 1975 there were 53 Americans for

311

every one employed on farms. This compares with 16 and 23 in developed countries like France and West Germany. The Soviet Union has five. In less developed countries like India and Pakistan there are less than four persons for every farmworker.[39]

The farm population has declined with the decrease in number of farms. This decline has been accompanied by a change in the rural social structure. Many villages and small towns, with their schools, churches, stores, and social life have declined and even disappeared. This has been offset, at least in part, by improved means of transportation, but the full significance of the changes are still to be determined.

The most important question, and one still to be both understood and solved, is what has happened to the displaced farm population. Earlier, surplus farm workers supplied some of the man power needed to industrialize America. Since the second American agricultural revolution, many have gone to the cities, some to a very uncertain future. Others are now part of the rural poor.

Another important question to be considered is whether or not we should permit or even encourage the persistent erosion of the farm population. Mechanization has helped keep the family farm viable by making it possible to farm the acreage needed for an economically sound unit. However, the investment now needed for establishing a new farm makes it almost impossible for the young family to enter farming unless it continues on a farm already in the family. Even the established farmer finds it difficult to finance the purchase of additional land and new equipment as technological developments seem to make this necessary. This is a major problem which must be solved in order for the family farm to continue to be a dominant force.

Who should be responsible for planning for the workers and farmers who might be displaced by new inventions and technologies? Certainly not the inventors and technologists. We cannot stop research and hope to maintain our agricultural production. As Henry A. Wallace said in 1940, when research was under attack as adding to farm surpluses:

> Science, of course, is not like wheat or cotton or automobiles. It cannot be overproduced. . . . In fact, the latest knowledge is usually the best. Moreover, knowledge grows or dies. It cannot live in cold storage. It is perishable and must be constantly renewed. . . .[40]

The implement manufacturers and other suppliers of agricultural technologies cannot and should not be forced to decide whether or not a particular technology should be released because it might force some people out of work. The Rust brothers found that such restraints did not work with their cotton picker. In our comparatively free economy, the implement manufacturer should not be asked to decide who and who should not be permitted access to a particular machine, nor should the American farmer permit any manufacturer or government employee to make such invidious decisions.

I suggest that the answer is not to limit research nor to stop the production and use of new machines, even though some changes in emphasis may be needed in research conducted with public funds. There can be no doubt that in the mechanization of American agriculture such leaders as Eli Whitney, Cyrus H. McCormick, C. W. Hart, C. H. Parr, Henry Ford, John Rust, and Roy Bainer have done away with much of the body- and mind-deadening drudgery always considered part of farming. Farmers and their families today live more healthy, and longer lives, in part, at least, because of the mechanization of American agriculture. We do not want to return a significant part of our population to dawn-to-dusk labor chopping cotton, thinning beets, or flailing grain.

The answer may be in a restructuring of American farming, so that young people can once again enter the field, or it may be in true rural development that would permit all of us to decide whether we wanted to live and work in a rural or an urban environment. This should be a responsibility of the U.S. Department of Agriculture, not in the sense of forcing any of us into one area or another but, rather, in the sense of making available viable choices of lifestyles while insuring the continued production of the food and fiber which America and the world need. That is another problem, and one not to be imposed upon our inventors, technologists, or manufacturing industries. But it is one which we must face.

In any case, there is no reversing of the mechanization of American agriculture. But, if it were possible, should we take that road? The answer is no, unless we wish to decide who, among Americans, let alone those elsewhere in the world, should live and who should starve to death. The mechanization of American agriculture has helped give us the most productive agriculture and one of the best diets at the lowest cost of any nation in the world.

REFERENCES

1. Theodore C. Byerly, "Systems Come, Traditions Go," U.S. Department of Agriculture, *Yearbook,* 1970, p. 37.
2. Jim Hightower, *Hard Tomatoes, Hard Times: The Failure of the Land Grant College Complex* (Washington, D. C.: Agribusiness Accountability Project, 1972), p. 66.

3. Byerly, p. 39.

4. Hightower, p. 3.

5. Rachel Carson, *Silent Spring* (Boston: Houghton Mifflin Co., 1962).

6. Ulysses P. Hedrick, *A History of Agriculture in the State of New York* (New York: Hill and Wang, c. 1933), pp. 287-288.

7. Rodney C. Loehr, "Arthur Young and American Agriculture," *Agricultural History* 43 (January 1969): 49.

8. Everett E. Edwards, ed., *Jefferson and Agriculture,* Agricultural History Series No. 7 (Washington, D. C.: U.S. Department of Agriculture, 1943).

9. Constance M. Green, *Eli Whitney and the Birth of American Technology* (Boston: Little, Brown and Co., 1956).

10. Clarence H. Danhof, "The Tools and Implements of Agriculture," *Agricultural History* 46 (January 1972): 83.

11. Leo Rogin, *The Introduction of Farm Machinery in Its Relation to the Productivity of Labor in the Agriculture of the United States During the Nineteenth Century* (Berkeley: University of California, 1939), 260 pp.

12. Edward C. Kendall, *John Deere's Steel Plow,* United States National Museum Bulletin, No. 218 (Washington: Government Printing Office, 1959).

13. William T. Hutchinson, *Cyrus Hall McCormick: Seed-Time, 1804-1856* (New York: Appleton-Century-Crofts, 1930).

14. Fred L. Holmes, *Badger Saints and Sinners* (Milwaukee: E. M. Hale & Co., 1939), pp. 305-314.

15. *American Farmer* 8 (1826): 55.

16. Clarence H. Danhof, "Gathering the Grass," *Agricultural History* 30 (October 1956), 169-173.

17. Clarence H. Danhof, *Change in Agriculture: The Northern United States, 1820-1870* (Cambridge: Harvard University Press, 1969), pp. 181-250.

18. For example: *Iowa Farmer* 4(1856): 88; *Michigan Farmer* 11(1853): 258. For a different view, *Homestead* 4 (February 3, 1859): 320.

19. Paul W. Gates, *The Farmer's Age: Agriculture 1815-1860* (New York: Holt, Rinehart and Winston, 1960), pp. 293-294.

20. Wayne D. Rasmussen, "The Civil War: A Catalyst of Agricultural Revolution," *Agricultural History* 39 (October 1965); 187-195.

21. Everett E. Edwards, "American Agriculture—The First 300 Years," U.S. Department of Agriculture, *Yearbook,* 1940, pp. 241-243.

22. George K. Holmes, "Progress of Agriculture in the United States," U.S. Department of Agriculture, *Yearbook,* 1899, p. 320.

23. Fred A. Shannon, *The Farmer's Last Frontier: Agriculture, 1860-1897* (New York: Farrar & Rinehart, 1945), pp. 145-147.

24. U.S. Country Life Commission, *Report* (Washington: Government Printing Office, 1909), p. 43.

25. Reynold M. Wik, "Steam Power on the American Farm, 1830-1880," *Agricultural History* 25 (October 1951): 181-186.

26. "Another Gasoline Engine," *Farm Implement News* 13 (Dec. 8, 1892), 24-25.

27. E. M. Dieffenbach and R. B. Gray, "The Development of the Tractor," U.S. Department of Agriculture, *Yearbook,* 1960, pp. 31-44.

28. *Farm Implement News* 9 (September 1888): 18-20.

29. Herbert F. Miller, Jr., "Swift, Untiring Harvest Help," U. S. Department of Agriculture, *Yearbook,* 1960, pp. 166-167.

30. Wheeler McMillan, *Ohio Farm* (Columbus; Ohio State University Press, 1974), pp. 87-95; Carl Hamilton, *In No Time at All* (Ames: Iowa State University Press, 1974), pp. 84-88.

31. Roy Bainer, "Science and Technology in Western Agriculture," *Agricultural History* 49 (January 1975): 60-64; Wayne D. Rasmussen, "Technological Change in Western Sugar Beet Production," *Agricultural History* 41 (January 1967): 31-35.

314

32. Coby Lorenzen and G. C. Hanna, "Mechanical Harvesting of Tomatoes," *Agricultural Engineering* 43 (January 1962): 16–19; Wayne D. Rasmussen, "Advances in American Agriculture: The Mechanical Tomato Harvester as a Case Study," *Technology and Culture* 9 (October 1968): 531–43; Raymon E. Webb and W. M. Bruce, "Redesigning the Tomato for Mechanical Production," U.S. Department of Agriculture, *Yearbook,* 1968, pp. 103–107.

33. H. P. Smith and D. L. Jones, *Mechanized Cotton Production in Texas,* Texas Agricultural Experiment Station Bulletin 704 (College Station, 1948).

34. Rex F. Colwick and Vernon P. Moore, "King Cotton Blasts Off," U.S. Department of Agriculture, *Yearbook,* 1970, pp. 39–46.

35. James H. Street, *The New Revolution in the Cotton Economy* (Chapel Hill: University of North Carolina Press, 1957), pp. 240–251.

36. President's National Advisory Commission on Rural Poverty, *The People Left Behind* (Washington: Government Printing Office, September 1967), pp. ix, 145.

37. Otha D. Wearin, *Before the Colors Fade* (Des Moines: Wallace – Homestead Book Co., 1971), p. 61.

38. "The Flue-Cured Tobacco Industry – Changes and Adjustments," in U.S. Congress, 93d, 2d Sess., Senate, Committee on Agriculture and Forestry, *1975 U.S. Agricultural Outlook,* pp. 295–302; Verner N. Grise, et al., *Structural Characteristics of Flue-Cured Tobacco Farms and Prospects for Harvest Mechanization,* Agricultural Economic Report No. 277, (January 1975), 46 pp.

39. Donald D. Durost, "The Farmer and His Farm," *Farm Index,* April 1975, pp. 8–11.

40. U.S. Department of Agriculture, *Report of the Secretary of Agriculture,* 1940, p. 143.

315

Commentary on the Mechanization of American Agriculture

By
Roy Bainer

It is difficult for someone who has spent a lifetime in agricultural mechanization research to agree with Hightower's statement that it has been a bad investment. For example, had he analyzed the labor situation involving the harvesting of tomatoes for processing prior to 1964, he would have found that 85 percent of the tomatoes produced in California were hand harvested by Mexican nationals. The termination of Public Law 78 shut off this supply of labor. Attempts to train domestic labor for this arduous task failed. Fortunately, research started 14 years prior to this action was timed about right to take over the production problems. As a result, an industry, which today, is worth approximately one and one-half billion dollars annually to California, was saved.

According to Raymond Roth of the California State Department of Employment Development (formerly Administrator for the Mexican National Program) the peak labor force for harvesting tomatoes in 1956 included 50,000 Mexican nationals and 5,000 domestic workers. By 1974, due to improved working conditions on the machine, 26,000 domestic workers harvested twice the acreage. In

Dr. Bainer is Professor Emeritus, Agricultural Engineering and Dean Emeritus, College of Engineering, University of California, Davis, California.

other words, the use of the machine created 21,000 new jobs which were acceptable to domestic workers. Many of these workers were local women. It should also be noted that the wages which were paid more than doubled. Furthermore, it has saved the jobs for the thousands of workers engaged in tomato production, steel making, lumbering, processing, transportation, can and paper manufacturing, sales, banking, advertising, etc.

The application of machines to agricultural production has been one of the outstanding developments in American agriculture during the past century. The results may be seen in practically every aspect of American life. The burden and drudgery of farm work has been greatly reduced, and the output per worker materially increased. Farm mechanization has released millions of agricultural workers to other industries and services, thus contributing to America's remarkable industrial expansion and to the high standard of living that now prevails in this country.

Some of the increased agricultural production during the past century must be credited to advances in non-engineering phases of agricultural technology such as improved crop varieties, the more effective use of agricultural chemicals, improved cultural practices, and irrigation. A major factor, however, has been the increased utilization of non-human energy and of more effective machines.

One may logically ask why the evolution of farm machinery attained its maximum rate in the United States during the past century. McKibben[1] suggested that it was "the result of a combination of favorable circumstances, a combination unique in the world's history and one which probably will not appear again." He listed 26 elements of this combination, including such factors as a stable, equitable government; our system of free enterprise; a rapidly increasing population occupying new lands; a surplus of clear, level land well suited to mechanization; a shortage or infrequent surplus of agricultural labor; three all-out wars that produced severe labor shortages; a rapidly expanding and effective industrial development, and a remarkable development of transportation facilities. The development of efficient farm power units has greatly broadened the horizon of mechanized agriculture. Without the tractor, much of the progress in fitting the machine to the land and to the crop could not have taken place.

Three important factors, not mentioned in McKibben's paper, also contributed to this evolution. The first was the signing of the Morrill Act in 1862 by President Lincoln which provided initially for the land-grant colleges in the areas of agriculture and the mechanical arts. Then came the Hatch Act that gave financial assistance to the state agricultural experiment stations. And, finally, the Smith-Lever Act that encouraged the development of the state agricultural extension services. It is interesting to note that the most unique contribution made by the United States in the field of education was the development of the land-grant system.

Aside from the tractor, the combined harvester-thresher patented in 1836 (five years after McCormick introduced his reaper) by Hiram Moore of Climax, Michigan, was by far the most important contribution to agricultural mechanization. Its acceptance in the Far West resulted in the development of a tremendous grain trade in the latter part of the nineteenth century. Whereas its acceptance in the winter wheat belt did not come until the mid-1920's (for example, 8,000 of these machines were sold in Kansas in 1926), it has become a universal harvesting machine. Its use has extended from harvesting wheat, barley and oats, to rice, soy beans, edible beans, flax, grain sorghums, corn, safflower, small seed legumes, etc. Even the principle of the straw-rack for separating grain from straw is employed on the tomato harvester for separating tomatoes from the vines. The combine has made it possible to produce a surplus of wheat for worldwide consumption and helped balance our foreign trade. A history of the combine alone could easily fill an entire volume.

Rasmussen mentioned the concern of Rust brothers for farm labor displaced by mechanical cotton pickers. Fowler McCormick was president of International Harvester when the decision was made to manufacture pickers. He was also concerned about the social implications. Therefore, the decision was made to manufacture the pickers at Memphis, Tennessee and use displaced labor in the factory. He insisted upon and finally convinced the City Fathers that the new plant would operate on the principle of equal opportunity. There would be no color lines in the cafeteria or separate wash rooms for the blacks. A training program was initiated to prepare workers for their new tasks.

During the introduction of the mechanical cotton picker in California, I, too, was concerned about displaced labor. While attending a three week seminar sponsored by International Harvester, I had the opportunity of studying the labor input for manufacturing a two-row picker. Much to everyone's surprise, the labor input from the mines through engineering design, manufacturing, transportation, and sales amounted to 7,500 manhours. All of the costs except royalties and rents were for labor. When a farmer purchased the picker, he made a substantial down payment for comparatively high cost labor. All of his operating costs, maintenance, fuel, etc., represents further labor input. It can be seen from this example that agricultural mechanization is not entirely a one-way street. If we consider farm labor in general, we find out that each agricultural worker is backed up by two and three workers in industry.

The literature covering agricultural mechanization is fragmentary with bits and pieces here and there. Many outstanding papers have been published in various publications. *Agricultural History* is a fine example. The *Journal* and *Transactions of the American Society of Agricultural Engineers* are other examples. During the golden anniversary year, 1957, of the founding of ASAE, a number of historical articles appeared in the June and July issues of the *Journal*. A typical example was "Highlights in the Development of the Combine" by Chris Nyberg. Many books have been written such as *The Century of the Reaper* by Cyrus McCormick (1931) and *Fifty Years on Tracks* by the Caterpillar Tractor Company (1954). A history of the development of the agricultural tractor for the period of 1858 to 1950 was prepared by R. B. Gray, formerly with the U.S. Department of Agriculture. This treatise is still available from the American Society of Agricultural Engineers, St. Joseph, Michigan; although it is in need of revision.

Probably the best single source of historical material concerning agricultural power and machinery is contained in the F. Hal Higgins Collection in the University of California Library on the Davis Campus, which contains between 300,000 and 400,000 items. Every effort has been made to keep the collection up-to-date.

Other sources of historical information are the trade journals such as *Farm Implement News* and farm magazines like the *Pacific Rural Press* (later changed to *The California Farmer*). The official publications of the various beet sugar companies carry running accounts of progress in the mechanization of sugar beet production. The bulletins and circulars published by state agricultural experiment stations have carried pertinent information. "Fruit and Vegetable Mechanization" compiled by Cargill and Rossmiller, of Michigan State University gives a review of the literature in this area. The development of oral history programs at many universities offers an entirely new source of historical information. For example, I have just completed an oral history program initiated recently by the University of California Library at Davis. It covers more than fifty years of the most productive period in the history of mechanization. Naturally, the emphasis is on contributions from the University of California Agricultural Experiment Station. The transcribed copy covers 450 pages.

A paper[3] presented at the symposium on "Agriculture in the Development of the Far West" held at Davis in June, 1974, stirred up a reaction among several key California farmers. They began to press the University administration for a complete history covering the contributions of the state of California toward the mechanization of agriculture. After having checked with the main libraries of the state, they were amazed that such a treatise had never been written. Such a history would be very informative since California has been one of the principal contributors in the mechanization of agricultural production.

From the limited examples cited above, it is evident that there is a tremendous amount of historical material available. A concerted effort is needed on the part of historians to gather, and to organize, and to prepare the necessary volumes covering the field. It will be a monumental but very worthwhile task.

No one refutes the claim that the new agricultural technology has introduced some serious environmental and social problems. They must be met in one way or another since agricultural mechanization is here to stay. Without it, there could be some very hungry people, including our own.

REFERENCES

1. Eugene G. McKibben, "The Evolution of Farm Implements in Machines," *Agricultural Engineering* 34 (February, 1953):91–93.
2. Michigan State University. Rural Manpower Center. RMC Report No. 16. 838 p.
3. Roy Bainer, "Science and Technology in Western Agriculture," *Agricultural History* 49 (January, 1975):56–72.

Man Made Famines: Past, Present, and Future

By
William A. Dando

INTRODUCTION

Since the beginning of time man has experienced hunger, starvation, and famine. Epidemic starvation or famine was a severe but temporary setback in man's long struggle to make food supplies available to a given population. Primitive man learned that food resources and supplies which had been adequate for one generation would not suffice for a new generation faced with many additional mouths to feed. Just as food shortages threatened the very existence of isolated civilizations thousands of years ago, poor food distribution in the last quarter of the 20th century now threatens man's interdependent world civilization. Potential for the first world famine seemed unlikely, since publicized accounts of successful scientific farming methods had all but dispelled the theories that population would increase until it exceeded food supplies. Then a series of events occurred, some of which were triggered by natural forces, although the majority were caused by intensified political, economic, and cultural factors. These events led to the contention by prominent demographers, human ecologists, and economists that

Dr. Dando is Associate Professor, Department of Geography, University of North Dakota, Grand Forks, North Dakota.

the balance between man and his food supply has reached a point more precarious today than in any period in history.[1]

Any analysis of human evolution and man's population growth must concern itself with the different ways in which men have supplied themselves with sustenance. All men must ingest food which, in turn, must come from animal and vegetable life. Earliest man lived by scavenging, hunting animals, catching fish, and gathering wild berries, grubs, roots, honey, and anything which by trial and error they found to be edible. This primitive means of gaining a livelihood, a hunting and gathering economy, fostered a life of great hardship and scarcity. Winter became a season of acute shortage since animals migrated, berries shriveled, and food plants died; unsurprisingly, many primitive hunters and gatherers perished from starvation every winter or spring. It has been estimated that one hundred thousand years before our era there were only about five million people in the world, since hunters and gatherers needed vast areas of land to supply them with sufficient food for survival.

Continuous experimentation with both alternate foods and new foods led man to discover that not only could seeds and fruits be consumed during the harvest season, but also that they could be stored for winter use. In addition, it was discovered that propagation occurred if the seeds of selected plants were scattered over the earth, and the ensuing crops could be harvested, providing sustenance for another winter. Soon, thereafter, man began to clear away unwanted plants from selected fertile sites and replace them with domesticated varieties which he used for his food. He became more sedentary and found time to tame animals, develop herds and flocks, and keep these animate food sources as "living larders" along with grain, dried fruits, or nuts. Animals could be slaughtered in winter, or as required, and families could eat meat and other foods regularly instead of only at harvest periods or after successful hunting trips. Milk from animals was found to be a nourishing drink and provided a reason both for keeping more female than male animals and for retaining only those males whose offspring were docile, meatier, and provided more milk. Skins and hides were found to be useful for making food containers, clothing, and household utensils. As man hoarded the treasure of his knowledge, his technical skill increased from generation to generation, in spite of occasional periods of retrogression.

Food production by simple agricultural methods exceeded that which could be secured from hunting and gathering. Larger numbers of people were able to survive in areas where agriculture was practiced. Man soon learned to till the ground and to train animals to assist in field tasks; his efforts and innovations provided him with security; winters were no longer feared as they were in the past. The development of simple agriculture, followed by a division of labor between pastoralism and vegetable-grain agriculture about ten to twelve thousand years ago was by far the most important revolution in human history; the human population growth stems from this fundamental change in the method of obtaining food.[2]

Man at last became aware of his mastery over growing things. He could calculate the seasons; he had discovered the virtues of sun and rain; he was able to distinguish good soil from bad. All men, however, did not grow the same crops, tend the same animals, or favor similar diets. Great variations in world climates, soil types, and food production potentials induced groups of men to develop distinct food preferences. Variations were not only confined to food basics such as meats, rice, wheat, corn, rye, barley, or potatoes, but also applied to a whole array of foods which later became important as items for trade.

A number of definite localities, most of which were confined to the muddy deltas or flood plains of large rivers, favored agricultural societies and they were able to provide more than adequate food in good years for their people and to store reserves for bad years. Each society had its own unique character and strengths and each supported non-agricultural specialists who produced no food themselves. As non-agricultural specialization developed and as the productivity of farmers increased, more people were able to be supported upon less land.[3] The first specialists were craftsmen who produced useful tools and weapons, closely followed if not preceded by chiefs, war leaders, and priests. Three or four millennia before the birth of Christ certain centers of high civilization had already arisen. While the rest of the world was content to languish in the conditions of prehistory, these favored spots were embarked upon the sea of history proper.

A few hundred years ago, societies which nurtured, through their agricultural surpluses, large numbers of specialists were divided into two types. The first, called the "vegetable civilizations," produced writers, teachers, doctors, lawyers, and traders, but few specialists in manufacturing. The second type, the "machine civilizations," not only produced the specialists of the vegetable civilization but, also elaborated upon the manufacturing segment of its economy, utilizing inanimate power extensively. Whole communities were created in which all or almost all of the inhabitants were involved with non-agricultural employment. In these highly specialized segments of machine societies, most of the people were and are to this day physically divorced from the agricultural resources needed to sustain their lives; they are still tied, however, to basic food supplies by critical transportation-communication networks.[4]

Commercial food suppliers for machine societies quickly identified regions on earth where specialty crops or animal products could be produced most inexpensively and transported most easily to urban markets. They delineated international and national trade areas where cultural or physical restrictions influenced consumptive patterns, crops grown, or animals produced for market, and created new markets for various foods which in turn, have shifted geographically over periods of time. Agriculture, one of the most respected of all economic activities throughout human history, slowly became the stepchild of machine civilizations. Still, the present distribution of people in the world is closely related to areas of food surplus. All advanced societies, including those classified as machine civilizations, are based on agriculture. Man lives on parts of the earth where he should live; the distribution of population is in essence an indicator of where man can secure food for survival.[5]

FAMINES OF THE PAST, 4000 B.C. to A.D. 1974

Famines have decreed untimely deaths for man since the beginning of time. They were a regular but unexpected calamity dispersed throughout the inhabited world and they varied in severity, location, and frequency of occurrence. A famine period in one part of the world in most cases was remembered as a good agricultural year by the inhabitants of another part. A famine, as defined in the chronicles of the learned men of the ages, was a protracted shortage of total food in a restricted geographical area, causing wide spread disease and death from starvation. In most instances, a famine cycle (crop failure/food unobtainable, hunger, death from starvation, epidemics, social disruption, relief, and a successful crop/food obtainable) was triggered by the failure of food crops in food surplus areas or the restriction of food imports to food deficient areas.[6] The primary natural factors in the creation of situations conducive for famine were drought, floods, frosts, disease, and insects; the primary human factors were war, internal disruption, fear, food speculation, panic, politics, poor communications, and inadequate transportation. Specific and general locations of high frequency famine

THE FAMINE CYCLE

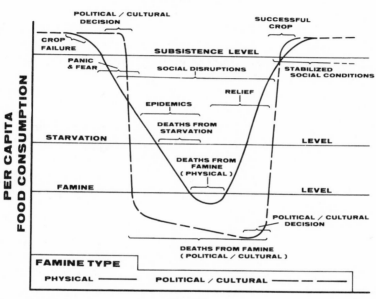

Diagram No. 1

327

regions shifted as civilizations or nations emerged, flourished, and declined, and as food demands exceeded food production in certain places. Famines have taken place in the world's best agricultural regions, in all natural zones and have not been restricted to one cultural area or one racial group.[7] The general areas affected by over 750 famines spanning nearly six millennia, the frequency of the famines, and what are believed to be the primary factors involving famine, were analyzed and then synthesized on Map No. 1, *World Famine Regions:4000 B.C.-A.D. 1974.* Although famines occurred throughout the world famine regions in *all* time periods, the highest percentage of total famines in each time period occurred in *specific* famine regions. This map identifies the location of five major temporal and spatial famine regions, the location of the "1975–80 Zone of Famine Potential," and the globe-girdling "Future Famine Zone."

Famine Region I: Northeast Africa and the Middle East, 4000–500 B.C. Millennia before the birth of Christ, centers of high civilization with advanced agricultural techniques for their time emerged in the Nile, Tigris, and Euphrates valleys. Muddy floodplains and deltas, because of periodic alluvial enrichment, provided man with the opportunity for producing food surpluses and economic specialization as well as prosperity. But these exotic rivers were not tranquil streams and their flows had to be controlled or else the people, who were confined by a harsh physical environment to their narrow floodplains, would experience alternating periods of floods and drought. Great works were constructed to mitigate the capricious mood of the waters and the heavens. This task imposed discipline and special forms of social organization. Although a proportion of the annual yield was set aside as a reserve to meet the eventuality of a lean year, famines did occur. One of the earliest authentic records of mankind's suffering in the days of famine was carved on a granite tomb on the island of Sahal, in the first cataract of the Nile. Egyptologists believe that the inscription was chiseled in the time of Tcheser, approximately 4247 B.C. Of equal importance is the fact that ten famines are recorded in the *Bible* and that the famine in Egypt of Joseph's day, 1708 B.C., is well documented. Cannibalism, as a result of famine, was first recorded within this region in the ninth century B.C. In *2 Kings,* 6:29, it states, " . . . so we cooked my son and ate him."[8]

Famine Region II: Mediterranean Europe, 501 B.C.-A.D. 500. Rome, it is said, never achieved a refinement of culture comparable to that of the Greeks. However, if the lesson taught by the

Greeks was one of beauty, then the lesson taught by the Romans was one of unity. Around the city of Rome coalesced an immense empire, which eventually numbered some 80 million subjects, all of whom bore the same seal. The Romans covered portions of Europe with an admirable network of roads and their waterways still remain the great economic arteries of Europe. Agricultural surpluses and specialties of many diverse geographical regions moved freely throughout the empire. To the people whom she subjugated and to all countries which she conquered, Rome provided the prime example of an organized civilization — yet Mediterranean Europe at the time of the empire experienced many famines. Although famines were recorded prior to 450 B.C., on this date began a famine which endured for more than 20 years and, in 436 B.C. thousands of tormented people committed suicide by throwing themselves into the Tiber River to escape the pain of starvation. Approximately 50 years later, raids and siege by the Gauls brought famine within the walls of the city of Rome. Thousands died in the famine of A.D. 6 and there was great suffering between A.D. 79 and A.D. 88 when a devastating drought encompassed the entire Italian peninsula. During this famine period, 10,000 people died on one day in Rome alone. A century later, locusts destroyed all crops and thousands of peasants perished daily along the roads as they fled from famine; the famine eventually reached the city of Rome, and for a brief period 5,000 city-dwellers also died each day. Many more famines were recorded in Rome, Judea, Greece, Antioch, Syria, Constantinople, and other sections of Asia Minor.[9] The two factors, however, which contributed greatly towards mitigating the shortage of food anywhere within Mediterranean Europe at this time were an excellent communications system and superb transportation networks.

Famine Region III: Western Europe, A.D. 501–1500. As a result of Rome's decadence in the third and fourth centuries, the economic axis of Europe moved from the Mediterranean to the north. Here, the general insecurity of life and property, absence of a highly organized state, and lack of trade and money as a medium of exchange, led to the development of feudalism. In Western Europe, there existed great physical isolation, distinct cultural differences, and variations in social organization. Each feudal state strove for self-sufficiency initially; each produced its own food, supplied its own clothing, and had its own court and army. Trade, which existed with towns or neighboring fiefs, was more or less a matter of barter. Transportation was restricted and communications were disrupted.

Isolation, fear, prejudice, jealousy, and mistrust nurtured and perpetuated horrible famines. In Western Europe, between A.D. 501 and 1500, more than 300 famines were recorded. England suffered at least 95 famines, France more than 75, and Ireland experienced in excess of 30 famines. Famines were recorded in Scotland, Wales, Germany, Denmark, Sweden and, at times, famines blighted all of Western Europe. Deaths per famine ranged from tens of thousands to one hundred thousand. Just when it seemed that Western Europe was awakened from the sleep into which it had lapsed after the fall of the Roman Empire, the Black Death and its accompanying famine killed from one-fourth to three-fourths of the population or, conservatively some 40,000,000 individuals.[10] Recovery was slow but, in time, the old system of self-sufficient feudal states gave way to a geographically arranged division of labor and homogeneous cultural groups. Western Europe began to tingle with vitality and the number of recorded famines declined.

Famine Region IV: Eastern Europe, A.D. 1501–1700. While Italy entered and passed through a period of economic progress, Portugal and Spain gathered in the wealth of new trade routes and a New World. France became the leading power of the world and Eastern Europe struggled to rid itself of the Ottomans and/or the legacy of the Mongol-Tatars. Ignorance of one another was abysmal, although contact between Western Europe and Eastern Europe was not altogether lacking. Eastern Europe was not indifferent to the religious controversies which shook the Christians of the West to their foundations, and was hardly susceptible to the enticements of trade which were felt strongly in Western Europe. The elective throne of Poland became the stake in a long battle between religious denominations. Russia seemed to belong to another world. She looked at the Europe of the Reformation as a place of lunatics while, in return, Western Europe regarded her as a nation of barbarians. The Ottomans were the masters of the Balkans from the Adriatic to the Black Sea. Eastern Europe, an area of great physical and cultural diversity, was caught between the ambitions and demands of Sweden from the north, Prussia and Austria from the west, the Ottomans from the south and, at times from the Muscovite princes or nomadic hordes from the east. Eastern Europe experienced more than 150 famines in a 200 year period.[11] Famines did not simply occur in Eastern Europe and portions of Novgorodian-Muscovite Russia; they were created and prolonged by war, political decisions or indecisions, non-recognition of starvation and famine, and refusal to provide aid. Food was a political weapon.

Famine Region V: Asia, A.D. 1701–1974. For the past two and three-quarter centuries, Asia has been the paramount famine area of the world. Three nations, in particular, have suffered the famine cycle to such a degree that they are now somewhat synonymously linked with the term famine, *i.e.*, India, China, and Russia/USSR. Each of these nations had a dense and impoverished rural population, and each contained significant agricultural regions where rainfall was limited and highly variable. In India, famine frequency is highest in the northwest and the Deccan Plateau; in China, the valley of the Yellow River; and in Russia/USSR, the Volga Basin. India, China, and Russia/USSR also have excellent agricultural regions with abundant and dependable rainfall where droughts rarely occurred – but famines did.

Indian legends cite almost continuous famines between 504–443 B.C. and a bad famine in A.D. 297. In all, mention is made of more than 90 famines in the past 2500 years; 66 per cent took place after 1701. Although the famine of 1769–70 was the first great Indian famine to attract world-wide attention, the 19th century was the time of India's most terrible famines. India's great population and spiralling population growth rate placed tremendous pressure on limited food resources, but famines occurred when there was adequate food for all; the fault was gross maldistribution of food.[12] China has had 1,829 famines between 108 B.C. and A.D. 1929, or 90 famines in each 100 years. Primarily seeking not conquest but the exquisite life, neglecting sciences and commerce but encouraging the poets, the population of China increased continuously. Existence in some areas became a perpetual struggle for food and the smallest deviation from a maximum yield destroyed the margin of safety between having barely enough and starvation. As in India, the 19th century was the century of China's most devastating famines. Four famines (1810, 1811, 1846, and 1849) were reported to have claimed nearly 45,000,000 lives. Nine million died in the famine of 1875–78. This famine occurred in four provinces of north China, about the size of France, called the "Garden of China". At least 2,000,000 lives were lost in the Hunan famine of 1929. Famines have occurred in China since 1929, but the scope of these famines are not comparable to the famines of the 19th century.[13]

Russian/USSR chroniclers and historians have described 77 famines in the last millenium. Famine occurrence increased gradually, reached a high point in the late 19th century, then declined. During the 19th century, rural population growth and rural food requirements equaled production in an average year. In poor agricultural years, local self-sufficiency came into conflict with national and international food commitments. Still the 20th century was the era of the great famines. In 1921–22, approximately nine million starved to death; in 1933–34, between four and seven million died; and in 1944–47 nearly two million died.[14] Overpopulation in marginal agricultural regions, drought, revolution, war, and political decisions worked simultaneously to produce senseless deaths for millions. Throughout India, China, and Russia/USSR, for the past 225 years, cultural changes and technological innovations did not keep pace with population and market pressures on food resources.

TYPES OF FAMINES

A spatial analysis of approximately 750 famines, spanning 6,000 years, has led to the identification of five basic famine types: physical, transportation, cultural, political, and overpopulation.

1. *Physical* or Egyptian famines in regions where the physical environment was naturally hostile to intensive forms of sedentary agriculture but man developed techniques which enabled him to temper natural hazards in all but their extreme form.

2. *Transportation* or Roman famines in highly urbanized, commercial, or industrial food deficit regions dependent upon distant food sources and supplied normally by a well developed transportation system.

3. *Cultural* or West European famines in food surplus regions induced by archaic social systems, cultural practices, and overpopulation.

4. *Political* or Eastern Europe famines in regions that are nominally self-sufficient in basic foodstuffs but where regional politics or regional political systems determine food production, food distribution, and food availability.

5. *Overpopulation* or Asian famines in drought-prone or flood-prone, overpopulated, marginal agricultural regions with primitive agricultural systems, whose inhabitants' perennial food intake was only slightly above starvation levels.

THE POTENTIAL FOR FAMINE

A decade ago, the world food problem was perceived as a food-population problem. It was argued that the human race did not reach its first billion people until A.D. 1830. Only a century later, in 1930, the second billion was reached; 30 years later, in 1960, the third; and it was estimated that in 1975, mankind would add the fourth billion. Relentlessly, human numbers were growing by 70

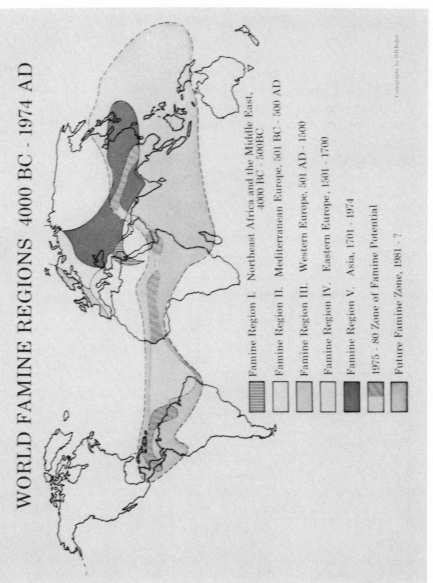

WORLD FAMINE REGIONS 4000 BC - 1974 AD

Famine Region I.   Northeast Africa and the Middle East,
                        4000 BC - 500BC

Famine Region II. Mediterranean Europe, 501 BC - 500 AD

Famine Region III. Western Europe, 501 AD - 1500

Famine Region IV. Eastern Europe, 1501 - 1700

Famine Region V.   Asia, 1701 - 1974

1975 - 80 Zone of Famine Potential

Future Famine Zone, 1981 - ?

Cartography by D.B. Baker

Map No. 1

333

million or more each year. If man were to avert famines, particularly in developing countries with high population growth rates, world food production had to double and this was thought unlikely. To the dismay of many concerned demographers, growth in world population exceeded the most pessimistic expectations.[15] Yet in developed nations, food production rose by three percent a year while population increased only one percent. Food production also increased in developing nations by about three percent, barely keeping ahead of a two and a half percent population growth. Gross world food production has kept pace with population growth, and per capita food production is now higher than in the 1960's (Graph No. 1).

Alarm about world food supplies and reserves in the mid-1970's is more than just a concern for a rapidly increasing world population; it is a concern for the modern famine triad of population growth, world affluence, and revolutionary dietary expectations. The current world food crisis was triggered by bad weather in the early 1970's; this reduced agricultural production in the USSR, China, India, Australia, Sahelian Africa, and Southeast Asia.

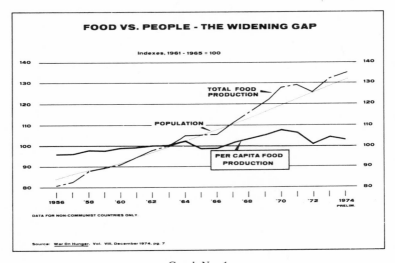

Graph No. 1

World food production declined for the first time in 30 years. Concomitantly, world grain stocks were at their lowest level since 1952. The food situation was aggravated by the unprecedented scale of USSR grain purchases, inflation, monetary instability, speculation in commodities, and the energy shortage. World demands

334

for food would have remained stable or experienced growth had not this unique spatial distribution of bad weather occurred.

A famine would have taken place in 1972 or 1973 in the USSR, China, and India had not the national affluence and the dietary expectations of most citizens in these and other nations led to massive food purchases not only to maintain people but also to provide food for animals. The national priorities and diets of nations change. As societies become wealthier, their consumption of animal products increase. This means that a greater proportion of basic foodstuffs, such as grain and soybeans that could be fed to humans directly, is converted into feed for poultry or large farm animals. Diets composed of wheat, rice, potatoes, or cassava are being replaced by diets dominated by meat, fats, oils, sugar, vegetables, and dairy products.[16] Not even the most totalitarian government would attempt to reverse such a trend in dietary improvement.

Through education, propaganda, and political action, the common man throughout the developing world has come to believe and expect marked economic progress and a sound basic diet for his family. There is a world revolution in consumer expectations and failure to meet these expectations in food and nutrition is more explosive than failure to reach non-food consumption goals. Hundreds of millions have felt the pangs of hunger, have seen their children go hungry, have been taught that malnutrition and hunger increase their susceptibility to infectious disease, sickness, and possible death. Workers know from personal experience that it is difficult to labor in the fields when one is weak from lack of food. Expectations differ from person to person, but most people want immediate relief from the fear of hunger and want a richer, more healthful diet.[17] If the common man in developing countries fails to receive food and economic progress, then agitators are there to tell them that a better diet, increased economic production, fairer distribution of income, and a higher level of living can be achieved in their lifetime if they follow the Marxist model for national development. Relative deprivation of expectations leads to social change; persistent deprivation of expectations leads to revolution.

The potential for famine in the 1975–80 period is greater than at any time since World War II. Barring a major catastrophy, food production in most of the developed nations of the world should be more than adequate to provide each citizen a rich and varied diet. Elsewhere, despite increasing total food production, *per capita* food production will remain low or decline slightly. Within the "1975–80 Zone of Famine Potential," delineated on Map No.1, five areas are

335

experiencing severe food problems today and are areas of high famine potential. These areas are: 1) the Caribbean; 2) the Sahel; 3) Ethiopia-Somalia-Yemen; 4) Trans Jordan-Syria; and 5) portions of South Asia (northern Pakistan, northern India, Bangladesh, Burma, and Laos). Cultural factors which inhibit increased agricultural productivity and the reduction of the world's highest percentage of natural increase, create serious food-population problems in the Caribbean area. Transportation and communication problems in the vast drought-prone Sahel and also in Ethiopia-Somalia-Yemen have inhibited agricultural development and relief efforts in time of crop failure in the past and will do so in the 1975–80 period. Political activities by external groups and power struggles among various internal groups in the Trans Jordan-Syrian area have created an environment conducive for famine. Overpopulation in marginal agricultural segments and areas of severe natural hazards in Pakistan, India, Bangladesh, Burma, and Laos have reached a point where only immediate resettlement, stringent birth control, and comprehensive development programs can avert an acute population-food imbalance in the 1975–80 period. With tremendous population growth in areas experiencing great nutritional difficulties, inequality in food production and utilization, and the revolution in expectations that have swept the developing world, mankind is running a desperate race with famine.

FUTURE FAMINES, 1981–?

The world food problem of the future will be similar to that of the past, namely, the problem of poor countries. Return to relative abundance and inexpensive food in developed countries will not remedy the problem of chronic food shortages in the developing world during the last 20 years of the 20th century. Despite the gradual improvement of *per capita* food supplies over the past quarter century, the situation in many developing nations will continue to be grim. Map No.1 delineates a globe-girdling tropical "Future Famine Zone." Thirty-nine nations and northeast Brazil, all within this zone, will have very serious food problems and, possibly, famines by 1985 or 1990. These nations and other poorer countries within this zone contained two-thirds of the world's population in 1975, produced only one-fifth of the world's food, and accounted for four out of every five births.[18] The current world population of four billion will double in 40 years if the present growth rate continues. Population in the "Future Famine Zone" will account for nearly 80 percent of the growth.

336

Short term natural events, such as droughts or floods, which cause local crop failures, can occur in the 1980's and 1990's as they have in the past, and a benevolent world climate can no longer be taken for granted. With the use of improved technology, superior seed, more fertilizers, new hybrids, improved insecticides, novel sources of food, reduction in waste, improved transportation and communication networks, and assistance from the developed nations of the world, these short term events, which in the past contributed to starvation or famine, should only at the most lead to food rationing in restricted areas.[19] The world of the 1980's and 1990's will have the capability to cope with short term crop failures, but the problem of the future may be long term shortages of total food.

The developing nations of the world within the "Future Famine Zone" have only a few short years to evolve from food deficient nations to nations which are self-sufficient in basic food products. These nations do not have time for trial and error, discovery, or invention; know-how must be transferred and aid made available. Developing nations with food problems must accept change in social and institutional patterns, land and/or animal ownership, birth control, and even food preferences. Famines can only be thwarted by all the nations of the world supporting massive agricultural development programs in those areas where the greatest potential for increased food production is located and where the greatest need for food exists.[20]

CONCLUSIONS

Famines in the past were short term events, confined to restricted geographical areas and taking the lives of limited numbers of people. No famines were recorded in North America, South America (except northeast Brazil), Central and South Africa, Australia and New Zealand; and no nationwide famine has been recorded in even India, China, or the USSR. However, future famines will last for extended periods of time, cover broad geographical areas, encompassing many nations, and will involve tens of millions. Future famines will undoubtedly be man-made and will be of a transportation, cultural, political, or overpopulation type. Famines can be averted by reducing population growth, modifying cultural food preferences and practices, changing social and political environments, improving world communications and transport, and by creating a world food bank. The solution to the man/food problem in the last quarter of the 20th century will necessarily require changes in the traditional behavior of most of the world's people.

337

For more than six millennia hunger has been a constant threat to man; starvation and famine were the silent deaths and more people have died of starvation than in war.

In the future, instead of silence, hunger may produce the resounding roar of violence. The next world war could be the First World Food War.

REFERENCES

1. P. Ehrlich, "Looking Backward from 2000 A.D.," in *The Crisis of Survival*, E. Odum, et al. (Madison: The Progressive Inc. and by Scott, Foresman and Company, 1970), pp. 238–245; N. Greenwood and J. Edwards, *Human Environments and Natural Systems* (North Scituate, Mass.: Duxbury Press, 1973), pp. 98–102; and T. Poleman, "World Food: A Perspective," *Science* 188 (May 9, 1975): 510–518.

2. N. Borlaug, *The Green Revolution Peace and Humanity* (Washington, D.C.: Nobel Foundation and Population Reference Bureau, 1971), pp. 1–18; and A. McKenzie, *The Hungry World* (London: Faber and Faber, 1969), pp.13–17.

3. E. Deevey, Jr., "The Human Population," *Scientific American* (September 1960) : 198.

4. K. Haselden, "The Social and Ethical Setting of the World Food Situation," in *Alternatives for Balancing World Food Production Needs* (Ames, Iowa: The Iowa State University Press, 1967), pp. 19–23.

5. J. Howe and J. Sewell, "What is Morally Right?," *War on Hunger* IX (June 1975): 1–5.

6. J. Mayer, "Coping with Famine," *Foreign Affairs* 53 (October 1974): 99–101.

7. W. Dando, "Man-Made Famines: Russia's Past and the Developing World's Future," *Proceedings of the Association of American Geographers* (Milwaukee, Wis.: fall 1975), p. 60.

8. *The New English Bible* (Oxford: Oxford University Press, 1970), p. 416; and R. Graves, "Fearful Famines of the Past," *National Geographic* XXXII (July 1917): 69–71.

9. A. Keys et al., *The Biology of Human Starvation*, 2 vols. (Minneapolis: University of Minnesota Press, 1950), II 1248–1249.

10. C. Walford, *The Famines of the World* (New York: Burt Franklin, 1970), pp. 3–10; and B. Nicol, "Cause of Famine in the Past and in the Future," in *Famine, A Symposium Dealing With Nutrition and Relief Operations in Times of Disaster* (Uppsala: Almquist & Wiksells, 1971), pp. 10–16.

11. S. Krasovec, *Clovestvo, Kruk in Lakota: Vceraj, Danes, Jutri* (Ljubljana: Drzavna Zalozba Slovenije, 1970), pp. 393–396; and M. Tikhomirov, *Novgorod: k 1100 Letuu Goroda* (Moskva: 1964), pp. 299–309.

12. *Cyclopaedia of India*, 1888 ed., Vol. I, "Famines," pp. 1072–1076; *International Encyclopedia of the Social Sciences*, 1968 ed., Vol. 5, "Famine," by M. Bennett, pp. 322–326; and A. Berg, "Famine Contained: Notes and Lessons from the Bihar Experience," in *Famine, A Symposium Dealing With Nutrition and Relief Operations in Times of Disaster* (Uppsala: Almquist & Wiksells, 1971), pp. 103–109.

13. J. de Castro, *The Geography of Hunger* (Boston: Little, Brown and Company, 1952), p. 29; J. de Castro, *The Black Book of Hunger* (New York: Funk & Wagnalls, 1967) p. 22; and W. Paddock and P. Paddock, *Famine 1975: America's Decision: Who Will Survive* (Boston: Little, Brown and Company, 1967), pp. 160–165.

14. F. Stefanovskii, *Materialy dlia izucheniia svostv golodnago khleba* (Kazan: 1893); H. Fisher, *The Famine in Soviet Russia* (Stanford: Stanford University Press, 1927), pp. 475–480; D. Dalrymple, "The Soviet Famine of 1932-1934," *Soviet Studies* XVIII (October 1965): 471–474; and N. Khrushchev, "Khrushchev's Report to Central Committee Session," *Current Digest of the Soviet Press* 15 (December 10, 1963): 5.

15. B. Ferris and P. Toyne, *World Problems* (Amersham, Eng: Hulton Educational Publications, 1970), pp. 212–213.

16. C. Kellog, "World Food Prospects and Potentials: A Longrun Look," in *Alternatives for*

Balancing World Food Production Needs (Ames, Iowa: University of Iowa Press, 1967), p. 99.

17. G. Borgstrom, *The Hungry Planet* (New York: Maxmillian Co., 1972), p. vii; and L. Brown and E. Eckholm, "Choices," *War on Hunger* VIII (November 1974): 1–3.

18. D. Halacy, Jr. *Feast and Famine* (Philadelphia: Macrae Smith Company, 1971), pp. 138–155.

19. K. Brandt, "Famine Is Not Inevitable," in *Can Mass Starvation Be Prevented* (New York: The Victor Fund, 1967), p. 25.

20. L. Blakeslee, *An Analysis of Projected World Food Production and Demand in 1970, 1985, and 2000,* Vol. 1 (Ann Arbor: University Microfilms, 1969), pp. 452–462; G. Bridger and M. de Soissons, *Famine in Retreat?* (Letchworth, Eng.: Aldine Press, 1970), p. 193; and G. Borgstrom, *Too Many: A Study of Earth's Biological Limitations* (London: Macmillan, 1969), pp. 316–340.

Commentary on "Man Made Famines: Past, Present, and Future"

By Surinder M. Bhardwaj

About a century ago Cornelius Walford attempted perhaps the first detailed and systematic study of the famines of the world.[1] He summarily rejected the Malthusian dogma:

> Some writers have appeared to look upon famines as furnishing one of the necessary checks, upon what they would term the inordinate growth of population; and in that sense as being one of the means devised for the regulation of the Universe.[2]

The occurrence of famines, observed Walford, ". . . would appear to me to be likely to result rather from the failure of human means and foresight in many instances than otherwise."[3] While Walford related famines to numerous individual causes, the emphasis throughout his study is on implicating human institutional factors.

One of the American classics in the literature on famines is Walter H. Mallory's *China: Land of Famine* written half a century ago.[4] Mallory, it may be recollected, was the Secretary of China International Famine Relief Commission. Even a cursory perusal of this work will show that more often than not a multiplicity of interrelated causes rather than a single cause produced the devastating famines. Mallory categorized the causes of Chinese famines into

Dr. Bhardwaj is Chairman of the Department of Geography, Kent State University, Kent, Ohio.

natural, economic, political, and social. Political disorganization, antiquated and deleterious social and economic practices, and the exercising of full human reproductive potential coupled with periodic natural calamities seemed to have created an ideal collusion to insure recurrent famines. Throughout Mallory's study the dominant determinent of famines is man himself and the malfunction of his institutions. History provides many examples of famines directly precipitated by the agency of man. Conflicting religious, economic, and political ideologies have resulted in the past in wars followed by famines and epidemics. In addition, the failure or inadequacy of human institutions and technology to respond to natural disasters is a crucial element in defining the extent and severity of famines. Dando's paper on man-made famines strikes the same keynote in light of his own research on this crucial issue facing mankind today. For those who have always had plenty to eat, it is not easy to grasp the meaning of famine. But for those, including this commentator, who have had a personal brush with famine or near famine conditions the threat of a possible future occurrence sends a chill through the marrow.

The history of the Indian subcontinent has recorded numerous famines. Many of these, it is true, have resulted from the legendary vagaries of the monsoons. Indeed, Indian agriculture has been often and aptly described as a gamble in monsoons. Nevertheless, many of the most disastrous famines have resulted from non-natural causes. For example, the tragic Bengal Famine in 1943 was primarily a man made disaster.[5] B. M. Bhatia, in his study on the famines of India quotes from the Famine Enquiry Commission Report:

> A million and a half of the poor of Bengal fell victims to circumstances for which they themselves were not responsible. Society, together with its organs, failed to protect its weaker members. Indeed, there was a moral and social breakdown, as well as administrative breakdown.[6]

Once again widespread severe food shortages occurred and persisted in this area resulting from the recent political upheavals and the bloody war in which the nation of Bangladesh was born. The fragile economy has been devastated and endemic malnutrition not only has intensified but also has become an "epidemic" throughout the country.

Paul Richard Bohr in his book, *Famine in China and the Missionary,* has recorded harrowing tales of the great famine of 1876–1879 in which nine and one half million people perished.[7] Despite strict government injunctions human flesh was sold openly in the markets.[8] While it is true that the precipitating natural cause of this famine was the long drought prior to 1876, it can also be said that ". . . suffering was aggravated by poor communication and inadequate transportation."[9] In short, Dando's contention is amply supported that man himself must bear the responsibility as a causative agent of famines.

Dando has painstakingly synthesized enormous amounts of information in his world map showing the spatio-temporal occurrence of famines in five famine regions. He has identified the 1975–80 zone of famine and the globe-girdling "Future Famine Zone." This geographic result is at once effective and thought-provoking. There are countries or parts of countries, however, for which data are extremely difficult to obtain. Nevertheless, famine potential exists in some areas not included in Dando's 1975–80 Zone and his Future Famine Zone. Dando has provided a cogent summary of the salient and related environmental, socio-economic and political conditions in each of his five famine regions. It is worth stressing that in his Famine Region II ("Mediterranean Europe 501 B.C.–A.D. 500"), the existence of the Roman transportation network helped to mitigate the effects of food shortages.

On the basis of about 750 famines spanning six thousand years, five famine types have been identified by Dando which correspond to the five famine regions, each with a distinctive (but not mutually exclusive) set of attributes. In the latter part of the paper, Dando studies the cardinal issue of potential and future famine regions in light of their human reproductive parameters, their related life support systems essentially based on terrestrial agriculture, and identifies their contributing natural, cultural, and socio-economic factors. The implications of this paper are far reaching and merit serious consideration both by famine prone countries and those with food surplus. Clearly there is urgent need to drastically reduce the high growth rates of population, improve the transportation-communication networks, and to increase agricultural productivity in the less developed regions. What still remains unclear, however, are the means by which fundamental transformation can be brought about.

It is not unreasonable to agree with C. P. Snow's pessimistic views and cite the present food scarcities in Bangladesh and the Sahelian and Ethiopian famines as the prelude to more widespread catastrophes. On the other hand, one may also share Robert McNamara's optimism that wholesale famine is not inevitable in light of the real gains in agricultural productivity registered by several countries which have made serious efforts to adopt the new agricultural technology popularly termed the "Green Revolution."[10] Unfortunately, international events in the recent past have underscored the fact that propagation of new agricultural technology can be heavily dependent upon events and policies extraneous to the less developed countries. Yet it cannot be denied that the famine prone countries have to effectuate an endogenous transformation of their social, political, and economic systems.

The world food situation today presents an ironical picture with reference to Dando's "1975–80 Zone" of famine potential and his Future Famine Zone. The imports of food by China are small, and India is importing much less food than it did a few years ago. On the other hand, although the Soviet Union (presumably one of the more developed countries) is obviously experiencing unprecedented food shortages at home, she seems to have the financial strength to import all that she needs. It is also clear that many industrially advanced countries of Europe continue to import substantial quantities of food. In view of widespread food shortages, the role of food surplus countries such as the United States, Canada, and Australia in averting possible famines is indeed crucial. Sharing C. P. Snow's pessimism regarding the future famines but with a much circumscribed wisdom, William and Paul Paddock propounded their "triage" philosophy and a strategy for American greatness, assigning the central role to the United States in time of the impending great famine.[11] One hopes that America's greatness has and will continue to have other more enduring moral and scientific bases rather than using its breadbasket as a political instrument for power.[12] The Paddocks, of course, advocate ". . . to use this food as an active tool to implement American policies abroad."[13] This commentator believes that true American greatness can be seen reflected by the classic works of such agronomists as J. L. Buck.[14] His monumental study of *Land Utilization in China,* even 40 years after its intial publication, continues to provide guidelines to the present People's Republic of China in planning their crop production. And this greatness is now reflected in the fundamental researches of Norman Borlaug in providing the only real tangible hope to the hundreds of millions of peasants across the world. It is a tribute to Borlaug's genius that several of the most populous nations of the world in the past few years have been able to substantially increase their food production. It may be noted that in 1974 the People's Republic of China purchased several thousand tons of high yielding wheat seed developed by Borlaug who directed International Wheat Improvement Program.[15]

It is quite obvious from Dando's paper that a world wide anti-famine strategy has to be developed. If mankind has been inadvertently or deliberately instrumental in causing the visitations of famines, he must develop a remedy for the situation. From mankind's collective ingenuity must be born a truly international cooperation, a transference of technology and a modernization of the institutional frameworks.[16] Divergent ideologies must join hands on earth in order to face a common enemy.

In developing an anti-famine strategy, however, it is necessary to redefine famines as has been suggested by Lester R. Brown and others.[17] To quote Brown:

> The modern version of famine does not usually confront the world with dramatic photographs, such as those of the morning ritual of collecting bodies in Calcutta during the Bengal famine of 1943, but it is no less real in the human toll it takes.[18]

While it is true that recent famine in the Sahel belt of Africa has dramatized the recurrence of the classical ghastly scenes of human wastage, it is no less true that persistent malnutrition is a far more serious problem in the major part of the developing world. It must be remembered that even a small percentage of inhabitants of the densely populated countries affected by food scarcity translates into very large absolute numbers. Thus, food scarcity affecting only 10 percent of India's population would mean distress for over 60 million people! Some famines, such as the recent Sahelian Famine, will, no doubt, be localized in certain marginal environmental settings; most, however, are likely to be far more diffused, hence they will be more difficult to cope with and will demand a more comprehensive strategy than the limited-time disaster relief measures presently being used. Both India and the Soviet Union provide instructive examples of periodic food self sufficiency followed by scarcity. Food production in both countries underscores the fact that self sufficiency is possible but only within favorable environmental and international parameters. The need for developing long term strategy to reduce dependence upon foreign imports is also emphasized by both countries.

All human societies and several nonhuman societies by design or instinct have developed some mechanism of food storage to tide them over unexpected or unanticipated seasonal shortages of food. Well-managed and fortified granaries, for example, were characteristic of all the ancient civilizations. Famines have resulted either because enough storage was not maintained and/or because the distribution system was inadequate or neglected. Quite clearly, due to low productivity per capita (a function both of their poor technology and population), many countries today, cannot always maintain sufficient buffer stocks for lean years. They must, therefore, depend upon the traditional food surplus countries. Ability to import food rather than reliance upon existing global stocks thus begins to determine the number of undernourished people in a given country. This ability to import food, of course, depends not only on the available purchasing power but also on a host of domestic, political, and ideological considerations. The present Soviet food grain purchased from the United States serves to highlight the complexity of effectuating grain imports despite the Soviet Union's willingness to pay for food grain. The impact of Soviet grain purchases on United States consumers cannot be ignored. In addition, should the Soviet Union be able to massively purchase grain to the extent of significantly depleting the surplus stocks of the major grain producing countries (including the United States), the effect on the purchasing ability of traditionally food deficient countries could be a potentially disastrous one. It is not inconceivable that the Soviet Union may purchase food grain far beyond its present admittedly dire need and then use it as a political and ideological instrument in food deficient countries. Lester Brown and Erik Eckholm have pointed out several consequences of increased international competition for food supplies.[19] The point of the matter is that global food needs and famine possibilities require the development of a well-planned, systematic, and truly international strategy so that hunger in some parts of the world does not occur while restrictions on exports or political ideology make it difficult to meet the needs in other parts of the world. The United States must assume a role of central leadership in the development of such morally sound strategy.

In order to develop effective anti-famine measures, a systems approach toward understanding the famine ecology of the potential regions is necessary. Weak links in the system of each such region must be clearly identified and strengthened through international sharing of technology and required adjustments in the existing institutional framework. The need at the international level for adopting the ecosystems framework for planning such strategy has been brought home by the grievous blows to the green revolution in several less developed countries due to the fertilizer shortages accentuated by mounting prices of petroleum based fertilizer. Here is a clear case of man made conditions strangulating the efforts necessary to increase food production in the famine prone areas of the world.

It must be stressed here that whether one approaches the famines in the traditional sense as a recurrent but localized disasters, or treats them as an intricately diffused malady of the world's poor, no amount of fragmentary solutions or aids based on sentimentality will ever provide an enduring solution. Commenting on the drought and food scarcity in India in 1974 and the response by India's Finance Commission, Amrita Rangaswami has rightly observed that recommendations for a massive time-bound program of action are naive.[20] Similarly, Morris David Morris, on the basis of his studies of famine problems in India, has pointed out that the position of the poor can be only marginally improved through crisis allocations, and that their salvation must come through decisions that accelerate the long rate of economic growth.[21]

Long lasting solutions for the problem of hunger demand the type of drastic global reforms boldly and thoughtfully articulated on the basis of systems theory by Ervin Laszlo in his *A Strategy For the Future*.[22] Traditionalists might consider his concepts utopian but there is little doubt that the time has come for giving serious consideration to his far reaching ideas. Laszlo proposed the establishment of four major world monitoring systems: security, economy, population, and ecology.[23] The World Ecology Monitor, for example, according to Laszlo ". . . investigates practices and trends which stress ecological balance, and centers attention on areas where disasters and catastrophes appear imminent."[24] It is a tribute to such ideas that the World Food Conference last year passed the resolution for the establishment of a "Global Information and Early Warning System on Food and Agriculture."[25] It is also most encouraging that the World Food Conference adopted the United States proposal for establishing a consultative Group on Food Production and Investment and endorsed the FAO resolution on International Undertaking on World Food Security. The World Food Conference, by adopting such significant ideas, has shown that the threat of mass starvation can be warded off only through international cooperation.

There are other encouraging developments along these lines. One such area of research in which considerable public interest now exists is natural hazard research.[26] Geographers, with their characteristic interdisciplinary outlook, have already contributed in this research. Although many ideological barriers toward this research

347

exist in terms of international cooperation, these barriers can be overcome through persistent efforts of international agencies. The Smithsonian Institution, as an example, has made efforts in this direction.[27] Similarly, the National Science Foundation has established a hazard research program. However, in all candor, a full-fledged, truly international and well coordinated program of famine research, inclusive of monitoring, policy evolution, coping strategy, and logistics has yet to take shape. A multidisciplinary approach towards the building of appropriate strategies is clearly called for because of the extreme complexity of causative factors.

It appears necessary that detailed attributes of the famine prone areas need to be clearly sorted out using the systems methodology. Dando's suggested typology of famines, therefore, should be elaborated upon and given spatial meaning by identifying multidimensional factor complexes and relationships in specific regions. Perhaps an ecosystems classification of famine prone areas can be developed based on the identification and interaction of the following:

A. *Demographic Parameters*
   This would require:
   Present population and future projections;
   Growth rates, age structure, density, nutritional density, etc.
B. *Physical Environmental Parameters and Environmental Stressors*
   Susceptibility to climatic hazards, droughts, cyclones, floods;
   Possible climatic changes;
   Soil capability;
   Effects of irrigation on soil;
   Physical effects of agricultural/pastoral practices on soil.
C. *Technological Parameters and Technological Support Systems*
   Present technology of agricultural productivity;
   Adoption rates of high yielding seeds, fertilizer, and irrigation;
   Flood control, water conservancy, and other such support systems;
   Food storage technology and capacity.
D. *Circulation Parameters and Support Systems*
   Nature of existing transportation and communication systems;
   Capability of the above systems under abnormal circumstances;
   Import handling and distributive channels and nodes.
E. *Economic Support Systems*
   Nature of flow of commodities within existing market system;
   Efficiency of marketing systems to respond to food scarcities;
   Land tenure and land taxation policies.

348

F. *Social Parameters and Support Systems*
  Rate of acceptance of population control measures;
  Present dietary pattern;
  Cultural attitudes toward changes in the dietary pattern;
  Existence and quality of non-governmental agencies for famine relief.
G. *Governmental Policies*
  Nature of governmental planning and policies;
  Specific policies against undernutrition and famines.

Using the systems methodology of information feedback it should become possible, as Laszlo has suggested, to make more explicit the implicit beliefs, value systems, and internal systemic inconsistencies of a people ". . . which could then motivate efforts to iron out the conflicting elements . . . The resulting shifts in motivation can be translated into concrete political action by providing opportunities to act on the new insights in an organized decision-making context."[28] These data then can be utilized by the Global Information and Early Warning System on Food and Agriculture, in order to activate the appropriate international agency which would implement specific steps to relieve short and long term famine distress. In this respect, the eight principles enunciated by the United States government for an international system of nationally held food reserves deserve special attention.[29]

In the antifamine strategy both the developed and developing countries have to play a cooperative role. According to the Chairman of the National Commission for the Observance of World Population Year, ". . . there are sufficient food producing resources and technology in the world today to provide for the feeding of whatever number of people may live in the world in the year 2000 better than mankind has ever been fed."[30] This can be realized, however, if the majority of developing countries can do as well as a few have done. One of the fortunate ironies in the famine picture is that potential for substantial additional food production does exist in the less developed countries.[31] Trends of food grain production in China, India, and several other countries have clearly demonstrated this potential. Henry Kissinger, in his keynote address to the World Food Conference, emphasized the need for realizing this potential in the developing countries.[32]

Dando is to be complimented for bringing into focus at this Bicentennial Symposium the most urgent issue of famines which faces not only the economically poor countries, but also the world community at large. Whether it is recognized or not, the basic reality is that the modern world is an integrated system and is likely

349

to become more so. Therefore, healthy maintenance of this system requires the use of the very best of its components if the World Food Conference's Declaration on the Eradication of Hunger and Malnutrition is to become a reality.

REFERENCES

1. Cornelius Walford, *The Famines of the World: Past and Present* (New York: Burt Franklin, reprinted 1970, originally published 1879).

2. Ibid., pp. 4–5.

3. Ibid., p. 5.

4. Walter H. Mallory, *China: Land of Famine* (New York: American Geographical Society, 1926).

5. B. M. Bhatia, *Famines in India 1860–1965* (Bombay: Asia Publishing House, 1963), p. 310.

6. Ibid.

7. Paul Richard Bohr, *Famine in China and the Missionary: Timothy Richard as Relief Administrator and Advocate of National Reform, 1876–1884* (Cambridge, Mass.: distributed by Harvard University Press, 1972), p. xv.

8. Ibid., p. 21.

9. Ibid., p. xvi.

10. Robert S. McNamara, *One Hundred Countries, Two Billion People* (New York, Washington, London: Praeger Publishers, 1973) pp. 42–43. McNamara obviously does not share C. P. Snow's pessimism and despair. John Maddox has argued that the doomsday psychology could actually undermine human spirit. See John Maddox, *The Doomsday Syndrome* (London: Macmillan, 1972).

11. William and Paul Paddock, *Famine 1975! America's Decision: Who Will Survive?* (Boston, Toronto: Little, Brown and Company, 1967), Ch. 10.

12. This is not to say that the United States has not used food aid for political purposes. In fact Lester Brown observed that the United States has been using food aid in this manner for twenty years. See Lester Brown with Erik Eckholm, *By Bread Alone* (New York: Praeger Publishers, 1974), p. 69.

13. Paddock, p. 172.

14. John Lossing Buck, *Land Utilization in China* (Shanghai: Commercial Press, 1937) 3 volumes. This is a detailed study of 16,786 farms in 168 localities and 38,256 farm families in twenty-two provinces in China (1929–1933).

15. Sterling Wortman, "Agriculture in China," *Scientific American* 232 (June 1975): 13–21. Wortman gives a first hand picture of China's agriculture and the efforts that have been made in achieving food self sufficiency.

16. The question of technology transfer has been admirably analyzed in Gunnar Myrdal, "The Transfer of Technology to Underdeveloped Countries," *Scientific American,* 231 (September 1974): 182. For a broader concept than the "transfer of technology" see Mahbub ul Haq, "Toward a New Framework for International Resource Transfers," *Finance and Development* 12 (September 1975): 6–9 and 40.

17. Lester R. Brown with Erik P. Eckholm, *By Bread Alone* (New York, Washington: Praeger Publishers, 1974), pp. 62–64.

18. Ibid., p. 64.

19. Ibid., pp. 69–72.

20. Amrita Rangaswami, "Financing Famine Relief: Calling the Bluff," *Economic and Political Weekly* 9 (November 9, 1974): 1885–1886.

21. Morris David Morris, "What is a Famine," *Economic and Political Weekly* 9 (November 2, 1974) 1855–1864.

22. Ervin Laszlo, *A Strategy for the Future: The Systems Approach to World Order* (New York: George Braziller, 1974).

23. Ibid., pp. 154–156.

24. Ibid., pp. 155–156.

25. U.S. Department of State, *Crisis in Food,* General Foreign Policy Series 293, Pubn. No. 8808 (1975).

26. James K. Mitchell, "Natural Hazards Research," in *Perspectives on Environment,* Eds. Ian R. Manners and Marvin W. Mikesell (Washington D. C.: Association of American Geographers, 1974), pp. 311–341.

27. Smithsonian Institute, *Natural Disaster Research Centers and Warning Systems: A Preliminary Survey* (Cambridge, Mass.: Center for Short Lived Phenomena, 1971).

28. Laszlo, pp. 115–116.

29. U.S. Department of State, "Crisis in Food" pp. 6–7.

30. U.S. Department of Health, Education and Welfare. Report to the President by the National Commission for the Observance of World Population Year, DHEW Pubn. No. (OS) 75-50016 (1975), pp. iii–iv.

31. W. David Hopper, "World Food—The Darkness and the Light," in *Agricultural Initiative in the Third World* (Lexington, Mass.: D. C. Heath and Company, 1975), pp. 185–186.

32. U.S. Department of State, *U.S. Positions at 29th U.N. General Assembly,* International Organization and Conference Series 119, Pubn. No. 8800 (1975), p. 12.

Index

AAA program, 203
AAEA, 204
Abercrombie, John, 38
ABLE, 228
Academia Economico-Agraria dei Georgi-
    fili, 220
Academie d'agriculture, 220
Account of an Expedition . . . to the Rockies
    (James), 82
Act of 1862, 151
Adams Act (1906), 260
Adams, Andy
    The Log of a Cowboy, 78
Adams, Henry Cullen, 165
Adams, John, 161
Adams, John Quincy, 151
An Address to the Farmers of Great Britain,
    with an Essay on the Prairies of the
    Western Country (Birkbeck), 72
Adlum, John, 51
    A Memoir on the Cultivation of the Vine in
    America, 113
Adventures of Captain Bonneville. See The
    Rocky Mountains — Adventures in the
    Far West (Irving)
Affleck, Thomas, 162
Africa, Central, 338
Africa, South, 338
Agee, James
    Let Us Now Praise Famous Men, 292
AGLINET, 229
Agrarianism, 26, 29, 165
Agricultural colleges:
    Development, 229-231, 243, 245-246,
        259, 261
Agricultural cooperatives, 152-153, 304
Agricultural development:
    Programs, 218
Agricultural education, 49, 150-157, 224,
    243, 245-246

Agricultural Enquiries on Plaister of Paris
    (Peters), 48
Agricultural Experiment Stations:
    Bulletins and circulars
    Establishment of, 152, 184, 231
        in American Colonies, 231
        in California, 231
        in Connecticut, 231
        in Texas, 243-256
        libraries, 231-232
Agricultural experimentation. *See* Experi-
    mentation
Agricultural fairs, 151, 161
Agricultural historians, 244-256,
Agricultural History, 26, 261, 320
Agricultural history, 245-253
Agricultural History Society, 244
Agricultural implements:
    cast iron plow, 297
    combine, 305, 307
    corn cultivator, 300
    corn shellers, 306
    cotton gin, 296
    cradle, 296
    cultivators, 300
    gasoline tractor, 305
    grain drills, 307
    hay-bailing presses, 306
    hemp brake, 296
    horse-drawn reaper, 297, 300
    internal-combustion engine tractors, 305
    manufacturers and suppliers, 305
    mechanical cotton harvester, 308, 313,
        319
    mechanical reaper, 297, 300
    mower, 300
    seed drill, 296
    sickle, 296
    sidehill plow, 296
    spindle picker, 308, 309

353

steam engines, 305
straw-rack, 300
threshing machine, 296
tomato harvesters, 307–308, 319
twine knotter, 300
Agricultural libraries:
European development, 219–220
history, 219
public, 224
service, 226
types, 225–233
U. S. development, 221–233
Agricultural literature, 33
cartoonist, 215
categories, 213–218
trade journals, 166, 225, 253
Agricultural Marketing Act of 1946, 261
Agricultural presses:
D. M. Dewey and Co., 120
Agricultural production:
in China, 265
Agricultural Publishers' Association, 188
Agricultural research, 57–61, 251–252, 260
Agricultural revolution, first, 300, 311
Agricultural revolution, second, 306, 311
Agricultural societies, 51, 150, 161, 166,
220–221, 229;
Agricultural Society of New Brunswick,
229–230
Columbia Agricultural Society, 151
Highlands and Agricultural Society of
Scotland, 220
local, 48
machine civilizations, 325
Maryland Agricultural Society, 244
Massachusetts Horticultural Society, 116,
220, 232
Massachusetts Society for Promoting Ag-
riculture, 220, 221
New York Society, 47, 220
Philadelphia Society for Promoting Agri-
culture, 49–50, 220, 221
Royal Hanoverian Agricultural Society,
220
United States Agricultural Society, 244
vegetable civilizations, 325
Agricultural Society of New Brunswick,
229–230
Agriculture:
Civil War, 78, 162, 297
commercial, 18, 20
economics, 9
exchange of information in American colonies, 9–32

farm labor shortages,
in American colonies, 297
in China, 341
in Great Britain, 12
in New England, 297
mechanization, 295–315
social conditions, 9
World War II, 306
AGRIS. See International Information Sys-
tem for Agricultural Libraries and
Technology
Allen, A. B., 194
Allen, Matthew, 38
Allen, R. L., 194
Allis-Chalmers Manufacturing Co., 305
America Moves West (Riegel), 86
American agricultural revolution. See Agri-
cultural revolution, first; Agricultural
revolution, second
American Agriculturist
"Eastman's Chestnuts", 194–196
American Antiquarian Society, 29
American Association of Agricultural Col-
leges and Experiment Stations, 231
American Documentation Institute, 226
American Farm Bureau Federation, 166
American Farmer, 161, 162
American Flower Garden Companion (Say-
ers), 127
American Flower Garden Directory (Buist
and Hibbert), 125, 127
American Fruit Grower (Green), 209
Buyer's Guide, 210
American Fur Trade of the Far West (Chit-
tenden), 73
American Gardener (Gardiner and Hep-
burn), 112–113
American Gardener's Assistant (1872)
(Bridgeman), 120–122, 127
American Gardener's Calendar (M'Mahon),
113
American Gardener's Magazine (Hovey),
124–125
American Handbook of Ornamental Trees
(Meehan), 130
American Heart Association, 248
American Hereford Association, 200
American Historical Association, 28
American Husbandry (anon.), 19
American Kitchen-Gardener (Bridgeman),
122
American Library Association. Notable
Books Council, 275
American Meat Institution Foundation Li-

brary, 232

American Silk-Growers' Guide (Kenrick), 116

American Society of Agricultural Engineers "Journal" and "Transactions", 320

American Stock Growers' Association, 95

America's Frontier Story (Ridge and Billington), 86

Anderson, James, 38

Andrus, Leonard, 297

Anna Karenina, 215

Annals of Agriculture, 38, 43, 48, 221

Appleby, John Francis, 300

Arbustrum (*sic*) *Americanum* (Marshall), 111

Asia, 336

Asia, South, 336

Ask the Fellows Who Cut the Hay (Evans), 292

Associated Advertising Clubs of the World, 188

Association of College and Research Libraries

Agricultural and Biological Sciences Section, 228

Astoria (Irving), 73

Atherton, Lewis

The Cattle Kings, 94–95

Atkinson, Wilmer

Farm Journal, 198

Atwater, Wilbur Olin, 165

Atwood, Alice C.

Plant Science Catalog, 226

Babcock, Stephen Moulton, 165

Bailey, Liberty Hyde:

vegetable gardening, 114, 120, 165

Bailyn, Bernard

Education in the Forming of American Society, 30

Bainer, Roy

"Science and Technology in Western Agriculture", 306, 313

Baines, Ella V., 145

Ball, E. D., 155

Bangladesh, 343

Banister, John, 63–68

Bankers and Cattlemen (Gressley), 101, 103

Bankhead, John Hollis, II, 165, 249

Bankhead-Jones Act (1935), 261

Barefoot doctors, 269–270

Barnett, Claribel, 225

Barrel plough, 43

Barrett, Charles S., 166

Barry, Patrick, 118–120;

Barry's Fruit Garden (1872), 118

"The Genesee Farmer", 120

"The Horticulturist", 120, 129

Mount Hope Nurseries, 118

Treatise on the Fruit Garden (1851), 118

Barry's Fruit Garden (1872) (Barry), 118

Bartlett, John R.

Personal Narrative of Explorations—in Texas, New Mexico, California, etc.—With the United States and Mexican Boundary Commission, 74

Bartram, John, 51;

Botanic Garden, 111

Bartram, William, 51

Bartram's Garden, 111

Baruch, Bernard Mannes, 187

Basler, Roy P., 163

Bauhin, Gaspar, 65

Bayard, E. S., 207

Bean drill, 47

Beard, Charles Austin, 21

Beaumont, Ralph, 176

Beecher, Henry Ward

Plain and Pleasant Talks About Fruits, Flowers and Farming, 132

Beef Bonanza; or, How to Get Rich on the Plains (Brisbin), 82

Bengal Famine of 1943:

Famine Enquiry Commissions Report, 342

Bennett, Hugh Hammond, 164

Benson, Ezra Taft, 228

Bercaw, Louise O., 226

Better Homes and Gardens, 175, 188

See also *Fruit*, *Garden and Home*

Bhatia, B. M., 342

Bible, 328

Bibliography of Agriculture, 226, 228–229

Bidwell, Percy W., 9, 11

Billington, Ray A.

America's Frontier Story, 86

The Far Western Frontier, 86

Binns, John Alexander, 51

Birkbeck, Morris

An Address to the Farmers of Great Britain, with an Essay on the Prairies of the Western Country, 72

Notes on a Journey in America . . . to the Territory of Illinois, 72

Black, George D.

"The Country Parson Ponders", 207

Blackhurst, Homer, 248

Blanc, A., 147

355

Block, Marc, 29
Blythe, Ronald, 291
Bobart, Jacob, 64
Bohr, Paul Richard
    Famine in China and the Missionary, 342
Book of Fruits (1838) (Manning), 116
Bordley, John Beale, 43, 48, 161;
    agricultural experiment station on Wye Island, 43
    Essays and Notes on Husbandry, 47
    Sketches on Rotation of Crops and Other Rural Matters, 43, 47
    A Summary View of Courses of Crops, In the Husbandry of England and Maryland, 43, 44
Borlaug, Norman:
    AAEA, 203–204, 217, 218
    awards, 204
    Nobel Prize, 204
Botanic Garden, 38
Boussingault, Jean Baptiste, 231
Botanical history, 63–69
Bowler, Metcalf, 51
Boyce Thompson Institute for Plant Research, Inc.
    Library, 232
Brake or Drage harrow, 40
Bratton, Arthur, 277
Braudel, Fernand, 29
Brazos blackberry, 248
Breck, Joseph
    The Flower Garden, 129
    The Horticultural Register and Gardeners' Magazine (Fessenden), 129
Bridgeman, Thomas
    The American Gardener's Assistant (1872), 120–122, 127
    The American Kitchen-Gardener (1867), 122
    The Florist's Guide, 127
    Kitchen Gardener's Instructor, 121
    The Young Gardener's Assistant (1828), 122, 127
Briggs, Harold Edward
    Frontiers of the Northwest: A History of the Upper Mississippi, 86
Brisbin, James S.
    The Beef Bonanza; or, How to Get Rich on the Plains, 82
British Board of Agriculture, 38
Broken Hand (Hafen), 73
Brown, Lester R., 345, 346
Brown, Thomas
    The Ohio Farmer, 206
Browne, William, 64

Bruce, David, 215
Buchanan, Robert
    The Culture of the Grape and Wine Making, 130
Buck, John Lossing
    Land Utilization in China, 344
Buck, Solon Justin, 58
Bucking the Sagebrush (Steedman), 86
Buel, Jesse, 144, 162
    The Cultivator, 162
Buist, Robert, 130
    The American Flower Garden Directory (Hibbert), 125, 127
    The Family Kitchen Gardener, 122–124
    The Rose Manual, 127
Burbank, Luther, 153
Burnett, Andy
    The Long Rifle, 76
Burns, Robert, 215
Burpee, 145
Burr, Aaron, 113
Burr, Fearing, Jr.
    Field and Garden Vegetables of America, 124
    Garden Vegetables and How to Cultivate Them, 124
    M. & F. Burr, 124
Burr (M. & F.), 124
Bush & Son & Meissner of Bushberg, Mo., 147
Butler, Burridge Devenal, 206
Butler, Tait
    Southern Farm Magazine, 197
"By the Way"
    column in *Nebraska Farmer*, 200
    ranch, 200

Cactus, 124
    thornless, 127
Cadwalader, John, 48
CAIN, 228
California:
    gold in, 71, 76–77
The California and Oregon Trail (Parkman), 76
California Department of Agriculture, 199
California Farmer (Warren), 320
    Wickson, Edward James, 199
California in 1837 (Edward), 76
California State Fair, 199
Campaign Sketches of the War With Mexico (Henry), 75
Campbell, Walter S.
    Joe Meek, 73
    Kit Carson, 73

Canada, 73
 Border disputes with U.S., 76
Capper, Arthur
 Capper-Volstead Act (1922), 200
 Capper's Farmer, 179, 20
 Michigan Farmer, 201
 Missouri Ruralist, 201
 The Ohio Farmer, 201
 Pennsylvania Farmer, 201
 U. S. Senator (Kansas), 165
Capper-Volstead Act (1922), 200
Capper's Farmer (Capper), 179, 201
Carleton, Mark Alfred, 153
Carroll, Boyd
 Missouri Ruralist, 201
Carter, Landon, 17
Carter, Robert G.
 On the Border with Mackenzie, 84
Carver, George Washington, 165
Case, John, 201
Cass (J. I.) Co., 305
Cast iron plow, 297
Caterpillar Tractor Co.
 Fifty Years on Tracks, 305
Cather, Willa
 Death Comes for the Archbishop, 74
Cattle
 agriculture
 economics, 94–98, 101–103, 104
 industry, 87–89, 106
 investors, 104–105
 land utilization, 91, 103
 longhorns, 92–93
 stock growers associations, 89, 200
Cattle associations, 95
Cattle drives, 88–89
The Cattle Kings (Atherton), 94–95
Cattle Raising on the Plains: 1900–1961
 (Schlebecker), 95–96
The Cattle Towns (Dykstra), 103–104
Cattlemen, 87–106
The Cattlemen's Frontier (Pelzer), 91–92
The Century of the Reaper (McCormick),
 297
Chamber of Commerce of the United States,
 188
Chandler, Robert, 217, 218
Chapter for Landscape Architecture and the
 Allied Arts. See Society of Architec-
 tural Historians
Charles Goodnight,
 Cowman and Plainsman (Haley), 86
Charleston, S. C., 18
The Cherokee Strip Live Stock Association:
 Federal Regulation and the Cattleman's

 Last Frontier (Savage), 105
Chew, Margaret, 43
Chew, Philemon Lloyd, 43
Children of God (Fisher) 75
China, 331–332
China International Famine Relief Commis-
 sion, 340
China: Land of Famine (Mallory), 341
The Chisholm Trail (Gard), 78, 93–94
The Chisholm Trail (Riding), 78
Chittenden, Hiram M., 73
Cholesterol, 248
Civil War, 78, 162, 297
Clark, Andrew Hill, 27
Clark, Josephine A., 225, 238
Clark, William Smith, 260
Clay, John
 My Life on the Range, 86
Clayton, John, 65
Clemens, Samuel Langhorne
 Roughing It, 77
Cobb, Cully, 249
Coke of Holkham, 220
Colcord, Mabel
 Index . . . to the Literature of American
 Economic Entomology, 226
Collison, Peter, 67
Colman, Gould
 Education & Agriculture, 247, 289
Colman, Norman J.
 Colman's Rural World, 201
Colman's Rural World (Colman)
 See also *Missouri Ruralist*, 201
Colorado Rancher and Farmer (Russell),
 200
Colter, John, 73
Columbia University. Oral History Research
 Office, 276
Columbian Agricultural Society, 151
*The Comanche Barrier to South Plains Settle-
 ment* (Richardson), 84
Comanche Indians, 73, 82
Combine, 305, 307
Commerce on the Prairies (Gregg), 73
Communes, 269–270
*Communicating Discoveries — By Captains
 Lewis and Clark, Dr. Sibley and Mr.
 Dunbar* (Jefferson), 72–73
Compton, Henry, 64, 65
Conklin, Howard, 277
Conrad, Joseph
 Heart of Darkness, 215
Cooke, Morris, 164
Cooperative Extension Service, 150, 154,
 156

Corn Cultivator, 300
Cornell University
  Library, 29
Correia, Dona Maria, 214
Cotton, 18, 28, 251, 308–309
Cotton gin, 309
Country Gentleman (Pickett), 199
Country Life Commission, 165, 304
"The Country Parson Ponders" (Black), 207
County agents, 153
Coxe, William, 51
  *A View of the Cultivation of Fruit Trees
    and the Management of Orchards and
    Cider*, 114
Coxey, Jacob, 176
Cradle, 296
Crane, Sylvanus B., 177
Craven, Avery, 249
Crawford, Nelson A., 187
Crist, John W., 230
Crop rotation, 40
  English Norfolk system, 43
Crops:
  in China, 263–264
*The Cultivation of the Grape and Manufac-
  ture of Wine* (Longworth), 130
The Cultivator (Buel), 162
The Culture of the Grape and Wine Making
  (Buchanan), 130
Cunningham, John F.
  Florida Grower, 206
  Wisconsin Agriculturist, 206
Curwen, M. E.
  *Sketches of the Campaign in Northern
    Mexico*, 75
Custer, Arline, 59
Cutter, William Parker, 225, 238–239

Dairy Farmer, 175
Dairymen, 264
Dairymen's League News, 196
Dale, Edward Everett
  The Range Cattle Industry, 89, 91
"Dales Laws", 15
Dana, Richard Henry
  Two Years Before the Mast, 76
Darlington, William, 51
Davis, William W. H.
  *El Gringo, or New Mexico and Her Peo-
    ple*, 74
Day of the Cattleman (Osgood), 87–89
Deane, Samuel, 51, 161
Death Comes for the Archbishop (Cather),
  74
Declaration on the Eradication of Hunger

and Malnutrition, 350
De Cordova, Jacob
  Texas: Her Resources and Her Public Men,
    75
Deere, John, 297, 305
Demos, John
  A Little Commonwealth, 29
"Descriptive Catalogue of Fruit and Orna-
    mental Trees, Shrubs, Seedlings,
    etc." (Leroy), 130
Developing nations:
  birth control, 324
  food preference, 324–326
  land and/or animal ownership, 325
  social and institutional patterns, 325
De Voto, Bernard
  The Journals of Lewis and Clark, 86
Dewey, D. M., 146
Dewey (D. M.) and Co., 120
Dewey, Melvil, 233, 238
*Dictionary Catalog of the National Agricul-
    tural Library, 1862–1964*, 226, 228
Dictionary of American Biography, 163–164
Dies, Edward Jerome
  Titans of the Soil, 249
Dobie, J. Frank, 84, 92
  *Guide to Life and Literature of the South-
    west*, 76, 78
  The Longhorns, 78, 92–93
Dodge, Jacob R., 164
Dorset, Marion, 164
Downing, Andrew Jackson
  Fruits and Fruit Trees, 118
  The Horticulturist, 118, 129
  *A Treatise on the Theory and Practice of
    Landscape Gardening*, 118
Downing, Charles, 118
Drill plough, 43
Drought, 326
Drums Along the Mohawk (Edmond), 215
Duffas, R. L.
  The Santa Fe Trail, 73
Duffus, J. H., 204
Duhamel du Monceau, Henri Louis, 38, 40
  A Practical Treatise of Husbandry, 40–41,
    43
Dunn, Richard, 28
Durham, Philip
  The Negro Cowboys (Jones), 98, 99, 101
Dykstra, Robert
  The Cattle Towns, 103–104
  The Early Far West (Ghent), 86

Eastman, Edward R., 196–197;
  The American Agriculturist, 196

Dairymen's League News, 196
Federal Land Bank's District No. 1, 196
Journey to Day Before Yesterday, 197
National Citizens Commission for the Public Schools, 196
White House Conference on Education, 196
Eckholm, Erik, 346
Ecology, 347
Edmond, Walter D.
  Drums Along the Mohawk, 215
Education and Agriculture (Colman), 247
Education in the Forming of American Society (Bailyn), 30
Edward, Phillip I.
  California in 1837, 76
Edwards, Everett E., 162
El Dorado (Taylor), 77
El Gringo, or New Mexico and Her People (Davis), 74
Eliot, Jared
  Essays on Field Husbandry, 110
Elliot, Edna C. (Mrs. Edwin T. Meredith), 177
Elliott, Franklin Reuben
  Elliott's Fruit Book (1859), 132
  The Fruit Book (1854), 132
  Hand-book for Fruit Growers (1876), 132
  The Western Fruit-Book (1859), 132
Elliott's Fruit Book (1859) (Elliott), 132
Ellwanger, George
  Mount Hope Nurseries, 118
Ellwanger & Barry, 120
Enclosure movement, 12
Engelmann, George, 147
The Enterprising Scot: Investors in the American West After 1873 (Jackson), 104–105
Essay and Notes on Husbandry (Bordley), 47
Essay on Calcareous Manures (Ruffin), 162
Essays and Notes on Agriculture (Ruffin), 162
Essays on Field Husbandry (Eliot), 110
Ethiopia, 336
Ethiopia-Somalia-Yemen, 336
Euphrates Valley, 328
Europe, 328
Europe, Eastern, 328
Evans, George
  Ask the Fellows Who Cut the Hay, 292
  The Pattern Under the Plow, 291
Evans, John, 68
Evans, Oliver, 51
Evelyn, John

Kalendarium Hortense, 64
"The Evolution of Farm Implements in Machines" (McKibben), 318
Experimentation, 48, 159

Fairchild, David Grandison, 164
Falconer, John I., 9, 11
The Family Kitchen Gardener (Buist), 122–124
Famine cycle, 326–328
Famine Enquiry Commissions Report, 342
Famine in China and the Missionary (Bohr), 342
Famine potential zones:
  Caribbean, 336
  Ethiopia – Somalia – Yemen, 336
  Sahel, 336
  South Asia, 336
  Trans Jordan – Syria, 336
Famine regions:
  Region I, 328
  Region II, 328–329
  Region III, 329–330
  Region IV, 330–331
  Region V, 331
Famines:
  anti-famine strategy, 346, 349
  famine cycle, 336–338
  famine ecology, 323
  famine regions, 328–330, 343
  population, 332
  potentials, 332–334
  types of, 332
Famines, Types of:
  cultural, 332
  overpopulation, 332
  physical, 332
  political, 332
  transportation, 332
The Far Western Frontier (Billington), 86
Farley, Richard A., 226
Farm Boys' and Girls' Club, 188
Farm Bureau, 206
"Farm Implement News", 320
Farm Journal (Atkinson), 198
Farm Journal, 198
Farm journals, 193
Farm life, 318
Farm population, 312
The Farmer (Webb), 203
  Wallace, Dan A., 203
The Farmer in the Second World War (Wilcox), 252
Farmers:
  gentlemen, 33, 47

in American colonies, 33–52
Farmer's Register, 162
Farmers' Tribune (Meredith), 176–183
Farming, 276
Farms, 275
Faville, E. E., 179
Febure, Lucien, 29
Federal Land Bank's District No. 1, 196
Fertilizers (Fertilizing):
  use in China, 265
Fessenden, Thomas Green
  The Horticultural Register and Gardeners Magazine (Breck), 129
Field and Garden Vegetables of America (Burr), 124
Fifty Years on Tracks (Caterpillar Tractor Co.), 305
First World Food War, 338
Fisher, Vardis
  Children of God, 75
Fite, Gilbert Courtland, 244
Fitzpatrick, J. C., 160
Fitzpatrick, Thomas, 73
Floods, 326
The Floral Magazine and Botanical Repository (Landreth), 113–114, 129
Florida Grower (Cunningham), 206
The Florist's Guide (Bridgeman), 127
The Flower Garden (Breck), 129
Flowers:
  books, 114, 127
Folded Hills (White), 76
Folklorists, 290–293
Food:
  imported, 346
  production, 17, 346
  shortages, 346
  surplus, 346
Food and Agriculture Organization of the United Nations, 228
Food maldistribution, 346
Food problems, 346
Food resources:
  domesticated animals, 324
  milk, 325
  primitive hunters and gatherers, 325
  seeds and fruits, 325
  skins and hides, 325
Ford, Henry, 313
Ford, Worthington C., 160
Ford Motor Co., 305
Forty Years on the Frontier (Stuart), 86
Francis, Mark, 248
Franklin, Benjamin, 20, 150

Frauenberger, George, 146
Froelich, John
  gasoline tractor, 305
Frontiers of the Northwest (Briggs), 86
Frost, Robert
  "You Come Too", 170, 215
The Fruit Book (1854) (Elliott), 132
Fruit cultures, 111
Fruit, Garden and Home
  See also Better Homes and Gardens, 175
Fruit growers, 111
Fruit trees, 110–111
Fruits and Fruit Trees (Downing), 118
Furnas, Robert W.
  governor of Nebraska, 199
  Nebraska Farmer, 199
Fusonie, Alan E., 57, 60, 61
Fussell, G. E., 26

Gadsden Purchase (1853), 71, 74
Gambrill, J. Mongomery
  The Westward Movement, 86
Gard, Wayne
  The Chisholm Trail, 78, 93–94
Garden Vegetables and How to Cultivate Them (Burr), 124
The Gardener's Calender for South Carolina and North Carolina (Squibb), 112
"The Gardener's Kalendar" (Logan), 112
The Gardener's Monthly (Meehan), 130
Gardening:
  catalogues
    mail-order blank, 110
    mail-order business, 144
    landscapes, 144
Gardening in the South (White), 132
Gardiner, John
  The American Gardener (Hepburn), 112–113
Garland, Hamlin
  The Westward March of American Settlement, 86
Gasoline tractor, 305
Gass, Patrick
  Journal of Voyages and Travels, 72
Gates, Paul Wallace, 27, 28, 300
General Foods Corp.
  Central Research Library, 232
"The Genesee Farmer" (Barry), 120
The Gentleman and Gardener's Kalendar (Thorburn), 125
The Gentleman Farmer (Home), 40
Gentleman of Virginia. *See* Randolph, John

Gerard, John, 63
German husbandry, 20–21
Ghent, W. J.
  The Early Far West, 86
Gibson, William, 38
Giddings, Luther P.
  Sketches of the Campaign in Northern Mexico, 75
"Global Information and Early Warning System on Food and Agriculture", 349
Glover, A. J., 207
Glover, Townsend, 163
Gold (White), 77
Gold rush, 71, 76–77
Goodnight, Charles, 95
Goubert, Pierre, 29
Gourley, J. H., 21
Grains:
  imports, 346
  production, 20
Granges, 152
Gray, A. B., 78
Gray, Lewis Cecil, 9, 11, 162
Gray, R. B., 320
The Gray Dawn (White), 77
The Great Plains (Webb), 86
Greathouse, Charles H., 224
Green, Charles A.
  American Fruit Grower, 209
Green Revolution, 218, 344
Green, Roland
  Treatise on the Cultivation of Ornamental Flowers, 125
Green's Fruit Grower (Green). *See American Fruit Grower*
Gregg, Josiah
  Commerce on the Prairies, 73
Gregory, Clifford V.
  Farm Bureau, 206,
  Prairie Farmer, 167, 206
Gressley, Gene M.
  Bankers and Cattlemen, 101, 103
Greven, Philip, 28
Gross, Robert, 29
Guest, Edgar, 170
Guide to Archives and Manuscript Collections in the United States (Hamer), 59
Guide to Life and Literature of the Southwest (Dobie), 76

Hafen, LeRoy
  Broken Hand, 73

Haley, J. Evetts
  Charles Goodnight, Cowman and Plainsman, 86
Hamer, Philip M.
  Guide to Archives and Manuscript Collections in the United States, 59
Hand-book for Fruit Growers (1876) (Elliott), 132
Hanna, G. C., 307
Harrar, J. George, 216–217, 218
Hart, C. W., 305, 313
Hart-Parr Co., 305
Harvester-thresher. *See* Combine
Harvesters:
  mechanical cotton harvester, 308, 313, 319
  tomato harvesters, 307, 308, 309
Hatch Experiment Station Act (1887), 152, 231, 260, 319
Hedges and Evergreens (Warder), 132
Hedrick, Ulysses Prentice, 67, 232
Hemp brake, 296
Henderson, Peter, 132
Henderson, Storrs & Harrison, 145
Henry, W. S.
  Campaign Sketches of the War with Mexico, 75
Hepburn, David
  The American Gardener, 112–113, 122
Herbs:
  garden, 120
  medicinal, 120
  pot (or sweet), 120
Hessian fly, 49
Hibbert, Thomas
  The American Flower Garden Directory (Buist), 125, 127
High Spots of American Literature (Johnson), 77
Higgins (F. Hal) Collection, 320
Highlands and Agricultural Society of Scotland, 220
Hilgard, Eugene W., 165
Hindle, Brook
  Technology in Early America, 26
Historia plantarum (Ray), 68
Histoire des Arbres Forestiers de l'Amerique Septentrionale (Michaux), 112
Historic Sketches of the Cattle Trade (McCoy), 78, 82
History of Carolina (Lawson), 67–68
Hoard, William Dempster
  Hoard's Dairyman, 207–209
Hoard's Dairyman (Hoard), 207

361

Holden, Perry G., 184
Ho Lei People's Commune, 266, 268
Holley, Mary Austin
  Texas, 75
Hollon, William Eugene
  The Southwest, Old and New, 86
Home, Henry (Lord Kames or Kaimes), 38
  The Gentleman Farmer, 40
Homestead Act (1862), 163
Hooper, E. J.
  Western Fruit Book, 130
Hope, Clifford Ragsdale, 249
Horse-drawn reaper, 297, 300
Horse-hoe plough, 296
The Horse-Hoeing Husbandry (Tull), 40
Horticultural publications:
  Catalogues:
    advertising and promotional techniques,
      110
    illustrations, 129, 146-147
    mail-orders business, 110, 147-148
*The Horticultural Register and Gardeners'
  Magazine* (Breck and Fessenden),
  129
Horticulture:
  history, 143
  sale of material, 110, 147-148
"The Horticulturist" (Barry), 120
The Horticulturist (Downing), 118, 129
Horticulturists, 143-148
Hortus Blesensis (Morison), 65
Hovey, Charles Mason
  The American Gardener's Magazine
    (1835), 124
  Magazine of Horticulture (Hovey, P. B.),
    129
Hovey, P. B., Jr.
  Magazine of Horticulture (Hovey, C. M.),
    129
Howard, Leland O., 164
Howes, Wright, 72
Hulbert, Archer Butler
  *Southwest on the Turquoise Trail: The First
    Diaries on the Road to Santa Fe*, 74
Husbandry:
  German, 20, 21
  English, 38
Husbandmen of Plymouth (Rutman), 14

*Index . . . to the Literature of American Eco-
  nomic Entomology* (Colcord), 226
India:
  monsoons, 342
Indians:
  agriculture, 11, 14

Mackenzie, Col. Ranald, 84
  Palo Duro Canyon, 84
India's Finance Commission, 347
Indigo, 18, 28
Institute of Agricultural Scientific Research,
  Nanking, 263
Institute of Early American History and Cul-
  ture, 30
Intercropping, 265
Internal-combustion engine tractors, 305
International Association of Agricultural Li-
  brarians and Documentalists, 228
International Harvester Co., 305, 319
International Information System for Agri-
  cultural Libraries and Technology,
  228
International Institute of Agriculture, 225,
  228
International Undertaking on World Food
  Security, 347
International Wheat Improvement Program,
  218
INTREDIS, 241
Iowa Homestead (Miller), 204;
  Duffus, J. H., 204
  Pierce, Dante, 204
  Pierce, James M., 204
  Wilson, W. P., 204
Iowa Tribune. See Farmers' Tribune
Irrigation, 263
Irving, Washington
  Astoria, 73
  *The Rocky Mountains . . . Adventures in
    the Far West*, 73
Ives, John M.
  The New England Book of Fruits (3rd
    ed.), 116
  The New England Fruit Book (2nd ed.,
    1844) (Manning), 116

Jackson, William Turrentine
  *The Enterprising Scot: Investors in the
    American West After 1873*, 104-105
James, Edwin
  *Account of an Expedition . . . to the Rock-
    ies*, 82
Jamestown, Va., 14-15;
  "Dales Laws", 15
  Labor problems, 15
  land division, 15
  land settlement, 18
  leisure time, 15
Jefferson, Thomas, 34, 113, 159, 160, 161,
  296
  Communicating Discoveries . . . By Cap-

tains Lewis and Clark, Dr. Sibley and Mr. Dunbar, 72–73
Jeffreys, George W., 221
Jensen, Merrill, 26
Joe Meek (Campbell), 73
John Deere Co.
  Library, 232
Johnson County War, 94
Johnson, Merle
  High Spots of American Literature, 77
Johnson, Samuel William, 232, 260
Jones, Everett
  The Negro Cowboys, 98, 99, 101
Jones, Marvin, 165
Josselyn, John
  New England Rarities Discovered, 120
"Journal" and "Transaction" of the American Society of Agricultural Engineers, 320
Journal of Voyages and Travels (Gass), 72
Journals
  horticultural, 129
The Journals of Lewis and Clark (DeVoto), 86
Journey to Day Before Yesterday (Eastman), 197

Kalendarium Hortense (Evelyn), 64
Kansas Department of Agriculture
  Kansas Farmer, 200, 201
  See also Mail and Breeze
Kansas Farmer, 200, 201
Kansas Flying Farmers, 201
Kansas Livestock Association, 201
Kansas State University, 201
Kellogg, E. A., 146
Kelly, Oliver Hudson
  "Patrons of Husbandry", 152
Kennedy, John, 38
Kenrick, William, 114
  The American Silk-Growers' Guide, 116
  The New American Orchardist, 114–116
Kern, Steber & Co., 147
Ketchum, W. F.
  mower, 300
Kiangsu Provincial Institute of Agricultural Scientific Research, 270
Kissinger, Henry, 349
Kit Carson (Campbell), 74
The Kitchen Gardener's Instructor (Bridgeman), 121
Knapp, Seaman Asahel, 164
Knox, William D.:
  American Dairy Association, 209

National Agricultural Advisory Commission (1961), 209
National Brucellosis Committee, 209
Kroger Co., 206
Kunkel, H. O., 244–245

Lacey, Mary Goodwin, 226
Ladies' Home Journal (Pickett), 199
Land, Aubrey C., 25–28
Land distribution, 15, 28, 264
Land Grant Act. *See* Morrill Land Grant College Act (1862)
Land grant colleges:
  creation, 151–152
  libraries, 229–231, 244, 255, 318–319
Land ownership:
  in China, 264
Land Utilization in China (Buck), 344
Landreth, David
  The Floral Magazine and Botanical Repository (Landreth, C.), 113–114, 129
Lane, John, 297
Laszlo, Ervin
  A Strategy for the Future: the Systems Approach to World Order, 347
Latham, Hiram
  Trans-Missouri Stock Raising: the Pasture Lands of North America: Winter Grazing, 82
Latrobe, Benjamin Henry, 26
Lawson, John
  History of Carolina, 67–68
Leadley, Tom, 200
Lelièvre, J. F.
  Nouveau Jardinier de la Louisiane, 130
Lemon, James T., 20
Leopold, Aldo, 164
Leroy, Andre
  "Descriptive Catalogue of Fruit and Ornamental Trees, Shrubs, Seedlings, etc.", 130
Let Us Now Praise Famous Men (Agee), 292
Lever, Asbury Francis, 165
Lewis, R. D., 246
Lewis and Clark expedition, 71, 72
Lewis and Clark seeds, 113
Lhwyd, Edward, 64, 65
Libraries, Traveling, 233
Library Company of Philadelphia, 29
Library of Congress
  Copyright office, 226
  National Union Catalog of Manuscript Collections, 59
Lincoln, Abraham, 162
  Organic Act, 51

Lindsay, Vachel, 170
Linnean Botanic Garden. *See* Prince Nursery
Lippincott, Miss C. H., 145
Lister, Martin, 65
A Little Commonwealth (Demo), 29
Livingstone, David, 215
Locke, John, 64
Lockridge, Kenneth, 29
Loehr, Rodney Clement, 26
The Log of a Cowboy (Adams), 78
Logan, Martha
  "The Gardener's Kalendar", 112
Long, Amos
  The Pennsylvania German Farm Family,
    292
The Long Rifle (Burnett), 76
Long, Stephen H., 82
The Longhorns (Dobie), 78
Longhorns:
  trail driving, 78
Longworth, Nicholas
  *The Cultivation of the Grape and Manufac-
    ture of Wine*, 130
Lorenzen, Coby, 307
Louisiana Purchase (1803), 71, 72
Lowdermilk, Colonel, 238

McAdoo, William Gibbs, 173
McCormick, Cyrus Hall
  The Century of the Reaper, 297, 319
McCormick, Fowler, 319
McCoy, Joseph Geating, 92, 93
  Historic Sketches of the Cattle Trade, 78,
    82
McKelvie, Sam:
  American Hereford Association, 200
  "By the Way" Ranch, 200
  Cattle business, 200
  Sandhills Cattle Association, 200
Mackay, Alexander, 97
Mackenzie, Murdo, 97
Mackenzie, Ranald, 84
McKibben, Eugene G.
  "The Evolution of Farm Implements in
    Machines", 318
McLoughlin, John, 76
McNamara, Robert S., 343
McNary, Charles Linza, 165
Magazine of Horticulture (Hovey), 129
Mail and Breeze. See Kansas Farmer
Mail-order business, 110, 147–148
Main, Thomas
  *Transplantation and Management of
    Young Thorn and Other Hedge
    Plants*, 113

Maize 14, 17
Mallory, Walter H.
  China: Land of Famine, 341
Manning, Robert
  Book of Fruits (1838), 116
  The New England Fruit Book (2nd ed.,
    1844) (Ives), 116
Manual of Roses (Prince), 116, 127
Mao Tse-tung, 267, 269
Marbut, Curtis Fletcher, 164
Marshall, Humphrey
  Arbustrum (*sic*) *Americanum*, 111
Marshall, William, 38
Maryland Agricultural Society, 51
Massachusetts Historical Society, 221
Massachusetts Horticultural Society library,
  116
Massachusetts Society for Promoting Agri-
  culture, 220
Massey-Ferguson, 305
Master Farmer-Master Homemaker, 201
Master Farmer program, 167, 206
Matador Cattle Company, 96–98
The Matador Land and Cattle Company
  (Pearce), 96–98
Maxwell, Robert, 38
May, Irvin, 259
Mayer, Andre, 237, 255
Mayer, Jean, 237, 255
Mechanical cotton harvester, 297
Mechanical reaper, 297
Mechanization, 266, 304, 306, 311, 318
Meehan, Thomas
  *The American Handbook of Ornamental
    Trees*, 130
  The Gardener's Monthly, 130
Mei Lung People's Commune, 266, 268,
  270
Meister, E. G. K., 209
*A Memoir on the Cultivation of the Vine in
  America* (Adlum), 113
Men and Milestones in American Agriculture
  (U.S. House Committee on Agricul-
    ture), 249
Meredith, Edwin T.:
  Agricultural Publishers' Association, 188
  Associated Advertising Clubs of the
    World, 188
  Chamber of Commerce of the United
    States, 188
  Dairy Farmer, 175
  education, 175–176
  Farmer's Tribune, 176–183
  National Committee on Boys' and Girls'
    Club, 188

364

publisher, 173–189
Successful Farming, 173–189
Meredith, Minerva J. (Marsh), 175
Meredith, Thomas
Farmers' Tribune, 176–183
Meredith, Thomas Oliver, 173
Mexican War (1846–1848), 71, 75
Mexico:
Green Revolution, 218
Rockefeller Foundation's Mexican Agricultural Program, 216–218
Michaux, F. Andre
Histoire des Arbres Forestiers de l'Amerique Septentrionale, 112
Michigan Farmer (Capper), 201
Michigan State Agricultural College, 243
Miles, Nelson A.
Personal Recollections and Observations, 84
Miller, Jarvis E., 246
Miller, Mack
Iowa Homestead, 204
Miller, Merle
Plain Speaking: An Oral Biography of Harry S. Truman, 275
M'Ilvaine, William
Sketches of Scenery and Notes of Personal Adventure in California and Mexico, 77
Minneapolis—Moline Power Implement Co., 305
Missouri Ruralist (Carroll & Capper)
See also Colman's Rural World, 201
Missouri State Corn Shucking Contests, 203
Mitchell, H. L., 166
Mixed Cropping, 265
M'Mahon, Bernard
The American Gardener's Calendar, 113
Mohrhardt, Foster, 226, 228, 241
Mono-germ seeds, 307
Monsoons, 342
Monticello, 34, 160
Moore, Hiram, 319
Morgan, Edmund, 15
Morgan, George, 49
"Prospect" farm, 49
Morison, Robert, 65
Hortus Blesensis, 65
Plantarum historiae universalis Oxoniensis, 65
Mormons, 71, 75–76
Morrill, Justin Smith, 162, 163, 229
Morrill Act (1862). *See* Morrill Land Grant College Act (1862)
Morrill Land Grant College Act (1862),

151–152, 163, 224, 318
Morris, Harry, 248
Morris, Morris David, 347
Morton, Julius Sterling, 164, 238
Mount Hope Nurseries, 118, 119
Mount Vernon, 34, 260
Mower, 300
Multigerm seeds, 307
Multiple cropping, 265
Murphy, Donald R., 204
My Life on the Range (Clay), 86

Nagana. *See* Trypanosomiasis.
National Agricultural Library, 29
History, 224, 225–229, 237–242
National Agricultural Library Catalog, 228
National Citizens Commission for the Public Schools, 196
National Commission for the Observance of World Population Year, 349
National Committee on Boys' and Girls' Club, 188
National Farmers Union, 166
National Grange, 166
National Historical Publications and Records Commission, 30
National Livestock and Meat Board, 201
National Science Foundation, 348
National Union Catalog of Manuscript Collections (Library of Congress), 59
Natural History of Oxfordshire (Plot), 64
Nebraska Farmer (Furnas), 199
"By the Way" (McKelvie), 200
Marvin Russell, 200
The Negro Cowboys (Durham & Jones), 98, 99, 101
Ness, Helge, 248
Nevins, Allan, 274
The New American Orchardist (Kenrick), 114
The New England Book of Fruits (Ives), 116
New England Farmer, 162
The New England Fruit Book (Manning & Ives), 116
New England Rarities Discovered (Josselyn), 120
A New System of Husbandry (Varlo), 47
New York Society
Transactions, 220, 221
Newbold, Charles, 297
Nile Valley, 328
Norris, George William, 165
North America, 328
Northern Farmers Alliance, 166
Norton, John Pitkin, 260

Notes on a Journey in America . . . to the Territory of Illinois (Birkbeck), 72
Nouveau Jardinier de la Louisiane (Lelièvre), 130
Nurseries and seed houses:
  Burpee, 145
  Childs, 145
  Ellwanger & Barry, 145
  Henderson, Storrs & Harrison, 145
  Kern, Steber and Co., 147
  Vick, 145
Nursery and seed catalogues, 143–148
Nurserymen, 143

Ohio Farm, 201
The Ohio Farmer (Brown & Capper), 201, 206–207,
Oliver Corp., 305
Oliver Farm Equipment Co., 305
Omaha Herald, 82
On the Border with Mackenzie (Carter), 84
O'Neal, Edward Asbury, 166, 206
Oral historians, 273–276
Oral history, 250, 273–288
Oral History Association, 274
Oregon Trail, 71, 76
The Oregon Trail (Parkman). *See The California and Oregon Trail*
Organic Act. *See* Act of 1862
Organization of Agricultural Experiment Stations in the United States, 262
Osgood, Ernest S.
  Day of the Cattleman, 87–89

Pacific Rural Press (Pickett), 199, 320
Paddock, Paul, 344
Paddock, William, 344
Palo Duro Canyon, 71, 84
Pammel, Louis H., 165
Park, Mungo, 214
Parker, Dorothy, 217, 218
Parkman, Francis, 147
  The California and Oregon Trail, 76
Parr, C. H., 305
Parsons, Samuel B.
  The Rose, 127–129
Parsons on the Rose, 129
Pasteur, Louis, 248
Patent plough. *See* Rotherham plough
The Pattern under the Plow (Evans), 291
Peaches, 67–68
Pearce, William M.
  The Matador Land and Cattle Company, 96–98

Pearson, John S., 197
Pelzer, Louis
  The Cattlemen's Frontier, 91–92
Pennsylvania Farm Show, 207
Pennsylvania Farmer (Capper), 201, 207
The Pennsylvania German Farm Family (Long), 292
Pennsylvania Horticultural Society Library, 221
The Pennsylvania Mercury and Universal Advertiser, 49
The People Left Behind (President's National Advisory Commission on Rural Poverty), 309
"People's" Party State Central Committee, 265
People's Republic of China, 264, 344–345
Personal Narrative of Explorations — in Texas, New Mexico, California, etc. . . . with the United States and Mexican Boundary Commission (Bartlett), 74
Personal Recollections and Observations (Miles), 84
Peters, George A., 194
Peters, Richard, 48–49
  Agricultural Enquiries on Plaister of Paris, 48
Petticoat Junction, N.Y., 216
Philadelphia Society for Promoting Agriculture, 47, 48, 151, 220, 233
Physick Garden, Oxford, 64, 65
Pickering, Timothy, 51
Pickett, John E.:
  California Department of Agriculture, 199
  Country Gentleman, 199
  Ladies' Home Journal, 199
  Pacific Rural Press, 199
  University of California, 199
Pierce, Dante, 204
Pierce, James M., 204
Pinchot, Gifford, 164
Pitkin, Timothy, 51
Pitts, Hiram Avery
  threshing machine, 300
Pitts, John
  threshing machine, 300
Plain and Pleasant Talks About Fruits, Flowers and Farming (Beecher), 132
Plain Speaking: An Oral Biography of Harry S. Truman (Miller), 275
Plant Science Catalog (Atwood), 226
Plantarum historise universalis Oxoniensis

(Morison), 65

Planters, 14, 19

Plot, Robert

Natural History of Oxfordshire, 64

Ploughs

"Barrel", 43

cast iron plow, 297

horse-hoe plough, 296

Rotherham, 43

sidehill plow, 296

Plukenet, Leonard, 64, 65, 68

Poe, Clarence, 167, 197–198

Polk, Leonidas Lafayette

Progressive Farmer, 197–198

The Pomological Manual (Prince & Prince), 116

Pork, 264

Powell, Sumner

Puritan Village, 28

A Practical Treatise of Husbandry (Duhamel du Monceau), 40–41

Prairie Farmer, 204–206

Butler, Burridge Devenal, 206

Gregory, Clifford V., 167, 206

Wright, John Steven, 204–206

Prairie Trails & Cow Towns (Streeter), 78

President's National Advisory Commission on Rural Poverty (1967)

The People Left Behind, 309

Prestele, Joseph, 146

Prestele, William H., 146

Price, Jacob, 28

Prince Nursery, 111, 116

Prince William

The Pomological Manual, 116

A Short Treatise on Horticulture . . ., 116

A Treatise on Fruit and Ornamental Trees and Plants, 116

A Treatise on the Vine, 116

Prince, William Robert, 116

A Manual of Roses, 116–117, 127

The Pomological Manual, 116

"A Treatise on Nature's Sovereign Rem dials, Eclectic Fluid Compounds Extracted from Plants, Humanized Electricity and Magnestism, the Fluid and Life Food", 118

A Treatise on the Vine, 116

Progressive Farmer (Polk), 167, 197–198

Pugh, Evan, 260

Puritan Village (Powell), 28

Puritans, 13–14

Purnell Experiment Station Act (1925), 261

The Queen of Flowers, 127

Quincy, Josiah, 164

Railroads, 71

Great American desert, 79, 82

in cattle trade, 103

Promontory, Utah, 78

Ramsey, J. L., 197

Ranchero (White), 76

Randolph, Vance, 291

Rangaswami, Amrita, 347

The Range Cattle Industry (Dale), 89, 91

Rasmussen, Wayne D., 27, 250, 319

Ray, John

Historia plantarum, 65

Reapers:

horse-drawn reaper, 297, 300

mechanical reaper, 297

Reid, Samuel G.

The Scouting Expeditions of McCulloch's Texas Rangers, 75

Reiser, Raymond, 248

Reports of Exploration and Surveys to Ascertain the Most Practical and Economic Route for a Railroad from the Mississippi River to the Pacific Ocean, 77

Research and Marketing Act (1946), 261

"Research and Education in American Agriculture" (Waggoner), 261

Researchers:

government records, 59

Guide to Archives and Manuscript Collections in the United States (Hamer), 59

historical documentary editing projects, 59

National Archives, 60

National Union Catalog of Manuscript Collections (Library of Congress), 59

primary sources, 58, 59

secondary sources, 59, 60

Revolutionary War (1775–1783), 33

Revolving horse rake, 297

Rhododendron, 129

Rice culture, 17–19, 28, 264–265

Richardson, Rupert Norval

The Comanche Barrier to South Plains Settlement, 84

Ridge, Martin

America's Frontier Story (Billington), 86

Riding, Sam P.

The Chisholm Trail, 78

Riegel, Robert E.

America Moves West, 86

Roberts, Job, 51

Robin, Vespacion, 65

Robinson, John, 38
Robinson, Solon, 162
Rockefeller Foundation's Mexican Agricultural Program, 216–218
Rockefeller, John D., III, 218
Rockefeller, Nelson, 218
The Rocky Mountain Saints: A Full and Complete History of the Mormons (Stenhouse), 76
The Rocky Mountains . . . Adventures in the Far West (Irving), 73
Rogers, Charles E., 187
Rolfe, John, 15
Roosevelt, Franklin Delano, 165
Roosevelt, Theodore, 165
  Winning the West, 72
The Rose (Parson), 127–129
The Rose Dawn (White), 77
The Rose Manual (Buist), 127
Rosebud, 84
Rosengarten, Theodore, 274
Roses, 127, 129
Roth, Raymond, 317
Rotherham (or patent) plough, 43
Roughing It (Clemens), 77
Rowley, William, 249
Royal Academy of Sciences, Paris, 40
Royal Hanoverian Agricultural Society, 220
Royal Palm Nurseries of Manatee, Florida, 147
Royal Veterinary and Agricultural College, 220
Ruffin, Edmund, 162
  Essay on Calcareous Manures, 162
  Essays and Notes on Agriculture, 162
Rummell, L. L., 206
Rupp, Robert, 204
Rural electrification program, 306
Rural free delivery, 179
Rural library service, 233
Rural life, 163
Rush, Benjamin, 51
Rush, Richard, 20
Russell, Charles Marion, 86,
Russell, Marvin
  Colorado Rancher and Farmer, 200
Rust, John D., 308, 313, 319
Rust, Mack, 308, 319
Rutman, Darrett
  Husbandmen of Plymouth, 14

Sahel, 214, 328, 345
Salmon, Daniel Elmer, 164
Sandhills Cattle Association, 200

Santa Fe Trail, 73
The Santa Fe Trail (Duffas), 73
Savage, William W.
  The Cherokee Strip Live Stock Association: Federal Regulation and the Cattleman's Last Frontier, 105
Sayers, Edward
  The American Flower Garden Companion, 127
  Treatise on the Culture of the Dahlia, 127
Schapsmeier, Edward Lewis, 249
Schapsmeier, Frederick Herman, 249
Schistosomiasis, 214
Schlebecker, John T.
  Cattle Raising on the Plains: 1900–1961, 95–96, 249
Schlesinger, Arthur M., 58
"Science and Technology in Western Agriculture" (Bainer), 306, 313
Scott, Roy Vernon, 249
The Scouting Expeditions of McCulloch's Texas Rangers (Reid), 75
Second harrow, 40
Secor, Alson, 184
Seed drill, 296
Seed firms:
  Burr (M. & F.) 124
Seed(s):
  Lewis and Clark, 113
  mono-germ seeds, 307
Seedsmen, 115
Sharecroppers, 309
Shaw, Ralph R., 226, 240, 241
Sherard, William, 64
Sherrod, John, 226, 241
Shoalmire, James, 249
A Short Treatise on Horticulture . . . (1828) (Prince), 116
Shryock, Richard H., 19–20
Sickle, 296
Sidehill plow, 296
Silo, 207
Sinclair, Sir John, 38, 47, 160
Singleton, John, 47, 49
Sketches of Scenery and Notes of Personal Adventure in California and Mexico (M'Ilvaine), 77
Sketches of the Campaign in Northern Mexico (Giddings & Curwen), 75
Sketches on Rotation of Crops and Other Rural Matters (Bordley), 43, 47
Skinner, John Stuart, 161
Slavery, 214, 296–297
Slaves, 214

Sleeping sickness, 215
Smith, Earl, 206
Smith, Erwin Frank, 164
Smith, John, 13
Smith, Justin H.
   The War with Mexico, 1846–48, 75
Smith, Theobald, 248
Smith-Hughes Vocational Education Act
   (1917), 153, 154
Smith-Lever Act (1914), 153, 154
Smithsonian Institution, 261
Snow, C. P., 343, 344
Society of Architectural Historians. Chapter
   for Landscape Architecture and the
   Allied Arts, 144
Soil conservation, 161, 162
Soil erosion, 161
Soil exhaustion, 47
Southern Alliance, 166
Southern Farm Magazine (Butler), 197
Southern Tenant Farmers Union, 166
The Southwest, Old and New (Hollon), 86
*Southwest on the Turquoise Trail: the First
   Diaries on the Road to Santa Fe* (Hul-
   bert), 74
Sovereign, Otto E.
   North American Construction Company
   of Bay City, Michigan, 187
Sowerby, Millicent, 221,
Sparks, Jared, 160
Spillman, William Jasper, 164
Spindle picker, 308, 309
Sprague, Isaac, 124
Squibb, Robert
   *The Gardener's Calendar for South Caro-
   lina and North Carolina*, 112
Stakman, E. C., 217
Stanley, John Mix, 77
Stanley, Louise, 164
Steam engines, 297
Steedman, Charles J.
   Bucking the Sagebrush, 86
Stenhouse, T. B. H.
   *The Rocky Mountain Saints: A Full and
   Complete History of the Mormons*, 76
Stephens, Philip, 64
Stockdale, Jerry, 277
Storey, Benton, 248
*A Strategy for the Future: the Systems Ap-
   proach to World Order* (Laszlo), 347
Straw-rack, 300
Streeter, Carroll P., 198
Streeter, Floyd B.
   Prairie Trails and Cow Towns, 78

Stuart, Granville
   Forty Years on the Frontier, 84, 86
Sturtevant, Edward Lewis, 232
Subsistence farmer, 311
Successful Farming (Meredith), 173–189,
   278
Such, George, 147
Sugar beet production, 307
Sullivan, Maurice S.
   The Travels of Jedediah Smith, 73
*A Summary View of Courses of Crops, In the
   Husbandry of England and Maryland*
   (Bordley), 43–44
Swan, Alexander, 96
Swynnerton, Charles, 215
Synder, Addison H., 184

Taber, Louis J., 166
Taylor, Baynard
   El Dorado, 77
Taylor, Henry Carl, 164
Taylor, John, 51, 161
Technology in Early America (Hindle), 26
Terkel, Studs, 273
Texas:
   annexation, 71
   republic, 74
   revolution, 74
   war with Mexico, 74, 75
Texas (Holley), 75
Texas (Von Roemer), 75
Texas A & M University, 244–253
Texas Agricultural Progress, 253
Texas: Her Resources and Her Public Men
   (De Cordova), 75
Texas tick fever eradication, 93, 248
Thorburn, Grant, 124, 143
   The Gentleman and Gardener's Kalendar,
   125
Threshing machines, 300, 306
Tigris Valley, 328
Tindall, John, 201
Titans of the Soil (Dies), 249
Tobacco, 15, 66–67
Tobacco culture, 15, 310
Tobacco production, 16–17
Tomato harvesters, 308
Tomato(es), 122–124, 125, 143, 199, 308
Toynbee, Arnold, 255
Tractors:
   gasoline, 305
   internal-combustion engine, 305
Tradescant, John, 65

Trans Jordan-Syria, 336
Trans-Missouri Stock Raising: the Pasture Lands of North America: Winter Grazing . . . (Latham), 82
Transplantation and Management of Young Thorn and Other Hedge Plants (Main), 113
The Travels of Jedediah Smith (Sullivan), 73
A Treatise on Fruit and Ornamental Trees and Plants (1820) (Prince), 116
"A Treatise on Nature's Sovereign Remedials, Eclectic Fluid Compounds Extracted from Plants, Humanized Electricity and Magnetism, the Fluid and Life Food" (Prince), 118
Treatise on the Cultivation of Ornamental Flowers (Green), 125
Treatise on the Culture of the Dahlia (Sayers), 127
Treatise on the Fruit Garden (1851) (Barry), 118
A Treatise on the Theory and Practice of Landscape Gardening (Downing), 118
A Treatise on the Vine (Prince & Prince), 116
Tree peddlers, 111
Trees:
  as shade in pastures, 112
  See also Fruit
True, Alfred C., 164, 261
Trypanosomes, 215
Trypanosomiasis, 215
Tsetse fly, 213, 215
Tukey, Harold B., 210
Tull, Jethro, 38, 43;
  and methods of farming, 38
  drill plough, 40
  horse-hoe plough, 38
  The Horse-Hoeing Husbandry, 40
Turner, Frederick Jackson, 58, 89
Twain, Mark. *See* Clemens, Samuel Langhorne
Two Years Before the Mast (Dana), 76

United States Agricultural Society, 51
U. S. Department of Agriculture:
  act establishing 51, 151
  Economic Research Service, 310
  Extension Service, 153
  Graduate School, 149–157
    enrollment, 155
    evening and correspondence programs, 155

independent study program, 156
  See also U. S. Department of Agriculture *Yearbook*
U. S. Department of Agriculture. *Yearbook*, 261, 308
U. S. House of Representatives. Committee on Agriculture
  Men and Milestones in American Agriculture, 249
U. S. Patent Office, 151, 224
Universal History of Plants (Morison), 65
University of California
  Regional Oral History Program, 275
University of California, Davis, 199, 228, 320

Varlo, Charles
  A New System of Husbandry, 47
Vegetables, 144, 269
Vestal, Stanley. *See* Campbell, Walter S.
Vick, 124
Vick, James, 120, 132, 146, 148
A View of the Cultivation of Fruit Trees and the Management of Orchards and Cider (Coxe), 114
Virginia:
  botany, 15
  plants, 15
Virginia Co., 15
Von Frauendorfer, Sigmund, 225, 228
Von Leibig, Justin, 260
Von Roemer, Ferdinand
  Texas, 75

Waggoner, Paul
  "Research and Education in American Agriculture", 261
Walford, Cornelius, 341
Wallace, Dan A.
  AAA program, 203
Wallace, Henry
  Wallace's Farmer, 203
Wallace, Henry Agard, 164, 312
  Secretary of Agriculture, 203
  Secretary of Commerce, 203
  Vice-President, U.S. (Harding), 203
Wallace, Henry Cantwell
  Secretary of Agriculture, 155, 203, 249
Wallace–Homestead Poll, 204
Wallace's Farmer (Wallace), 203
  See also Iowa Homestead
Walters, Thomas, 51
The War with Mexico, 1846–48 (Smith), 75

Warder, John A.
Hedges and Evergreens, 132
Warren, Col.
The California Farmer, 199
California State Fair, 199
Washington, George, 33–34;
and agricultural societies, 34, 49
and agriculture, 38, 47, 150, 159, 160,
161, 296
on federal support for agriculture, 49–50
Watson, Elkanah, 51, 161
Watson, Jack, 112
Watts, Frederick, 260
Wearin, Otha D., 310
Weaver, James Baird, 176
Webb, Edward A.
The Farmer, 203
Webb, Walter Prescott
The Great Plains, 86
Wellhausen, E. J., 217, 218
Western Fruit Book (Hooper), 130
The Western Fruit-Book (Elliott), 132
Western Newspaper Union, 181
The Westward March of American Settlement
(Garland), 86
Westward movement, 71–86
The Westward Movement (Woestemeyer &
Gambrill), 86
White House Conference on Conservation in
1908, 165
White House Conference on Education, 196
White, John, 65
White, Stewart Edward
Folded Hills, 76
Gold, 74
The Gray Dawn, 77
Ranchero, 76
The Rose Dawn, 77
White, William Nathaniel
Gardening in the South, 132
Whitney, Eli
cotton gin, 296, 313
Wickson, Edward James
California Experiment Station, 199
California Farmer, 199

Wilcox, Walter
The Farmer in the Second World War, 252
Wiley, Harvey Washington, 164
Wilson, James, 164
Wilson, M. L., 249
Wilson, W. P., 204
Winning the West (Roosevelt), 72
Wisconsin Agriculturist (Cunningham), 206
Wittwer, Sylvan H., 243
Woestemeyer, Ina Fay
The Westward Movement (Gambrill), 86
Wood, Jethro
cast iron plow, 297
Wood, Peter, 28
Woodburn, Elisabeth, 143, 144
Woodward, Comer Vann, 249
World Ecology Monitor, 347
World Food Conference (1974), 347–349;
Consultative Group on Food Production
and Investment, 347
Declaration on the Eradication of Hunger
and Malnutrition, 347
"Global Information and Early Warning
System on Food and Agriculture",
347–349
International Undertaking on World Food
Security, 347
World War II, 306
Wye Island, Md., 43

Yarnell, Sid, 248
Yearbook (U.S. Department of Agricul-
ture).
See U.S. Department of Agriculture
Yearbook
"You Come Too" (Frost), 215
Young, Arthur, 38, 39, 160, 220, 296
Annals of Agriculture, 38, 43, 48
The Young Gardener's Assistant (Bridge-
man), 122, 127
Youngblood, Bonney, 246

Zinfandel grape, 116
Zirkle, Conway, 26